TRANSITION IN ACTION

TOTNES AND DISTRICT 2030

AN ENERGY DESCENT ACTION PLAN

Published 2010 by Transition Town Totnes

Scripted and Edited by Jacqi Hodgson with Rob Hopkins

Cover and Graphic design by Ishka Michocka at Lumpy Lemon (lumpylemon.co.uk)

  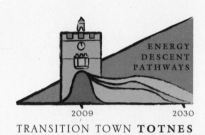

Transition Town Totnes,

43 Fore Street,

Totnes,

Devon.

TQ9 5HN

Tel: 01803 867358

Email: transitiontowntotnes@googlemail.com

Website: www.totnes.transitionnetwork.org

Printed by Cambrian Ltd. on recycled paper

TRANSITION IN ACTION

TOTNES AND DISTRICT 2030

AN ENERGY DESCENT ACTION PLAN

by **Transition Town Totnes**

Scripted & edited by

Jacqi Hodgson

with **Rob Hopkins**

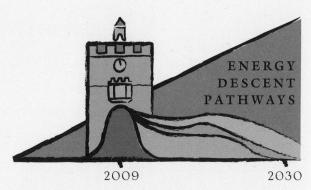

ENERGY DESCENT PATHWAYS

2009   2030

TRANSITION TOWN **TOTNES**

Acknowledgements

This document and the research that led to it has been funded by the Esmee Fairbairn Foundation, Artists Planet Earth, Land Share CIC, the Ashden Trust, the ESRC and Ashoka. We are deeply grateful to them all for seeing the importance of this work. We are also grateful for all the support we have received from Totnes Town Council, South Hams District Council and Devon County Council. This Plan stands on the shoulders of the many community plans that have gone before it, in particular the Totnes Community Plan, created by the Totnes and District Strategy Group, the Community Response to South Hams District Council's Development Plan Document, and the 'Leading the Way' report, produced by the Devon Association for Renewable Energy. A list of all the people who have contributed to this document would run over several pages, suffice to say without the input of many hundreds of people, Transition Town Totnes would not exist and this Plan would be a scant and insignificant document.

We would also like to thank the many people involved in TTT working groups and projects who have supported the development of this EDAP, all those who participated in the public workshops, discussion groups and consultation processes which have fed into and created this EDAP. Totnes Image Bank and Rural Archive for permission to use their archive photos, Ernest Goh for fast-forwarding photos to 2030, Ian Campbell for his data analysis, the children of Grove School for their pictures, students at KEVICCS for their insights and visions, the many artists for their drawings, cartoons, illustrations and artworks, the valiant proofreaders, the many local organizations. Totnes Town Council and the surrounding Parish Councils who have contributed to this EDAP

Many thanks to everyone for their encouragement, enthusiasm and patience.

At the close of producing this EDAP, we have heard sad news about 2 people who have made substantial contributions to this work. Philip Gibbon of Lower Longcombe, Totnes and Councillor Ian Slatter of Totnes Town have died. Philip with his nuclear engineering and naval background and enthusiasm for all forms of energy, played a huge part in the development of the Energy Sections of this EDAP and indeed his support for the TTT Energy Group which he attended regularly. Ian, a former Mayor of Totnes shared many of his early memories of Totnes to help build a picture of Totnes just after the last war, through oral history. We wish to acknowledge the extensive support both Philip and Ian gave to the work of Transition Town Totnes.

Disclaimer

Dedication

We would like to dedicate this Plan to the community of Totnes and District, to their wisdom and collective genius, and to their good health and prosperity in the times of change ahead. We would also like to dedicate it to all those unsung heroes who, in various aspects of their lives, and when the conventional wisdom has for so many years run in the opposite direction, have striven to live in harmony with this planet.

CONTENTS

4

APPENDICES 289

Note:
  *   Edited version - full text appears in web version
  **   Included only in web version: www.totnesedap.org.uk

INTRODUCTION

When *RMS Titanic* set sail on her maiden voyage in 1912, she headed across the Atlantic with full confidence that her journey would go according to plan, and all her passengers would arrive safely in New York. So confident that she was unsinkable were her designer and captain, that they took scant notice of warnings about possible icebergs floating in her path. When the *Titanic* hit an iceberg she sank within 3 hours; the lack of adequate lifeboats and evacuation preparations resulted in less than a third of the passengers surviving. Most of the lives lost were amongst the third class passengers.

As has often been explored, this story could have had a different outcome; saving more of the 2,240 people on board that night. There were many reasons (known at the time) for Captain Smith to be more cautious about the threat and sighting of icebergs, the law should have required ships to carry adequate lifeboats, there should have been better responses to Morse code signals between the Titanic and other ships close-by, the inadequate bilge pumps and cheaper rivets in the hull were a false economy, and no-one should have had preferential opportunity for survival because of the ticket they carried. But did the officers also ignore a key resource that fateful night? Could involving the passengers in the emergency have saved more lives? With creative thinking it is possible to imagine a scenario where passengers were given the freedom and encouragement to flex their resilience and threw together some life rafts from the deckchairs, masts, beds, doors etc. Perhaps some lateral thinking and more hands on deck could have changed this episode of history.

© Jenny Band

In setting out to write an Energy Descent Action Plan (EDAP), three simple yet substantive questions soon emerged: First, "What is an Energy Descent Action Plan?" then "Who is it being written for?" and thirdly "Where does one get this kind of information from?" Another more significant question also became apparent as progress with the EDAP got underway, "Who is going to do all this?"

An Energy Descent Action Plan is a guide to reducing our dependence on fossil fuels and reducing our carbon footprint over the next 20 years, during which we expect many changes associated with declining oil supplies and some of the impacts of climate change to become more apparent. In this EDAP we have built a picture of this future scenario based on visions of a better future. In the process, we have invited the community to dream how the future could be, and to then work out the practical pathways by which we actually get there.

This EDAP is written for the community of Totnes and District, a market town and its fifteen encircling parishes. It is for people from all walks of life, all sectors; individuals, families, organisations, businesses, policy makers and service providers; people who want to become part of the solution to some of the biggest challenges civilisation has ever faced. This EDAP provides a guide to our common future, with information about the issues, ideas about how the future may look as we move across the timeline and suggests many small and large actions which can contribute towards this vital process.

The material in this EDAP has been drawn from a wide range of sources. The creative visioning, assumptions and many suggestions for actions have been drawn from over 500 members of local society in Totnes and District; at public workshops, at Transition Town Totnes meetings and events and from individuals who have shared their ideas. The scientific framework which informs the timeline and the depletion of fossil fuels, in particular peak oil and the case for climate change due to fossil fuel use, is drawn from reliable published scientific research, which is referenced throughout the text.

In asking who is going to do all this, we now pass this question back to you as a request to engage in this EDAP, to pick it up and to make it happen. We say this with a sense of urgency, but also as an invitation to participate in one of the greatest possible initiatives open to us. Those who have contributed to this EDAP we hope will lead the way and help us to galvanise. If we wait for the Government to do this, it will be too late. If we try and do it all on our own, it will be too little. But by organising with friends, neighbours and our community, it may just be enough, and it may just be in time. We urge you to be brave, cast aside your fears and shyness, and enjoy the ride.

"The choice is ours – yours and mine. We can stay with business as usual and preside over an economy that continues to destroy its natural support systems until it destroys itself, or we can adopt Plan B and be the generation that changes direction, moving the world onto a path of sustained progress. The choice will be made by our generation, but it will affect life on earth, for all generations to come"
Lester R. Brown.[1]

HOW TO USE THIS DOCUMENT

This document is intended to offer ideas and inspiration for individuals, the community and local service providers in the area of Totnes and District, in their efforts to plan responses to volatile energy prices, climate change and a deeply uncertain economic future. It is in three main sections.

PART ONE, 'Where we start from', sets out the assumptions that underpin this report. It sets out the 3 key assumptions, namely the imminent peaking in world oil production, climate change and the economic crisis, upon which the strategies proposed here are based. It also introduces the concepts of resilience and localisation, which are key elements of the responses proposed. It closes with a look at Totnes and District, drawing together some of the key information about the area.

PART TWO, 'Creating A New Story', looks at why, as a culture, the stories we have about the future aren't up to the job, and why we need new ones. This Plan is, in effect, a story about how the community could make the transition away from its oil dependency. It is a story that starts with a reflection on the past, and the bulk of Part Two is based on oral histories conducted in and around Totnes, looking at how food, work, energy and other aspects of life functioned in the last period when Totnes and District had a more localised economy and much less energy availability than the present day. Finally, the story of Transition Town Totnes is told, how it began, and the process that has led to the creation of this Plan.

PART THREE 'A Timeline to 2030' looks at a range of subject areas, Energy, Building/Housing, Economy and Livelihoods, Education, Governance, Art and Culture, Health and Wellbeing, Transport, Food, Biodiversity, Water, Waste and Community Issues. For each it sets out the challenges that Transition presents to them, and how things might progress if we carry on as usual and do nothing to start embracing the changes already underway. It then presents a Transition Timeline for the topic, setting out, year by year, what such a response might look like. Part Three is also illustrated with a number of stories of 'Transition in Action', that is, local initiatives and projects that have emerged from the Transition Town Totnes process that may have a key role to play in bringing the Transition Timeline about. It also contains two stand-alone sections, which

offer a deeper look at the practicalities of the changes proposed. The first 'Can Totnes Feed Itself?' is a ground-breaking piece of research which looks at the degrees of food self-reliance that could potentially be achieved in the area, and the second, 'An Energy Budget for Totnes' - a further unique study - estimates the demands and supply of energy in the district and offers a detailed look at the potential of local energy generation from macro to micro scale.

This published Plan is accompanied by a website, www.totnesedap.org.uk, where longer versions of many of the sections of this Plan can be found, and where you can comment and suggest changes. Many of the links, photographs, references and appendices that we didn't have space for here, can also be found on the EDAP website.

NOTES & IDEAS

WHERE WE START FROM

1

This plan is different from the many Community and County Development Plans that appear regularly in our lives. It is based on a set of different, and we feel more realistic, assumptions. It assumes that we have reached a pivotal and historic moment in history, a time when we can afford to think big and to think beyond what one might call 'business as usual'. The economy of Totnes and District is starting to feel the impacts of the global downturn, and the record oil prices of last summer hit the economy hard. What if those two trends turn out to be a permanent and growing feature of our everyday lives? What will it look like if the area takes proactive steps to live within its carbon balance, playing its part in avoiding runaway climate change? This section looks at the thinking that underpins this Plan.

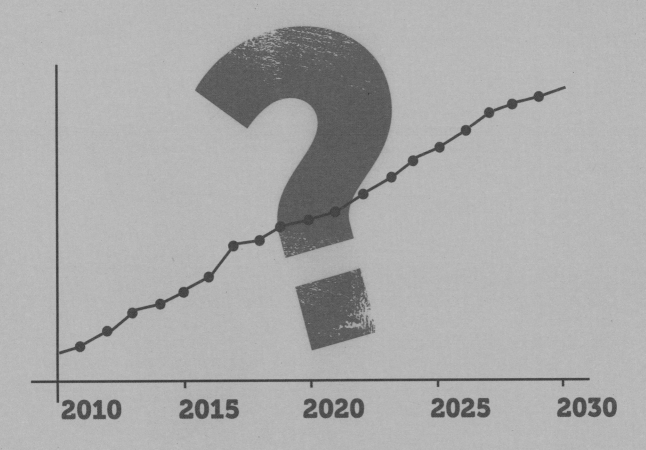

2010   **2015**   **2020**   **2025**   **2030**

TELLING A NEW STORY ABOUT OUR FUTURE

Introducing the Wonder of the Oil Age

Here is a litre of oil. It is an extraordinary thing. The oil in this bottle contains more energy than you would create doing hard physical work for five weeks. Just in this small bottle. It has made us powerful beyond the imaginings of previous generations, able to change landscapes, eat foods from the other side of the world in defiance of the seasons, travel the world as though we had Seven League Boots, and break, for the first time, our connection to the land beneath our feet.

It can also be transformed into the dazzling array of plastics, glues, materials and products, which fill our homes, workplaces and shops. We make our medicines from it, and our food system has become a system for turning it into food. Were we to pick our lives up and wring them out, they would drip with oil. Yet this level of oil dependency, which once determined our degree of prosperity and success, now determines how vulnerable we are. While in many ways the oil in this bottle has brought us wonderful things and extraordinary opportunities, we need, as Fatih Birol, head of the International Energy Agency is now telling the world's governments, to "leave oil before oil leaves us".

As part of the oral history interviews that start in part two, we asked the late Douglas Matthews of Staverton, shortly before his 100th birthday, whether he considered the Oil Age he lived through to have been a blessing or a curse. "A blessing. But it was also a blessing for the type of wars we were able to fight. Is it a blessing if you put the two together? I don't know. I am very glad though to have lived through the period that I have lived through".

The Assumptions that Underpin this Plan

When most Councils, businesses or Governments sit down to plan for the next 20 years, they still start by assuming that in 20 years the settlement in question will have more jobs, more energy, more cars, more houses, more businesses, more economic growth and so on. In the past few months it has become clear to many people that each of those assumptions is becoming increasingly questionable.

We are moving from a time in history when our degree of economic success and personal wellbeing is directly linked to our level of oil consumption, to a time when our degree of oil dependency is our degree of vulnerability. For many people, it is increasingly clear that we cannot continue as we have been, and that three key trends are forcing our hands, making major and far-reaching change inevitable. These include:

The Beginning Of The End Of Cheap Fossil Fuels

Nobody yet knows for sure when the world will pass the peak in oil production, although this historic moment may well have already happened in July 2008[1], when the price reached $147 a barrel, which dampened demand to an extent from which it has yet to recover, and indeed may never do so. Indeed some argue that the current economic situation was, in large part, caused by the oil price spike[2]. Our lifestyles depend on cheap oil for virtually everything in our homes, from our food to our toothbrushes, from our carpets to our shoes. The 21st century way of living is literally built out of oil. The peak oil argument does not say that one day soon we will 'run out' of oil, we may well never see that day; what it says is that we will soon see that end of the age of cheap oil and all that that has made possible. It will prove to be a historic shift. During the Oil Age, we have extracted and burnt 1200 billion barrels of crude oil, nearly half of all the ancient sunlight laid down in prehistory. That is an astonishing amount of any material, never mind one that has the long-term impacts that it has had on the climate, the environment and on humanity. As the Chief Economist at the International Energy Agency now tells world government leaders, "we should leave oil before it leaves us"[3].

The Impact We Are Having On The Climate

Every day brings increasingly grim news about the speed and scale of climate change. Most of us have noticed weather patterns changing during our lifetimes; snow and cold winters are now a

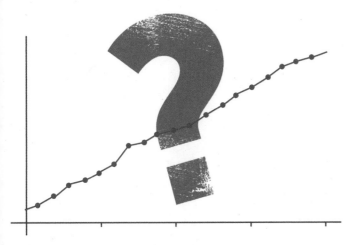

rarity in Devon, whereas as the oral histories section of this report will show, they used to be commonplace. The average temperature in Devon has increased 1.5°C since 1960[4], and is predicted to rise by the same again between now and 2030. Globally, of most concern, is the scale of the melting of the ice in the Arctic, long seen by climate scientists as one of the crucial indicators of climate change. The pace of melting is far faster than anyone expected. The last report by the Intergovernmental Panel on Climate Change, an unprecedented scientific consensus that climate change is underway, suggested that, in its worst-case scenario, the arctic ice might start to break up by 2010. If current trends continue it could all be gone by 2014[5]. Governments are now responding, but are working to targets of 450 parts per million. The latest science tells us that we need to cut to 350 parts per million[6]. We have already passed 387ppm. Our time for postponing action and for procrastination has long passed. The scale of the cuts we need to make in our carbon emissions is profound, yet achievable, and could be the catalyst for an extraordinary revolution for industry and commerce.

The End Of The Economic Growth Bubble

Money is brought into existence by being lent to people, so money, really, equals debt. The UK has become the second most indebted nation in the world (second only to Ireland), with astonishing levels of personal credit and a total national debt 336% of GDP[7]. The Government has also borrowed heavily in order to carry out its objectives, and more recently, to bail out the UK banking industry, debt for which we will be liable for many years to come. The trouble with generating debt is that it is based on the assumption that the future will be wealthier than the present, in order to repay that debt. Underpinning that is the assumption that there will always be the cheap energy to enable the economic growth required. The current unravelling of international finance, and the realisation that much of that debt is 'toxic', i.e. un-repayable, will prove to have far deeper implications than currently realised.

Also of importance is the fact that the UK, situated at the end of many long energy pipelines, sold much of its own indigenous energy at a time when prices were very low, and has become a net importer at a time of great energy volatility. Moreover, the level of national debt incurred in the bailing out of the banks recently has necessitated deep cuts across the economy, which will put in question our ability to rely on pensions and the Welfare State in the way that we have done.

For the past three years, Transition Town Totnes has co-ordinated a programme of awareness raising on these three key issues in the town, bringing many of the world's experts on the subject to the town. Peak oil specialists have included Richard Heinberg, Jeremy Leggett and David Strahan, climate change experts have included Aubrey Meyer, Mayer Hillman and Tony Juniper, and leading thinkers on economics have included Andrew Simms, Colin Hines, David Fleming, Molly Scot Cato, Bernard Lietaer, Richard Douthwaite, David Boyle and others. It has been an illuminating journey, and much of the wisdom that they have brought to this community is captured in this document.

The Context of this Plan

Totnes is not the first town or city to start to explore the practicalities of moving away from oil dependency and high levels of carbon emissions. One of the first such plans was the Kinsale Energy Descent Action Plan, developed in 2005 by students at a college in southern Ireland, which was partly responsible for the formation of the Transition concept. It set out to explore how the town could make the move away from its oil dependency, seeing a huge potential opportunity in these inevitable changes. The Kinsale report became a viral phenomenon, being downloaded many thousands of times.

Since then, plans that relate to responses to peak oil have fallen into four categories. There are those that are local government-led, those that explore the wider impacts of peak oil on society, those that look at solutions in a wider context, mostly national 'power down' style responses, and finally there are those which, like this Plan, are community driven re-localisation plans, known as 'Energy Descent Action Plans' (a more detailed round up of other communities who have produced such plans can be found on the website). Some local authorities have passed 'Peak Oil Resolutions' (see box), and some local authorities, most notably Somerset and Leicestershire have passed resolutions in support of their local Transition initiatives.

Nottingham City Council's Peak Oil Resolution

(passed 8th December 2008)

This Council acknowledges the forthcoming impact of peak oil. The Council therefore needs to respond, and help the citizens it serves respond, to the likelihood of shrinking oil supply but in a way, which nevertheless maintains the City's prosperity. It acknowledges that actions taken to adapt to and mitigate against climate change also help us adapt issues around peak oil.

It will do this by:

Developing an understanding of the impact of peak oil on the local economy and the local community

Encouraging a move across the city towards sustainable transport, cycling and walking throughout the city

Pursuing a rigorous energy efficiency and conservation programme through its carbon management plan, the work towards EMAS[8] accreditation and on leading on raising energy awareness across all sectors to reduce dependency on oil based energy in the city

Supporting research and production within the city which helps develop local effective alternative energy supplies and energy saving products in order to encourage a move away from oil based fuels and also in order to create local 'green collar jobs'

Co-ordinating policy and action on reducing our city's carbon dependency and in response to the need to mitigate and adapt to climate change and peak oil.

In this way Nottingham City Council will not only be helping the city to rise to the challenge of peak oil but also encourage the city to grasp the opportunities which peak oil offers.

Recent UK Government Policy

While the UK Government continues to state that peak oil is not an issue that needs to be considered until sometime beyond 2030, it is increasingly taking the issue of climate change very seriously. Its 'Low Carbon Transition Plan' (its very name inspired by Ed Miliband's visit to the 2009 Transition Network conference where he was invited as a 'keynote listener') sets out a bold and visionary plan for the UK. It includes some of what is proposed here: microgeneration, energy efficiency and conservation and a concerted, cross-sector push to reduce the nation's emissions by 80% by 2050. It contains much to commend it, and is also frustratingly unspecific on actual measures, especially in relation to food and farming[9].

A couple of months later, the Cabinet Office released its latest document on the UK's food policies, and, for the first time, put the issue of food security centre stage. Although it didn't promote the idea of increasing regional food self-reliance, it was a significant step forward from DEFRA's statement in 2003 that 'food security is neither necessary, nor is it desirable'. We feel that what is set out in this Plan is ahead of Government thinking and policies, and will contribute to raising the national debate considerably, given that it is a community-led process, asking questions which Government still finds it uncomfortable to ask.

Resilience

The concept of resilience is central to this plan. One of the best ways to explain what this means is by looking back to the year 2000 and the truck drivers' dispute of that year. Angered by the proposed rise in fuel tax, lorry drivers across the UK picketed fuel depots, and within a short period of time, the nation's fleet of delivery lorries and its entire just-in-time distribution system began to grind to a halt. Supermarket shelves started to empty and within days, the UK had gone from a nation with abundant food supplies and an illusion of plenty, to one that was 2 days from a major food crisis and which, just for that short window of insight, could see that the local food system that had supported it historically had largely been unravelled.

In 2008, staff at the Grangemouth oil refinery came close to going on strike, which would have led to a situation similar to that of 2000. The media was filled with editorials along the lines of "how dare these people hold the country to ransom with their demands?" The question that no-one asked was how we had so spectacularly failed to learn the lessons of 8 years previously, and why it was that we were still in the position where an interruption to our liquid fuels supply could still bring our economy to its knees.

Central to this is resilience. Resilience is, in a nutshell, the ability of a system, whether an individual, an economy, a town or a city, to withstand shock from the outside. As the credit crunch has highlighted, the global economy is now so highly networked, that a shock or crisis in one part can pulse very fast through the rest of the system. Resilience is about building the ability to adapt to shock, to flex and modify, rather than crumble. You can think of it as being like building surge protectors into an electrical system.

A resilient Totnes would have an economy that cycles more money locally, creates more local jobs, is less at the mercy of major employees deciding to relocate elsewhere (e.g. Dairy Crest, Dartington College of Arts). It would be more diverse, in terms of skills, livelihoods, land use, businesses, housing provision and so on. It would also bring the impacts of its consumption closer to home, and take more responsibility for its impacts. It would be a Totnes that learned to live more in place, and to appreciate the vulnerability that current approaches bring. While it is wonderful, and historically unprecedented, to be able to eat strawberries in March, the system that makes that possible has at the same time unravelled our local systems, deskilled our farmers and growers and left us more vulnerable. Resilience thinking offers a key insight for those planning for our future. The starting place for this plan is not a judgemental list of the things that are 'right' and 'wrong' in the world. Rather it is an acknowledgement that change is inevitable, and that we need to pull together in order to make Totnes and District as resilient as possible, in such a way as to inspire the rest of the country to do the same.

Localisation

This Plan explores the nuts-and-bolts practicalities of relocalising the economy of the area. It argues that in a world of highly volatile oil prices, the need for stringent cuts in carbon emissions and economic uncertainty, the globalised economy upon which we are so dependent can no longer be relied upon, indeed it leaves us highly vulnerable. At the moment, Totnes and its surrounding parishes act like a large leaky bucket. Money pours into the area through wages, grants, pensions, funding, tourist revenues and so on. In our current economic model, most of it pours back out again, and its ability to make things happen locally is lost. Each time we pay our energy bill, that money leaves the area. Each time we shop in a supermarket, 80% of that money leaves the area. Every time we shop online, that money that could have bolstered our economy leaves the area. All the while, pressure grows on our local shops and businesses.

At the same time, local agriculture employs fewer and fewer people each year, more and more food is imported, new buildings are created from materials from around the world, and most of the goods sold in the shops of Totnes have travelled long distances to get there. The concept of localisation is about shifting the focus of production closer to home. It is not something that can be done overnight, it is a long-term process that requires planning, design and innovation. In many ways, the area is poised to take a national lead here, being home to a strong local food culture, and many innovative businesses.

Localisation is a powerful concept. Clearly Totnes cannot become self-sufficient, nor would it want to be. It will never be able to make computers or frying pans. However, as the oral history section of this report shows, it used to be far more self-reliant than it is today, functioning far more like a bucket than its present day leaky sieve. There is significant potential for Totnes and District to, for example:

◎ Produce most of its food locally, and create a range of livelihoods, processing and value-adding that food in the locality

◎ Source a significant proportion of its building materials, for both new build and retrofits, either from the local area or from recycling from the local waste stream

◎ Buy its energy from locally owned and managed energy companies rather than distant ones

◎ Maintain and enhance the proportion of shops in the town that are locally owned, and avoid the 'Ghost Town Britain' phenomenon seen in so many High Streets across the country

◎ Bring land for development into community ownership, so that the financial gains from that development accrue to the community, rather than to speculative developers

◎ Make medicines using local plants to treat common ailments

◎ Use its food wastes to create bio-methane to power vehicles

◎ Use local currencies and local investment mechanisms to enable more money to be invested in the immediate area

None of this will happen by accident, it needs careful planning and design. This Plan is a first attempt at trying to map out what the process of re-localisation might look like.

Introducing our Survey

As part of the process that led to the creation of this Plan, a survey was carried out on 220 households in Totnes and Dartington. The survey was conducted by the University of Plymouth during April 2009. Where findings relate to specific areas (food, energy and so on) they appear in the relevant sections in Part Three. The more general findings from the survey are presented here.

Transition Town Totnes (TTT) has been in existence for just over 3 years now, so we were fascinated to know the extent to which knowledge of it had percolated into the community, and also what depth of engagement it was attracting. It was encouraging to discover that 74.9% of those questioned had heard of TTT and its work.

The respondents were then asked whether they had ever participated in any of its events. 60.6% said never, 33.3% occasionally, 3.9% regularly and 2.2% often. Taking a rough figure for the population of Totnes as 8,416, extrapolated to all the survey respondents, this means that around 155 people are often involved, 328 regularly involved, and around 2800 occasionally involved since the launch of the project in late 2006.

Those who said they had participated in TTT events were then asked which ones. 59.1% said they had attended a talk or workshop, 7.7% had had some involvement in the Garden Share scheme, 36.9% had been involved with the Totnes Pound initiative, 21.5% had taken an active role in one of TTT's 11 working groups, 6.2% had got involved with the Transition Tales project run at KEVICC and 12.3% had participated in the creation of this Energy Descent Plan for the area.

When asked whether they thought the work of TTT was relevant to their lives, 57.2% of respondents said it was either highly relevant or relevant. Only 11% felt it to be completely irrelevant. People were also asked for their thoughts on community. The next section looked at how people perceived the community in which they lived. When asked whether they felt adequately consulted in public consultation processes that affect the area, opinion was fairly neatly divided. 50.7% of people agreed that they did and 49.3% said they did not. When asked whether they felt it was hard to get their voice heard, there was again, a neat divide, 59.1% agreeing that it is hard, 40.9% that it isn't.

When asked whether they felt that in the event of a crisis the community could pull together, 83.2% agreed that it could. They were then asked whether the sense of community the respondent felt from their neighbours had decreased over the past few years. 65.7% disagreed or strongly disagreed with this, only 8.3% strongly agreeing that their sense of community had declined.

Many of the questions will allow TTT to redo the survey in two years and to see whether the community's resilience and thinking have continued to grow and evolve.

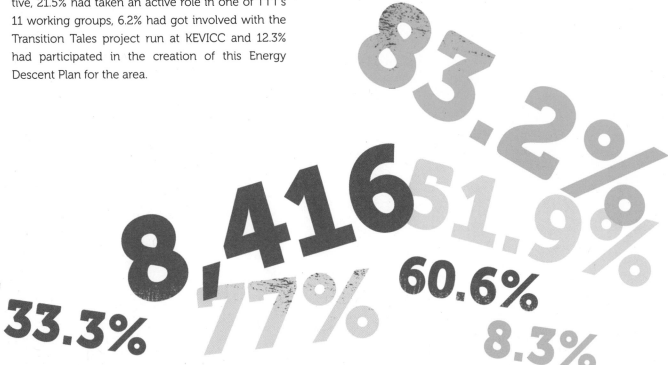

NOTES & IDEAS

CREATING
A NEW STORY

Part Two sets the context for the new story we are about to tell. It starts by looking at why, at this time of rapid change, we need new stories. We then start this section by telling, through a series of oral history interviews, the story of the last time that Totnes and District experienced energy shortages while still having a more localised food system. This is important in rooting this plan in the history of the area, in the stories and lessons learnt by those who experienced those times.

It then goes on to look at the approach that created this plan, and how the community of Totnes and District were engaged in the process of its creation. The plan you hold in your hands is the result of many hundreds of people's input over a 3-year period of creative engagement. It is also intended that that process doesn't stop with the creation of this plan, but is ongoing. We also set out how that is intended to work.

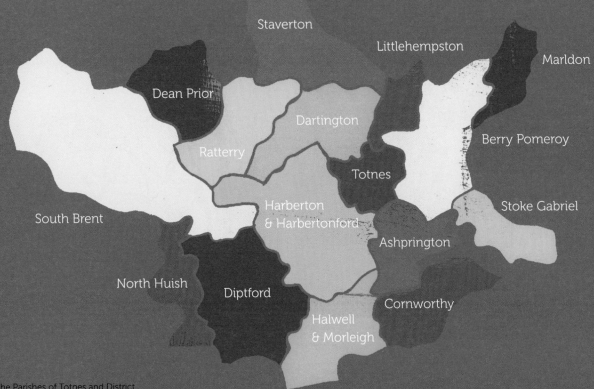

Staverton

Littlehempston

Marldon

Dean Prior

Dartington

Berry Pomeroy

Ratterry

Totnes

South Brent

Harberton & Harbertonford

Stoke Gabriel

Ashprington

North Huish

Diptford

Cornworthy

Halwell & Morleigh

WHY WE NEED NEW STORIES...

What you are about to read is as much a story as it is a community plan. It is a story about how a Devon town and its surrounding parishes embarked on an extraordinary journey, starting in 2009, harnessing all of its creativity and brilliance to re-imagine itself for a rapidly changing world. It is the story of ordinary people who came to see that their future would be very different from the present, and that that change was an inevitability. Rather than panic, switch off or slump into denial of the changes building around them, they took the braver, more testing, but ultimately more nourishing route, of seeing that change as a tremendous and historic opportunity.

Like all great adventure stories, it begins with ordinary people faced with a task the scale of which initially looks impossible. By taking the first steps and rediscovering how to work with each other, skills, strengths and previously unimagined inner resources were uncovered, and a scale of transformation was achieved that 20 years later, is the subject of the songs and stories of the generation that followed them. It is a story, but it is also a statement of intent.

As a culture, we struggle for lack of appropriate cultural stories in these times of great change. If you asked 30 people chosen at random in Totnes High Street to describe their mental picture of the world in 20 years having begun to reduce its carbon emissions by 9% each year starting in 2009, the likelihood is that it would probably be somewhere between the Flintstones and Steptoe and Son. We have many cultural stories, and their telling in mainstream movies and novels, of societies that collapse in various ways (Mad Max), those that invent their way to a space age future (Star Trek) or those that just continue with business as usual, where the future is like the present, except there's just more of everything. What might the stories look like of the generation that looked peak oil and climate change square in the face and responded with creativity and imagination? That is what this document tries to do.

While on the theme of stories, we might wonder what future generations might make of this time as they look back. What will those in an energy-lean world make of an age like ours, which wasted their

The Unleashing of Transition Town Totnes in 2006. © Sally Hewitt

Hop o' My Thumb stealing the Seven-league boots. Copy of a drawing by Gustave Dore

energy inheritance, and destroyed their climate, with such profligacy? How will people, who never got to experience such a thing, think about cheap flights around the world, or the idea of eating strawberries in February? One hint might come from looking at the stories that people told before cheap oil, when their lives were constrained by the realities of living without fossil fuels. These included:

◎ **The 7 League Boots,** which enabled the wearer to cover 7 leagues (around 21 miles) with each stride

◎ **The Magic Porridge Pot,** which enabled the owner, provided they knew the magic words, to create an endless supply of food without having to lift a finger to produce it (they also had to remember the magic words to stop it, or there was a danger of their entire town being submerged in porridge)

◎ **The Elves and the Shoemaker,** where someone who made their living from a manual trade found that magically all the work was done for them without the need for them to do anything, the shoes being mysteriously manufactured overnight, and all they had to do was sell them.

Although these are stories, in effect they are fantasies about a world with fossil fuels. The 7 League Boots are now Ryanair, the Magic Porridge Pot is Tesco, and the Elves and the Shoemaker? That is the sweatshops of China, without which, as a nation that has dismantled much of its manufacturing, we would be without many of life's current essentials.

At a workshop run by the Wondermentalist Cabaret and Transition Town Totnes in January 2009, participants were invited to write a piece from the perspective of someone in the future looking back on our time now.

Nostalgia

I remember a world

Where I could get up

In the middle of the night

And drive 3 hours

Just to be with you

On a whim

Now I'd have to swim

It was okay back then

Cause you could get a frozen coffee at 3am

Now in Winter I can't get a cup of tea till noon

But I still get twitchy under a fool moon

And want to do something crazy

Go garden ferociously

By the ever encroaching sea

I smile as I remember how

Stupid and impulsive I used to be

by Liv Torc
(member of the Wondermentalist Collective)

My grandma

My grandma ate a mango every morning in her day.
And each one wrapped in a plastic pack
that she'd just throw away
She had strawberries in winter – and apples in the spring
She must have been quite special to deserve so many things

Grandma's house had many rooms but she resided all alone
And a hideout in the countryside made up a second home
And she had energy to burn at the flick of any switch
If everything she says is true she must have been quite rich.

The Garden of my grandma was the prettiest you've seen
She never grew a single grain or vegetable or bean
She never had to work the land and get her clothes all mucky
She never had to lift a hand, how could she be so lucky?

Grandma had her very own car, to go just where she'd like
One didn't have to walk so far, or take the bus, or bike
She didn't need her neighbours, she knew city folk instead
I hope that she was grateful for the amazing life she led.

Gran would get on aeroplanes if she fancied taking flight
She'd disappear once every year – for maybe just a fortnight!
She must have been contented when her life was so carefree
I like to hear her stories and pretend that it was me...

by local poet Roz
(AKA. Beryl the Feral)

HOME: WHERE WE START FROM

TOTNES AND DISTRICT

Totnes is a rural market town whose fortunes have fluctuated greatly throughout history. In Medieval times it was a wealthy market town, which prospered through the wool trade, resulting in its legacy of many fine buildings built by prosperous merchants of the time. Its success was due to 3 things, its role as a market town, as a river port and as the lowest bridging point on the River Dart. In the 19th century, a long-running legal dispute nearly bankrupted the town, since when its fortunes have gradually improved. Many businesses have been central to the economy of the town, in particular the Dairy

Crest milk processing plant, Reeves Timber yard, Harris' Bacon Factory, Dartington College of Arts, Symonds Cider, Tuckers Toffee, all of which no longer exist.

Totnes has been a vibrant centre for arts and culture, initiated by the establishing of the Dartington Hall Trust in 1923, which turned the Dartington Estate into place, which, to this day, attracts many leading artists to the area. In 2009, Totnes finds itself an economy based on tourism, a number of small and medium enterprises, and not much else in terms of employment opportunities. Many people now travel

2.4 Totnes from Fishchowters Lane near Ashprinton. © Jacqi Hodgson

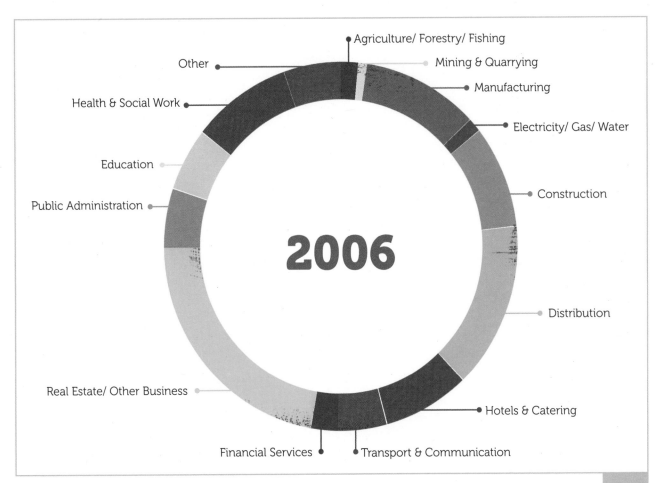

Agriculture/ Forestry/ Fishing
Mining & Quarrying
Manufacturing
Electricity/ Gas/ Water
Construction
Distribution
Hotels & Catering
Transport & Communication
Financial Services
Real Estate/ Other Business
Public Administration
Education
Health & Social Work
Other

2006

Sectors Contribution to GVA in Devon. Source: Devon GVA   2.5

to Exeter and Plymouth, or even to London, for work. The use of the river for importing goods has all but ceased, being used more for recreation and tourism than for commerce. As Walter King[1] puts it, "the problem is not that old industries are fading, but that nothing of substance has been put in their place".

Totnes and District: Some Socioeconomic Data

Totnes is seen as one of the significant towns in the South Hams, what South Hams District Council refer to as an 'Area Centre', that is, a settlement that plays a distinctive role in the county. Devon County Council (2006) has identified some of the key data about the town and its surroundings ("Totnes and District" is defined as the 16 parishes, of which Totnes parish is one). The area has seen significant population growth since 1991, with Totnes parish seeing a 17.2% rise between 1991 and 2004 (the last year for which data is available). The proportion of ethnic minorities is about average for Devon. Compared to the

average, Totnes and District has slightly high levels of unemployment, although in Totnes parish the percentage of people claiming Income Support is 50% over the national average.

The main sectors of employment are wholesale and retail trade, health and social work, manufacturing and education. Totnes has more part-time and less full-time and self-employed workers than the national average. Also, the number of households with an income below £20,000 in Totnes parish is 50% more than the national average. One in fifteen households in Totnes parish is occupied by a lone pensioner, and the percentage of people claiming Incapacity Benefit and Severe Disability Allowance is well above average. According to the 2001 Census, in Totnes and District 5.54% of people in the area work in food, forestry and fishing (although an exact figure of how many work in agriculture is unavailable) (ONS 2001). This clearly differs between the urban and the rural populations. 2.4% of Totnes work in food, forestry and fishing, while 7.33% of the rest of Totnes and District do (ibid).

STORIES OF OUR RECENT PAST

Is there anything that we can learn from the last period during which this area experienced energy shortages and had a more localised food system than it does today? What insights can be drawn from that period to inform our choices and decisions over the period of Transition that we are facing? Those are the questions this section sets out to address. The following is based on 12 oral history interviews conducted in and around Totnes during 2008/9. They focus on the period between 1930 and 1960, the last period in the history of the town when energy was in short supply, and a more localised food system was still functioning, albeit declining over the period in question.

This collection of histories makes no claim to being authoritative, being, after all, based on the recollections of just a handful of people, but it does offer some useful insights. Their implications for our planning for a lower energy world will be explored below[2].

Setting the Scene

Totnes has long been an important market town for the South Hams, and during the period focused on here, its population was around 4,000 (it is now more than twice that). During the period being explored here, Totnes was passing through, and emerging on the other side of, a World War. Alan Langmaid (now Museum Administrator of Totnes Museum) sets the scene.

"The whole of Britain was a tired, weary, drab place. It had gone through six years of a very serious war, only 20 years after another very serious war that had completely wiped it out. Totnes was empty. It was dirty, and like everything else it was tired. Nobody could afford anything, very few people had cars. We had no car, we didn't even have a telephone or a television".

This is, however, at some variance with Ken Gill's recollection of Totnes as having "the feel of a prosperous town", and also David Heath, who said, "when I was growing up in Totnes in the late 40's and 50's it was a thriving market town well served with a wide range of shops of that time. Large numbers of people came in to shop from the surrounding villages on market day and generally the town had a feel of prosperity about it."

Food

Food was by necessity, until recently, a far more local affair than it is today. Most people, apart from the wealthiest, would have grown some of their own fruit and vegetables, and would have had a far deeper connection with where their food came from than our supermarket-focused generation of today. This arose, in the main, from necessity. Rationing was, after all, still in place the mid 1950s. Val Price recalls in the late 1950s the first time she became aware of the idea that food was something that could actually come from further afield than the local area, when she was asked to do a school project which involved collecting the paper sheets that oranges came wrapped in at that time and compile a list of where they had come from. Until that point, she told me, the idea had never occurred to her.

Attitudes to food were very different. Alan Langmaid describes the attitude of the generation who had lived through the war. "My grandmother's attitude to food was if it is put in front of you, you must eat it. You had no choice. You must not leave a crumb. Food was very precious and most of it was vegetables. It was a good healthy diet, proper, fresh food". Similarly, Val Price remembers being made to stay at the table for long periods of time until she had finished eating all of her meal. "If you didn't eat it", she said, "it was back again for the next meal. I was very envious of friends who had dogs, and could feed them bits under the table!"

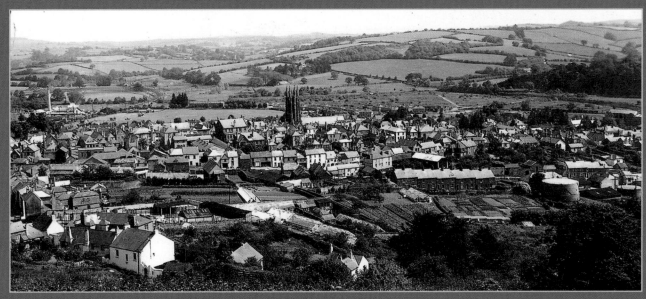

2.6   Totnes town in the 1940s. Note market gardens and greenhouses on what is now called 'The Southern Area'.
© Totnes Image Bank and Rural Archive

2.7   Mason's Butchers at the top of Totnes Town, 1930s. © Totnes Image Bank and Rural Archive

2.8   George Heath in one of his heated greenhouses'.
© Totnes Image Bank and Rural Archive

George Heath in his nursery, in what is now 'Heath's Nursery
Car Park'. © Totnes Image Bank and Rural Archive   **2.9**

The production and processing of food was also a far greater generator of employment than it is today. Three of the town's main employers, Harris's Bacon Factory, Tuckers Sweet Factory and the Milk Factory, were food producers, and a far higher proportion of the town's shops were food shops.

Home Growing and Allotments

Home-grown food was commonplace until the mid-1960s. Most people interviewed remember the town itself having a diversity of food gardens, allotments and small livestock. Marion Adams, whose parents ran the bed and breakfast in Bridgetown in which she grew up, recalls the garden behind the house, managed by her father, which grew the large majority of the vegetables used by the family and by their business, as well as their chickens and fruit trees.

For most people, growing some of their own food was just a fact of life, a skill acquired almost by osmosis during childhood, and the landscape of the town reflected this. Val Price, who grew up on Sparrow Road, remembers every garden in the street being used to grow food, mostly done by the men of the households. "Dad grew all our food in our garden", she said. "Potatoes, runner beans, beetroot, carrots, onions, raspberries and strawberries". Gardening was, she recalls, the main topic of conversation for the men of the street who would "stand around, leaning on their forks, and telling each other they were doing it all wrong."

Small livestock was also common. Alan Langmaid estimates that one in ten homes kept chickens, recalling "there was always someone with a big wire netting chicken coop", but Marion Adams remembers it as being even more than that, closer to being every third house. Pigs were also kept in the town. Ken Gill, who ran one of the three market gardens in the town, kept three styes of pigs, whose manure fertilised the garden.

Villages and farms tended to be more self-sufficient, as Douglas Matthews in Staverton (who recently passed away shortly after his 100th birthday in Staverton and who still slept in the bedroom he was born in), recalled;

"I suppose we might have had an orange on very special occasions. Our main meal was lunch, not supper, if the husband worked at home. Evening meals were

a professionals' thing. Lunch was normally roast beef, mutton, hot or cold. Hot or cold chicken, stews, potatoes and veg, peas and beans, potatoes baked or boiled. We ate meat every day, hot or cold, depending on how the husband and wife were getting on! For tea we had bread and butter, jam and cream. For breakfast it was bacon and eggs. Supper was just a snack meal, bits and pieces of what you liked. For fruit we had apples, pears and plums. Apples could be kept all year round. They were kept in a cellar under the house. Certain kinds of pears could be kept. We had greengages and plums; we usually made those into jams".

In the late 1960s, the need for productive gardens began to diminish, and the new generation began to see it as boring and unnecessary. Andy Langford, whose father was a keen gardener, and who initially kept an allotment at Coplands Meadow (now housing), and subsequently a very productive third of an acre home garden at the top of Barracks Hill, said "We used to consider gardening to be something you did because he'd caught you! My generation was the one that broke the link with gardening. It was much more fun to take your bicycle to bits, put it back together again and go off racing around the countryside". Similarly Val Price recalls never being taught to garden, as gardening was "something Dads did", and that by the early 60s it had become something that young people only did if they had to, most seemed to agree that with the beginnings of pop music and teenage culture they had far better things to do.

The Market Gardens

Totnes featured 3 commercial market gardens within the town itself: Heaths, Gills and Phillips/Victoria Nursery. The largest, at least initially, was Heath's, started in 1920 by George Heath senior, and then run by his son, also called George, until its closure in 1981. Much of the south-facing area of the town has been dedicated to food production back through history, and the gardens serve as a powerful reminder of the potential of urban market gardening.

Heath's Nursery was in two sections: there was the open area, which grew mainly vegetables and had one small propagating house, now "Heath's Nursery car park", and the lower area, now also a car park known, just as "The Nursery", which was covered in greenhouses. He grew a wide range of vegetables and salad crops in season. To support the florist side

Totnes Mayor Lewis Major showing the cleared site of Heath's Nursery following its acquisition by South Hams District Council and its earmarking for re-development as a car park, early 1980s. © Totnes Image Bank and Rural Archive **2.10**

Gills Grocers shop. © Totnes Image Bank and Rural Archive **2.11**

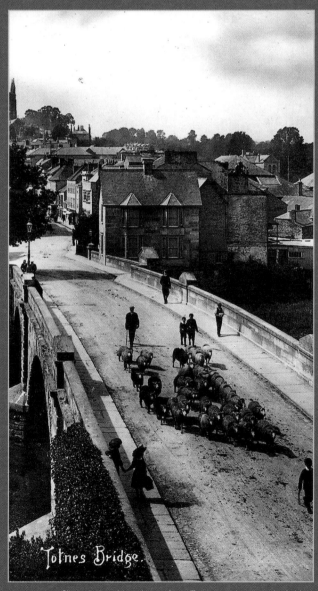

2.13 Sheep being driven home from Totnes market over the bridge. © Totnes Image Bank and Rural Archive

The glasshouses of Gills Nursery (now housing). © Totnes Image Bank and Rural Archive **2.12**

of the business he also specialised in chrysanthemums, dahlias and pot plants. The greenhouses were heated and allowed the production of large quantities of tomatoes (a specialty), lettuces and chrysanthemums out of season.

The garden's fertility came mainly from manure brought up from Harris' Bacon factory. The outlet for Heath's produce was his shop on the Butterwalk (now Harlequin Bookshop), which was frequently beautifully decorated for special occasions, such as the 1977 Silver Jubilee.

Andy Langford recalls going to Heath's shop on Saturday mornings with his father, Eric, who was a teacher at the Redworth Secondary Modern School. "My dad and he were both in the amateur operatic society and would be singing in the same Gilbert and Sullivan show, so they would sing little bits to each other, and then him saying "oh no, tomatoes, we got no tomatoes, but let's go get some then"... and then we all went over. That's what we did. We all went over to the greenhouses at the nursery and picked tomatoes, and they sang songs to each other wandering up and down and talked about this and that".

Douglas Matthews, farming out at Staverton, remembers recalls George Heath's business style. "He had a miserable manner. If you took anything to him to see (I used to take Bramley apples), he would plead poverty. "I can't pay you what I paid you last week Mr. Matthews, business is very bad". I used to say, "George, you're talking rubbish!" He was a very good businessman and he did nobody any harm. He was very go-ahead and he worked hard".

When George Heath retired, his land was sold to the South Hams Council and it was only after this that the Southern bypass road was opened up and the car parks put in as they are today. The closure of the nurseries took place in 1981 ending with the dismantling of the greenhouses. George Heath passed away in 1985.

Gills Nursery (which adjoined Heath's), was run by Jack Gill until 1973, when his son Ken took over, who managed it until the nursery closed in 1981. Running a series of glasshouses, which were kept warm all year round, required a lot of energy. Initially they were heated using coke, which required 10 tons a year, but they later moved to the less labour intensive oil, necessitating the burning of 2000 gallons of oil a year in order to generate sufficient warmth.

The site behind the shop was not the only one Gills managed. They also had a site on Harpers' Hill, where they grew potatoes and sprouts, and one on North Street, where, Ken recalls, "we grew raspberries, in spite of it being north-facing, and somehow it was warm enough for raspberries". Later they also acquired a 3½-acre site beside the bypass, which was used for field scale vegetable production. We had no complaints with our fertility", he said, "one year we grew 20,000 lettuces", an extraordinary output from a small piece of ground.

Although running a business like Gills was hard work, it was a good living. Unlike Heath's, the closure of which was forced by retirement, Gill's was driven to close by a less predictable challenge. "A Highways engineer from Devon County Council came into one of the greenhouses one day, and told me and my father "you won't be picking many more tomatoes here, we're going to build a road through the place".

Although the proposed road linking South Street and the newly built Heath's Way was never built (part of the road building phase which saw Heath's Nursery opened up), it created enough uncertainty, hanging in the air as a possibility for at least 10 years, that when Jack Gill died, it fell to his son, Ken, to decide whether or not to invest in modernising and expanding the Nursery. Given the degree of uncertainty, he decided it would be unwise, and the nursery was slowly wound down.

Running a market garden and a shop was hard work. Ken Gill recalls working 12-14 hour days, seven days a week during the summer months, and David Heath describes his father's choice of career as 'bloody hard work'.

Local Farming

The farmers who surrounded Totnes were much more directly engaged with the town than they are now, as the town provided the key markets for their produce. Douglas Matthews farmed 250 acres (which had grown to 300 by the time of his retirement in 1989). When he started work on the farm, it was still run by working horses. The farm had around 30 cows, 40 acres of cereals and about 50 breeding ewes, but by the time he had retired, it had been turned into a purely dairy farm, with nearly 80 cows.

He recalls the post-war push to increase productivity, driven, at least in part, by the Agricultural Committees of which he was a member. One of the other key drivers in agricultural innovation was Dartington, which started the first artificial insemination centre in 1944, one of the first in the country, and also hosted the Agricultural Discussion Society, which brought many leading agriculturalists to the area to give talks on new developments and innovations.

Andy Langford recalls picking up lots of casual work on local farms from the age of 13 onwards. He said that in the late 1960s there were "lots of small family farms all over the place. The average farm size would have been 30-40 acres, 120 acres would have been considered quite upper class sort of farming". Many of the farms were short of labour during the summer, especially during haymaking and straw baling times. His favourite was one at East Allington. "We were out there a lot. We used to go out there and the farm was pretty much run by the young people. Andy Strutt was a classmate of mine. He had 6 sisters, which was part of the attraction. Suddenly I found myself in charge of a little tractor moving around the farm picking up hay bales with all these young women about and these big lunches and suppers where you could eat as many roast potatoes as you could get in yourself, that was very lovely. We basically ran the place".

A Market Town

For most farmers, the two markets in the town were absolutely essential to their economic survival. Totnes had two markets, the Cattle Market, held initially at the Lamb every other Tuesday, before later transferring for a short period to Totnes Racecourse (now the Industrial Estate), and the Friday Pannier Market, held in what is now the Civic Square but which was, until it was destroyed by fire in the 1950s, a traditional covered market with stalls, the front of which came right out to the High Street. Douglas Matthews recalls the Pannier Market as being "all covered, with old stalls with top and bottom doors, and a separate bit in the middle. Anyone could sell anything, rabbits (this was pre- days) and so on".

The Cattle Market was a key element of the local economy. Not everyone recalls it favourably. Alan Langmaid said "on Tuesdays, the town became what you would imagine the Somme to be. It was muddy, dirty, dingy, smelly, drunken, bloody and crowded". On market days the pubs closest to the market, the

Kingsbridge, the Bayhorse, the Plymouth and the Bull Inn were open all day. For Andy Langford, a young teenager at the time, market day was the day when, as an underage drinker, one could get served in the pubs.

Shopping

Clearly the markets weren't the only source of food. The High Street contained a far higher proportion of shops selling food than today. The way the shops were run was also very different to today. Muriel Langford describes a trip to the shops in the early 1950s;

"I used to go to the grocers and I could sit down, lovely. They'd go through your list and say, "yes, yes, we've some new whatever it is, would you like to taste some?" You'd have a little snippet of cheese or something, "great, yes, we'll have that". "Now we've got a tin of broken biscuits, but they're not too bad (half price you see), would you like them?" As soon as you put a biscuit in your mouth it's broken isn't it! Then they'd say, "Now Mrs. Langford, you're going to the butchers, yes, yes, and going to get some fish? Yes, yes, and paraffin? Yes, yes... and they used to say to me now bring any parcels in, we'll put it in the box with your groceries and bring the lot up for you. And they did. They'd come and deliver and you'd go through it and say that's fine and would you like a cup of tea...."

Reflecting on the changes seen in the local economy, Ken Gill is unsure change has necessarily been for the better. He reflected "it has been progress of a sort, or has it? I'm not sure. We lost something we will never be able to regain. The loss of a lot of small shops has been hard, although we have replaced them with what we might call 'slightly unusual shops'... We've lost the dairies, the independent grocers, although we have retained a good selection of butchers and some good cheese and fish shops. When you consider what we used to have...."

The supermarket age began at the end of the period we have been exploring here, on May 28th 1968, with the opening of Gateway, in what is now the chemist besides the Market Square. Nowadays the opening of a new supermarket in the town would be front-page news, but Alan Langmaid, then a reporter for the Totnes Times, says that it "didn't even register" for him, and was only reported in the Totnes Times on page 5.

Marion Adams remembers the shops until the mid-60s as being very different from today. "Everyone seemed to buy everything in the town, they didn't go anywhere to buy it". The idea, which began to emerge in the late 1960s, that shopping meant driving to another town, would have been baffling in the 40s and 50s.

Food Gleaning

Vera Harvey's father worked on the railways, and often returned home with rabbits and turnips collected along the way. Marion Adams recalls getting the bus to Redpost and visiting a friend who lived near there, with whom she would go for walks in the country which often involved returning home with a pheasant, or other 'available' produce.

Energy

Until the 1950s, Totnes was powered mainly by 'town gas', that is, gas made in situ from coal. The gas was produced in three large gasometres sited near the Grove School. These took in coal and used them to produce the gas that was used to run street lighting and also for domestic supply. This was superseded as natural gas supply arrived.

Lighting

When electrification arrived in the 1950s, Ian Slatter's family in Collapark were one of the first houses to have it installed. The first appliances installed were electric lighting. Marion Adams recalls growing up with gas lights in the house, and when Vera Harvey's house was electrified in the 1950s, their landlord only put it in downstairs, so they had electric lights downstairs, but still needed candles upstairs. Similarly, Muriel Langford, living in a flat above the High Street after the war recalls having "gas, no electricity. We had gas lights".

Heating

Keeping warm was a perennial problem in the days before central heating. Alan Langmaid describes winters thus; "from morning to night you were chilled right through to the bone. Even coming into the house you got warmer but never really warm. You'd go to bed cold and warm up in bed. You'd have a hot water bottle. It sounds romantically tough, but it was just the way it was, everyone was like that".

Most people heated their homes with coal fires, or with firewood if they could get it. Marion Adams recalls the peasouper fogs that the coal fires could generate in the winter, Totnes being a town that sits in a natural valley. As a child it was her job to get up in the mornings and light the fires around the house.

Alan Langmaid recalls his grandmother, with whom he and his mother lived, keenly moving out of an old house that was a converted cider press. "She just wanted modern. She wanted electric fires, electric cookers, electric everything. She wanted automatic this, that and everything. So we moved, at my grandmother's insistence, from this wonderful rambling old building.... to a brand new house, typical of its time. Wooden framed, single glazed windows, open fire for a chimney, which she quickly replaced with an electric fire, "I'm not having any more of that dirty coal business". The winters were actually colder than the previous house! You'd wake up in the morning, and your breath would have condensed on the window, frozen on the inside. Inside it was cold, outside it was cold".

Appliances

Speaking to people about their memories of this time, one is struck by the extraordinary impact that one domestic appliance has had on society, and in particular on the position of women. The washing machine. Before its invention, doing the family laundry was hugely time consuming. For Muriel Langford, living in a one-roomed flat above the High Street just after World War Two, washing for herself, her husband and their young baby was hard work. "We bought a big boiler (known as a copper, a ubiquitous piece of everyday domestic life then), a big pan with a lid, and I used to fill that with water. I'd put it on my gas ring in our main room, and when it was warm enough I'd do my washing on a little table. Once I had done it, I hung it up in our room and opened the window".

Vera Harvey also grew up with her grandparents, and the work of doing the family washing fell to her grandmother, although Vera and her sister were expected to play an active part. Their house in the centre of Totnes had a washhouse, which had two large bathtubs and was, initially, lit by candles. When electricity was installed in their house, they ran a cable out to the washhouse. The hot water was produced in a copper, and once washed, clothes needed to be

2.14 Sheep being bought and sold in the market held in the Lamb every other Tuesday. © Totnes Image Bank and Rural Archive

2.15 The front of Totnes market, before it was destroyed by fire in the 1950s and opened out into the public square of today. © Totnes Image Bank and Rural Archive

International Stores, the first supermarket in Totnes. © Totnes Image Bank and Rural Archive **2.16**

put through a mangle. She recalls the arrival of the first washing machine. "As soon as we got a washing machine that was it. 'I'm not going out in that wash house like Gran!' In the 1950s, our first washing machine had a wringer on top. I remember when we used the washhouse, being out there with my Gran, and it was snowing, getting deeper and deeper, saying 'Gran! We can't stay out here!'. People worked so hard in those days".

Refrigeration wasn't a part of peoples' lives until the early 1960s. Muriel Langford recalls that until then, for her, a fridge was "a good pantry, and for milk, a bowl on the floor full of cold water with a wet cloth over it". Ian Slatter recalls in 1959, working behind the bar at the Seymour Hotel (now flats), at the annual Police Ball. There was a raffle to win a small refrigerator, a novelty at the time. His fellow barman failed to turn up and it was extremely hectic. "This bloke came along, he said do you want any tickets for this fridge? I said get me a book of tickets to write out and I'll pay you later on. At the end of the evening the band struck up when the draw was done. Who won it? Yours truly".

The next day when it was delivered, he didn't tell his mother what was to be delivered. He continues, "knock, knock, knock on the back door, and they said, "We've brought your fridge". My mother said "Fridge?! Fridge?!" Nobody had a fridge. My mother said nice to have, but it was so new, nobody had fridges".

Transport

In the 1930s, Douglas Matthews, living in Staverton, relied on horse-drawn traps to travel into Totnes. By the 1940s, cars were becoming a more common sight, although during the war petrol rationing had ground most of them to a halt. As a child growing up in Totnes in the 1960s, the sum total of the transport devices owned by Alan Langmaid's family was his roller-skates, or later, his bicycle. For most people, transport consisted of public transport. Alan recalls "I didn't travel very far. Nobody travelled very far. My mum took the bus to work in Paignton and it was a regular service, like clockwork. She disappeared at 8.25am and reappeared at 4.30pm every day". The pre-Beeching railway network made a great difference to some of Totnes's outlying villages. John Watson, the founder of Riverford Organic Farm, recalls setting off on the train from Staverton station for a romantic ski holiday in the Alps, complete with skis.

Val Price's father bought a car in late 1952, and lovingly built a garage to keep it in. However, she recalls that he rarely used it, never using it to pick her up from school, and never taking it out during the week, given that everything he needed was within walking distance. It was only ever used on weekends, for trips to visit relatives.

By 1963 Totnes was busy in terms of traffic. Alan Langmaid recalls, "there was just as much traffic as there is now, cars, vans and trucks. Not very big trucks, the biggest you would get would be like a horsebox. Just enough to get under the arch, it would usually be heading up to the cattle market". He remembers traffic by the 1960s being noiser than it is today. "Although there was less of it, exhausts were louder and tyres made more noise. People hooted a bit more".

Traffic was still, at that time, two-way up and down the High Street (see Figure 4 above), which necessitated, as Margot Vickers relates, "a man standing at the corner (where the entrance to Castle Court is now), where the road turns left. He had a board which said stop or go".

Reflections

At the end of the interviews, the interviewees were asked what, from the period in question, they felt were the elements that we would do well to carry forward with us into a new period of increased localisation and energy scarcity. There was a fairly high degree of unanimity on those things best consigned to the past. They were: **Life with no washing machine, Coal, Life without central heating, Cold houses and the resultant feeling of being permanently cold in winter months, The mangle.**

In terms of the things that people felt strongly ought not be consigned to history, and which would serve a valuable role if we were successful in carrying them forward with us into a lower energy future, the list ran as follows: **Computers, Double glazing, The Internet, Solar panels, Cavity wall insulation and household insulation in general, The National Health Service, Good public transport, The washing machine, The vacuum cleaner, (In terms of gardening) reusable seed trays and clay pots, Jobs for life, The pre-Beeching railway network.**

Early shoppers in the Gateway supermarket, 1960s. © Totnes Image Bank and Rural Archive **2.17**

The first washing machines for sale in Totnes in Paul Pinch's electrical shop. © Totnes Image Bank and Rural Archive **2.18**

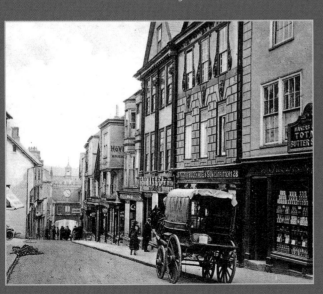

2.19 Totnes High Street, with horse-powered transport very visible. © Totnes Image Bank and Rural Archive

Twenty years later, the car has arrived, and has two way access up, and down, the High Street. © Totnes Image Bank and Rural Archive **2.20**

THE STORY OF TRANSITION TOWN TOTNES

TTT has been a story of ordinary people motivated not by fear and despondency, but rather by inspiration and the desire to create a positive response to peak oil and climate change. Initiated in late 2005, it has grown, since its 'Official Unleashing' in September 2006, to become a significant influence in the town. TTT has always been seen as a catalyst, its role being to inspire and nurture projects, and to support them with fundraising, office facilities, networking and so on. The work done here has gone on to inspire an international movement, as thousands of communities around the world draw from the Totnes experience in designing their own similar projects.

Transition is based on the following four assumptions:

◎ That life with dramatically lower energy consumption is inevitable, and that it's better to plan for it than be taken by surprise

◎ That our communities presently lack the resilience to enable them to weather the severe energy shocks that will accompany peak oil

◎ That we have to act collectively, and we have to act now

◎ That by unleashing the collective genius of those around us to creatively and proactively design our energy future, we can build ways of living that are more connected, more enriching and that recognize the biological limits of our planet

Since its inception, it has catalysed, supported and fundraised for projects as diverse as the Totnes Pound, the Garden-share Scheme, the Transition Together group study course, the Totnes Local Food Directory, the Nut Tree Plantings, re-skilling courses around gardening, run a wide and extensive programme of events and courses, run Transition Tales, a visioning the future project, with all of Year 7 at KEVICC (two years running)[3], donated almost £2,000 worth of books to Totnes Library, run an International Youth Music Festival, held a series of Open Space events, run World Cafe events with local councillors, Oil Vulnerability Audits for local business, the Solar Thermal Challenge, Totnes Renewable Energy Society (a community owned energy company), regular seed exchanges and much more[4].

It has also become a catalyst and an inspiration for one of the fastest growing social movements in the world, the Transition movement. Inspired by the model and the tools developed here, groups in places as diverse as San Francisco, the Isle of Wight, Fujino in Japan and Biggar in Scotland, have begun their own Transition initiatives. Somerset County Council and Leicestershire County Council have both passed resolutions supporting their local initiatives, and Ed Milliband, Secretary of State for Energy and Climate Change, recently said, "how do we build a popular movement on these issues? Movements come from individual experiences that raise consciousness of the issues and are translated into bigger demands. So local campaigns and action whether it's the Transition Town movement or pioneering local authorities - are absolutely essential. Not just because they are important in themselves but because they can help create a movement for change".

This Energy Descent Action Plan has been one of TTT's key initiatives. It is a drawing together of all the threads of TTT's work thus far, creating a unique perspective on the future. As well as creating an EDAP for Totnes, it has also been a process of developing a methodology for doing them, which will be of use to hundreds of other communities. One of the things that Transition Town Totnes has done is to put the town on the map as a centre of innovative thinking about sustainability and how to implement it. While this plan sets out just one story of how that might come about, the process by which it actually happens will, similarly, be of great inspiration to many other communities facing the same challenges.

Cider Press Dartington. © Lou Brown

Totnes Littlehempston Railway Station 2009. © Lou Brown

Transition Town Totnes display cart at The Eden Project, Cornwall. © Jacqi Hodgson

2.21

CREATING AN ENERGY DESCENT ACTION PLAN

This EDAP has been created as an output of Transition Town Totnes's 'Energy Descent Pathways' project, which was funded by Esmee Fairbairn Foundation and Artists Planet Earth. It is a process that has not been undergone before, and a number of tools and approaches were developed during the process, which unfolded through a series of steps.

Step One: Developing a Framework

The initial decision was to focus on the area defined by the Market and Coastal initiative in 2003, which identified market towns and their traditional hinterland and trading area. Research included reading about peak oil, climate change and economics, identifying key players, conducting extensive oral histories, some broader historical research, and a detailed survey of around 220 households.

Step Two: Key Tools

We produced a postcard, showing an artist's impression of what two familiar scenes of Totnes might look like in 21 years time. A leaflet was also developed, and a 10 meter long 'Transition Timeline' was made and taken to all events and talks. This was used to indicate the future we are looking at, and to enable people to contribute their ideas on post-it notes about future dates. A series of large board posters were created to cover the content of the introductory presentation, and allow people to browse during the workshop. All proved very popular.

Step Three: Engage the Community

The starting point was to build on what Transition Town Totnes (TTT) had already catalysed. This included public events, Open Space sessions, the TTT working groups and practical projects, and also giving talks and running sessions with many local groups, Parish Councils and other bodies, getting media coverage and meeting with relevant local people.

Step Four: The Public Launch

This was held at St. John's Church in Bridgetown, in September 2008. Speakers included the Mayor of Totnes, the Chief Executive of South Hams District Council, the head of Totnes Chamber of Commerce and Chairman of the Devon Small Farmers Association. The celebratory event included a short improvised piece of theatre acted with the storyline built with the audience. It closed with time for people to add their visions of the future to the Transition Timeline.

2.22 Timeline and other display tools at EDAP workshop.
© Richard Hodgson

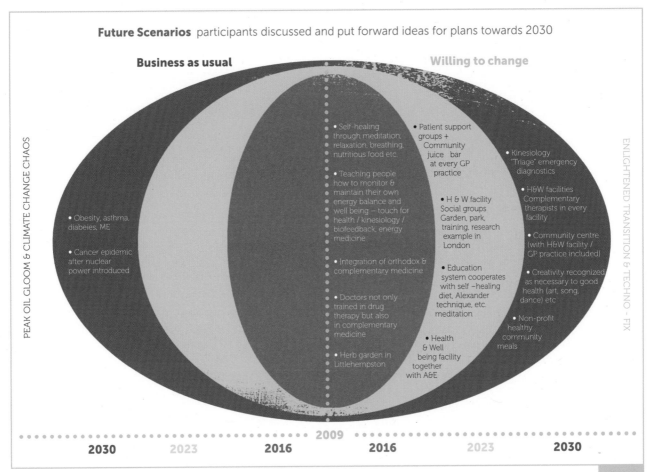

Future Scenarios participants discussed and put forward ideas for plans towards 2030

Business as usual

Willing to change

PEAK OIL GLOOM & CLIMATE CHANGE CHAOS

ENLIGHTENED TRANSITION & TECHNO - FIX

• Obesity, asthma, diabetes, ME

• Cancer epidemic after nuclear power introduced

• Self-healing through meditation, relaxation, breathing, nutritious food etc.

• Teaching people how to monitor & maintain their own energy balance and well being – touch for health / kinesiology / biofeedback, energy medicine

• Integration of orthodox & complementary medicine

• Doctors not only trained in drug therapy but also in complementary medicine

• Herb garden in Littlehempston

• Patient support groups + Community juice bar at every GP practice

• H & W facility Social groups Garden, park, training, research example in London

• Education system cooperates with self –healing diet, Alexander technique, etc. meditation

• Health & Well being facility together with A&E

• Kinesiology "Triage" emergency diagnostics

• H&W facilities Complementary therapists in every facility

• Community centre (with H&W facility / GP practice included)

• Creativity recognized as necessary to good health (art, song, dance) etc

• Non-profit healthy community meals

2009

2030   2023   2016   2016   2023   2030

Future Scenarios Planning at an EDAP Public Workshop.   **2.23**

Step Five: Public Workshops

Two series of public workshops were hosted. At the first round of 9 themed workshops based on TTT working group themes (plus others identified) such as food, education, biodiversity etc, the project was introduced and some creative methods to be used during the workshop were discussed. As a group, the participants identified assumptions about the key drivers and changes they anticipated influencing the future.

The second part of the workshop was based on future scenarios planning. Participants worked in smaller groups and a scenario was set for which they considered possible futures. In most cases, participants found it much easier to imagine a creative future where people were willing to change rather than continue as usual (Fig 2.23).

The workshop finished with some visioning exercises. Participants were invited to close their eyes and imagine themselves in the early morning, one day

in 2030. They called out their thoughts and feelings, and then added them on post-it notes to the large timeline on the year 2030.

A second round of workshops was hosted which started from the Visions from the earlier workshops, and invited participants to suggest ideas for plans

Building the Timeline at the EDAP project launch.
© Neil Chadbourne   **2.24**

© LocalEyes. www.localeyes.org

and actions which would work towards these, a process sometimes referred to as 'back-casting'. Many ideas were put forward through this process. People could move about between the tables, the informality of which people enjoyed.

Step Six: Back-casting on Strategic Themes

The hard work of constructing the EDAP commences from this point, as there is a lot of material, much of which is very disparate. A mini-exhibition of the Draft Plan was hosted at Totnes Civic Hall for a week to enable many people to browse all the input in its primary form. Schools were also invited to visit the plan and contribute ideas in pictures. A '2030 Cabaret Night' was also hosted during the event.

Step Seven: Drafting the EDAP and Consultation

The complex task of drafting the EDAP commenced after the exhibition. Strategic themes were identified from the back-casting worksheets and a general process for evolving idea and building the pathways was developed:

◎ Awareness, education, audit, gather info – take some simple actions

◎ Education, make plans for change & develop skills – take more informed actions

◎ Engagement - Invest time etc. in more involved actions, lifestyle changes, time with others

◎ Foster links – share ideas, skills, knowledge with others. Form groups and act together

◎ Empowerment – nurture good citizenship, give good example, think and act strategically

◎ Strive for joined up thinking; be open to creative ideas and find ways to implement them

◎ Greater equity and life balance - Work with others to share hope, dreams and resources

◎ Give something back to society - Share what can be spared and nurture others who need support

Consultation on the drafts has been widespread, so as to enable many parties to engage with the process of developing this EDAP. This, it is hoped, will ensure greater ownership of the Plan and its actions. Essentially this has evolved through three stages.

The first round of consultation with the drafted document was with the TTT working groups, many of whom took on a more prolonged process of working on the preliminary drafts of their topic section. Slightly later but in parallel, a wider round of consultation was commenced with revised drafts which were posted on the TTT website and information circulated to those involved in TTT (groups, projects etc). As revised drafts of the sections evolved they were posted for viewing and commenting. Two months, and several drafts later, with a number of revisions made, a wider audience was invited to comment. The later drafts were also posted on the Localeyes website to allow people to view each other's comments, and post their own. At all stages browsers could download the most recent version of a section as Word document from the TTT website and propose suggestions using Track Changes; this was used for suggestions by many people.

Step Eight: Implementing the EDAP

This is the most important and vital aspect of the work, and it will be essential to bring the EDAP back to the individuals and groups who have contributed. As a fairly complex document, many people and organisations would probably appreciate the opportunity to have an introductory session on how to use the EDAP and possibly further advice and support such as networking and linking up with others also getting involved.

2.25 Mirror Mirror players perform at EDAP 2030 Cabaret Night.
© Jacqi Hodgson

www.totnesedap.org.uk

This published Plan is accompanied by a website, where longer versions of many of the sections of this Plan can be found, and where you can comment and suggest changes. Many of the links, photographs, references and appendices that we didn't have space for here, can also be found on the EDAP website.

The full text of the extended EDAP can be downloaded free from the website as pdfs. However, be aware that this on-line version is over 350 pages long and the files are quite large.

You can also use the website to order the published book on-line.

Revised editions will be uploaded to the website from time to time. These will be based on feedback and the implementation of transition through activities, projects, new services, systems, infrastructure and changing habits and lifestyles.

You can contact the Energy Pathways project by email at edap.totnes@transitionnetwork.org

Next Steps

Now it's over to you! This EDAP is being made available both as an online document and as a printed document. The finished document you are holding in your hands is just one step along the way. The online version of EDAP allows us to revise and update the plan more readily and invite continued comment through blogging.

Use this EDAP to get involved in energy descent, use it for ideas and suggestions that you can do in your own home, in your community, at work in your social life. Make your own energy descent plan. Get involved in Transition: come along to our events, join the TTT groups and projects. Tell others about this EDAP. Get others to come along with you on your energy descent journey.

Updating the EDAP

The EDAP is an on-going interactive process. We hope to review, revise and update the EDAP as the plan unfolds across its timeline, ideas and innovations evolve, attitudes and behaviour change and the biosphere responds to mankind's impacts and interventions. We expect to update the web version annually and the printed version as needed and resources permit.

How to Contribute

Tell us what you think. Share your ideas and suggestions with us, so that we can use future revisions of the EDAP to share your ideas with other people. Drop us a line with your views and ideas in writing to EDAP Updates at the TTT office. Use the EDAP website to add ideas on-line and use the blog for shared discussion.

The Grove School visit the Draft EDAP Exhibition.
© Jacqi Hodgson

2.26

NOTES & IDEAS

A TIMELINE TO 2030

This section is the heart of this Energy Descent Action Plan. Grouped into 5 themed sections, we explore the challenges, issues and pathways to transition across 15 key topics. We consider and compare within the topics how 'business as usual' might look if we are 'willing to change'. Having outlined our collective visions for 2030 we provide pathways across the timeline to 2030 for each topic, describing ideas and actions that individuals, communities and policy and decision makers can take on to contribute and participate in our transition together.

TOTNES: PAST, PRESENT AND FUTURE – A VISUAL JOURNEY

The following photojournalism has taken some views of Old Totnes, revisited those same places with a camera, and taken the liberty of applying modern technology to show what some of these familiar sites might look like in future. The created future views show these places prepared for providing more local food, producing renewable energy, a Totnes with fewer cars, and more people active in the landscape.

Heath's Market Garden in Totnes

© Totnes Image Bank and Rural Archive

circa
1970

© Jacqi Hodgson

2010

© Photo Enhancement Ernest Goh

2030

The Cattle Market in Totnes

circa
1960

2010

2030

© Totnes Image Bank and Rural Archive

© Jacqi Hodgson

© Photo Enhancement Ernest Goh

The Rotherfold in Totnes

© Totnes Image Bank and Rural Archive

circa

1950

© Jacqi Hodgson

2010

© Photo Enhancement Ernest Goh

2030

NOTES & IDEAS

Joined up Thinking

3

Water, Cycle and Railway Interchange in Totnes. © Lou Brown

A VISION OF TOTNES AND DISTRICT IN 2030

"Can we rely on it that a 'turning around' will be accomplished by enough people quickly enough to save the modern world? This question is often asked, but whatever answer is given to it will mislead. The answer "yes" would lead to complacency; the answer "no" to despair. It is desirable to leave these perplexities behind us and get down to work."
E.F. Schumacher[1]

"Saving our civilisation is not a spectator sport."
Lester R. Brown[2]

The Totnes of 2030 is a town which has weathered difficult times, but has now emerged as a resilient, diverse and prosperous community. The surrounding parishes have undergone a similar transition, and the parishes and the town are now much more economically intertwined and more dependent on each other. The area is now 60% self-reliant in terms of food, and has reached a similar percentage in terms of energy provision.

Many more people now work closer to where they live, and have become active members of the community, more engaged in a more vibrant and effective local democracy. The south-facing rooftops of the town now glint on a sunny day with their solar panels and many members know that the wind turbine visible from the town is making them money each time it turns.

A walk through the town reveals a quieter, happier and calmer town than that of 2009. The ATMOS Project by the river became, in 2012, a key driver for the rebuilding of the local economy, and led to the creation of hundreds of new small businesses, providing revitalised local markets with building materials, food, skills, advice, and so on. Rather than the town's economy now being at the mercy of international financial events, it has transformed into a more resilient settlement, one that has led the way and inspired many other communities to start taking their future into their hands.

Key Challenges

◎ Peak Oil; power down from 9 barrels pp/y in 2009 to (possibly) 1 barrel per person by 2030

◎ Climate Change: keeping the lid on global temperature rise, getting carbon below 350ppm

3.1 Totnes from Fishchowters Lane Nr Ashprington in 2030. © Photo Enhancement Ernest Goh

◎ Carbon sequestration: removing some carbon from the atmosphere

◎ Stabilising Population growth to around 7 billion and reducing thereafter

◎ Increasing renewable energy supplies to meet 50% of current energy demand

◎ Reducing consumption and waste to zero

◎ Repairing biodiversity

◎ Maintaining adequate clean water supplies with less energy inputs

◎ Society making an inner transition and taking responsibility

"Our latest report finds that despite significant steps towards reducing waste, water consumption and emissions from road travel, Government departments are still not on course to meet their own target for reducing carbon emissions by 12.5%, and far more remains to be done if they are to make a real contribution towards meeting UK-wide targets for 80% emissions reductions by 2050" Sustainable Development Commission 2009[3]

At current growth rates the global population is expected to grow to between 8 and 10.8 billion by 2050[4]. increasing population poses an enormous challenge to all nations. Population stability requires the cooperation of both policy makers and people. In poorer countries, access to education and family planning, can reduce pregnancy rates. In many richer countries, pregnancy rates have fallen below replacement level, but we cannot afford to be complacent as we are likely to witness significant short-term population increase through 'baby boomers', still in their fertile years, increasing life expec-

tancy and 'climate and immigrants', people displaced through their homelands becoming uninhabitable, as well as economic and internal migrants. In 2005 population projections suggested that South Hams could expect an increase of 3% by 2011 rising to 19% by 2031.[5] A comparison of estimated population data[6] from 2006 to 2008 indicates a rise of 4%, i.e. greater than the predicted rise in the first 2 years. A rise of 19% would bring the total population of Totnes and District from 23,863 in 2008 to 28,397 by 2031.

Business as Usual or Willing to Change?

If we continue to ignore these perceived problems facing society and continue Business as Usual in Totnes and District, by 2030 it is likely that we will see decreasing happiness and personal respect, and increasing fear, denial, austerity, poverty, climate chaos, severe environmental degradation, over-crowding, civil strife and an acceleration towards chaos, fragmentation and the decline of civilisation as we know it. The symptoms of a society in collapse[7] may be clearly upon us. Most of society could be living in extreme hardship and ill placed to take responsibility or actions to reverse the impacts of climate change. A willingness to initiate change and build on a strong ray of hope and positive visioning can guide us to a better life. There are many unresolved issues and problems to be dealt with. The biggest challenges are relearning to live within the carrying capacity of one earth; stabilising population growth, reducing energy and material consumption, and repair and regeneration of biodiversity and ecosystems.

Indicators –
Key Characteristics of a
Resilient Community[8]

These can be regularly revisited to see if the community is making progress in the right direction.

1. Leadership is diversified and representative of age, gender, and cultural composition of the community
2. Elected community leadership is visionary, shares power and builds consensus.
3. Community members are involved in significant community decisions.
4. The community feels a sense of pride.
5. People feel optimistic about the future of the community
6. There is a spirit of mutual assistance and co-operation in the community
7. People feel a sense of attachment to their community
8. The community is self-reliant and looks to itself and its own resources to address major issues.
9. There is a strong belief in and support for education at all levels
10. There are a variety of Community, Enterprise and Development (CED) organisations in the community such that the key CED functions are well served.

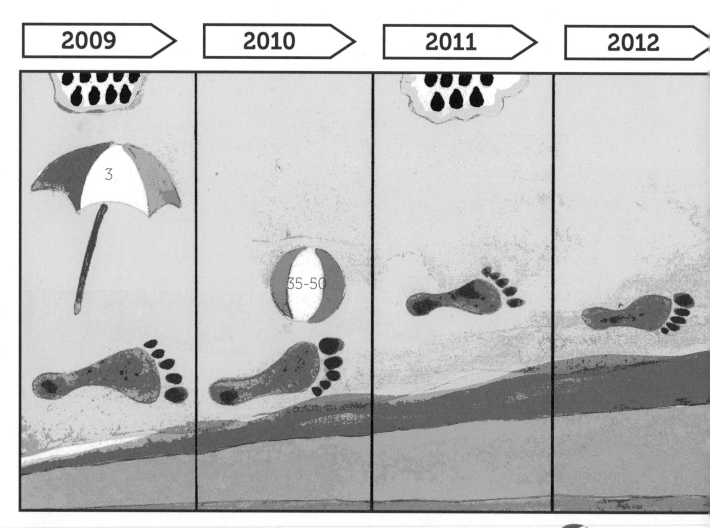

2009 > 2010 > 2011 > 2012 >

3.2   © Richard Hodgson

Oil available to UK
per capita / per annum
2009: 9 barrels
> 2030: 1 barrel
(source: The Oil Drum)

Growth of UK Renewable Energy
supplies per annum
2009: 3 TWh
> 2030: 200 TWh
(source: Zero Carbon Britain)

11. Organisations in the community have developed partnerships and collaborative working relationships
12. Employment in the community is diversified beyond a single large employer
13. Major businesses in the community are locally owned
14. The community has a strategy for increasing independent local ownership
15. There is openness to alternative ways of earning a living and economic activity
16. The community looks outside itself to seek and secure resources (skills, expertise, finance) that will address areas of identified weakness

17. The community is aware of its competitive position in the broader economy
18. Citizens are involved in the creation and implementation of the community vision and goals and have a CED Plan that guides its development.
19. There is on-going action towards achieving the goals in the CED plan
20. There is regular evaluation of progress towards the community's strategic goals

Key Challenges across the Timeline to 2030 with declining oil supplies and climate change

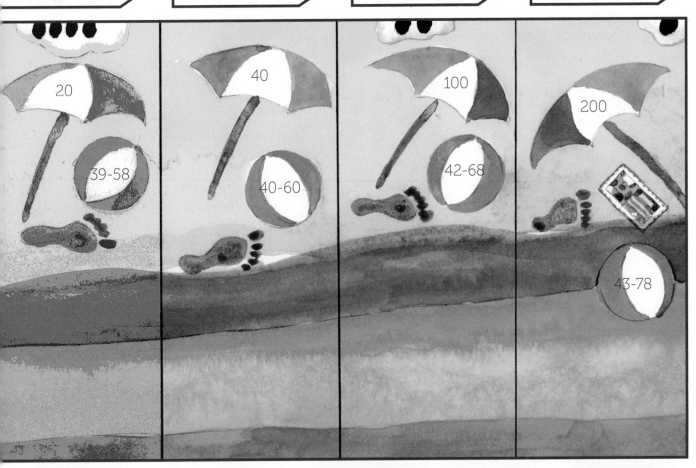

| 2013-15 | 2016-20 | 2021-25 | 2026-30 |

Global Greenhouse Emissions
2010: 35-50 G CO_2-equivalent
> 2030: 43-78 G CO_2-equivalent
(anticipated range)
(source: IPPC)

UK Carbon Budget (based on Contraction & Convergence)
2009: 150 MtC
> 2027: 1 MtC
(source: Zero Carbon Britain)

Rising Sea Levels
3-10mm per annum
(source: K. Steffen University of Colorado)

Global Population estimates
2009: 6.5 Billion
> 2030: rising 9.5 Billion or declining to 5 Billion
(source: Earthtrends)

Global Surface Warming
above pre-1800 levels
2010: 0.1 – 0.2 °Celsius
> 2030: 0.2 – 0.9 °Celsius
(source: IPCC)

JOINED UP THINKING -

Strategic themes: • Peak Oil • Climate Change • Stabilising Population • Reducing excess consumption and waste to zero

The following timeline illustrates the suggested key challenges faced by UK society today and offers some solutions for mitigation. We have used a timeline of the next 21 years to show the widening gap between "business as usual" (if we don't make and changes) and how small but significant steps can lead to substantial and meaningful improvements if society is willing to change

2009

Economic Downturn is Good News for DIY Enthusiasts

The economic downturn puts many people out of work; many use their newfound time to start growing food, insulating their homes to keep bills down, and looking for other ways to make and save money.

Transition goes mainstream in Totnes

Through the local Transition Town initiative, the rising cost of energy is becoming more widely understood to be linked to the depletion of reliable oil supplies. A new awareness and concern is evolving as people respond to news about global warming. The concept of environmental limits to growth is gaining momentum as the populist media cover stories of over population.

Major Report shows potential for behaviour change

The IPSOS Big Energy Shift Report reveals huge potential for people to change their energy use and that people are overwhelmingly positive, but that "they will need to be nudged along by the Government and other principal stakeholders." [9]

Community invests in Dairy Crest site

The Atmos Project for the Dairy Crest Site is swamped on its first day of trading as it opens for local investment. Investors in community bonds include prospective (affordable) home buyers, retirees, eco-commerce interests, green builders, community groups and railway companies, who all want to be part of this comprehensive sustainable development. At the close of the day the investors symbolically switch on the solar powered lights behind a brightly coloured billboard with a 3D picture of the proposed development and raise a glass of local wine. The Whistlestop café has done a roaring trade.

South Hams District Council hosts a Community Partnership Forum

to invite proposals under The Sustainable Communities Act. The event attracts a wide attendance and discussion leading to over 180 proposals coming from the community, with eleven proposals going forward to national government with SHDC backing.

A TIMELINE OF CHANGE

- Increasing renewable energy supplies • Repairing biodiversity
- Maintaining clean water supplies with less energy inputs

Major national and international reports are released about possible impacts of climate change and plans for renewable energy.

They emphasise the urgency of political and international cooperation and strong leadership to avert catastrophe.

UN Copenhagen Summit fails to secure a global agreement to reduce carbon emissions

in line with atmospheric levels of 350ppm and a range of measures to achieve this. They agree in principle that subsequent agreements to reduce carbon emissions to reduce global warming to just 2 degrees above pre-industrial averages is desirable and will form the basis of future UN agendas.

Global warming causes 300,000 deaths a year

says Kofi Annan of the UN think-tank. It is affecting 300m people, according to the first comprehensive study of the human impact of global warming[10].

The Prime Minister puts out a national call to everyone to rise to the challenge of climate change and support the stringent yet realistic outcomes from Copenhagen

He says he will lead by example and has started by putting his car on ebay and will use the profits to put solar hot water and PV panels on the roof at no.10. He has promised to use UK produce for all food at no. 10. He has further given a personal guarantee to reduce the carbon footprint of Parliament. The media has a field day.

People are feeling fitter

from all the DIY and use their newfound energy to walk and cycle instead of using the car for many short journeys; some children complain about the new family walks but enjoy the other children who tag along.

Widespread popular interest is shown in local development planning

in the wake of the 2009 Enquiry by Design process and the revised DPD is publicly debated. Public meetings about significant developments and valued sites in the locality attract large attendance and the need for affordable and social housing as well as co-housing is widely supported. A broader debate about how to support a more diverse society is evolving at grass-roots level and there is a rising call for high quality housing to ensure that those on lower incomes can live comfortably and better understanding of how everyone benefits from getting involved in local issues.

2010

JOINED UP THINKING -

Strategic themes: • Peak Oil • Climate Change • Stabilising Population
• Reducing excess consumption and waste to zero

Community events are gathering momentum

The weekly markets, the annual festivals, the Lantern Procession and the Christmas markets are all gaining in popularity as giving pleasure and local economic benefit. Many people of all ages are putting a lot of effort into these events as they find a renewed pleasure in being involved in local activities, wondering how and why they previously spent so much time and money on retail therapy. Homemade jams and chutneys are back in fashion.

The UK Government announces 'Green Transport' plans to electrify public transport, which will run off renewables.

This will be fast-tracked, commencing with trains and move swiftly to national buses. Grants are to be made available for local transport providers to convert their vehicles to electricity, bio-diesel from waste cooking oil and methane from anaerobic digestion. All public service vehicles will gradually be replaced with lighter models to reduce weight and resources. The replaced and scrapped vehicles will provide metals for the additional railway infrastructure, which will also create more local employment as we move towards reopening many old lines.

Devon County Council and South Hams District Council adopt Transition.

Their first stated goal is to rapidly improve the position of SHDC of 15th from the bottom of the UK 434 Local Authorities with the worst CO_2 emissions per capita. They also wish to improve community consultation, and agree to develop a Kitemark for Public Meetings to maximise community participation and partnership in building resilience and localisation. Being in Transition means we will make strong positive changes a priority says a spokesperson.

2011

The 'Big Lunch' is a bumper event in over 50 streets in Totnes and District.

Home grown food is a popular theme, and this summer's glut of peas dictates the main dish for many of the tables. Conversations at these parties lead to several ad-hoc car share schemes starting up, people clubbing together to buy Heat Pump units in bulk and informal child-minding arrangements with retirees.

A TIMELINE OF CHANGE

- Increasing renewable energy supplies • Repairing biodiversity
- Maintaining clean water supplies with less energy inputs

Teachers are inspired by Transition

throughout Totnes & District, and actively encourage their schools and students to become sustainability centres in the local community. Weekly goals for change are leaning on parental support for the cycle trains and walking buses. Some parents are starting to wonder how they ever had time to work full-time; but enjoy the additional time they are now spending with their children.

Unified religious events

such as the harvest thanksgiving are becoming more popular and some take place on the land as more people are growing fruit and vegetables they are proud of.

The UK has become the holiday destination

of choice for many UK residents and European tourists as heat waves, floods and forest fires become more severe in Southern Europe. For 3 years in succession Greece and Spain are badly burnt out and their tourism market is declining. A flurry of new B&B's appear all around Totnes and District, with many proprietors pulling in the extended family and neighbours to help run the business; many are promoting home grown and organic breakfasts. Local wildlife routes for pedestrians and cyclists are gaining popularity with visitors and residents.

UK government proposes a ban on fuel hungry cars

The ban will apply to the sale of cars using more than 80kWh per 100km and is widely hailed as a very positive step. The government decides to make this a stepping down process from 80kWh to 60kWh to 40kWh with additional design improvements to lower fuel consumption further over an 8-year period. This is welcomed by health workers who have been calling for legislation to reduce emissions in cities and towns to improve air quality. The slowing of traffic in all urban streets to 20mph also reduces fuel consumption, emissions and improves road safety, encouraging cyclists and pedestrians.

Health and Safety regulations reviewed as objections rise to Nanny State

These will "loosen restrictions and simplify local systems". Transport of waste will be reviewed to ease transport of materials for bio-digestion. DIY fitting of renewable energy supplies to houses will be reviewed along with packaging and freezing requirements for food products. This is just the start says the Minister for Enterprise, "we want to encourage people to take actions and take more personal responsibility to improve life for themselves and others. A multi-agency approach to the review will ensure safety yet flexibility for increased personal responsibility."

Green Space Initiatives

are supported at all 3 tiers of Local Authority in Devon. A new comprehensive Public Space Plan to support local food production, biodiversity, wood fuel and recreational public space, and which will involve the public is welcomed by many community groups.

JOINED UP THINKING -

Strategic themes: • Peak Oil • Climate Change • Stabilising Population
• Reducing excess consumption and waste to zero

Letters Page makes the News

As the media is bombarded by letters from inspired people who want to share their ideas about a better life with less material goods. A rising wave of positive thinking is supporting strong initiatives from the grass-roots and elected public representatives at all levels are responding by making change easier and giving strong leadership.

Celebrities lead on Population Challenge

In the wake of yet another African famine threat, a number of celebrities join together to highlight the need to stabilise the global population. The Invest in our Future - 2 is plenty campaign calling for voluntary limitation to family size is welcomed by many national leaders and development organisations around the world. Small is Beautiful was never more true says Stephen Harding at Schumacher College.

Readathon clocks up 24 hours for new library opens in Totnes

as part of the community rooms and services. Community groups are delighted with the new enlarged facilities and supports including hot desks, meeting rooms and their own section in the library. A voluntary Ex-libris bookstall in the market will help provide on-going funds for new books and facilities in the library.

Great Retrofit shows tangible benefits as fuel prices rocket.

Some older houses have proved more of a challenge to insulate and install with renewable energy; however this has increased interest and understanding of many traditional crafts and trades and has created many new jobs. Recycled materials are being utilised wherever possible and many old buildings are looking funky

Community tax on second homes and empty houses is

piloted in response to local pressure groups to discourage this practice. The money will be used to buy more land for allotments.

Trains, Buses and Bikes win favour.

A re-appraisal of public transport finds that all forms are running at much higher efficiencies than predicted as most trains and buses are running at an average of 80% full. Working in conjunction with the Dept of Education, new road designs to improve safety for cyclists are introduced as a pilot in Devon; this includes roundabouts with an outer separate cycling lane, where cars exiting the inner lane must give way to cyclists. The Devon network of off-road cycle and walkways is to be completed. School cycling clubs and community groups will be consulted on preferred routes and signage.

Community Right to Buy legislation introduced nationally.

This will allow land to be transferred from local authority ownership to community groups at less than market value, giving community groups 'first refusal ' on any land disposal by the local authority. Totnes & District Allotments Association are delighted and put in an offer for land at Follaton.

2012

A TIMELINE OF CHANGE

- Increasing renewable energy supplies • Repairing biodiversity
- Maintaining clean water supplies with less energy inputs

UN hosts world summit on Climate Change and Energy Poverty.

20 years on from Rio, major negotiations take place to secure energy for overcrowded countries from over-heating countries that are predicted to become uninhabitable for several decades. Old oil pipelines are to be used to bring dessert energy to many parts of Europe that are expected to host climate migrants. TEQs (Tradeable Energy Quotas) and energy rationing are discussed as citizen based currency in some of these deals. Unlike the Johannesburg Summit, there is positive cooperation, and US President Obama takes a key role in pressing for international implementation agreements.

2013-15

Worrying reports from the polar regions

are exacerbated when summer storms and major heat waves strike Europe, US and Australia. People are getting more active. A number of public commentators take substantial leadership in their media columns and programmes. 3 local radio stations in Totnes and District link together to provide daily programmes to highlight enterprising ideas. First to call in is Jamie Hanson from Berry Pomeroy who offers to help people convert abandoned large cars into useful space including chicken shacks and cloches for seedlings.

Most families are growing some of their own food.

Food swaps at Totnes Market's Glut Stall provide a great meeting place and exchange of seeds, ideas and information about food growing. Children are becoming very aware and informed about food growing and there is a rising interest from young people going into jobs in agriculture. Farming has risen in popularity and status and is providing more families with income and food. Different farming systems and crop and farm animal varieties are attracting interest, in particular those that can sequester carbon, support wildlife, are naturally resilient to pests and moulds and can adapt to hotter climes.

Age of Scarcity

is coined by the media, but letters to the popular press indicate that many people feel living more frugally is okay, and there are expressions of pride in tightening belts and making ends meets. Plastic materials and goods are far less dominant in shops and recycled paper and card is replacing plastic for many uses; the latest bankcards are made from a new cellulose laminated card. The Good Ideas notice boards lead to a national competition for "The Ten Best Things YOU Can Do To Make Do and Mend."

The great compost versus bio-digestion debate heats-up

as both sides defend the benefits of their systems. Methane assessments of open composting and compost toilets are to be trialled at Landmatters in Cornworthy, while the comparative fertilizer value of bio-digestate and compost will be the subject of a study at KEVICCs students with funding from South West Water. Bio-Digesters for waste are coming on stream in nearly all the parishes. SWW announces plans to pipe all soft biodegradeable

JOINED UP THINKING -

Strategic themes: • Peak Oil   • Climate Change   • Stabilising Population
• Reducing excess consumption and waste to zero

wastes and agricultural effluents to the biodigester units to save energy from overland transportation and risk of contaminating waterways.

UK Government adopts the Citizens' Income

which will be paid to all UK residents regardless of whether they are in or out of work. It is estimated that this help those without paid work yet will save money by simplifying benefits and removing a large layer of bureaucracy that will be redirected to implementing the energy saving initiatives and grants. The news is welcomed by many sectors including Trades Unions who say this will provide opportunities for people to become more independent and help people to find time to grow food etc.

Shopping list of measures to support local businesses and energy initiatives are introduced by Westminster

that will be administered locally. Business rate relief for businesses that trade in locally grown or locally made produce. Local energy suppliers will be able to bring local renewable energy supplies on-stream at competitive prices with major suppliers. The Post Office network will be supported to provide a service in every village and town throughout the UK by allowing them to perform new functions and local community services.

2016-20

Grey Power becomes hip

as the number of people in Totnes and District aged 65 or over hits 35%. Elders are given a number of supports in the community and with safer streets, many are able to be more mobile. Public transport and local deliveries becomes more viable with more people using the services. Health and wellbeing spaces, gardens and cafés are widely used by young and old and are meeting places for community across the generations. Extended families are living under the same roof as housing has become more expensive and less available and many children are learning from and sharing domestic tasks with grandparents. Public Health services are reporting a rise in general health and well being for older and younger people, reflected with a decline in the number of children going in to foster care, and youth crime rates are decreasing.

A TIMELINE OF CHANGE

• Increasing renewable energy supplies • Repairing biodiversity
• Maintaining clean water supplies with less energy inputs

Sign up for your Local SWAT Teams

Local Territorial Army members, volunteers from the over 50's and others with occasional days to spare have formed work-parties to prepare and help out with emergencies or urgent needs. Their emergency planning is well rehearsed and they provide training to school and community groups who enjoy the sessions. Totnes Arts has designed a very visible and popular temporary shelter which most people can make quickly should a flooding or migration emergency arise; the prototype Swelter is used as a marquee for the annual festival. Suprisingly the shelter is found to be more energy efficient than some of the commercial buildings in Babbage Road.

Food & Travel Hubs keep the wheels turning

A survey into the use and benefit of the Food and Travel hubs operating in and around Totnes finds they are working like clockwork. National interest has grown in the 'linked up system' which was piloted in Totnes in 2010. Over 90% of local people use their local hub at least twice a month, making them one of the most successful initiatives to support local food production. Food producer reports in the survey show that 60% rely on the hubs to be viable. Amongst the other initiatives that have arisen at the hubs are reading rooms, crèches, health cafés and cycle repairs.

Happy people as more affordable houses are eco-homes

In the wake of national legislation for affordable and sustainable homes, new local planning and development policies reflect an emphasis of meeting social and environmental needs rather than economic development. Community housing co-operatives and parish councils can apply for grant aid to buy up empty houses and convert large houses and other buildings according to the number of local people on their housing lists. Compulsory sustainability checks called Integrated Impact Assessments on all new builds and refurbishments of 5 or more dwelling units will be required to ensure the local community's health and well-being; this will require a locally based, multi-agency approach.

Public representatives slash travel budgets

The increasing government levies on aviation fuel have almost brought commercial flights to a standstill. The investment in solar planes is still controversial and yet to reap reliable results. Few people take flights for holidays or business trips, preferring to use the fast trains with improved dormer units. Local public representatives have agreed a voluntary energy budget, encouraging them to minimise travel.

JOINED UP THINKING -

Strategic themes: • Peak Oil • Climate Change • Stabilising Population
• Reducing excess consumption and waste to zero

Wild about Totnes

Recognising the need for pollinators and with an increased interest in the science of growing food, many local food growers are setting aside a section of their garden to support wildlife. A group of growers have formed Wild Totnes, an advisory group that will advise and help people carry out wilderness regeneration to support biodiversity going through difficult times, reduce extinctions and plant trees to sequester carbon. Schools have formed support units for this initiative and some students monitor named species in their home gardens. Tree planting expeditions take place most weekends across the winter.

Water rationing saves on butts

Severe water shortages are being coped with by stringent water rationing and extensive reuse of grey water. Flush piping and buckets are being supplied to all households to enable people to collect grey domestic water and refill toilet cisterns. Clothes are lasting longer as they are washed less. Rainwater butts are being extended with additional barrels on most buildings, as the hotter weather is bringing flash rainfall that needs to be collected. Many growers and gardeners have dug extended wastewater irrigation schemes for watering plants and many have created covered horticulture units.

Climate migrants to be allocated around Devon

Totnes and District is expecting to host an additional 1,000 people over the next 5 years, although this figure may rise. Many people are worried about the impacts and whether all the services will cope, but Community and Voluntary Services host a number of community evenings to introduce the idea and later the new migrants to the area. Migrants are hosted as lodgers in family homes and a number of flooded units in Babbage Road are to be rebuilt on raised bases to create co-housing units for the incomers. Many migrants have skills for growing different vegetables, which are more adapted to the warmer climate.

Totnes and District Agricultural show blooms

The variety of stands has expanded including many advisory stands for food growers and agricultural services. Local public representatives host a stand to invite ideas and initiatives that the public are interested in. Many people take the opportunity to discuss the new locally based income taxation system and how they would like to see the money spent.

Totnes Water Back on Tap

SHDC agrees to investigate some of the old aquifers including the old Ashprington springs in and around Totnes to the delight of many. A pilot Totnes Water supplies in returnable glass bottles springs to life.

Paid volunteers opens the way for better local services

A restructuring of Local Authorities as they take on more duties in line with localisation of services improves dialogue between the sectors. The changes away from privatised services has opened very localised employment opportunities and in response to public meetings, many of the new posts are part-time to enable people to have time to grow food, mind their children, help the elders etc. Many voluntary groups will be able to claim for paid volunteer workers under the new localised services and this is widely welcomed.

2021-25

A TIMELINE OF CHANGE

- Increasing renewable energy supplies • Repairing biodiversity
- Maintaining clean water supplies with less energy inputs

2026-30

The family is flocking back

A survey shows that more young people are likely to return to their home town, after they finish their studies, than head for the cities. The opportunities for interesting and meaningful work has reversed in recent years and many are opting to work from family bases, often supporting older members of the family. Living units are more diverse reflecting extended family and friends sharing co-housing units.

Better health with less wealth

Local public health units are benefiting from reduced workloads due to people being more healthy, resilient and enterprising in addressing their own needs. The health gardens and increased community supports are popular and having a marked effect on the general health and happiness of local people. Many people are claiming that having fewer possessions is less stressful, others consider the greater diversity of tasks in their day gives them an increased sense of achievement, others put their increased sense of well-being down to less isolation and the strong sense of community they feel.

Happiness and calm reigns on the streets

Totnes and District has quite a different ambience. There are more people on the streets and there is a general air of being busy yet conversational. The shops in the town and villages have gone through many changes and there are many new food and general hardware shops as well as repair and reuse shops. Many of the products on sale are locally produced, more utilitarian and there are generally fewer exotic and luxury goods for sale. Most businesses offer a local delivery service which is generally by bicycle. The local Nostalgia Society has commenced horse and cart street deliveries for daily bakery and dairy products, much to the delight of local small children and elders alike.

Global response to climate change

The international call to arms to implement severe carbon mitigation is met with enthusiasm by the general public. While many measures have already been undertaken, it is widely recognised that not enough is being done by the developed nations, and Ethiopia shows strong leadership again by calling for universal stringent energy rationing and carbon sequestration requirements per capita. The UK Government debates where it will plant all the trees to manage its carbon quota and enters into negotiations with other European countries to mobilise communities. We have still got too many people observes Karen Chinner age 10 from South Brent.

Contingency Planning for Sudden Change

Assumptions around Contingency planning (From EDAP workshops)

◎ People will respond and pull together (as per WWII)

◎ Contingency planning – need to cope with National requirements to supply food to outside areas (e.g. 50%)

◎ We will be forced to think about food security and other securities – energy and water

◎ Enduring peace / expect violence over resource shortages

◎ Strategic rationing i.e. oil in many products

◎ Catastrophic fluctuations in commodities – including volatility

◎ Governments will start to look at alternative energy supplies: nuclear, bio-fuels, quick-fix centrally controlled

◎ The military are likely to have a role in domestic disaster management

Contingency planning is essential when difficulties and serious challenges face society. While the main mobilisation plan will be at national and regional level, locally a strong plan can help mitigate the worst impacts of difficulties likely to be experienced due to sudden energy shortages and climate change. In conjunction with community representatives, local leaders need to agree a clear set of priorities and make preparations in the event of any national emergency due to sudden extreme changes in weather, sea-level or energy cuts.

As in the last world war, a plan for rapid mobilisation of a plan is also essential. The following list provides a brief outline that can be built on by public bodies who wish to prepare:

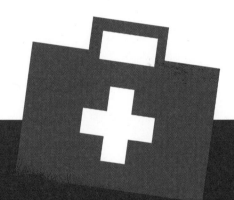

Contingency - First Aid Starter Kit

◎ A clearly identified team of Trained Emergency Personnel including a local volunteer back-up force and local people trained in First Aid and veterinary experts.

◎ Battery operated communications equipment including radio and telephones

◎ Emergency local contact numbers in all community halls and key public notice boards

◎ Local food growing, storage and security of supply. An emergency food distribution plan

◎ Adequate access to non-energy dependent, clean water supplies, and containers to carry water

◎ Non-grid dependent local renewable energy supplies

◎ Safe weatherproof shelter for large numbers of people spread across the district, e.g. community halls with access to blankets, first aid and emergency equipment, medical supplies, candles, matches and rope

◎ Isolation plans in the event of a pandemic disease of people, animals or plants

◎ Flood mitigation procedures in place, ability to check quality of possibly contaminated water

◎ Rescue boats, bicycles, sandbags and bales of straw.

◎ Local supplies of antidotes in the event of a nuclear incident.

◎ Preparations to ensure elderly and disabled people can be checked on and helped as needed.

© Transition Town Totnes

Transition Streets

Transition Streets is an exciting project that will make a real difference to the carbon emissions, energy bills and depth of community for at least 10% of households in Totnes. Based on a funding pot of £625,000 awarded by the DECC's Low Carbon Communities Challenge and announced just before the publication of the Totnes EDAP, this project has 2 main streams – one that works with householders directly, and one which uses public assets for the benefit of the whole community.

Households are invited to join the existing Transition Together programme (see page 272) which helps them, in small groups with friends or neighbours, to take practical low or no cost actions to minimise energy and resources across all parts of their lifestyle. In addition to this standard programme, groups eligible for Transition Streets 'extras' then have access to personal advice from the Energy Saving Trust about relevant grants for things like loft insulation and cavity wall insulation. They then also have the option of a £3,000 towards discounted solar PV systems, with further support available to low income households thanks to South Hams District Council.

Meanwhile the community's Civic Hall will undergo a total energy retrofit, including installation of around £60,000 of solar PV. The income generated from this system will be used to support further projects and provide a highly visible manifestation of the work TTT is doing in the town.

**For more information see
www.transitionstreets.org.uk
and www.transitiontogether.org.uk**

NOTES & IDEAS

Working with Nature

Allotments at Castle Meadow in Totnes © Lou Brown

FOOD SECURITY
CAN TOTNES AND DISTRICT FEED ITSELF?

Exploring the practicalities of food relocalisation

Rob Hopkins, Mark Thurstain-Goodwin and Simon Fairlie. This paper has been produced by Transition Town Totnes (www.totnes.transitionnetwork.org) and Transition Network (www.transitionnetwork.org), with funding from Land Share CIC (www.landshare.org), research and GIS input from Geofutures (www.geofutures.com) and advice from Simon Fairlie and Martin Crawford.

1. Introduction

Interest in local food has grown steadily in recent years, with people seeing not just its nutritional and taste benefits, but also its political role, alongside its ability to strengthen local economies. Increasingly, movements such as the Transition Network[1] are seeing, in the light of climate change and resource depletion, that the role of local food is no longer an optional extra, but a key necessity in a resource-constrained future. In the wider context of economic localisation, economist David Fleming writes, "...localisation stands, at best, at the limits of practical possibility, but it has the decisive argument in its favour that there will be no alternative" (Fleming 2006). This paper explores the degree of relocalisation in the food sector that might be possible, through a drawing together of the concepts of 'foodzones' and 'foodsheds', as well as Simon Fairlie's work on 'Can Britain Feed Itself?' It utilises GIS (Geographical Information Science) technology and a range of datasets to look at Totnes and District in Devon, England, to assess the degree to which the area could achieve a significant degree of self-reliance for food and other essentials. Totnes and District is chosen for this paper as it is home to Transition Town Totnes, the first such project in the UK, and this paper is part of a larger project into food relocalisation that they are undertaking.

The research and findings presented here are very much work-in-progress, and raise many areas for further research. Many of the key datasets that a thorough version of this work would need are not in the public domain and are prohibitively expensive to access, some of the data around land use is out of date, and many of the statistics have to be inferred from an overlapping of several sets. However, in spite of its limitations and imperfections, the findings of this paper are fascinating, with far-reaching implications for other settlements and for the UK as a whole. The conclusions identify the need for a rethink of how agriculture is practiced, as well as the urgent need for research into new models of food production. Also identified is the need for national version of this research, a larger project, but in the light of the fast moving issues of peak oil, climate change and the economic difficulties facing the UK, a profoundly urgent one.

2. An Opening Caveat

Beginning to ask the question of whether anywhere "can feed itself" is like opening a set of Russian dolls. At which scale does one start? Can a village feed itself? A town? A city? Can Europe feed itself? Indeed, can the world? This is surely one of the key questions of our time, but where to begin? The research and contemplations presented in this paper start at the level of a small area of Devon, but by doing so, the intention is to explore the challenges and opportunities of doing the same on a national scale, a project Transition Network is planning to develop in partnership with a range of other organisations. Also, this paper just looks at food and fuel. Clearly though, there is also a need for research on whether Britain can power itself, clothe, medicate, house and furnish itself. This is a huge area of potential research but it is hoped that this paper initiates a long-overdue debate on these vital questions.

3. Why Food and Farming Needs a Plan B

It is increasingly clear that we are moving from a time in history where our degree of economic success and sense of personal prowess are directly linked to our degree of oil consumption, to one where our degree of oil dependency equates to our degree of vulnerability. This is felt nowhere more keenly than in agriculture. In the US, the food system has been estimated to require 10 calories of fossil fuel for every 1 calorie that lands up on our plates (Giampietro and Pimentel 1994). The UK can no longer rely on the assumption that cheap fossil fuels will continue to be available into the indefinite future.

The global economy is entering a world where, as a report commissioned by the US Department of Energy predicted in 2005, "liquid fuel prices and price volatility will increase dramatically", and the high prices of July 2008 (over $147 a barrel[2]) are predicted by many to be just the first of many such surges, attributed by some as being one of the principal causes of the current economic downturn (Rubin

2009). Christophe de Margerie, CEO of Total, stated recently that the economic downturn means that world oil production will be unable to exceed 89 million barrels a day (Hoyos 2009), and a growing number of observers argue that July 2008's price spike coincided with the peak in world oil production (Oil Drum 2009).

Francisco Blanch of Merrill Lynch was recently reported as saying that oil companies must find another Saudi Arabia every two years just to maintain current production levels. Referring to the July 2008 price spike, he recently said, "the commodity supercycle is not over, just resting" (The Economist 2009: 76). It is clear that the next 10-15 years will see increasing price volatility, and possible interruptions to supplies of the liquid fuels that make our current economic model viable. Being oil dependent is already becoming a high-risk strategy, for individuals, businesses and whole economies.

Climate change is the second issue that underpins this paper. The government has set a target of reducing emissions by 80% by 2050, based on the assumption that the aim is to stay below 450ppm. Recent research by the Tyndall Centre for Climate Change Research (Anderson and Bows 2009) argues that 450ppm actually has a 50% risk of runaway climate change, and is deeply inadequate as a target[3]. They argue that shifting the focus to cumulative emissions, leads to a shift from thinking of "long term gradual reduction to urgent and radical reduction" (ibid). What is needed, they argue, is the total decarbonisation of the economy by 2035-2045, which raises huge questions for the present-day food system. This was reflected in a 2008 Cabinet Office paper, which stated "existing patterns of food production are not fit for a low-carbon, more resource constrained-future" (Cabinet Office 2008). The task this paper sets itself the task of exploring

what a pattern of food production that is fit for that future might look like, taking Totnes and District as a microcosm for that debate.

Based on the need to address these two issues, we might set out the following qualities of any system capable of feeding Totnes and District in the future:

◎ Fully contributing to the 80% or higher cut in carbon emissions by 2050

◎ Resilient: resilience (see further below) being the ability at all levels to withstand shock, must be key, embodied in the ability of the settlement in question, and its food supply system, to adapt rapidly to rising energy costs and climate change. UK Climate Projections 2009 estimate that by 2050, the climate for the South West in 2050 will be 2-3°C warmer than present, with around 30% less summer rainfall[4]).

◎ Delivering improved access to nutritious and affordable food[5]

◎ Delivering far more diversity than at present, in terms of species, ecosystems, produce, occupations, etc.

◎ Providing a significantly greater source of employment than at present

◎ Enabling agriculture becoming a net carbon sink, rather than the net emitter it has become

◎ Being lower carbon in terms of transportation, at all stages in the growing, processing and delivering of foodstuffs

◎ Providing a much-reduced dependence on fossil fuel-based fertilisers and pesticides and other agrochemicals

◎ Maximising the contribution of food produced from back gardens, allotments and other more 'urban' food sources, collectively referred to as 'urban agriculture'[6].

In essence, it is argued that the need to build a re-silient food system goes far deeper than the UK Government's interpretation of the concept of re-silience. This interprets resilience as referring to the need to broaden the base from which food is sourced, rather than a focus on increased produc-tion of local food for local markets (Cabinet Office 2008) and which also sees resilience in the context of emergency preparedness, stating that resilience

Basic town food foodprints – South West England

Key:
- Towns over 800 population
- Totnes & Dartington

Source: Geofutures

3.3 Food Footprints of settlements in the South West with a population of over 800, note location of Totnes and Dartington (Geofutures 2009. www.geofutures.com/2009/07/food-fooprints-re-localising-uk-food-supply/). © Mark Thurston, Geofutures

is about reducing "the risk from emergencies so that people can go about their business freely and with confidence" (Cabinet Office 2009). This paper argues that increased resilience is a potentially positive process, rebuilding food security, stronger communities, healthier food and more skilled and active communities. In the context of peak oil and climate change, the Government definitions of resilience could perhaps be seen as being about resisting change, whereas this paper argues that we need to fully accept that change is inevitable, and in order to develop a strategy to manage that change.

Increasingly, the concept of local food, and of the 'foodshed' (Kloppenburg et al. 2006, Hedden 2009, Peters et al. 2008), or the 'urban foodshed' (Getz 1991), is helping us to conceptualise a local food economy, focusing on the need to rebuild around our settlements the food systems which supply the bulk of their needs, designed to function beyond the availability of cheap liquid fuels. Peters et al. (2008) define a foodshed as "the geographical area from which a population derives its food supply"; while for Kloppenburg et al. (1996) it is "a more locally reliant, alternative food system that reduces the negative social and environmental impacts of agriculture". It is this foodshed concept, along with that of the 'foodzone' (see below), and how they could be applied to assessing the potential food resilience of Totnes and District, using GIS mapping to estimate that underpin the rest of this paper.

4. 'No Man is an Island': the Concept of Food Footprints

Clearly, one cannot look at Totnes and District in isolation. While this paper suggests a rebuilding of food resilience, and of a local food economy primarily built around meeting local needs and thereby living more within its energy budget, it is not suggesting an isolationist approach, or of somehow intentionally choosing to deny ourselves a certain amount of imports while they are available. Rather, it is about building resilience, the ability of the area to withstand shocks from the outside. A recent paper by DEMOS, 'Resilient Nation', defined resilience as "the capacity of an individual, community or system to adapt in order to sustain an acceptable level of function, structure, and identity" (DEMOS 2009: 18).

What is explored in this paper is the hypothesis that living within the food footprints set out in map 3.5,

were it to prove possible, need not mean a marked impoverishment of our current quality of life, a hairshirt lifestyle set in an apocalyptic worst-case scenario. Rather, what is presented here explores the potential for a new food culture, one that becomes more rooted in healthy, fresh food, with a wide variety of local livelihoods offering meaningful and productive work, with rich soils, abundant wildlife, a resurgence of skills and craft, and a renewed interest in healthy eating[7]. It would result in a more populated countryside being home to a range of businesses and a greater range of land use types, and an urban landscape fully integrating food production and intensive market gardening. It is not about "going back" to some dimly imagined rural idyll, rather it is about going forward into the future in such a way as to be able to thrive and flourish in uncertain and volatile times, and to live within realistic energy constraints.

One of the most fascinating places to start this exploration of the degree to which Totnes and District could build a more self-reliant food economy is to look at its geographical context, and how the food footprints of neighbouring larger settlements overlap with that of the area. The term 'food footprint' refers to the amount of land in total that it would take to meet the basic food needs of a given settlement. The food footprint of Totnes town itself (that is, the amount of land required to feed its population if it were to be entirely self sufficient) covers an area of 19.4 square kilometres[8]. This might lead one to think that given that it sits in a mostly rural landscape, building a relatively self-reliant food system is easily achievable. Figure 3.3 soon dispels this idea by showing composite food footprints for all settlements in the South West with estimated populations of over 800 people. It is based on the assumptions that all back garden space is utilised for food production and that the diet is Fairlie's Livestock Permaculture model (see Figure 3.9).

When one looks at the food footprint of Torquay and Paignton to the east of Totnes and District, it passes beyond Totnes heading west, passing into the footprint of Plymouth, which extends nearly as far as Totnes from the opposite direction. The area we are looking at in this paper is intersected and overlapped by these two other much larger population centres. The most sobering footprint is that of Greater London (not shown in Figure 3.3), which extends almost as far west as Bristol, and as far north as Birmingham. Feeding the UK's cities will be a huge challenge, and raises many questions, including what degree of re-ruralisation will be required.

5. Defining Totnes and District

Totnes is a town in the South Hams in Devon with an urban population of around 8,416[9], while Totnes and District (that is, Totnes and its surrounding 15 parishes, Figure 3.4) is a largely notional concept, developed by the Market and Coastal Towns Initiative (MCTI), with a total population of 23,914 (15,498 excluding Totnes town) (Devon Primary Care Trust (PCT) 2008). Although its southern boundaries reflect traditional and geographical relationships based on Totnes' history as a market town, its northern border is a politically generated boundary, forming the north-eastern boundary of South Hams district. The total land area is almost 24,000 ha., which, when roads, buildings, water and so on are taken out, translates into around 22,000ha of land (DCLG 2005).

One last challenge that a more localised food system will need to address is that of who will do the

farming. It has been estimated that a post-oil agricultural community will need to employ something like 20% of its population in food production[10]. According to the 2001 Census, in Totnes and District 5.54% of people in the area work in food, forestry and fishing (although an exact figure as how many work in agriculture is unavailable) (ONS 2001). This clearly differs between the urban and the rural populations. 2.4% of Totnes work in food, forestry and fishing, while 7.33% of the rest of Totnes and District do (ibid). The other challenge is the area's age profile. Farming requires fit and able-bodied people, but Totnes and District has a more aged population than most other parts of the region, as the graph below (Figure 3.5) highlights.

In 2008 at the Soil Association conference, Richard Heinberg looked at the increase in the number of people working in agriculture in Cuba before and after their 'Special Period' that lasted throughout the 1990s, when the Soviet Union collapsed and the country lost 80% of its fossil fuels and agrochemicals. The percentage of people working in farming rose from 1% to 20%[11]. The wider link between the avail-

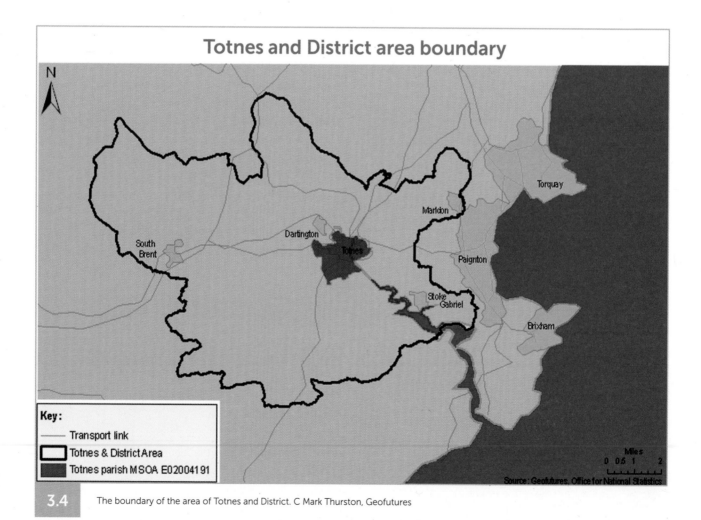

Totnes and District area boundary

Key:
— Transport link
☐ Totnes & District Area
■ Totnes parish MSOA E02004191

Source: Geofutures, Office for National Statistics

3.4 The boundary of the area of Totnes and District. C Mark Thurston, Geofutures

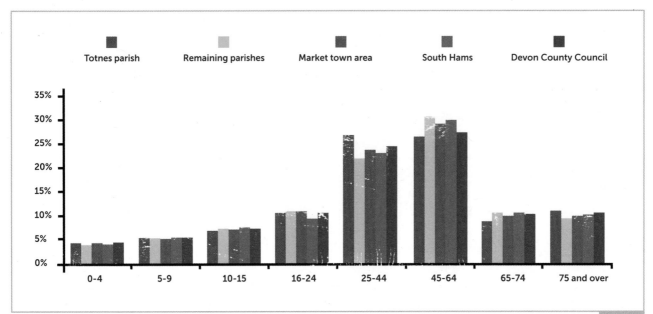

Legend: Totnes parish | Remaining parishes | Market town area | South Hams | Devon County Council

The population age profile for Totnes and District. Source: based on data from Devon PCT (2008)   3.5

ability of cheap oil and the number of people required in agriculture can be seen, for the US, in Figure 3.6.

For the UK, this would translate into an increase from half a million to 10 million employed in agriculture in some way[12]. More people working on the land will in turn necessitate more people living on the land. This implies a process of increased ruralisation, and also raises planning issues in terms of where these people will live.

6. The Land, and How it is Currently Used

In rough general figures, Totnes and District contains around 23,700 ha of land (DCLG 2005). Of that, agricultural land consists of approximately 19,282 ha; woodland and set-aside land covers around 1,273 ha (Defra 2004); buildings, roads, water, paths, railways and 'other' account for about 1,272 ha., and gardens around 329 ha (DCLG 2005). Our starting point in this paper is to look at the quality of the land that is available in the area, which will in turn inform our land use options. Clearly it makes no sense to graze sheep on Grade 1 land, nor to try to grow wheat on Grade 5 land[13]. The land base beneath our feet will inevitably constrain and inform our land use choices. Figure 3.7 sets out the land use classes for Totnes and District.

Having identified these land use classes, the next step is to pin down how land in Totnes and District is

currently used. This has proven a difficult task given that the area we are looking at straddles several of Defra's data areas, but pinning this down is key to our being able to explore the potential productivity of the area. The most recent data available at a suitably granular level is that from 2004. After that point, Defra issued statistics in a more general format, and specific data is harder to come by. As a rough thumbnail sketch, based on the 2004 data, land use in the area is composed as shown in Figure 3.8; A more detailed breakdown is as follows;

In terms of the regional enhancing of self-reliance this paper is exploring, it is interesting to note that the 2,669 ha dedicated to cereals production in 2004 would yield, under organic systems, roughly 8,000 tons of wheat annually, enough for around 24,000 people if they ate a diet consisting mostly of wheat, but clearly able to support far more people as part of a more balanced diet.

7. "Can Britain Feed Itself" and the "Livestock Permaculture" Model

In his paper in The Land magazine (Winter 2007-8), Simon Fairlie asked the question 'Can Britain Feed Itself?' (Fairlie 2007). So far as the authors are aware, this question had not been asked in print since 1975, when Kenneth Mellanby wrote a book of the same name (Mellanby 1975). Fairlie identified and

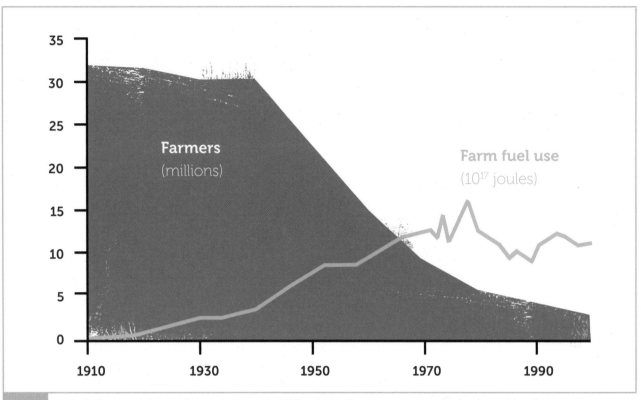

3.6 The US farm population and direct fuel consumption, 1910 to 2000. Much the same pattern can be observed for UK agriculture. Source: Miranowski 2004

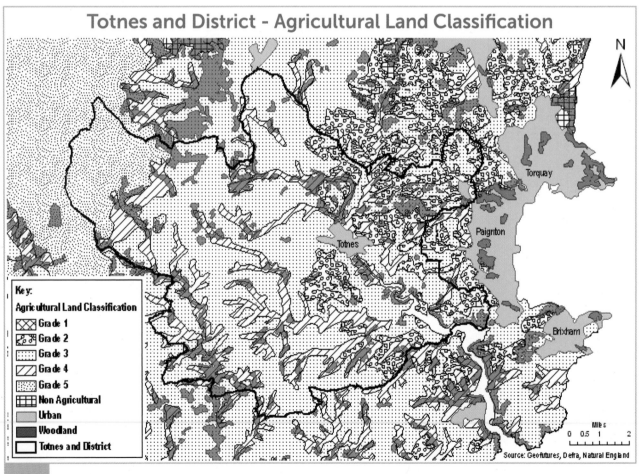

3.7 Land use classes across Totnes and District, showing the Totnes and District area boundary. Source: Natural England 2002, 2008

Total Cereals:
2,669 ha

Wheat: 869 ha
Winter Barley: 604 ha
Spring Barley: 877 ha
Oats: 189 ha
Other cereals: 130 ha

Total other arable:
944 ha

Potatoes: 34ha
Beans 67ha
Peas 43ha
Oilseed rape 149ha
Linseed 70ha
Turnips 55ha
Other stock feed 70ha
Maize: 295ha
Other arable: 54ha
Bare fallow: 9ha
Total peas and beans: 1ha
Vegetables (salads): 64ha
Orchard fruit: 24ha
Bush fruit: 5ha
Nurseries: 6ha

Total pasture:
12,062 ha

Permanent grass: 8,911ha
Temporary grass: 2,638 ha
Grazing: 513 ha

Fallow land[14]:
3,607 ha

A general indication of land use in Totnes and District in 2004. Table data Source: Defra (2004) June Agricultural Survey Data

3.8

evaluated six possible scenarios by which the nation might attempt to feed itself. He dismissed conventional organic livestock production on the basis that it is too hungry in its demand for land, and the two models that emerge as most viable are 'Livestock Permaculture' and 'Vegan Permaculture'. This paper focuses on 'Livestock Permaculture' because it is felt to be the most socially acceptable of the two. He states some of the key elements:

◎ Feeding livestock upon food wastes and residues

◎ Returning human sewage to productive land

◎ Dispersal of animals on mixed farms and smallholdings, rather than concentration in large farms

◎ Local slaughter and food distribution

◎ Managing animals to ensure optimum recuperation of manure, and

◎ Selecting and managing livestock, especially dairy cows, to be nitrogen providers rather than nitrogen stealers.

He acknowledges that this approach would require more labour, a more even dispersal of agricultural workers around the country, and a more localised economy with some degree of agrarian resettlement. As he puts it, the purpose of this model is;

"... to go another step further and see whether the UK could become more self reliant, not only in food, fodder and fertility, but also in fibre and fuel? Our environmental footprint currently stretches across untold ghost acres across the world; if suddenly we had to shoehorn it into the 22 million hectares of non-urban land we have in this country, how would we cope? Could this be done organically, whilst keeping a reasonable amount of meat in our diet for those who wanted it, and ensuring that a reasonable proportion of the country is reserved for wildlife?"

(Fairlie 2007: 22)

The 'Livestock Permaculture' scenario features the following elements:

◎ It aims to provide 2,767 calories per person per day

◎ Meat is produced to meet demand at 1975 levels (around 83 grams of red meat per person per day, for a family of four the equivalent of a traditional Sunday roast, as well as some chicken and fish, totalling around half of present meat consumption), resulting in a reduction in stocking levels, especially for cattle

◎ Agriculture is more localised, producing as close as possible to the point of consumption

◎ Production of milk is kept as it is today, but cows are grass-fed, rather than eating a grain based diet, and some eggs are also available

◎ Pigs are fed, as they were traditionally, using human food wastes[15], supplemented by grains

◎ The model allows for a doubling of woodland cover, mostly for increased firewood production

◎ Sufficient land is also factored in either for feeding working horses, or for the growing of enough bio fuels to power a tractor

◎ Land is also included to grow 7kg of fibre per person per year for clothing

◎ Fruit is grown in orchards which can also double as grazing land

Figure 3.9 shows this model in more detail.

On a national scale, this would produce an agricultural system whereby the UK "produces all its food, a substantial proportion of its textiles, and the energy for cultivating its fields on 13.4 million ha., a little over half the entire country" (ibid: 24). This paper explores whether Totnes and District could feed itself, and whether it could do so from its 'foodshed', that is, the land surrounding it, using the assumptions behind the 'Livestock Permaculture' model. It would be very useful, however, to repeat the modelling being undertaken in this paper for Fairlie's other five models as well.

Livestock Permaculture

Population 60.6m Total agriculture and forestry land 22.205m ha

Including pigs, poultry, textiles, tractor or horse power and timber	7.9m ha arable and ley 5.9m ha pasture	6m ha woodland 2.4m ha spare

	Consumption (grams/person/day)	Calories in diet (kcal/person/day)	UK production (million tons/yr)	Yield (tons/ha)	Arable land (1000 ha)	Perm pasture (1000 ha)	Other land (1000 ha)
Cereals for human food	448	1526	9.9	4.3	2302		
Potatoes	453	300	10	25	400		
Sugar	32	100	0.707	7.5	94		
Vegetables and fruit	500	150			100	50 (100)	
Hemp and flax	5 kg/yr		0.303	3	100		
Horse or biofuel					876		
Green Manure					430		
Milk (incl. butter, cheese)	568	330	12.5	3.7 (3.26 net)	2825	1765	
Beef (grass reared)	33	86	0.735	0.4		1740	
Cereals for pigs	bacon 36	180	1.2	4.3	279		
Cereals for hens/eggs	(egg/chicken) 30	50	2	4.3	465		
Sheep	9	24	0.2	0.084			2372
Leather and sheepskin	1.46 kg/yr						
Wool	750 kg/yr						
Fish	11	11	0.243				
Timber & firewood				3			6000
Spare land/wild meat	5	10	0.11	0.031			2407
Land used [total calories]		[2767]			7871	3555	8372

1 ha arable plus 0.8 ha pasture supplies 7.5 people

3.9   The detailed breakdown of the Livestock Permaculture model. From Fairlie 2009

What a sustainable re-localised food system might look like in the future

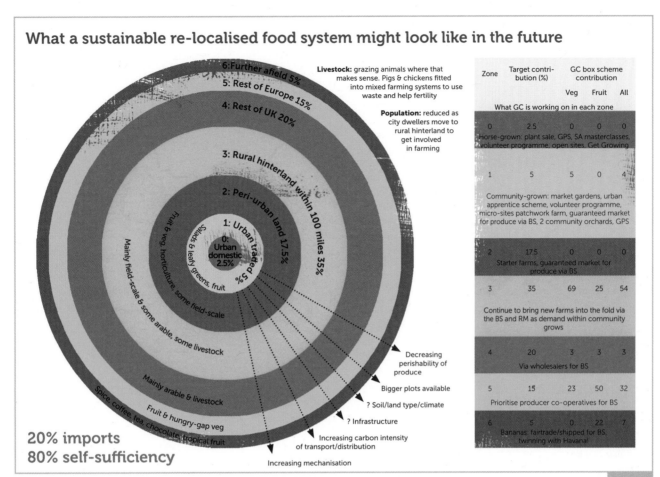

The Growing Communities Food Zone Diagram. Source: Brown 2009

3.10

Zone	Target contribution (%)	GC box scheme contribution		
		Veg	Fruit	All
What GC is working on in each zone				
0	2.5	0	0	0
Horse-grown: plant sale, GPS, SA masterclasses, volunteer programme, open sites, Get Growing				
1	5	5	0	4
Community-grown: market gardens, urban apprentice scheme, volunteer programme, micro-sites patchwork farm, guaranteed market for produce via BS, 2 community orchards, GPS				
2	17.5	0	0	0
Starter farms, guaranteed market for produce via BS				
3	35	69	25	54
Continue to bring new farms into the fold via the BS and RM as demand within community grows				
4	20	3	3	3
Via wholesalers for BS				
5	15	23	50	32
Prioritise producer co-operatives for BS				
6	5	0	22	7
Bananas: fairtrade/shipped for BS, twinning with Havana!				

8. Weaving in the Foodzones

Julie Brown of Growing Communities[16], an urban organic food social enterprise in Hackney, London, has developed a model she called 'foodzones'. It attempts to put figures on the percentages of food that would feed London, and from what distance they might need to travel. It assumes an 80% national self-sufficiency, a more seasonal diet, and factors in domestic and urban food production. The result is the foodzone diagram shown in Figure 3.10. Brown's model offers a fascinating model for how a city might feed itself utilising the principles of the foodshed; that is, giving priority to foods grown as close as possible to the settlement. Although clearly stylised, might it be that settlements could create food systems based, at least loosely, on the stylised 'target' type model shown above?

In this research, the combined food footprints of 5 settlements within Totnes and District (see Figure 3.11) were calculated for their populations' main requirements, fruit and vegetables, sheep, dairy and arable. Taking the foodzone model above and applying it to the locations of Defra-defined agricultural land types in Totnes' hinterland, the foodshed analysis identifies the land types in closest proximity to the town which are best suited to different production needs.

Figures 3.11 and 3.12 break this down into more detail, looking at specific kinds of agricultural production that are possible on the land types available. Perishability and labour intensity are the drivers that give first priority to the required amount of fruit and vegetable production on the Grades 1 and 2 land in the urban area and its periphery. Next priority is Grade 1 and 2 land for arable production of cereals, sugar, hemp, flax, green manures, biofuels and fodder crops.

Defra sub-categorises its Grade 3 land into sub grades 3a and 3b, 'good' and 'moderate' quality land; the difference is potentially significant but data distinguishing the two sub-grades are not consistently available nationwide. For this model, Grade 3 and 4

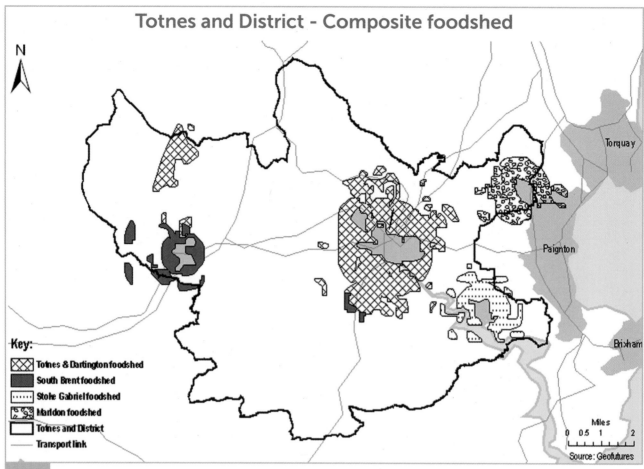

Totnes and District - Composite foodshed

Key:
- Totnes & Dartington foodshed
- South Brent foodshed
- Stoke Gabriel foodshed
- Marldon foodshed
- Totnes and District
- Transport link

Miles
0 0.5 1 2

Source: Geofutures

3.11 Composite Foodsheds for the four largest settlements in Totnes and District, showing how they do not accord with the 'foodzones' model. © Mark Thurston, Geofutures

land is all allocated to dairy and beef pasture. Theoretically, food zoning in the Brown model would place this activity further from the settlement, but for Totnes much of this land is in immediate proximity to the town – reflecting the wider region's strong current livestock farming economy. Grade 5 land is best suited to sheep farming, and the nearest suitable location is some distance from Totnes, near South Brent on Dartmoor. Equally, the population here has insufficient land to grow enough grain, and the nearest place for them to grow it is close to Totnes.

This analysis has been subject to a number of data issues. Fine-scale soils data would provide a deeper insight into land suitability than the basic Defra classifications. We also lack access to comprehensive Defra data for productive urban areas or for woodlands, and our calculations use additional datasets from Natural England to identify the latter. In section 8 below we highlight the key issue of insufficient woodlands being available to provide enough wood

for fuel; for the purposes of this model, woodland is regarded as an area to maintain biodiversity and offer a source of wild meat as well as providing wood for fuel.

Also, we need to acknowledge that the agricultural land classification is of itself, fairly crude. For example, it is highly likely that there is land closer to Totnes that is well suited for sheep grazing, whereas the model suggests that Dartmoor is the closest location best suited to this type of farming. We plan in future versions of the model to be able to integrate local knowledge more fully, by using more granular datasets and also by enabling local experts to modify land parcel information. However, at this stage, the cruder method we have employed does begin to give us an insight to the food security issues not only at the local level, but also just as importantly at the sub-regional, regional and indeed national level.

In section 10 below we touch on a number of additional important future research directions, including the need to understand the potential for mixed farming systems. Currently, this model takes no account of existing land ownership or actual agricultural usage, and it may also be that mixed farming systems such as agroforestry offer greater opportunities to increase overall yields, especially on Grade 3 land.

9. So, Could Totnes and District Feed Itself?

The foodzones we have specified in the previous section are fairly crude, and represent our efforts to calculate the amount of land required to feed Totnes and its neighbouring settlements. In this section, we explore some of the yield calculation we employed in the model.

Vegetables and Fruit

The UK presently imports 60% of its vegetables and 95% of its fruit (Defra 2005). Feeding the area with vegetables is the easy part. Guy Watson of Riverford Farm[17] has stated[18] that one acre of ground[19] can produce, organically, sufficient vegetables to fill 30 vegetable boxes around the year (enough to meet most of a household's vegetable needs). Given that the population of Totnes town is 8,416, a total of around 3,500 households, this suggests that around 47.35 ha. would be required, and that for Totnes and District, with its total of around 10,000 households, organic vegetables could be provided for all on around 142 ha. Oral history work conducted by Transition Town Totnes[20] suggests that the three urban market gardens that the town used to have were able to produce around 60% of the fresh vegetable requirements of the town, supplemented by that brought in to local markets from nearby farms, and also during World War Two, the nation was able to achieve yields of up to 40 tons per hectare from allotment and back garden vegetable production[21].

Given that Totnes and District contains 319 ha. of back gardens (ONS 2001), were these all to be adequately fertile, south-facing, unshadowed and accessible (that is, not covered in concrete slabs, gravel or decking), and were they to be in the hands of skilled growers reaching the kinds of yields achieved by World War Two allotment gardeners, they could theoretically produce 13,840 tons of fresh

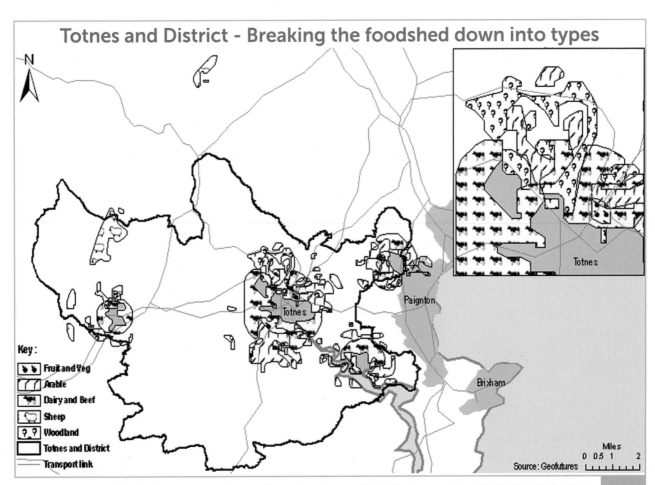

Key:
- Fruit and Veg
- Arable
- Dairy and Beef
- Sheep
- Woodland
- Totnes and District
- Transport link

Source: Geofutures

A more detailed look at the foodsheds for the five largest settlements in Totnes and District, broken down into agricultural production types.
© Mark Thurston, Geofutures

3.12

vegetables. Although all of the above would take a great deal of work, clearly supplying vegetables is not an impossibly onerous task, especially to feed a population eating more seasonal produce. Meeting demand for cereals is harder, and for meat, harder again.

Cereals

In 2004, 3237 ha. of land were dedicated to the production of cereals, mostly spring barley (Defra 2004). However, most of this is grown as feed for cattle eating a grain-based diet, an approach which consumes a vast amount of grain. One of this paper's conclusions is that living within our foodshed will require our consuming significantly less meat than at present, which raises the possibility of much more grain being grown for local consumption. If the land currently dedicated to growing cereals were to instead grow for local, human consumption, it would be able to feed around 24,000 people (if they ate little else, and a lot more people if that wheat were part of a balanced diet). Cereals are hard to replace with anything else, but can easily be part of an organic rotation.

In terms of wheat grown for bread production, the damp climate of Devon doesn't make it the ideal place, increasing the susceptibility to moulds and fungal diseases. Also, bread makers tend to prefer wheat with a gluten level above 12, whereas locally grown wheat struggles to get above 8. More research into other grains, such as spelt, is needed.

Meat

As set out above, this scenario requires the consumption of much less meat than is presently consumed. In particular, it requires a move away from grain-fed cattle, moving towards grass-fed animals, especially using systems such as foggage[22], which require fewer inputs. Conversely, it needs more consumption of chickens and pigs, and their being used as part of integrated, mixed farming systems.

A significant proportion of the protein required, currently supplied by meat, could be provided instead by nut production. The Agroforestry Research Trust, based in Dartington, has been researching nut varieties and their potential productivity in a Devon context, and their research suggests that hybrid walnut and sweet chestnut varieties could produce, after 15 years, 1 ton of walnuts per acre, roughly equivalent to the organic production of wheat. This agroforestry approach carries the advantage that it can be worked in around current farming without requiring an overnight change in conventional farming practices, although it is an element that requires a longer lead-in time than other approaches. Furthermore, one ton of walnuts is estimated to yield 60% of its weight in edible oil (Crawford 1996).

Alcohol

There are no figures for the amount of land required to provide alcoholic drinks for Totnes and its surroundings, but Sharpham vineyard has calculated that its current level of production, were it to be focused purely on local markets, would provide 1 bottle of Sharpham wine per month for each of the 22,000 people within Totnes and District. Traditionally, the area drank more cider and beer. Many of the cider orchards have now been lost, and even when they existed, the area was still a net importer of apples (from Brittany) for cider production. Beer should be easier; 1 ton of hops and 100 tons of barley produces around 800,000 pints of beer. At present, however, little or no hops are grown in the area.

Dairy (Milk and Cheese)

Fairlie's Livestock Permaculture model (see above) suggests that meeting a national, per capita demand for 568g per person of milk (slightly over a pint) per day, which is sufficient for milk and dairy products, requires 2,825,000 ha of arable land and 1,765,000 ha of permanent pasture nationally. This figure is for grass-fed, organic cows, which includes calves and heifers, so there would also be the potential to produce some beef from this. Scaled to a Totnes and District population of 23,914, this requires 1072 ha of arable land and 669ha of permanent pasture, making a total of 1741ha of land required for dairy production, which is about 1/13th ha. per person. Devon has, of course, long been a milk-exporting part of the country.

Little remains of the infrastructure of local dairy processing that was once a feature of life in the area. Gone is most of the network of local creameries, local bottling plants and the idea that milk produced locally is consumed locally. Exceptions are a biodynamic farm near Totnes which sells unpasteurised milk directly into the town, and Riverford Organic Farm, who produce a range of organic dairy produce, sold within Totnes and District but also further afield. Riverford's dairy has a throughput of 2,287,680 pints of milk per year, which equates to 96 pints per person per year, around one quarter of the area's demand. The recent closure of the Dairy Crest milk processing plant in Totnes has led to a further demise of the capacity of the area to supply its own dairy needs. One interesting observation[23] from Riverford is that its processing of the milk into skimmed and non-skimmed milks, yoghurt, cream and butter creates far more jobs than the actual milk production, emphasising the benefits to the local economy of more localised milk processing. Riverford state that their milk processing facility is currently only working at half its potential capacity[24], so were more organic milk to be produced, they would be able to supply more than half of Totnes and District's needs.

Timber for Fuel

At present, only 585 ha. are dedicated to woodland in the Totnes and District area (Defra 2004). The woodland owned by the Dartington Hall Trust, if sustainably managed, is estimated to produce insufficient firewood even for the Dartington Estate's proposed woodchip boilers, and the same is the case for the Sharpham Estate. The Forestry Commission (1988) estimate that yields from well designed coppice can range from 2 tons per hectare for most varieties (i.e. oak, alder, sweet chestnut) and up to 6 tons for poplar and willow. We have therefore taken an average of 3 tons per hectare for this paper. We do note, however, the probability that the impacts

of climate change may well include increasing risks of pest or disease outbreaks and of fire, although for some species, yields may turn out to be higher, and plantings will need to take this into consideration.

The average house, retrofitted and with an efficient woodstove and solar thermal panels, using wood for central heating and backed up by solar panels for hot water, would require around 7 tons of dried timber per year. Totnes and District contains around 10,000 households, which at 7 tons of dried firewood per household, would need around 70,000 tons of firewood. At an output of 3 tons of firewood per hectare, meeting this demand would require 23,3000 ha. of well-managed coppice woods, of which around 22,750 would need to be newly planted. Unfortunately, Totnes and District only contains 23,443 ha. of land in total. There is clearly a major role for energy conservation, other technologies such as heat pumps, and also for anaerobic digestion (which could also play a role in cycling fertility). The answer to the question 'Can Totnes Heat Itself?' appears to be a resounding 'no'. We have also been unable to establish figures for the potential timber output from the management of hedgerows, which may make a significant contribution in more rural areas.

10. Maintaining Fertility

Currently, most conventional agriculture depends on imported fertility, usually nitrogen fertilisers made from natural gas as well as phosphorous and potassium. This is unsustainable in many ways, most notably in the precarious nature and affordability of the UK's natural gas supplies (see Figure 3.12).

The provision of fertility is one of the principal limiting factors in UK agriculture. Well-designed farming systems are able to provide for their own fertility, through a combination of good waste management and return of fertility to the soil, as well as well-managed rotations of pasture and arable. Land under pasture will accumulate nitrogen, potassium and potash, and will deplete them if grazed year on year. The balance, in the Totnes and District land base, of arable and temporary grassland is ideal for the area to be able to provide for its fertility without the need for external inputs. This can be speeded up with the addition of clover to the temporary grass leys. The area at the moment has about 5 ha. of grass for every 2-3 ha. of arable land, which is the ideal proportion.

The 'bringing home' of food production will also require a reduced dependency on imported fertility. This will require a fresh look at how the area treats its human waste, as human waste contains, per person, nitrogen and phosphorous equivalent to that which agriculture requires to produce its food. Systems for safely and hygienically collecting and utilising human urine as a replacement for nitrogen fertilisers exist in other European countries, and systems for the safe composting of human waste have also been developed[25].

11. Other Questions and Challenges

The move from Totnes and District being merely one consumer in a vast and profoundly unsustainable globalised food system towards being a more self-reliant and resilient local 'foodshed' is a vast undertaking. Nonetheless, given the impending, or possibly already historic, peak in world oil production and the need to reduce emissions from agriculture by 80% over the next 40 years, this is a shift

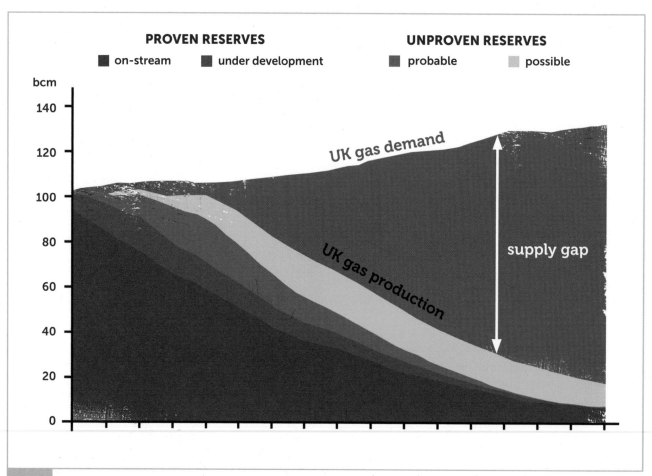

PROVEN RESERVES
■ on-stream ■ under development

UNPROVEN RESERVES
■ probable ■ possible

bcm

UK gas demand

UK gas production

supply gap

3.13 The forecasts for UK natural gas production to 2020, showing a precipitous decline over the next seven years. Source: Parliamentary Office of Science and Technology (2004)

which is inevitable, and the sooner it is embarked upon, the greater chance it has of success[26].

This research is in its early stages, but it may be useful at this point to identify some of the challenges and issues that have emerged thus far:

◎ An unknown percentage of the land that would be needed for this kind of approach is low-lying and at risk from flooding and other climatic and meteorological impacts that will arise from climate change. Furthermore, the Livestock Permaculture model itself is based on our understanding of our current temperate agriculture's system; how applicable this will be in a couple of decade's time is moot. More research is needed on this and on the amount of land it might remove from food production, or the changes in land use it might necessitate.

◎ Many of the datasets required to do this research more fully, and on a national scale, are not in the public arena and are hugely expensive to obtain. These include one set which allows a calculation to be made of the exact amount of land currently utilised by back gardens in any given settlement. Accessing the appropriate data sets will allow this work to be much more thorough.

◎ No exact data are included here with regards to the amount of fish that could be included in such an approach. The proximity of Totnes and District to fishing ports such as Brixham offers the possibility of significant input of protein, although at the moment most of that fish goes to markets elsewhere.

◎ This paper has explored the supply side of such an approach. The equally difficult aspect is that of creating the demand for locally grown produce, in the age of supermarkets and convenience foods. Although some models exist[27], the generation of sufficient demand to support such a transition presents major challenges in the current economic digm.

◎ A calculation is needed for the potential generation of energy from anaerobic digestion, utilising slurry and other farm wastes, as well as waste food, and their ability to provide space heating, thereby reducing the demand for firewood, shown above to be potentially insatiable if viewed as the only source of space heating.

◎ Much of the land in the area being looked at here is hilly, unsuited for grain production. Exploration of new ways of using such land productively will be needed.

◎ Can this land use model be expanded to include other essentials like building materials, and medicines?

◎ The thorny issue of population needs to be explored, both the question of whether there are too many people in the area, and also in terms of the fact that Devon County Council states that in 2009, one in five households are pensioners living alone. Also of concern is the current average age of the Devon farmer, raising the important question of who will actually do the work required by this approach to feeding the area.

◎ Another challenge revolves around issues of nature conservation. The expansion of food production requires us to reassess current concepts of nature conservation, in which food production and habitat protection are often viewed as being mutually exclusive (as indeed with energy and chemical intensive agriculture they often are).

◎ Another challenge lies with the planning system, and the tensions that will arise as more people need to live in agricultural areas.

◎ The area of reskilling is also vital. The huge majority of people no longer have any experience or knowledge of food growing on any kind of scale, and farming as a profession has also become deskilled over the last 40 years. The training question is key; who is to be trained, where, and what will they be taught?

◎ One of the key challenges the authors of this paper have faced has been the data available for yields from different land uses. Data exists for yields from dairy and arable production, but little exists for more mixed, integrated approaches such as agroforestry. More data on this is urgently needed.

12. Getting from Here to There: the Nuts and Bolts of the Transition

It is, of course, not possible to implement such a change overnight. It would require an unprecedented collaboration and shared sense of urgency and purpose, akin to that seen in 1939, when the amount of land under cultivation increased from 12.9 million ha. in 1939 to 19.8 million by the end of the war. Food production during that period had risen 91%, and the UK was able to feed itself for approximately 160 days a year, rather than the 120 days it had been in 1939 (Gardiner 2004). There was also, of course, the famous 'Dig For Victory' campaign, which led to a significant proportion of the nation's diet coming from back gardens and allotments. One of the challenges facing us today is how to design the business models required to bring this about in such a way to make them financially viable in the current economic situation, which is very different from that in which they will need to function in 20 years' time. Models that offer potential for being integrated into existing farming enterprises will be vital.

Part of making such an approach possible will be the implementation of new models for getting food to people. These will include (but not be limited to) Community Supported Agriculture, consumer/farmer co-ops, farmers' markets, local procurement, local processing, local investment mechanisms and many more. There will also need to be a huge programme of reskilling, given the small number of people with broad scale food growing skills. Engagement will need to be deep and cross-sectoral. The Transition movement is one of many that are looking at the practicalities of rebuilding local economies, and this paper is an indication of the scale of its thinking. How the various models and approaches might fit together is a key part of the thinking that Transition initiatives do, and this paper identifies the need for a national-scale version of the research that underpins this paper, as part of a food plan for the UK.

Conclusions

This paper has offered a very rough, broad-brush attempt at addressing the question "Can Totnes and District feed itself?" Utilising GIS mapping and the datasets that are currently accessible, it has explored the current land classes and how farmland is currently used, and then, using Simon Fairlie's 'Livestock Permaculture' model, has tried to assess whether or not Totnes and District could actually feed itself. Even if we were to assume roughly stable climate conditions, the answer is that yes, it could, but only if:

◎ It lived in isolation from its neighbouring major conurbations of Plymouth and Torbay; when these settlements are factored in, it becomes far more difficult;

◎ Far far more people lived on, and worked, the land; and

◎ We ate a very different diet from the one we consume today.

Those current eating habits, current levels of meat consumption, as well as the long supply chain, just-in-time distribution models on which the food system is based, are all key factors in the inability of the area to meet its food needs. The approach explored here has looked at an alternative to the current paradigm, arguing that interests of sustainability, resilience, health and nutrition and long-term economic stability are best served by a move, through a well designed and integrated approach, towards the area meeting its food needs as close to home as is practicably possible.

It raises the question as to whether, in times of increasing unemployment and economic contraction, the 'outsourcing' of food to whoever can produce it cheapest in the world is an economic own goal. It could be that the relocalisation of the food economy would have huge benefits to the local economy, creating a wide range of jobs. Although the mechanisms and structures needed to make this possible are, in some cases, still at a very early stage of evolution, this paper contends that they are possible and indeed are urgently needed.

This paper has taken an approach that assumes forms of agricultural land use are separate and unintegrated, so that dairy farming happens in one place, forestry in another, and fruit growing some else again. One of the areas for future research that emerges from this paper is the need for more hard data about integrated systems, well designed forms of land use which integrate the production of fuel, medicine, freshwater fish, fruit, vegetables, herbs and so on. One such a model exists in agroforestry, and one of the primary research centres into this, the Agroforestry Research Trust[28] is based just outside Totnes. A more widespread adoption of this model could prove a key element in the UK's ability not only to feed itself, but also to fuel, warm and heal itself too. Ultimately it could turn out that Totnes and District can feed itself, and could be healthier, wealthier and wiser for having done so.

Bibliography and Further Reading

Anderson, K. & Bows, A. (2009) Reframing Climate Change: How recent emission trends & the latest science change the debate. Tyndall Centre for Climate Change Research.

Cabinet Office (2008) Food: an analysis of the issues. The Strategy Unit. Revision D. August 2008. Retrieved from www.cabinetoffice.gov.uk/media/cabinetoffice/strategy/assets/food/food_analysis.pdf

Cabinet Office (2009) UK Resilience Homepage. Retrieved from www.cabinetoffice.gov.uk/ukresilience.aspx

Crawford, M. (1996) Walnuts: their production and culture. Agroforestry Research Trust.

DCLG (2005) General Land Use Database, 2005 – LSOA level.

Defra (2004) June Agricultural Survey Data 2004 - MSOA level.

Defra (2005) The Validity of Food Miles as an indicator of Sustainable Development, July 2005

DEMOS (2009) Resilient Nation. Retrieved from www.demos.co.uk/files/Resilient_Nation_-_web-1.pdf?1242207746

Devon County Council (2006) Devon Town Baseline Profile. Retrieved from www.devon.gov.uk/totnesbaselineprofile.pdf

Devon PCT (2008) Family Health Services Authority (FHSA) population estimates: South Hams parishes 2008. Available [online] at www.devon.gov.uk/index/councildemocracy/improving_our_services/facts_figures_and_statistics/facts_and_figures/thepeople/peopleestandproj/peoplepopestimates/peoplepopulationestandproestimatestotnes.htm. Accessed on 28/05/2009.

Economist, The. (2009) Briefing: The outlook for the oil price. Boom and Bust. The Economist May 23rd 2009 pp76-78.

Fairlie, S. (2007) Can Britain feed itself? The Land 4 (Winter 2007-08)

Fleming, D. (2006) The Lean Economy: a survivor's guide to a future that works. Unpublished manuscript. Draft dated 27th July 2006.

Forestry Commission (1988) Farm Woodland Planning. Forestry Commission Bulletin 80. London, HMSO.

Forestry Commission of Scotland (2008) Research Note: Impacts of climate change on forestry in Scotland – a synopsis of spatial modelling research. Retrieved from www.forestry.gov.uk/pdf/fcrn101.pdf/$FILE/fcrn101.pdf

Gardiner, J. (2004) Wartime Britain 1939-1945. Headline Book Publishing.

Getz, A. (1991) Urban foodsheds. The Permaculture Activist 24 (October): 26-27.

Giampietro, M. and Pimentel, D. (1994) The Tightening Conflict: population, energy use, and the ecology of agriculture. www.dieoff.org

Hedden, W.P. (1929) How Great Cities Are Fed. Boston: D.C. Heath and Co. [Watersheds, Milksheds, and Foodsheds chapter] [later: Journal of Business of the University of Chicago (Apr. 2, 1930) Joseph G. Knapp vol. 3, no. 2, p. 263: Watersheds, Milksheds, and Foodsheds]

Heinberg, R. & Bomford, M. (2009) The Food and Farming Transition: towards a post carbon food system. Post Carbon Institute. www.postcarbon.org/files/PCI-food-and-farming-transition.pdf

Hopkins, R. (2008) The Transition Handbook: from oil dependency to local resilience. Green Books, Dartington, Totnes.

Hoyos, C. (2009) Total says oil output is near its peak. Financial Times [online]. Retrieved from: www.ft.com/cms/s/0/1df0bc9c-fbc7-11dd-bcad-000077b07658.html

Kloppenburg, J.; Hendrickson, J. and Stevenson, G.W. (1996) Coming in to the foodshed. Agriculture and Human Values 13(3) (1 June 1996), pp. 33-42.

Mellanby, K. (1975) Can Britain feed itself? London: Merlin Press

Miranowski, J. (2004) Energy consumption in U.S. agriculture (presented at USDA/Farm Foundation "Agriculture as a Producer and Consumer of Energy" conference, Arlington, Virginia, 24-25 June 2004)

Natural England (2002) Agricultural Land Classification Provisional, www.magic.gov.uk/datadoc/objecttypegb.asp?geoid=4

Natural England (2008) Ancient Woodland England www.magic.gov.uk/datadoc/objecttypegb.asp?geoid=60

Oil Drum, The (2009) World Oil Production Forecast - Update May 2009. May 19th 2009. Retrieved from www.theoildrum.com/node/5395

ONS (2001) GLUD

Parliamentary Office of Science and Technology (2004) The Future of UK Gas Supplies. Postnote. October 2004. No. 230. Retrieved from www.parliament.uk/documents/upload/POSTpn230.pdf

Peters, C.J.; Bills, N.L.; Wilkins, J.L. And Frick, G.W. (2008) Foodshed analysis and its relevance to sustainability. Renewable Agriculture and Food Systems 23(4).

Rubin, J. (2009) Why Your World is About to Get a Whole Lot Smaller: What the Price of Oil Means for the Way We Live. Virgin Books.

Walker, B. And Salt, D. (2006) Resilience Thinking: Sustaining Ecosystems and People in a Changing World. Washington: Island Press

FOOD PRODUCTION AND FARMING

"Not only is our entire agricultural and food system based upon the availability of cheap fossil fuels – we do not even use them in a wise and frugal manner. We squander them on flagrant consumerism in order to maximise short-term profit, while destroying the localised systems that once sustained our culture".

Dale Allen Pfeiffer

The Challenge

A walk down Totnes High Street could leave one under the impression that the whole town feeds itself from locally grown, seasonal, organic produce. The town's vibrant local food culture has long been one of its defining features. Yet, we shouldn't be misled into thinking Totnes is genuinely using local food production to feed itself; only a fraction of what is eaten in Totnes is locally grown. As we have seen in the history section of this Plan, it was not always like this. Totnes used to be situated firmly in what one might call a 'foodshed', a catchment around the town that provided for its key food needs. It was a highly diversified approach: there were market gardens, back gardens, small mixed farms, orchards, abattoirs, creameries, gleaning from the surrounding countryside. Now most of that system is gone, and although we might celebrate the fact that we personally no longer have to grow anything, we find ourselves in a far, far more vulnerable place in terms of food than we were 40 years ago. The present system is a fragile illusion.

The way we feed ourselves is coming under increasing stress, greatly compounded by the twin challenges of peak oil and climate change. For the last 30 years we have been almost literally 'eating oil', such is the degree to which our food supply system is underpinned, and indeed made possible, by the uninterrupted flow of cheap oil and gas. Each calorie of food that lands on our plates has needed at least 10 calories of fossil fuel to grow, process, store and transport it to us[29]. We have also become increasingly dependent on just-in-time distribution systems, with the result that although we now have access to a greater variety of foods from all corners of the world than at any point in our history, we are also, at any one time, only a couple of days away from a major food crisis should the lorries that make it possible stop running, as we saw starkly in 2000 during the lorry drivers' dispute. Clearly this is not a desirable, nor a sensible, state of affairs.

Our challenge is to rebuild the foodshed that supported the area, although what we will be putting back will be very different from what was there before. Based on a detailed analysis of the land base of Totnes and District and how it is currently used, as well as the food needs of the population, we attempt to define what the land in the area might look like if its aim is to support the population of the area. In short, we aim to answer the question "Can Totnes Feed Itself?" It is a question no one has asked in this context before, and one that we should have addressed long ago.

9.9 million kilos

10.2 million kilos

Where we are Now

Our current approach to food is to assume that the market will always provide. The British Government has become increasingly hands-off in terms of food production, assuming that the market will build a wide enough base across the world to ensure reliable supplies. It also associates local farming increasingly with supplying niche markets, rather than providing essential foodstuffs. Here are a few facts about our current food production system:

◎ At present, the UK imports 40% of its food, 25% of which is food that we could have grown here in the first place.

◎ We import 95% of our fruit.

◎ The UK exports 15.5 million tons of potatoes to Germany, and imports 17.2 million back into the UK

◎ We export 9.9 million kilos of milk and cream to France, and import 10.2 million

◎ 80% of our shopping is done in supermarkets, local food accounts for less than 1.5% of total UK food sales.

◎ UK agriculture is still largely dependent on natural gas for manufacturing fertilisers, which, given that 80% of UK gas will be imported by 2016, leads to a high degree of vulnerability.

◎ Global reserves of potash are running low. The UK currently imports 80% of our potash, and the price rose by 700% last year. Some argue that given its essential role as a fertiliser, 'peak potash' could be more of a problem than peak oil.

A business-as-usual scenario would mean that by 2030, Totnes and District has fewer farmers, grows less food for local markets, and has fewer skilled people working in agriculture. The quality of its soils will have continued to deteriorate, and the nutritional quality of the food it does grow will continue to decline. The grip of the supermarkets will have become absolute (given that they already sell over 80% of the food purchased in this country, one could say it already has). The challenge for the area in terms of food production can be best summed up by use of the analogy of a cake. Totnes and District, until round 1850 when the railways arrived, was largely self-reliant for food, with its core needs produced locally. In 1850, the cake was produced locally, and what was imported was the icing and the cherry on top of the cake. Now this is reversed. By 2030, we will be buying our cake wherever in the world we can find it cheapest, and the local farmers that remain will be producing the meagre icing and the cherries on top. This will leave us vulnerable, under-skilled, and ill prepared for times of increased uncertainty and insecurity.

According to SouthWestID[30], the average South West household spent £45 per week (2006) on its food shopping[31] (£10 lower than the UK average). Given that Totnes and District contains 9,481 households[32], this would make the total spent on food in Totnes and District currently around £450,000. While this may seem a very low amount, even half of this spent on local food would encourage the further development of locally based food producers with the wider beneficial impact on our environment, economy and wellbeing.

95%

15.5 million tons

17.2 million tons

A strategy to encourage the more localised, resilient approach to feeding Totnes and District that this Plan sets out, would need to be based on the following principles:

◎ It will need to be well on the way to the 80% cut in carbon emissions by 2050 (as stated by UK Government policy)

◎ The concept of resilience, the ability at all levels to withstand shock, must be key, embodied in the ability of settlements and their food supply system, to adapt rapidly to rising energy costs and climate change

◎ The need for improved access to nutritious and affordable food

◎ The need for far more diversity than at present, in terms of species, ecosystems, produce, occupations, etc. to support food production systems

◎ The need to increase the capacity of our soils to act as a carbon sink requires us to adopt more perennial, farming systems supporting grass and tree systems, as well as making good soil management and the building of organic matter in soils a priority

◎ Stronger links to local markets than at present, supplying local markets by preference where possible

◎ A much reduced dependence on fertilisers and other agrochemicals (ideally enabled by a shift to organic practices)

◎ Accompanying this will also be the need for a large increase in the amount of food produced from back gardens, allotments and other more 'urban' food sources

◎ The use of genetically modified crops has no place in a more sustainable agriculture

This gives rise to the oft-asked question, "can organic farming feed the world?" The answer to this question is really that in the coming years, given the degree of oil dependency of conventional farming and the amount of natural gas required by fertiliser production, farming in the future will at least be organic, from necessity, cost and practicality rather than choice. What else farming will be is still open

3.14 Grow More Fruit and Veg by students at Grove School.

to debate. One last challenge that a more localised food system will need to address is that of who will do the farming. It has been estimated that post oil agriculture will need to employ around 20% of its population in food production.

What follows is one vision of how food and farming might become more localised and sustainable over the next 21 years.

Achieving the Vision - Creating Demand

The section 'Can Totnes Feed itself' has looked at whether it is feasible to feed Totnes and District from its foodshed. The answer is yes, with certain changes to what we eat. The question that then follows is how to we put in place an infrastructure in our current economic paradigm in such a way that it will be in place for an almost unimaginably different one? This is not easy, but fortunately there are already many parts of the solution already in place in and around Totnes. At a Transition Town Totnes event in May 2009 called 'Can Totnes Feed Itself?' the audience were asked to identify all of the ingredients of a stronger local food system that already exist. Here are some of the ideas they came up with:

◎ Transition Town Totnes Garden Share Scheme

◎ Many orchards growing different varieties of fruit

◎ Many shops that sell local food

◎ Productive vegetable gardens at the Steiner school & KEVICCs

◎ Dartington Estate (around 1000 acres on the edge of Totnes (with an interest in enlightened rural regeneration)

◎ Knowledge about wildfoods (i.e. Wildwise and others)

◎ Many people who 'grow their own'

◎ Freshwater fish in the River Dart

◎ Sharpham Estate (home to 4 farms, active in cheese making, winemaking & an interest in pursuing enlightened land use policies)

◎ Brixham, a nearby fishing port

◎ The Community Herb Garden and its education programme

◎ Schumacher College providing inspirational short courses championing sustainable food

◎ TTT's Nut Tree Capital of Britain scheme

◎ The many local small and independent farmers

◎ Community Supported Farming at 14 local landholdings

◎ Landmatters, an off grid permaculture community

◎ SHDC's Agriculture Forum

◎ Young Farmer's Association

◎ Totnes Allotments Association

◎ Riverford Organic Farm: one of the UK's most successful organic farm businesses

◎ Orchard Link supporting the development of traditional varieties of apples

◎ The Small Farms Association, of local independent farmers

◎ Totnes and Kingsbridge Beekeepers

◎ Trees for Health

◎ Volunteer groups providing active practical support to farmers and growers

◎ Strong and active group of local biodynamic farmers and growers

◎ Agroforestry Research Trust providing information and training in the development of forest gardens

◎ The 'Seedy Sisters' (regular events on swapping seeds)

◎ Land available in Public parks

◎ Consumers interested in buying local food

In relation to the powerful supermarkets however, all of the above are tiny. What models might allow local food to come to the fore and make the re-establishment of local market gardens and the ongoing viability of existing farms possible? Below are some possibilities:

◎ Food hubs where consumers and producers can link for direct sales

◎ Local branding to identify local products and indicate quality

◎ Changes in land use policies and legislation to open up more land to small producers

◎ Allowing more people to live back on the land as small producers

◎ Research and education in local food production

Mapping Local Food Webs

Mapping Local Food Webs is a national project led by the Campaign to Protect Rural England. The project aims to engage local people in finding out about their local food webs in up to 24 towns and cities across England. The project has been being piloted here in Totnes, along with five other locations across England. A team of local volunteers have been carrying out interviews with shoppers, shopkeepers and suppliers with the aim of finding out more about the importance of the local food network or 'web' and its impact on local people's lives, livelihoods, places and the countryside. The project aims to use the information gathered across the country to increase support for more local food production and better supply in local outlets, and to strengthen and secure local food webs across England. [33]

Summarising The Key Objectives for Food in Totnes and District

Summarising all of the above, we can state the following as being our priority actions over the next 10-15 years:

◎ Build and increase the market for local food

◎ Increase the physical and political infrastructure for local food growing, processing and distribution

◎ Changes to land legislation, including planning laws to open up land for food production

◎ Decrease the distance between producers and consumers

◎ Utilise available resources for urban agriculture

◎ Produce food with minimal imported materials in a sustainable manner[34].

From Our Survey

97% of local household respondents stated that they always or mostly cook at home from fresh ingredients. 43% said that a member of their household grows some of the food that is eaten there. We asked people how they would rate their skills in growing food. 66% felt that they were either excellent or good at food growing, although only 8% said they had access to an allotment. We asked people to rank the priorities they attached to the choices that underpinned their thinking when they went shopping. The order in which those surveyed ranked their choices were as follows; good quality, local, low price, organic, fair trade and finally, brand. Finally, respondents were asked how far from them food would need to be grown in order for them to consider it 'local'. 40% said within 10 miles, and 20% within 20 miles.

3.15 The Food Chain: Field to Fork.© Jenny Band

Vision 2030

By 2030, Totnes and District has become a pioneer for local food production, having proactively reorganised its food system based on the principle of a 'foodshed', applying the idea of the watershed[35]to food, producing food that can be grown as close to where people live as possible. 80% of food consumed locally is now grown within 50 miles of Totnes, and the proportion of the population employed in agriculture has grown sharply. The Dartington and Sharpham estates on the edge of the town have now re-directed their land use to focus mainly on the production of food for local markets. The towns and villages have seen a huge increase in 'urban agriculture', growing food in back gardens, public spaces and on any available land. In Totnes, as a result of 'peak cars' in 2009, when the number of cars on the road began to fall sharply due to the recession and high fuel prices, around two-thirds of car parking spaces have now been converted back into the market gardens they were until 1980.

The drop in the oil and gas dependency of food production to a ninth of what it was in 2009 has led to less intensive but more productive food production. Garden food production systems are now recognised as the most productive use of land and enable people of all ages to be actively involved in producing fresh healthy food or local use.

KEVICC now prides itself on being a farm school, the only lawn now visible being the playing fields, with every other available space now being used to grow food, providing many business opportunities for enterprising students. Local farms have experienced a renaissance, often by forging direct links with more urban-based communities by becoming community supported farms (CSAs). Farmer's incomes are now more diverse and secure, with farms producing much more than food, having also become providers of building materials, energy, and other vital supplies.

A walk around the town of Totnes in 2030 reveals food production in most gardens and back yards, productive trees (fruits and nuts mainly) planted in most public spaces, and a much increased number of allotments. Many more people are now able to cook using fresh ingredients, cookery having become a core part of daily life from an early age. Food is eaten in season, and meals are less meat oriented. Levels of obesity have fallen, and all health indicators have improved significantly. Across the area, a number of centres have been established to act as catalysts for food production and healthy living, the first of which was opened in Totnes in 2010.

Resilience Indicators

From the research that led to this Plan, we have identified a number of key indicators by which we can be sure that we we are moving forward. These include:

- The percentage of the population with basic food production skills

- The percentage of the population who feel confident in cooking with fresh produce

- The percentage of food consumed locally which has been also grown locally

- The number of people who feel they have access to good advice, skills and retraining in basic food production

- The percentage of land (agricultural & urban) under utilisation for food production

- Rates of obesity and chronic heart disease

- The average body mass index

These can be revisited regularly to see if the community is making progress in the right direction.

FOOD PRODUCTION AND FARMING
PATHWAYS ACRO

Strategic themes: • Localising Food consumption • Linking Farmers, Growers &
Develop skills, resources & capacity • Develop land use

2009

Community

- Hundreds join Billy Bragg for the TOSCAs, where hundreds of people make scarecrows as part of Totnes Allotments Association's campaign for more allotments.

- Local primary school leads campaign to source 5 a-day fruit & veg locally

- The TTT Gardenshare project leads to 30 gardeners growing food in 14 gardens across Totnes town

- 'Totnes, the Nut Tree Capital of Britain' initiative reaches a total of 100 fruit and nut trees planted in and around Totnes

- Gardening continues to grow in popularity. The summer of 2009 sees more back gardens in use for food growing in the area than at any point since 1978

- 39 people complete TTT's Basic Gardening course

- The Diploma in Sustainable Horticulture at Dartington opens, set up and run by Duchy College. Based at Foxhole, it covers a range of Sustainable Horticulture skills, as well as placements at School Farm Organics, Schumacher College and the Dartington gardens. In its first year, bookings exceed expectations.

- Dartington Hall Trust begin a process of rethinking how they will use their 1,000 acres of land when its current lease expires in 2014. A 2 day event is held to explore the options, and concludes with a vision of the Estate being planted as a mixed agroforestry system, designed to produce fruit, nuts, fuel, medicines and field crops, drawing from the 15 years experience of the Agroforestry Research Trust, who have a demonstration garden on the Estate. A design and a feasibility study is commissioned.

- KEVICC begin growing food in the walled garden behind Kennicott, with students in their spare time, and also set up a Forest School in the nearby orchard, teaching brash hedging, clay oven building and other skills.

- The TTT Energy Descent Plan food section sets out a clear model for the relocalisation of food in the area.

Producers

- Sharpham Estate management look into growing cooking oil crops to supply local cooking that can subsequently be recycled for transport fuel.

- The former Organic Training Centre at Foxhole in Dartington, which had been closed, reopens as 'School Farm Organics', a no-dig, intensive market garden, with the intention of supplying local markets

- In February 2009 half of all farmers surveyed in England as part of the NFU Farming Futures project said they were already affected by climate change and more than 60% expect to be affected in the next ten years.

Policy Makers & Service Providers

- In the news: the Sun reports that Manchester City Council plans to spend £200,000 planting fruit and nut trees as well as herbs and vegetables, in every park in Manchester. Readers' comments include the concern that people with nut allergies might eat the nuts by mistake and sue the Council[36]. Vegetable growing is established at Buckingham Palace and Michelle Obama, wife of the new US President, digs up the South Lawn of the White House and creates an organic vegetable garden.

- Totnes is chosen as one of 6 towns nationally to pilot the Mapping Local Food Webs Project, which looks into retail, supply and consumption of local food in the area as a first step towards changing local shopping habits. Local report to be launched by the end of the year alongside national report.

SS THE TIMELINE

Consumers – promoting awareness • Produce more local food
• Legislation for Localising • Food Production & Consumption

Community

- Dartington Hall Trust makes land available for new allotments. 48 new allotments are created on two sites close to Totnes town. (Totnes Allotments Association celebrates with a 'Come As Your Favourite Vegetable' fancy dress ball.)

- The first year of the Totnes Town Makeover Festival includes, among other things, the planting of a forest garden and vegetable garden on public land in Bridgetown. Local residents design the garden, and more people turn up for the planting, inspired by the 'permablitz' concept'. Edible areas replace need for council mowing.

- The Totnes Retrofit Street Challenge results in 8 of the houses putting raised beds in their front gardens. A team of students from South Devon College offer the muscle for their creation, and that summer, the streets host community parties to celebrate; all the salads consumed come from the new raised beds.

- Training for Dartington & Sharpham Estate management teams in productive tree species begins. It is agreed that outside of the main gardens, any new plantings on the estate must be productive in some way. 50 almond trees are planted in the first 2 months and dozens of fruit trees are offered to residents on the estates to plant in their own gardens.

- Adult education classes now teach composting, care of fruit and nut trees and food preserving skills such as drying, pickling and bottling.

- Gardenshare expands to include land owned by businesses, public bodies, churches etc.

Producers

- A farm at Sharpham transports farm produce to Totnes market by horse.

- Ten Totnes restaurants begin supplying local sustainable fish – starting with crabs.

- Local fishermen set up a sustainable fish cooperative.

- The Linking Local Food project is launched – Farmers increasingly supply to local shops and consumers.

- Sharpham begins recycling waste grape seed into massage oil. Local therapy centres are delighted.

- More farmers extend grass fed livestock systems, reducing grain feeding.

Policy Makers & Service Providers

- Totnes Hospital joins the Soil Association's 'Food for Life' initiative, and implements a target that 30% of its fresh food purchases will be locally produced and 40% will be organic. This proves to be a great boon to local producers.

- TTT's Totnes Garden Share scheme passes its 50th garden, and South Hams District Council decides to begin funding the scheme as a key strategic tool for creating access to growing land. The scheme decides not to take up the funding, as it already operates well with very little input, and it is felt to be more resilient in the longer term for not having funding. Instead, the funding is used to set up a sister project, called 'Eat my Street', which looks to stimulate more commercial use of unused urban land. Within 6 months of it starting, a local couple start a business called 'Salads Direct'. Instead of renting land on the edge of Totnes, they assemble at no cost (aside from the occasional gift of some produce), over 1½ acres of land within the town, some private gardens, some owned by South Hams District Council in the centre of town, and some just off the Plymouth Road. They supply fresh salads and herbs through a variety of outlets in the town.

2010

FOOD PRODUCTION AND FARMING
PATHWAYS ACRO

Strategic themes: • Localising Food consumption • Linking Farmers, Growers &
Develop skills, resources & capacity • Develop land use

Community

- The Totnes Food Hub forms, as an innovative way of linking local food to local people. Modelled on the Stroud Co model, developed in Stroud[37], it links local producers to consumers and creates viable markets for the increasing number of small local growers/producers. Members order their food online and pick it up once a week, every Saturday, from a venue in town. Cutting out the middleperson means more profit for growers, and cheaper food for members. Initially it launches in the still-empty Woolworths store in the middle of Totnes.

- Restaurants scale up the Responsible Fish project to serve local sustainable fish.

- Rates of obesity decline as school PPE (practical physical education) classes include regular crop maintenance and harvesting.

- Community-shared tools, seeds, expertise and root cellars for storing root vegetables established.

- Many students now opt to take their gap year working in agriculture.

- Taking the lead from Dartington, local housing associations make land available to their employees and residents, to enable them to build their own food security. It becomes a vital part of the in-house training available to staff.

- As part of their greening of the school, KEVICC launch their Sustainable Food Policy. It sets targets that within 3 years, the school will be sourcing 40% of its food locally, 30% will be organic, and 25% will have been grown in the grounds of the school. They make a successful application to the local food fund for infrastructure for creating an intensive food garden at the school, 3 polytunnels, tools and a watering system.

- Torbay Housing Association makes land available in the South Hams for CSAs to produce food for tenants and staff in South Hams and Torbay.

Producers

- Sharpham plant 4 acres of mixed nut trees on the estate, and also turn 2 acres of land that are closest to Totnes town into allotments for the community.

- A survey shows that gardening is now more popular than golf and jogging combined.

Policy Makers & Service Providers

- SHDC launch a grant scheme to promote new food processing businesses. The criteria are that businesses must be adding value to locally grown produce.

- Devon and Cornwall Police, initially through a pilot run by Totnes Police Station, start promoting TTT's Garden Share scheme as part of their Crime Prevention work. When visiting the elderly living on their own, businesses with land around them, or public buildings, they discuss the benefits of having their gardens/lawn/land used by others to grow food, so the land is better kept, more frequently visited, and 'kept an eye on' by more people.

2011

SS THE TIMELINE

2012

Inspired by the new BBC series featuring Sir Alan Sugar, 'The Appleprentice', where 15 young hopefuls compete for the job of Sir Alan's head orchardist - programme catchphrase "You're Grafted" - interest in rare apple varieties booms across the area.

Individuals

- Sharply rising food prices, as a result of the oil price surge, mean that the weekly shopping basket for Totnes and District rises sharply. A new supermarket announces proposals to build a new store in Totnes to exploit the demand for cheap food. A public campaign to prevent this is launched, with weekly demonstrations, and an awareness campaign about the benefits of local food. A shocking Channel 4 documentary "The Real Costs of Cheap Food" brings new energy to the campaign, and the application is refused.

- Transition Town Totnes launches its 'Make an Orchard of Your Street' project, and collaborates with similar groups in the 16 parishes, making fruit trees available to people in the area at very low prices. In the first 4 months, over 400 trees are purchased and planted, and all the local schools get involved and plant trees.

Community

- A new Totnes Farmers Market opens on the first Saturday of every month as part of the existing market. There is great competition for spaces and the public flock to it.

- Riverford fund the installing of a 'rooftop kitchen garden', which covers all of the buildings that form Phase One of ATMOS. The garden, which has railings around the edge, and pathways between the raised beds, mainly grows salads and herbs. It prevents water runoff from the buildings, and provides a source of great fascination to the trains as they pass through the station. It turns out to be a fabulous marketing ploy. The restaurant is packed every day.

- The new food garden at KEVICC is now producing 5% of the food used in the school canteen; other schools start to follow suit.

- Work begins on the Totnes Health and Wellbeing Garden, providing much first hand experience of the process of reverting a car park to a growing space.

- The final designs for the Dartington Agroforestry Plan are submitted to the Dartington Trustees, and unanimously approved. The CEO of Dartington announces the plans to the press, telling them "Dartington has always been about innovative solutions to pressing problems. Our plans to plant most of the estate as a diverse, abundant and high-yielding agroforestry farm puts Dartington on the cutting edge of ideas and practice in this fast-changing world".

- Edible landscapes replace the need for council mowing and maintenance (potatoes, fruit and nuts grown).

- Riverford open 'The Riverford Town Kitchen' as part of Phase One of ATMOS. The kitchen is designed as a restaurant, but also as an opportunity for people to learn to cook. The kitchen is seldom closed, when it is not being used by staff to cook for the restaurant, it is home to classes and workshops.

FOOD PRODUCTION AND FARMING
PATHWAYS ACRO

Strategic themes: • Localising Food consumption • Linking Farmers, Growers &
Develop skills, resources & capacity • Develop land use

Producers

- Farmers are now over-wintering cattle outside, reducing feed costs and improving the health of livestock, biodiversity (and humans).

- Training now popular with farmers on building soil fertility without the use of chemical inputs, and managing pastureland, improves fertility and enables livestock to be kept without supplementary grain feeding.

- Pilot studies comparing traditional 4 year crop rotation on growing land with more recent agro-chemical supported agriculture show more productive results from traditional methods when combined with modern types of crops. Crops of hemp for building prove to be an excellent green manure that can be followed with food crops and grazing land using land rotation and crops closely matched to the local soil type

Policy Makers & Service Providers

- TTT, Community Supported Farming and Trees for Health launch a major initiative in partnership with SHDC to increase the Follaton House Arboretum into a neighbouring land with a rich mixture of productive species, to be planted by and harvested by the community. The model is based on a CSA approach.

- 10% of food used by the public sector is procured locally

- Planning laws are changed to allow buildings for seasonal farm worker accommodation on farms.

2013-15

Celebrity Love Allotment' wins 2 BAFTAs after topping the ratings all summer. The winner, Letitia Lloyd, becomes an icon for the rapidly growing home-growing movement.

Individuals

- A survey of Totnes finds that gardening is now one of the key ways that people meet new friends.

- Quality gardening tools are the most popular Christmas presents in the area.

Community

- Due to disruptions to fuel supplies and the resultant industrial dispute in 2013, Morrisons and Somerfields are both forced to close for periods, first for a week, and then for 3 weeks, during June and July. It is the first time the food resilience of the area is really tested since 2000 (when it failed miserably). Local food shops report a huge increase in turnover, and although they struggle to meet demand, they manage, combined with the percentage of food now grown within the town. KEVICC sends some of its more disadvantaged children home with vegetable bags from the school's gardens, but acknowledges that it grows nowhere near enough at present to be able to

SS THE TIMELINE

Consumers – promoting awareness • Produce more local food
• Legislation for Localising • Food Production & Consumption

cope in a similar situation that lasted for longer. When the Prime Minister broadcasts to the nation saying that there is every likelihood of such occurrences happening in the future, given the world oil crisis, the Principal of KEVICC announces that an additional 3 acres of the school's grounds will be going into food production, with 3 more polytunnels being installed.

- So many people in Totnes town start keeping chickens that the Totnes Hen keepers Society is formed, holding regular events and providing a newsletter of tips and ideas. In its first year, membership passes 200.

- In 2014, work begins on planting Dartington land. The first winter's planting sees 40 acres contoured and planted with nearly 10,000 trees and shrubs.

- Local churches make land available, including cemeteries for family and community use. Fruit trees are planted on graves.

- Schumacher College begins offering an MSc in Transition Land Use, which includes modules on permaculture, agroforestry and making sustainable food production financially viable. There is huge interest in the course.

Producers

- Squirrel is enjoyed as a delicacy in Totnes – Rumour, McCabes and the White Hart all include squirrel pot roast and stew on their menus.

- Prisons grow food on site and within the community, building connections, skills and vital produce.

- Quinoa is adopted by producers as a key crop; grains used for fallow crop in rotation system.

- Sharpham Estate sets 5 acres of sunflowers for its first cooking oil production trial

- Local beef and dairy farmers begin to struggle as grain prices and fertiliser prices rise sharply. Many decide, with help from DEFRA's Post Oil Farming team, to move to completely grass-fed systems, which require a change in the mixes of grasses used, to develop a stronger root mat enabling the cattle to stay out longer. Clover becomes a part of the mix for farmers as they reduce their dependency on nitrogen fertilizers.

Policy Makers & Service Providers

- The Government introduces the Home Growing Act, as an outcome of the Green New Deal passed the previous year. This uses the Working Tax Credit system to, in effect, pay people to stay home 2 days a week and grow food. Supported by a Community Gardening Officer, those in receipt of the support grow food at home, and are provided with free tools and equipment. The scheme takes off rapidly and is a huge success, supported by an inspiring television series. Within a month of its launch, nearly 300 families in Totnes are participating.

- Devon County Council offers local landowners a temporary '5s' land rent scheme. The pilot scheme will initially last for 5 years make parcels of land available to groups of 5 people or more to grow food within 5 miles of where they live

- Deregulation of health and safety regulations encourages farm visits and volunteers.

- Deregulation encourages more mobile abattoirs

FOOD PRODUCTION AND FARMING
PATHWAYS ACRO

Strategic themes: • Localising Food consumption • Linking Farmers, Growers &
Develop skills, resources & capacity • Develop land use

2016-20

David Reilly from Cornworthy became the winner of the National Runner Bean Growing competition, run by DEFRA to inspire the new generation of young gardeners. His runner bean plant reaches 48ft 3 inches, beating the previous world record of 46ft 3 inches. He put the extraordinary growth of his Scarlet Emperor bean down to the compost he grew it in which was made in school, through the 'Master Composter' training. The bean was grown up a telegraph pole in the school grounds, and was fertilized organically using comfrey liquor from comfrey harvested from the school's garden. Headmistress Amanda Pike told the Herald Express "we are very proud of David, he is turning into a gifted gardener. It has been wonderful for the school, we bring the juniors out and read 'Jack and the Beanstalk' next to it. They love it, brings it all to life..."

Individuals

- Competition for muck from local horse stables is fierce. Some enterprising stable-owners start selling their manure on 'Totnes Swap Shop'.

- A survey of the 5 car share schemes operating across Totnes town finds that cars without tow-bars are those that are taken out the least, as peoples' gardens and allotments become their key weekend recreational activity, and they increasingly take out cars in order to shift manure, collect sea weed and other gardening-related equipment around. The car share schemes each add two trailers to their 'fleets'; they are well used.

Community

- After months of increased intermittency, Morrisons closes, with the loss of 60 jobs. Despite constant reassurances that the business is safe, and is looking for new buyers, media reports speculate that the cost of transportation has made the business model unsustainable. One day, the shop was open with no sign of trouble, assuring customers that the recent occasional closures were now behind them, the next the shop was closed. For the next year, the building stands empty, becoming an eyesore in the middle of town.

- Dartington's own catering now uses 40% produce from on the Estate, and many local shops now source from Dartington's food co-op.

- Dartington Tinctures go on sale. Developed through a partnership with the University of Plymouth, they are based on a range of medicinal plants grown on the Estate, including various medicinal mushrooms.

- For the first time, demand for hands-on, practical courses at Schumacher exceed demand for the more academic ones.

- The International Sustainable Agriculture Summer School starts.

Producers

- The Sharpham Estate expands their vineyard, and also starts growing hops, adding 'Sharpham Ale' to their outputs. The ale proves so popular in local pubs that Sharpham opens its own pub in Totnes town, called 'The Sharp Ham'.

- Totnes and District is now producing a food surplus that can be 'exported' to Torbay and Plymouth.

- Soil fertility levels in Totnes and District have risen to such an extent that chemical inputs have been halved.

- By 2017, the planting of the planting of the agroforestry farm at Dartington is completed for the northern half of the Estate

SS THE TIMELINE

Consumers – promoting awareness • Produce more local food
• Legislation for Localising • Food Production & Consumption

- All vehicles on Sharpham and Dartington estates are now powered by biomethane generated with the estates' waste cooking oil, food and farm waste.

- Old watermills, such as Crowdy Mill, are put back in use for grain milling and textile production.

- Red squirrels return to the area as grey squirrels are culled to protect nut crops.

- Herds of Devon Red cattle and hardier livestock breeds grazing in fields are now a common sight, now that grain feeding and indoor housing is too expensive an option for local farmers.

- In 2016 the costs of importing organic fabrics from abroad became exorbitant, forcing Greenfibres to look at restarting local fabric manufacture. Trial crops of hemp, flax and jute grown at Sharpham, are the first crops grown in the area specifically for their fibre potential for over 100 years.

- Two years after the initial fabrics trials, Greenfibres declares the experience as a "surprisingly wonderful" one. Company manager Rick Pike said "Initially we had great difficulties, partially with the raw material but also with the lack of skills. For example, with flax after our first failed season one of the community's elders came forward who remembered how to set flax in the field (using a land roller!). We're now starting to get final products, and many of them are of a much higher quality than anticipated." The company has recently signed contracts with local farmers to produce four times as much of each of the crops in the following year (2018).

- Devon's inspired 5s land use scheme has proved popular and is extended to 10 years. Other County Council's are catching on and finding this opens up more land for very productive use.

- The Duke of Somerset makes land available for a CSA scheme in Berry Pomeroy, and begins to roll out an agroforestry plan across his estate, as well as setting up woodchip processing to supply the growing market locally for woodchips

Policy Makers & Service Providers

- New land reform laws make it easier to acquire land for food production. Many hundreds of young people and permaculturists set up new innovative farms, smallholdings and forest gardens across the South Hams.

- All local authority owned businesses procure their food from local sources, apart from 'luxury' (out of season) produce, which chefs are trained to minimise use of.

- 60% of food used by the public sector is procured locally.

- Devon County Council state that all of the Old Age People's homes under their management must make their grounds into food producing landscapes. Some funding is made available and many of the residents are able to pass on their gardening skills to the staff and join in with some lighter tasks.

- South Hams District Council decide to remove their ornamental gardens and put in intensive, organic, well-designed and highly attractive edible landscapes. Although some initially bemoan the loss of the box hedging and the ornate shrubs, the sense of excitement about the new landscape rapidly builds, and after the first crop of salad harvested, in April 2017, complaints soon quieten.

- Community composting schemes replace the use of brown bins.

FOOD PRODUCTION AND FARMING
PATHWAYS ACRO

Strategic themes: • Localising Food consumption • Linking Farmers, Growers &
Develop skills, resources & capacity • Develop land use

Individuals

- Lawnmowers are little used now, given that all available land that can be used to grow is under production. A few are kept for public open spaces, but now, in some local pubs, lawnmowers hang from the ceiling in the same way that old ploughs hung from pub ceilings 20 years previously.

- Everyone leaves school with a basic knowledge of growing, able to grow at least 10 vegetables to a basic level. Many now take the advanced course in 'Organic Plant Husbandry', learning to graft as well as acquire a much deeper set of gardening skills.

Community

- Diets are now much more seasonal, with less meat and more nuts and other locally produced carbohydrates. People enjoy cooking, and the desire to share new recipes leads to the revival of the dinner party as a key tool for creating social interaction.

- By now, on average, 5% of the food consumed in Totnes and District is produced in back gardens and allotments, 10% from the new market gardens on the edge of the town, and 50% from the Totnes and District area. It is an amazing achievement, and it brings with it a newfound sense of security and confidence. People no longer miss the supermarkets, although they occasionally speak of them with something approaching awe, being unable to imagine the concept of a starfruit in February.

- The first pairs of Totnes Jeans go on sale. "How did they get the sting out of the nettles" says TeenMag

- Local entrepreneur, Imelda Platt, starts a business called N·Pee·K, who pay the major pubs, hotels and schools in the area to install urine-separating toilets, and large tanks to collect the liquid. The price of nitrogen fertilisers (due to the astronomical cost of gas) has hit farming hard. Imelda tells the Totnes Times "the average adult produces roughly the same amount of nitrogen in their urine as agriculture requires to grow their food. We decided to stop being squeamish and start being practical". The urine is diluted and sold to local farmers. Despite initial reluctance, once farmers start telling each other how good the product is, N·Pee·K starts growing rapidly.

2021-25

Policy Makers & Service Providers

- A survey among staff shows that one of the top three reasons that people still work for South Hams District Council is the edible landscaping and the discounted produce they are able to buy there. The same trend is observed across the UK, as businesses that transformed their gardens and surrounding land into food gardens are by far the most popular places to work.

- South Hams District Council agree to take vegetables as part payment for Council Tax.

- Local Authorities are coordinating the New Land Army; groups of young people and newly arrived migrants who are formed into working groups on local farms to increase the number of agricultural workers and increase productivity. Like a revival of their wartime predecessors, these young people enjoy a healthy life and improve their agricultural skills.

TRANSITION IN ACTION

Walnut trees being planted in Bridgetown with aul Hussell of Wills and Probate. © Totnes Times

The Nut Tree Planting Project

The vision behind this scheme is to provide another source of nutritious food for the Totnes community in the future, while also raising awareness and locking up carbon. In March 2007, TTT started the scheme with a few varieties of nut trees on Vire Island. Further plantings took place during the winter of 2007-2008 on Longmarsh, Borough Park playing fields, Follaton gardens and Bridgetown. Some people volunteered to be guardians of the trees, to watch their growth, and nurture them. Most of the trees have survived, despite a lot of flooding on Longmarsh and some battering of trees surrounding playing fields in Bridgetown

In December 2008, a small group of residents of Meadow Close in Bridgetown, including several children, planted a new orchard of apples, pears and almonds on a site adjacent to the close. A further planting session took place in January 2009 – a combined effort between the TTT project, Trees for Health and South Hams District Council - planting more trees in Follaton Gardens, mulching some of the ones planted last year, and putting in 3 almond trees in the Town Cemetery.

On March 1st 2009, we had another sunny planting day on Longmarsh, putting in more sweet chestnuts, walnuts and hazel trees. On the same day, we re-planted 4 trees on the Pathfields playing field that had got damaged last year, and on March 4th we planted another 7 fruit trees on the Town Cemetery site amongst the old graves.

More plantings planned for this winter (2009-10), in Bridgetown, in the Town cemetery again, on the Sharpham estate, and possibly on the KEV-ICC land. One date already planned is in December when the nut tree planting in Totnes will be part of a national tree planting campaign sponsored by the BBC 'Breathing Spaces' programme.

**For more information, visit
www.totnes.transitionnetwork.org/nuttrees/
home**

HEALTH AND WELLBEING

"If I had my way I'd make health catching instead of disease."

Robert Ingersoll

The Challenge

The general health of our population arises from healthy lifestyles and good access to healthcare services. Currently those services are creaking at the seams as health statistics show that despite the high levels of health care available, we have deepening trends of avoidable ill health due to our lifestyles and diet. People are also living longer, and our aging and growing population in turn puts greater pressure on those public services. In addition, there are the challenges presented to our healthcare system by climate change, succinctly summed up by Dan Bednarz and Kristin Bradford:

"Through our unrestricted use of energy and resources in the health care industry, as well as our production of greenhouse gases, we are actually contributing to the ill-health of our planet and ensuring future suffering of the Earth's inhabitants." [38]

An Unhealthy Lifestyle? © Jenny Band

Unhealthy Lifestyles - What are we Doing to Ourselves?

We walk less, cycle less, drive more, eat more fatty foods and carbohydrates, spend more time sitting in front of TVs and computers and work for longer hours. The wellbeing effects of healthy exercise, healthy diets, taking quality time out and relaxing and connecting with nature have been widely publicised and promoted but are not widely adopted in the majority of people's lives, often simply because we find ourselves too busy. Obesity, cancer, high blood-pressure, diabetes, chronic heart disease, many of these are increasingly being linked to the way we live in the early 21st century, eating easily-prepared processed food, working long hours in sedentary jobs, driving rather than walking so as to save time, as well as the stress arising from just trying to keep our heads above financial water. If current trends continue, these illnesses and their causes will only increase. Perhaps, however, it is time, as part of the wider rethink this plan represents, to stop and re-evaluate, and to think what a truly healthy society might actually look like, and then, how we might get there.

A Health Services Health-Check

Without abundant and cheap oil, our healthcare services would look very different. Whether it's energy-intensive NHS buildings, heating and lighting for hospitals, electronic equipment such as scanners, basic medical products such as gloves and syringes or the actual medicines themselves (which are largely made from oil), the current healthcare system is perilously reliant and therefore vulnerable. Current trends indicate that this dependence is growing.

Healthcare expenditure across the board is increasing, making many services highly vulnerable to the impacts of the credit crunch and rising energy costs. The NHS drug budget is increasing by 7.5% a year, meaning that it will double in 10 years. In 2002 the direct cost of treating obesity was estimated at around £47m and around £one billion for treating the consequences of obesity[39]. Hospital services are being increasingly centralised requiring patients, staff, goods and visitors to travel further for both hospital and GP services. As in other realms of society, healthcare is also undergoing its own de-skilling. Over-reliance on machines and technology is leaving the medical skills base vulnerable to loss of experienced and knowledgeable staff who can apply a more hands-on diagnosis based on touch, feel, sound and careful observation. Orthopaedics and midwifery are examples of diagnoses previously reliant on experienced touch and feel which have been largely replaced by machines (e.g. x-ray and ultrasound).

Added to this, there is an increasingly widespread concern within the NHS that climate change will bring additional challenges:

◎ Heat waves will become more common
◎ Sunburn, skin cancer and poor air quality rates will increase
◎ The risk of hurricanes and flooding will increase, with associated health consequences
◎ It may also cause an increase in infectious diseases in the UK, affecting food-borne, water-borne and vector-borne disease.

As with other aspects of our lives, this assessment of the vulnerabilities of our healthcare system can also reveal the possibilities inherent in a new approach. A more localised healthcare system, combining the best of modern medicine with complementary therapies, the promotion of healthy eating and exercise, and with health centres re-conceived as market gardens, re-skilling centres, apothecaries, energy generators, cookery schools and much more, would not only be an improvement on the present, but could also become a key player in the wider transition of society.

7 Local Hospitals

Totnes Community Hospital
Paignton Hospital (4.9m)
Torbay Hospital, Torquay (6.6m)
Mount Stuart Hospital, Torquay (6.8m)
Ashburton & Buckfastleigh Hospital, Ashburton (6.8m)
Dartmouth Hospital (7.1m)
Newton Abbot Hospital (7.7m)

45 GP Surgeries
2 in Totnes
1 in Harbertonford (2.9m)
1 in Ipplepen (4.3m)
9 in Paignton (4.3 – 5.5m)
1 in Dittisham (4.8m)
1 in Buckfastleigh (5.7m)   1 in Dartmouth (7.0m)
1 in Blackawton (5.8m)   4 in Brixham (7.6 – 7.8m)
14 in Torquay (6.2 – 8.0m)   4 in Newton Abbot (7.7-8.0m)
1 in Kingskerswell (6.5m)   1 in Strete (8.6m)
1 in South Brent (6.8m)   1 in Kingsteignton (9.0m)
1 in Ashburton (6.8m)   1 in Slapton (9.6m)

Within a 10 mile radius of Totnes

37 Dental Surgeries
with a similar geographical spread as the GP Surgeries

55 Pharmacies
similarly dispersed, though none in any of the villages

Midwifery and A&E Services
Only Torbay Hospital (6.6m)

Community Clinic
the closest is in Epsom (163miles away)

Other Specialist Services
such as alcohol clinics are available in the locality, in the towns

Health and Wellbeing in Totnes & District

Currently Totnes and District enjoys the benefit of a broad range of health services mostly centred in Totnes and South Brent, with Torbay Hospital providing A&E, midwifery, general surgery and outpatient procedures. Totnes has a small community hospital that provides some procedures, outpatient clinics and community care services for elderly people, some of whom are collected on a Friday and brought to Totnes hospital where they enjoy a communal lunch and some socialising before being taken home again.

As the hinterland is essentially rural, there is currently a high dependence on travelling for services, but for villages like Diptford that are not served by a public bus, access to health services relies on access to private transport or taxi hire. Of a total population of 23,863 living Totnes and District, 12,926 people live in the town of Totnes and the villages of South Brent and Harbertonford (8,416, 3,109 and 1,401 respectively) that are served by local GP services. The remaining 10,937 people live in the rural villages and hinterland and need to travel to visit their GP or dentist or to collect medicines.

Totnes and District does however have a wide variety of complementary and alternative therapies available. Local directories carry long lists of private therapists from homeopaths to acupuncturists. Most of these alternative practitioners are not registered and their services are not available under NHS, although they are well used.

Emerging Trends: Business as Usual or Willing to Change?

The risks of continuing with a Business as Usual approach to healthcare have been set out above.

On the other hand, a Plan B, based on principles of resilience, localisation and health promotion, would need to be based on the following principles:

◎ Investment in reducing energy use in hospitals and health care centres, through retrofits and the installation of renewable energy systems

◎ Investment in reducing travel for patients and staff – e.g. virtual/remote support for major procedures

◎ Green procurement policies such as:
  • Reversing the high dependence on plastic products, moving back to glass, metal etc and reusable products
  • Reversing the trends in use of expensive and oil-dependent pharmaceutical products; advocating simple remedies, herbs, diet etc., focusing on those with a proven efficacy, and preferably that have been locally grown
  • Sourcing local food and other supplies and services (the potential boost this shift in procurement can bring to local growers is huge)

◎ Restructuring public health services to increase very local access for simple procedures and therapies

◎ Continued high investment in promotion and support for healthy lifestyles

◎ Free preventative care (including dentistry) as in the original NHS vision.

◎ Broader support and mainstream inclusion of alternative therapies and remedies in public health system

◎ Recognition and support for public parks, open spaces, gardens, pedestrian and cycle ways as therapeutic for relaxation, stress relief and exercise

◎ Giving good examples of healthy eating in hospitals and healthcare centres (healthy meals & snacks)

What Might Healthcare in Totnes and District Look Like in a Transitioned 2030?

◎ Growth in the number of people taking responsibility for their own health

◎ People motivated to be healthy

◎ People eat less junk food, sugar is rationed

◎ Better health on less food

◎ Reduced need to travel to healthcare

◎ More localized provision with technical assistance / webcams (CAT–Computer assisted technology)

◎ New developments in healthcare & resources

◎ Research more patient centered and connected

◎ More integrated health care

◎ A blur between regular and complementary medicine.

Vision 2030

By 2030, Totnes and District has become a shining light for vibrant health in the southwest. All of its indicators for health and wellbeing are improving, leading to experts from far a-field coming to the town to understand what has become known as 'The Totnes Effect'. Some put it down to the integration of complementary medicine, especially herbalism, which has not only transformed the types of treatment for common ailments, but also the landscape around the town, which now has many farms which have diversified into herbs in order to supply demand.

Others put it down to the transformation in 2012, of the town's schools into centres of excellence in intensive food production. This led to increased exercise for young people, healthier food in the school canteens, and has also led to hundreds of families taking the idea home from school, raised beds are now common place, and, when accompanied by the training in cooking what you have grown, has led to families being better exercised and fed.

Another school of thought puts it down to the impact of the Health and Wellbeing centres, the first of which opened in 2011, which prescribed for people suffering from stress, obesity and other related illnesses, time spent learning to garden and cooking. Thousands of people on the surgery's lists took up the training.

The final argument goes that increased community cohesion has played a major role. The slowing down of life and people working more together and depending on each other more has had unexpected knock-on effects. It has been observed that there is a quantifiable connection between the amount of time spent caring for others, and one's own wellbeing. Whatever the reason is, it is clear that the change in direction embarked on in 2010 has led to a population that is not only more healthy, but one that has much to share with the rest of the world.

Resilience Indicators

From the research that led to this Plan, we have identified a number of key indicators by which we can be sure that we are moving forward. These include:

- Depression trends / rates
- Obesity rates in children & adults
- Frequency of visits to the doctor
- The proportion of babies exclusively breastfed for six months or more
- Acres of land used to cultivate medicinal herbs
- Average age of dying
- Number of hours spent walking
- Number of meals per capita eaten alone by over 65s

These can be revisited regularly to see if the community is making progress in the right direction.

Further Reading

Tackling Obesity: Future Choices Foresight (2007), UK Department of Health. www.foresight.gov.uk/OurWork/ActiveProjects/Obesity/KeyInfo/Index.asp

Making the Invisible Visible: the real value of park assets. Commission for Architecture and the Built Environment (2007) http://www.cabe.org.uk/publications/making-the-invisible-visible

http://www.ic.nhs.uk/news-and-events/press-office

The Department of Health commissioned a group of independent scientists to produce the report Health Effects of Climate Change in the UK, which was published in 2002

Draft Carbon Reduction Strategy for England (2008), NHS, www.sdu.nhs.uk/page.php?page_id=94

Change4Life, NHS, www.nhs.uk/Change4life/Pages/Default.aspx

HEALTH AND WELLBEING
PATHWAYS ACRO

Strategic themes: • Nature as Therapy - Health & Wellbeing Gardens • Public Health

2009

Individuals

- People take a far greater interest in gardening

- The major upsurge of interest indicates more exercise is being taken by older people. Jogging is starting to return as a cool pastime and the off-road pedestrian ways are well used in mornings and evenings

- Diets are still worryingly laden with empty carbohydrates, but there is a rising interest in tackling children's eating and exercise habits. A lot of people sign up for the healthy cooking and eating adult education classes at the Mansion House

Community

- All local schools adopt healthy lunch-box code based on plenty of fresh local vegetables

- The benefits of a healthy life are widely publicised in the media and schools and workplaces

- A healthy menu appears in the Totnes Times each week.

- Work gets underway at a public space in Totnes for the first Health and Wellbeing Garden in T&D

Local Service Providers

- Choice4Life campaign gets lots of publicity and local healthcare workers visit schools to advise on lunch boxes

- The economic downturn is causing concern for hospices that rely on voluntary funds. A review of hospice needs with a view to a more localised and community- integrated provision in T & D is scheduled for 2010.

Individuals

- Families have begun getting together to walk with their children in the summer evenings to the local park to cut down on TV viewing. This started with the local swimming pool opening a family session every Thursday and Sunday afternoon

- People are using the 'Green Gym' in the green space by Heath's car park

Community

- Schools now start the day with a daily exercise work-out which includes a weekly yoga session for all students

- TTT sets up local Health & Wellbeing on-line directory on its website to enable people to track down local practitioners, alongside an Ebay-style system for people to rate the practioners they have been to see

- The Fit 4 Work unemployment scheme for local deliveries has been very successful with local businesses and is helping people get fitter

- The newly planted Leechwell Gardens opens to the public who wax lyrical over the intensive herb beds and wonderful fragrances. Totnes Healthy Futures project gets underway, working with Leatside surgery to engage those most at risk of chronic heart disease and high blood-pressure in learning to garden and how to prepare the resultant produce

Local Service Providers

- SHDC has a new staff policy which gives all staff an extra fifteen minutes at lunchtime to work out in their new Green Gym in the Arboretum at Follaton House – all staff have been supplied with a track-suit and locker and showers, and have agreed to the use it or lose it policy. The Green Gym at the Arboretum is also open to the public and for staff to use before and after work. The

SS THE TIMELINE

& Social Support Services • Wide Choice of Therapies • Foster Healthy Lifestyles

CVS and CAB are among the first to follow suit

- Totnes Community Hospital carries out a resilience audit based on TTT's Health & Wellbeing principles.

- DPCT carries out an audit of all community halls in T&D to see whether they are suitable for weekly clinics and fitness programmes

- Totnes Community Care links with surrounding communities and public health workers to expand its weekly lunches for the elderly into surrounding parishes

- Overpopulation issues are being widely discussed and the FPA initiates a new leaflet and TV promotion aimed at reducing birth rates

2010

Individuals

- People are buying and swapping a large variety of herbs and medicinal plants as interest has grown in self-help, with many gardens now containing the ten most commonly used medicinal herbs

- The resurgence in the oil price has led to local chemists struggling to obtain some key medicines. As a result, the newly renamed 'Department of Health and Wellbeing' equip and retrain local chemists to manufacture some key medicines on the premises, as happened during World War 2. It is a move widely welcomed by chemists

- Walkers are becoming more noticeable as are cyclists. Fewer children are being driven to school. 'Walk to School' days and 'Walking Buses' become an everyday occurrence as more parents find the costs of running a car becoming prohibitive

2011

Community

- Medicinal herbs as well as food are bought in the local shops, small guides for their use are very popular

- Pharmacists are looking into returning to preparing remedies on their premises to keep down costs and reduce packaging

- Car share schemes are being used to give lifts to people in villages with no public transport

Local Service Providers

- Totnes Hospital implements a target that 30% of its food will be locally produced and 25% will be organic. Salads are on every main menu for inpatients. The snacks and drinks machines in all hospitals in the south-west are being reviewed with the idea of bringing back small café services with herb teas, home-made soups and a personal touch

- NHS retrofits are scheduled for Totnes Hospital with the target of halving the energy use

- Local Community halls are being offered Government funds to upgrade their buildings to provide rooms suitable for GP and dental clinics

- A medical herbalist is engaged by Leatside Surgery to advise on complementary therapies

- The Totnes Food and Wellbeing Centre opens in Totnes. This is a collaboration between TTT, the Primary Care Trust and Leatside surgery, and provides training in food production alongside horticultural therapy and a range of related services.

HEALTH AND WELLBEING
PATHWAYS ACRO

Strategic themes: • Nature as Therapy - Health & Wellbeing Gardens • Public Health

2012

Individuals

- Rising numbers of people wanting to plant trees have created a 'Tree Force' who meet most weekends to plant and manage plantations of productive trees in the countryside, as part of the rollout of a wider agroforestry plan for the area. Teenagers have been particularly enthusiastic as they receive vouchers for 'Leechwells café'

- Summer evening walks around Totnes have inspired a Scented Route which links some of the many gardens with aromatic herbs and other plants

- Totnes Town park is very busy in the evenings with families organising get-togethers, sports parties and open yoga sessions

Community

- 'Leechwells' Communal Health & Wellbeing café opens in Totnes serving a wide range of popular and tasty fare

- TTT's event to plant up the new herb garden at the top of Heath's car park is oversubscribed and so another herb garden is planted out in the smaller car park

Local Service Providers

- Totnes & District Hospice Service is established with Government funding to set up three new community hospices. These will be set up in local villages where public transport is available

- A new debate on euthanasia invites discussion on whether this should be available in hospices; living wills are widely used. The first trial of the mobile GP Village Clinic takes place in Diptford

Individuals

- More elderly people are attending fitness classes and helping out in the local soup kitchens. Losing weight is being supported by care workers and home helps who assist people with developing their own fitness programme

- Cycling is becoming increasingly popular and many people have invested in tandems.

- Totnes markets record major sales in vegetables as diets improve

- The Duke of Somerset gifts parcels of land for community benefit in all sixteen parishes

Community

- The Mansion House opens its 'Space for Nature' Garden in the former playground and sets off a spate of similar nature gardens on former tarmac playgrounds. The old café reopens with 'Healthy+' menus and a Friday soup kitchen

- As part of the Dartington Estate's Agroforestry makeover, ten acres are dedicated to medicinal plants, shrubs, trees and herbs that can be used to make herbal medicines. Also, the first medicinal mushroom facility in the UK is established on the Estate, growing Trametes, Shiitake and other powerfully medicinal mushrooms, for their powerful anti-cancer properties

- Children in schools are learning about herbs and are growing medicinal herbs in their school gardens.

- Schumacher College has opened an Apothecary Garden in Dartington Hall courtyard based on the Chelsea Physic Garden to train people in identifying medicinal and beneficial plants

2013-15

SS THE TIMELINE

& Social Support Services • Wide Choice of Therapies • Foster Healthy Lifestyles

- Local evening classes help people to measure their own energy levels through kinesiology and biofeedback

- Parent and child together programmes at pre-school facilities are helping families to improve their diet and fitness. Leechwell Gardens community group introduce 'a quiet day with stories in the garden'

- The rising cost and gaps in supply of formula baby milks lead to a huge increase in women wishing to breastfeed their babies. NCT and La Leche support groups form, and new mothers benefit from the help and encouragement of experienced friends and family as well as the excellent services provided by midwives and health visitors

Local Service Providers

- National evaluation shows benefits from people using Heath and Wellbeing gardens

- Totnes Hospital initiates a feasibility study to install a biodigester to deal with some hospital waste and to produce energy. The Sterilising suite is extended and two more staff are employed as more reusable equipment is used. Hospital waste has decreased noticeably

- Hospital menus now include their recipes as patients are keen to recreate the meals at home. The in-patient gym is expanded and opened to staff and community care users

- SHDC finally gives Totnes Leisure Centre a makeover and another solar swimming pool and sauna complex is opened in Bridgetown to cater for all the new enthusiasm. A further three new mini leisure centres are earmarked for Dartington, South Brent and Marldon

- Major debate on health and safety regulations to allow for calculated risk and commonsense so that people can become more self-reliant.

2016-20

Individuals

- The population is clearly becoming more healthy and active. Few people still smoke. Young people are openly more health conscious and generally much slimmer than five years before

- 'Dartington Health' is launched, making a range of herbal tinctures, creams and ointments made from materials grown on the Estate. Leatside Surgery provides training to its doctors in how to prescribe them, providing guaranteed sales

- Teenage pregnancy rates are starting to drop

- A rise in interest in natural cleaning products has led to a revival of old methods and the 'Tried and Tested' cleaning company sells more vinegar for window cleaning than the chip shop uses

- Swimming has replaced shopping as a national pastime. People are less stressed with the three-day week and spend more time relaxing and enjoying the local nature walks.

Community

- The mobile apothecary service working out of Totnes Herbs Ltd has expanded to two vehicles calling to all the villages. It plans to replace the mobile service with new permanent centres in three villages this year

- T&D Health & Wellbeing internet Co-op has been established where members can share ideas, products, remedies and recipes via a website

- Local tourism has received boost from the extensive interest in Totnes' healthy success; all the B&Bs serve healthy organic breakfasts.

HEALTH AND WELLBEING
PATHWAYS ACRO

Strategic themes: • Nature as Therapy - Health & Wellbeing Gardens • Public Health

Local Service Providers

- A&E usage has dropped with the reduced levels of car traffic. Totnes Hospital has introduced a water respect programme to cut water consumption and pollution: all its sewage and waste food goes into the biodigester and the kitchen staff bake or steam all the vegetables

- The mobile GP service is now operating in six parishes around Totnes and is very popular. Care services are less stretched as fewer people are unsupported by families, friends and neighbours

- The Community Care in Our Street programme covers most support needs such as meals for the elderly, child and disabled persons care and help with hospital appointments

- Trials of doctors trained in remote operations are now underway and proving successful; some of the specialists being used are based in Australia and America

- Torbay Hospital achieves full WHO / Unicef Baby Friendly accreditation, in acknowledgement of the high standard of care it provides to support mothers to breastfeed successfully. The number of women breastfeeding is growing fast, leading to less gastro-enteritis in infants, an expected reduction in allergies and heart disease in the future, as well as less waste and emissions from the processing, packaging, transport and heating of formula milks

Individuals

- Public health checks indicate that weights are coming down in adults and children, people are much healthier, with diabetes and heart attacks reduced

- Most people find time to spend with their families, neighbours and friends each day

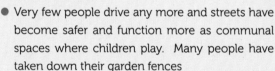

2021-25

- Porches are appearing on the front of many houses for people to socialise with their neighbours and many neighbours have taken down their garden fences so as to create shared space with their neighbours

- Vitamin supplement sales have dropped as diets have improved

- Cooking healthy communal meals has become common and people contribute vegetables and herbs to the pot, the virtues of various remedies are widely shared at these meals

- Many people have taken up the First Aid Courses being taught in schools for pupils and parents

Community

- Very few people drive any more and streets have become safer and function more as communal spaces where children play. Many people have taken down their garden fences

- KEVICC has won the Totnes Terrific Garden award for its physic garden that boasts the largest herbal apothecary in Totnes. Patient support groups are linked in with GP surgeries and talks about self-help techniques and diet are provided

- Community Care days take place every Friday in Totnes and on other days in the surrounding parishes; they usually include a cooking demonstration of a healthy meal which everyone then eats; most people bring some food they have grown to contribute

- The majority of mothers now breastfeed long-term. This is helped by all mothers receiving a year of well-paid maternity leave, and being able

SS THE TIMELINE

& Social Support Services • Wide Choice of Therapies • Foster Healthy Lifestyles

to take nursing breaks at work, if they wish. Some employers even allow mothers to work with their babies. Local shops and cafés all make it clear that breastfeeding mothers are welcome, and everyone is now used to mothers giving their infants 'the healthiest and most locally produced food there is'. Mothers feel truly comfortable feeding their babies when they need to.

Local Service Providers

- Totnes Hospital has achieved its 50% energy reduction goal and its budget is benefiting

- Care-worker transport expenses have been invested in the local Transport Co-op scheme to help provide transport for care workers, outpatients and hospital visitors

- Hospital car parks have been reduced to open up space for apothecary gardens and horse troughs and posts for tying up horses have been installed.

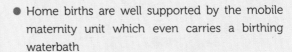

Individuals

- Older people share their knowledge about beneficial plants and remedies with local school children under the Wise Elders programme

- Children of all ages spend more time with their parents and families and less time in formal child care

- Most able-bodied people walk about 10 miles a week

- The major reduction in meat consumption and increased amounts of vegetables is benefiting diets.

Community

- Society is well linked to support local child care, disabled needs and provide help to neighbours, elderly people living alone

- Home births are well supported by the mobile maternity unit which even carries a birthing waterbath

- Wellbeing gardens are available for all residents in Totnes and South Brent and ten of the local parishes also have developed their own, which provide medical herbs and are linked with local GP practices and other health-care facilities. The workers & people involved in their gardens have become very knowledgeable about herbs.

Local Service Providers

- Health care provision has become more balanced towards individual responsibility with health care providers supporting the public's increased self-reliance and preventative care

- Community Clinics are well attended and provide a cost-effective system for delivery of public health

- The extensive budgets once allocated to tackling obesity and unhealthy lifestyles have diminished and the focus of investment is now on supporting access to services for rural communities

- Health and safety regulations have long been readjusted to enable more common sense approach and allow calculated risk so that people can become more self-reliant.

2026-30

TRANSITION IN ACTION

© Richard Hodgson

Totnes Healthy Futures

"If I'd known I was going to live so long,
I'd have taken better care of myself."
Leon Eldred

The Totnes Healthy Futures Project (THFP) is being
co-ordinated by a partnership of Totnes Development Trust, Transition Town Totnes, Leatside Surgery and the Faculty of Health and Social Work at
the University of Plymouth, which aims to provide
a practical solution to integrating local food production, well-being and health, horticulture and re-
skilling in order to increase localisation, and to build
communal and individual resilience.

The objectives of the project are to grow local food
to support food security with the involvement of all
sectors of the community; to provide a therapeutic opportunity with local medical care practices to
improve mental and physical health through 'green
prescriptions'; to provide an education/skills resource and self-supporting business model, and develop an evaluation programme.

A feasibility study has been completed, with help
from the Wakefield Trust, and a number of sites are
being explored for the project.

WATER MATTERS

"Water is the best of all things."
PINDAR (C. 522-C. 438 B.C.)
Olympian Odes

The Challenge

Water is the world's most precious commodity; there is no other substance more crucial to survival. As humans we are dependent on access to abundant uncontaminated water for public water supplies as well as for agriculture and fisheries. It is an integral part of the natural heritage and cultural life of all human societies. Rivers, lakes and the sea have affected patterns of human and animal movement and settlement, and influenced our beliefs and myths for thousands of years. In the UK our personal use of water alone, amounts to about 50 litres each day[42]. Industry uses twice this. 90% of all water used by humans is for agriculture. Water quality is the clearest indicator of environmental quality.

There are many reasons to be gloomy right now about global and local water supplies. Currently over a billion people in the world do not have access to safe water and over two million people die from diseases related to drinking contaminated every year. The lack of clean water close to people's homes also affects livelihoods and quality of life. Unstable weather patterns are likely to create droughts and floods. The rising global population will increase demand on diminishing water supplies. The melting of the glaciers will increase flooding, such that large low-lying coastal areas and estuaries may be lost under water

Strategic Themes Across the Timeline

Drinking water quality

Water conservation measures

Back-up, low energy water supplies

Flood plain planning & management

The detailed timeline developing the themes on this topic are available in the web version of this publication at www.totnesedap.org.uk

1kg = 15,500 litres

SUPPORTING BIODIVERSITY
THE WEB OF LIFE

"Adopt the pace of nature: her secret is patience."

Ralph Waldo Emerson

Business as Usual or Willing to Change? Emerging Trends 2009-2030

A Business as Usual approach to biodiversity assumes that nature can endlessly repair itself and that humankind can exist fairly independently and in control of natural systems. It also assumes that biodiversity is something that happens in reserves and parks, not in our everyday lives. New developments in the area make no space for wildlife, and farmers, driven by Government subsidies to grow as much food as possible, take back out all the hedgerows and other conservation measures put in over the 80s and 90s, in order to maximise production. This results in sharp declines in water quality, pollution and wildlife.

The extensive impact of the loss of this diversity is largely ignored, while research intensifies into genetically modified organisms (GMOs) to replace lost species. Little remains of native woodland and landscape features like hedgerows. The push for greater national food security meant that nature conservation became seen as an expendable luxury. The increased acidification of soils due to leaching and lack of earthworms leaves them sterile and exposed to severe erosion.

The bee population is severely damaged and growers have to pollinate food plants by hand. Few people use nature walks for pleasure, nature is something people watch on television, rather than experience firsthand. The sharp decline in the bird populations mean that the dawn chorus becomes more of a solo performance; people compensate by downloading tracks of birdsong onto their IPods.

If we are willing to change or make a Plan B on the other hand, this would need to be based on the following principles:

◎ Recognition by the planning system that protecting and enhancing biodiversity is an essential function of any development

◎ Full habitat protection is afforded to any species threatened with major population losses and/or extinction

◎ Production of food and the protection and enhancement of biodiversity are not mutually exclusive, all food production must do both. Biodiversity is a conservation and production strategy

◎ Policies from local authorities to national and international governance, must be realigned to enhance the health and viability of eco-cultural systems

◎ Increasing understanding of the importance of biodiversity

3.17   Bees on Their Knees. © Jenny Band

- Broadening awareness of the fragility of ecosystems
- Increasing the protection afforded to biodiversity & enable it to flourish
- Increasing the number and size of wildlife havens
- Supporting a plan that protects the marine environment and fish stocks
- Ensuring a full consideration and prioritisation for sustaining biodiversity with the implications of the impacts of global warming and sea level rise

What follows is one version of how biodiversity might become more localised and sustainable over the next 21 years.

Strategic Themes Across the Timeline

Land-use Supporting Biodiversity

Regenerating Species

Public Education & Awareness

Research & Legislation

The detailed timeline developing the themes on this topic are available in the web version of this publication at www.totnesedap.org.uk

Vision 2030

In 2030, Totnes and District is now home to a rich and diverse mosaic of habitats, from productive woodlands, agro-forestry systems, field-scale herb production, more lakes and ponds. The villages and towns are now as diverse and buzzing with flora and fauna as the countryside, if not more so. Over the 20 years since 2009, the landscapes in urban areas have changed markedly. There are now far fewer large expanses of impermeable car parks or hard standing, more than half of it, due to the sharp decline in car use, has been converted to food production, those gardens buzz with bees and butterflies. The concrete jungle has been overrun by nature reclaiming softened edges and gentle curves to buildings and roads. Woodlands

managed for coppice timber offer highly diverse habitats, from open, wild flower-rich open habitats, to dense woodland. Hedgerows full of birds and butterflies and wildflowers have been replanted to protect fields and soil and provide fuel and foraging. Recently planted native tree stands have become a significant feature of the landscape, their beautiful understory host to primroses and bluebells in spring.

People value and enjoy the nature around them. Families take nature walks on weekends. Schools prioritise nature and outdoor studies for all ages. Gardens are less manicured, and are now burgeoning with vegetables, fruits, vines and trees. Bird tables, beehives and bat boxes are tucked away in many places, all very busy. Many bird species have returned to farmland, fish to rivers and people to nature. The dawn chorus can be very noisy.

Resilience Indicators

From the research that led to this Plan, we have identified a number of key indicators by which we can be sure that we are moving forward. These include:

- Hectares of deciduous woodland managed for nature conservation.
- Monitoring of Red Shanked Carder bumblebee population.[40]
- The total km of hedgerows.
- Number of mating pairs of otters (Operation Otter at Dartington / Devon Wildlife Trust).
- Numbers of Skylarks[41] in the district.
- Monitoring of key bat species.
- % of households with bird tables and bat boxes.
- Cleanliness of main waterways in the area.
- Number of people actively involved in nature conservation.

These can be revisited regularly to see if the community is making progress in the right direction.

NOTES & IDEAS

Creative Energy Systems

ENERGY SECURITY

"Sometimes people ask me, "Surely we used to live on renewables just fine before the industrial revolution? Yes, but don't forget that two things were different then: lifestyles and population densities."

David J C Mackay, Professor of Physics, Cambridge University[1]

The Challenge

At present, despite plenty of Governmental talk about the need to create a low carbon economy, 90% of the UK's energy supply in 2009 still comes from oil, gas and coal, fossil fuels which are finite and non-renewable, and high emitters of carbon. Renewable energy use is now over 5 times the level it was in 1990, but in 2007 contributed to only 3.3% of our energy demand. We lose energy due to inefficient conversion and use of supplies and poor conservation of the energy.

The UK's energy situation is deeply perilous. We are at the end of lots of very long pipelines, and North Sea oil and gas peaked several years ago and are now falling sharply. Much of our indigenous energy production was sold during the 1980s at a time when oil and gas prices were very low. Now we have become a net importer of energy, at a time when those prices are highly volatile. The imperative to reduce our consumption of fossil fuels is driven by the need to reduce carbon emissions with huge urgency, and also by the fact that we need to build energy security; as Fatih Birol, Chief Economist at the International Energy Agency puts it "we must leave oil before oil leaves us".

The Government's response is to talk of a new generation of coal fired power station, and also nuclear energy. Both of these responses are problematic. The UK has also seen a doubling over the last 4 years of the number of residents living in fuel poverty, that is, needing to spend more than 10% of their income on energy.

The National Energy Picture: Where our Energy Comes From at the Moment

Although different kinds of fuels are used for producing different types of energy, it is important to note that not all are interchangeable.

Fossil fuels

Oil has a high energy density and its liquid nature makes it easily transportable. It is used for over 90% of the world's transport and is an important raw material for the plastics, chemical and pharmaceutical industries. Oil is also used for making pesticides and other agrochemicals. The UK was self-reliant for oil, and for gas, profiting from exports of both, until 2003.

Gas requires more stringent measures to contain and transport and is more suited to static applications such as cooking, space heating and water heating and electricity generation. It is also used as a raw material for fertilizer production. Global peak gas is expected around 10 years later than oil, but when that peak comes it will be more abrupt than the oil peak. The UK is more dependent on natural gas than most other countries. 38% of UK primary energy comes from gas, as opposed to, for example, 25% in the US.

Coal is the least energy dense (but most carbon rich) of the fossil fuels. Its primary use in the UK is electricity generation; worldwide use is growing more rapidly than any other fuel. Global peak coal is expected around 2025 and the quality of the coal being mined around the world is falling sharply.

Other non-conventional oil resources include deep-water oil, polar oil, heavy oil, tar sands and oil shale. These require high investment in energy (giving a low EROEI[2]) to recover them and their carbon implications are such that their use should be avoided.

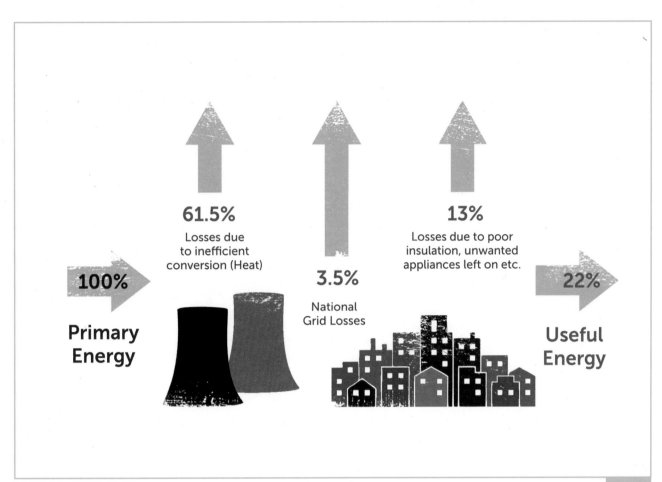

61.5%
Losses due
to inefficient
conversion (Heat)

13%
Losses due to poor
insulation, unwanted
appliances left on etc.

100%

**Primary
Energy**

3.5%

National
Grid Losses

22%

**Useful
Energy**

Loss of Energy due to inefficient Conversion. Source: Greenpeace　3.18

Nuclear power

Nuclear energy is produced as electricity from fission of uranium oxide, a finite resource. It currently accounts for about 3% of total UK energy supply. The EROEI of nuclear power is worsening as stocks of high quality uranium ore deplete although there are clearly differing ideas about how long reserves may last. The DARE report states that under current consumption levels the world's known reserves may last 60 years[3] However in another scenario Professor David MacKay suggests thorium could yield 120 kWh/day per person for 60,000 years[4] Dr Colin Campbell of ASPO has stated that "if the all the world converted to nuclear tomorrow, this would last about 3 years"[5]. Production of nuclear power also uses fossil fuels at most stages of its production.

Global warming is also having an impact on nuclear power production. Natural streams are used for cooling purposes; as global temperatures and sea temperatures rise these streams will reach the power plants at higher temperatures, thus less cooling is possible. Nuclear power plants in France have already had to operate below capacity due to this effect and their legislative upper limit of 24 C for receiving waters post discharge.

Nuclear fusion (based on light elements, e.g. hydrogen & lithium) has been researched for over 2 decades, but has not yet provided a reliable source of clean or cheap energy. Its potential contribution towards energy provision remains speculative. Lithium - a likely vanishing resource - is relatively uncommon in the earth's crust (and China has been buying up lithium mining rights over the past decade); this could also have serious implications for electric cars and similar vehicles, as lithium is currently a key component of their batteries.

Energy from renewable supplies

In 2007 just 1.5%[6] of the total UK energy supply came from renewable sources, and much of that was methane gas reclaimed from landfill sites. Renewable energy is an integral part of the Govern-

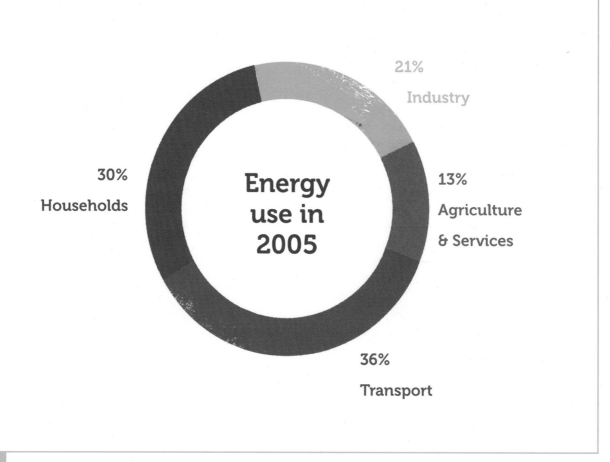

21%

Industry

30%

Households

Energy
use in
2005

13%

Agriculture

& Services

36%

Transport

3.19   Energy Use in Britain. Source: Zero Carbon Britain

ment's longer-term aim of reducing CO_2 emissions by 80% by 2050, a figure now matched by the rest of the G8 countries. In 2000 the Government set a target of 10% of electricity supply from renewable energy by 2010, and in 2006 announced an aspiration to double that level by 2020[7].

How we Use Energy

Before exploring solutions, it may be useful to firstly look at the ways in which we produce energy for use at present.

Electricity is currently produced in the UK using 78% fossil fuels; 1% oil, 43% gas and 34% coal. Nuclear electricity contributed 15% to electricity production in 2007, but has been declining in the past decade and will continue to do so over the next 20 years. Renewables continue to grow but in 2007 contributed just 5%. Electricity generation currently accounts for about one third of the UK's total carbon emissions.

Transportation – mainly uses oil

Heating, cooling and cooking – mainly uses gas, but in rural areas also relies heavily on oil, electricity and some wood.

Industry and Services – generally uses gas coal & oil

The Coming Energy Gap

In 2007, the UK imported 20.2% of its consumption of primary fuels[8]. With UK oil and gas production in the North Sea in sharp decline this gap, in effect, the UK's energy deficit is widening sharply, and we will need to find alternative domestic energy supplies or increase imports. However, fossil fuel supplies world wide are also in decline, with more than 65 of the 98 oil producing nations having passed their peak in oil production, and those nations whose production hasn't yet peaked will need more and more of it themselves; therefore less and less imported energy will become available to the UK.

As fossil fuels become scarcer, they become more costly and energy intensive to extract. The ratio of the amount of energy a resource provides and the amount of energy required to recover that resource is known as Energy Returned on Energy Invested (EROEI). EROEIs for fossil fuels decline as resources decline and are likely to indicate that other sources of energy such as renewables are more profitable for short-term as well as long term investment.

The UK has a security of supply problem looming, this is known as the "energy gap". A substantial number of old coal and nuclear power stations (around 30% of the current total generation capacity) are scheduled to close by 2020. These currently produce 22.5 gigawatts (GW) of energy production; leaving a risk that energy demand will exceed supply unless alternative energy supplies are available. As former UK Chancellor of the Exchequer Nigel Lawson said in 2008, "all in all, the likelihood of the lights going out in Europe at some point over the next 20 years has never been greater". The question that really must arise from looking at the graph above is, where is our energy going to come from?

Renewable Energy

Renewable energy supplies can be captured from:

Solar

Wind

Hydro

Biomass

Waste organic material

We can also harness additional energy by using technology such as heat pumps to increase supplies we are already using.

In the T & D Energy Budget section we explore these different technologies.

Managing the National Grid, Fluctuating Supplies, Seasons and Storage

There are a number of technical challenges in providing and storing electricity supplies from inter-

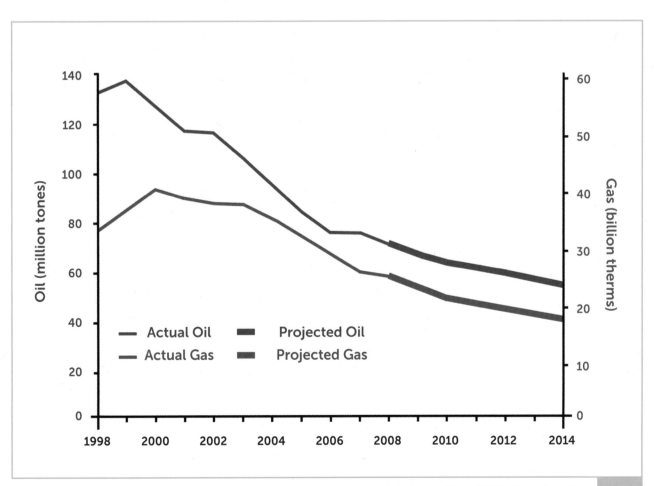

Actual & Possible Future UKCS Oil & Gas Production.
Source: UK. Dept. Environment and Climate Change (DECC)

3.20

mittent sources such as renewable supplies. Solar supplies are generated in variance with time of day, season and cloud cover. Wind and hydro supplies can vary enormously by the day. Wave and tidal are generally more predictable but still have daily tidal variance. Continuous feed in anaerobic digestion can provide a steady supply, but this energy generation is more efficient at producing methane for vehicle fuel.

The Sustainable Development Commission while postulating an overall reduction in energy use of at least 30% by 2050 nevertheless forecast an increase in electricity consumption of 16% due to expectations of changes such as diesel trains and road transport switching over to electric vehicles. This has major implications for the Grid.

Local short-term fluctuations (SLEW) can be accommodated by the Grid provided there are sufficient back-up reserves on-line e.g. pumped up storage, emergency generators, quick response gas turbines etc. We need to be able to store energy off grid, which then feeds back into the grid to meet demand. Electric cars are being considered as a useful

multiple system of storing electricity which can be left plugged in when idle, drawn on as needed by the grid and used for travel when energy supplies permit.

Water pumping systems can be used, whereby excess electricity is used to pump water up a height to store energy, to be released with the energy recaptured by turbines feeding back into the grid as needed. The large water reservoir at Roadford (which currently supplies Totnes and District) could be part of a regional energy storage scheme. Smaller schemes in conjunction with weirs and turbines on some of the smaller local rivers (e.g. near Sharpham) could also be utilised. In Spain desalination plants are used to store energy.

At the supplier level it is generally most convenient to be able to plug into and feed or use from the national grid using either 2 separate meters or just one 2-way meter (as in Oregon for the last 20 years!). Government set feed-in tariffs for consumer produced power supplies are famously ungenerous to smaller suppliers, however these are set to improve.

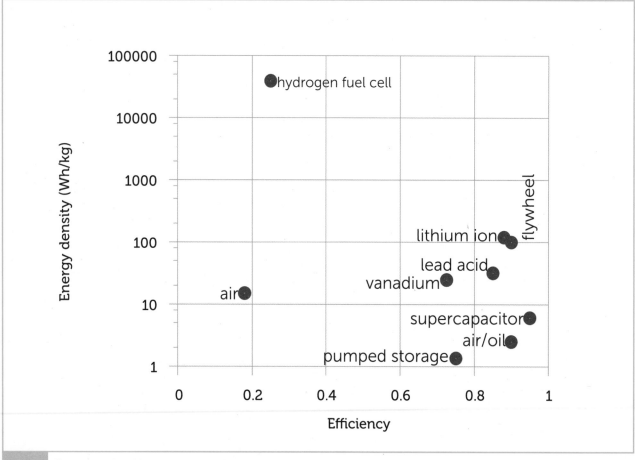

3.21 Some properties of storage systems and fuels: Energy density versus efficiency.
Source Sustainable Energy Without the Hot Air

The national grid needs to be able to match demand with supply, there are a number of ways that this can be achieved, for example 'smart metering' to encourage customers to use 'off peak' electricity at cheaper rates. Smart metering can be used to manage both electricity and gas supplies; power companies can:

◎ Vary the price according to hour by hour supply and demand

◎ Monitor usage remotely (no need to read meters manually)

◎ Provide users/consumers with an easy to understand indication of energy usage

◎ Access customers' appliances to switch them on and off remotely (this will require modifications to the wiring in individual premises) to reduce loads (peak-lopping)

A maximum allowance or consumer ration can be set. On the Island of Eigg, households have a warning noise when they are reaching their maximum allowance for the day (if they exceed this the electricity cuts out and they are fined).

We need to question whether we can practically or realistically expect the electricity supply to be available 100% of the time on the national grid. It will be easier for us to get through the coming energy transition if we can accept and prepare for some interruptions in supply. There is an ongoing debate at the time of writing that there could be an upper limit to the amount of renewable energy supplies the National Grid could accommodate, however experience from Germany suggests 100% is possible. A renewables based grid will be easier to put in place if we can accept some management of demand, including short interruptions in supply.

Resilience in the national grid at the local level poses many challenges; however there is speculation that resilience could be achieved by creating regional grids linked nationally using interconnectors (as currently used between countries). There is a need for research and trials in grid management for renewable supplies and storage.

Energy Demand and Supply in Totnes and District

In the Energy Budget in the next section we have made the following estimations:

Totnes & District Baseline estimated
total DEMAND of all energy
= 709.5 GWh/y in 2009

reducing to 354.7 GWh/y by 2030
(in line with ZCB 50%)

T & D Baseline estimated potential
renewable energy production
= 138 GWh/y in 2009

rising to 163.8 GWh/y by 2030

(2030 T&D estimated total renewable energy
production INCLUDING per capita share of
National potential large scale
renewable energy capture
= 234.4 GWh/y)

(2030 T&D estimated total renewable energy
production INCLUDING per capita share of
National + International potential large scale
renewable energy capture
= 299.2 GWh/y)

While this would indicate that large scale national and international energy capture technology could provide the bulk of renewable energy supplies there are 2 key considerations:

◎ The full off shore renewable potential is likely to take a long time coming on stream

◎ As an essentially rural locality, T & D is probably more able to generate renewable energy than other places e.g. cities in the UK; the overall UK picture may therefore be, a lower share of nationally produced renewables available to rural areas.

Please refer to the Energy Budget Section for further details and analysis of potential energy demand and supply of renewables in Totnes and District

Fuel Poverty in Devon

Fuel poverty demonstrates the social dimension of equity of access to affordable home heating. The Devon Affordable Warmth Strategy[9] of 2004 stated that the average level of fuel poverty in Devon is 24%; this is just above the English average of 23%. In South Hams the average is 20%, however as the map below shows, there are small areas in Totnes and District, particularly in Totnes town with red areas indicating 26-40% households in fuel poverty.

The temperatures recommended by the World health Organisation are 21 degrees C in the living room and 18 degrees C in other occupied rooms. Households living in fuel poverty cannot afford to heat their homes to these temperatures when outside temperatures fall.

The causes of fuel poverty are:

◎ Low household income
◎ Homes with poor energy efficiency
◎ Under occupancy
◎ Fuel prices

Those most at risk of fuel poverty are:

◎ The elderly
◎ Families with young children
◎ The long term sick / disabled
◎ The long term unemployed

Zero Carbon Britain?

The Centre for Alternative Energy in Wales commissioned a report in 2008 to consider the challenge of having our energy supplies produced entirely from renewable resources. Their findings were that by the year 2030 in order to meet energy needs, we need to be producing 50% of current usage through renewable energy and 0% from conventional fuels. To achieve this a number of obstacles will need to be overcome. ZCB 2008 estimates that we can reduce consumption by 50% through energy efficiency and energy conservation measures, in particular through major improvements in insulation of buildings, energy efficiency, and substantial reductions

in use of individual transport. With rising costs of energy, households are likely to reduce their consumption further in small but accumulatively significant ways. Other measures such as rationing may be applied by the government to curb demand in line with supply problems as they arise.

Please refer to the Energy Budget section for discussion on the ability of T&D to meet this target

Imported Energy

National estimates of energy consumption are based on the use of energy within the UK. Goods from foodstuffs to plastic goods that are imported carry embodied energy that is not included in the UK calculations and carries energy produced in other countries. Various estimates have been made to assess the energy consumption of imported goods we use[10].

The total estimate based on the more conservative DEFRA study is around 60 kWh/day per capita nationally[11].

Locally this translates to about (365 x 60kWh x 23,863) 522,600 MWh/y energy from imports and adds about 6.5 tonnes of carbon from emissions per person in the UK.

Adding this total to our other current energy use (estimated above): 709.5 GWh/y

Almost doubles our 2009 total energy use in T&D to 1,232.1 GWh/y

This highlights our current dependence on imports and pinpoints a key challenge to becoming nationally and locally resilient.

Managing a Global Carbon Budget: Energy Rationing

The science shows that we cannot afford to burn all the oil, gas, and coal left on the planet, as this will lead to run away climate change, in fact we have burnt too much already and need to take measures to reabsorb some of those carbon emissions. Contraction & Convergence is a proposal for nations to adopt to reduce carbon emissions[12]. Having identified national annual allocation of carbon emissions,

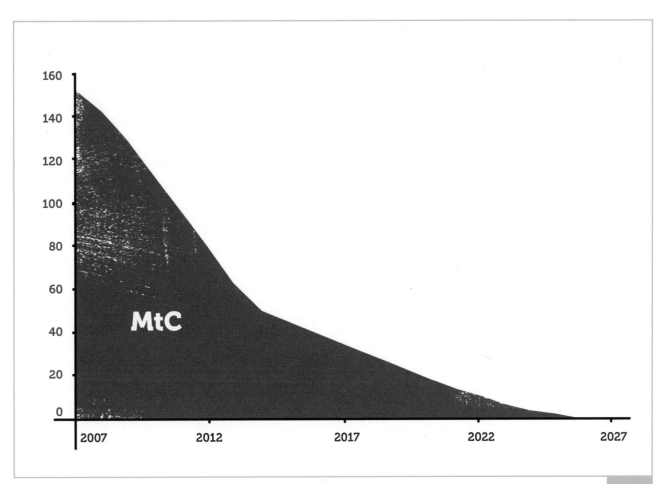

Carbon Budget Britain. Source: Zero Carbon Britain.   3.22

this budget will be divided into annual allocations with a year on year reduction (Contraction), bring all nations to a position of emission equity (Convergence). Major emitters like UK and US will have to make drastic cuts initially, whereas countries like Bangladesh would reduce by less. Where nations use less than their quote they could trade these with other countries as Tradable Energy Quotas (TEQs)

Energy Efficiency

It is clear that to generate enough energy to meet current energy demand will require an investment over many years. Reducing our energy demand by investing in energy efficiency is an essential prerequisite to introducing renewable energy and will have a double benefit[13]:

◎ A once off investment in energy efficiency will continue to save money indefinitely

◎ This will reduce the capital investment needed for renewable energy infrastructure

Energy efficiency covers a very wide range of measures from fitting a condensing boiler to switching off a light. It is estimated that 10% of all energy could be saved by simply changing our behaviour and switching off unwanted appliances. Space heating is by far the biggest use of domestic energy and this is where the best possibilities of energy efficiency occur.

The DARE report assessed that 58% of energy can be saved through simple measures applying energy efficiency, the main one being good insulation (see T&D Energy Budget section)

Funding Local Energy Security

Energy Action Devon (EAD) is a not for profit, charitable business working with the public, private, and voluntary sectors to deliver energy efficiency and awareness through action in Devon. It also raises awareness of the many local and national grants and schemes, offering free or discounted cavity wall and loft insulation, heating and renewable energy systems. The Charity is part of a consortium which manage the South West Energy Saving Trust's advice centres, providing free and impartial home energy efficiency and transport advice via the Trust's free helpline for advice (0800 512 012) and a home energy check.

We need to guard against the Rebound effect!

The Rebound effect happens where increased energy efficiency due to better insulation in the home brings fuel costs down, so people turn up the thermometer. "Domestic temperatures are estimated to have increased from 16 degrees in 1990 to 19 degrees in 2002" [14] Ideally this idea (also known as Jevrons Paradox) should not apply in the post-peak oil world.

Business as Usual or Willing to Change? - Emerging Trends - Where we are Now

If we pursue business as usual to its logical conclusion; assuming that economic growth is still possible in a world needing a drastic cut to its carbon emissions and fail to prepare for the reality of dwindling oil supplies, the world will be one which has done nothing to adapt its energy system for the inevitable shocks it is facing. Nationally, the failure to engage in a concerted programme of far-reaching energy conservation could be catastrophic. As the UK struggles to import sufficient gas to make up the shortfall of its own plummeting supplies, the UK may have to make some tough choices about where the priorities for that energy lie. By 2010, the UK will be importing one-third of its natural gas, and by 2020, 80%. By 2013, the cost of importing oil and gas could reach £100bn a year, which if nothing is done will continue to grow each year, having a disastrous impact on an economy already reeling from the recession [15].

We will see highly volatile oil prices, interruptions to supply, geopolitics shifting increasingly in favour of those who still hold energy reserves, sharply rising fuel poverty, and, most probably, blackouts and rationing. With focus, determination and an honest assessment of our situation, these are all avoidable. Like any addict whose addiction is out of control, without a co-ordinated, focused and committed 'detox' programme, the likelihood of the addiction taking the addict down with it is very high. From a climate change perspective, we need to break our dependence on fossil fuels as soon as possible.

While climate change says we should break our oil addiction, peak oil says we will have no choice in the matter.

Any approach that strategically navigates our way out of our energy predicament must be based on the following principles:

◎ Clear understanding and awareness of how energy is used

◎ Major reduction in use of energy at all levels of society

◎ Severe reduction in use of products with high embodied energy

◎ High priority for investment of time and finance in energy efficiency

◎ Recognition of the vulnerability of conventional energy supplies

◎ Development and provision of renewable energy supplies must be prioritised and brought on stream

◎ Rapid reduction in use of fossil fuel based energy

◎ Equitable approach to the sharing of all resources

What follows is one version of how energy security might become more localised and sustainable over the next 21 years.

Vision 2030

By 2030, the relationship that Totnes has to energy has undergone a transformation. Over the 20 years of this plan, the area successfully reduced its energy consumption by 50%, and installed the capacity to generate the other 50% from number of different renewable technologies. One of the keys to this was the setting up in 2009 of the Totnes Renewable Energy Society. This proved to be a powerful driver in the installation of large-scale renewables, as it invited the community to invest in them, and to share in the return. Renewable energy became not only something people wanted for environmen-tal and energy security reasons, but also because they accrued a financial return from them. What cars and other vehicles there are in Totnes now are powered either by bio-methane or electricity, and every south-facing surface is now clad in solar panels. The two wind turbines installed close to Totnes are now a source of great pride to the town, and the money they generate has made a significant contribution to funding the establishment of many of the new businesses vital to the localisation of the local economy.

'It is not the strongest species that survive, nor the most intelligent, but the ones who are most responsive to change' - Charles Darwin

Resilience Indicators

From the research that led to this Plan, we have identified a number of key indicators by which we can be sure that we are moving forward. These include:

- % of houses with insulation to Passivhaus standards
- % of energy produced from local renewable sources to meet local (estimated) demand
- % of buildings with solar hot water collectors
- Number of people who feel well informed about energy issues
- Number of people concerned about energy security/climate change
- Reaching the Government target of reducing carbon emissions by at least 20% by 2020 (80% by 2050)

These can be revisited regularly to see if the community is making progress in the right direction.

ENERGY SECURITY
PATHWAYS ACRO

Strategic themes: • Renewable electricity generation • Energy efficiency measures

Individuals

- The TRESOC share option (see below) raises £250,000 within the first 6 months.

- 3-fold rise in interest in DIY low energy housing is reflected in huge attendance at TTT's tour of buildings with retrofits and solar panels.

- The Great Retrofit pilot solar panel installation takes place at 10 houses in Totnes as interest widens in investing in PV and Solar hot water combined systems.

- Farmers put forward land parcels for tree management plans to generate wood fuel

- Many people get enthusiastic about changing their incandescent lights for low energy bulbs and cutting back on car use

- Engineers call for Smart metering to be prioritised by power companies and in Government plans.

Community

- The Totnes Renewable Energy Society launches its share prospectus, inviting people within Totnes and District to buy between £20 and £20,000's worth of shares. The Totnes Times feature about the launch quotes TRESOC's Managing Director, Ian Bright, as saying "TRESOC offers a unique opportunity for the Totnes community to take control and benefit from local renewable energy production, a key component of a sustainable energy future".

- TRESOC submits planning application for a 4.6kW wind turbine on land close to Totnes.

- The RSPB announces that birds and wind turbines can co-exist

- The woodchip boiler installed at Sharpham becomes fully operational after some initial teething problems. Later in the year, as does the 44kW Guntamatic Synchro 44 log boiler in the Barn Retreat and a 20.16Kw Photovoltaic array on the Creamery.

- Members from Sustainable South Brent (SSB) and the Dartmoor Circle pay a visit to the PGE-32 wind turbine at Bodmin. SSB have measured the average wind-speed in South Brent at 5.18m/s during 2008.

- KEVICC has a comprehensive Energy feasibility study carried out on whole college starting with current energy usage. This finds that two thirds of electricity use is for computers and related systems - servers, air conditioning and peripherals. The report makes a long list of recommendations, starting with several easy-win energy efficiency measures and a 500kW biomass boiler to replace the ancient gas boilers on Redworth site. Cavity wall insulation is installed where possible and loft insulation is topped up where there are ceilings, but the 1970's design with sloping roof spaces is difficult to retrofit.

Policy Makers & Service Providers

- April - The Chancellor announces an extra £1.4 billion in support for low carbon industries ranging from energy efficiency and renewables through to carbon capture and storage. These measures, together with announcements made since last autumn when the downturn started, will enable an additional £10.4bn of low carbon investment over the next three years. The extent of the UK's investment in low carbon is set out in "Investing in a Low Carbon Britain", published today in the News pages of their new website. Whitelee 300MW Wind Farm opens near Glasgow, the largest on-shore wind farm in Europe with 140 turbines.

- July 2009, Government announces rates for Feed-in Tariffs (FiTs) of 42p/kWh. Reeling in delight and almost disbelief at the news, Andrew Knox from DARE said "42p/kWh could make a domestic PV installation an investment on par with investment in the market and would make

SS THE TIMELINE

• Energy conservation measures • Sustaining grids and network

investment in TRESOC something only a fool would refuse. Please let me know when I can buy shares".

- The new parking metres installed in Totnes High Street are powered by photovoltaic cells on the top.
- SHDC grants permission to SSB for a 225kW turbine (hub height 30m). This is estimated to potentially supply about 10% of South Brent's electricity need.
- DPNA grant planning permission for the reinstatement of the 12' diameter waterwheel at Lydia Mill and the Environment Agency grant an abstraction (transfer) licence, SSB set to work clearing the leat.

2009

2010

Individuals

- Carbon footprint calculation, wireless home electricity meters & Smart meters gain popularity as self-assessment gets a grip on householders. Rising energy bills are met with major reductions in domestic use. Computers are being switched off twice as often as before. Fridges are having their heat exchangers dusted.
- Smart Energy demonstration street in Totnes self selects as part of major retrofit initiative. All

houses will be fully insulated, all light bulbs will be low energy, every roof will carry both Solar PV and Solar HW and one house is to be fitted with under-floor heating generated by a heat pump.

- Sales of pyjamas and Long Johns increase as people invest in clothing to cut heating bills.
- Totnes Men's Probus Society organise a visit to Plymouth University Energy from Algae trials.

Community

- Phase One at ATMOS features a photovoltaic roof, installed by Totnes-based Beco Solar[16], who operate out of Totnes Industrial Estate.
- Work begins on TRESOC's hydro scheme on the weir in Totnes.
- Department of Communities and Local Government give a grant to TRESOC to fund their planning work and set-up costs.
- KEVICC installs a woodchip boiler to replaces its defunct gas boiler. Also installed is energy monitoring software that tracks electricity and gas use in real time and heat production from the biomass boiler. This is accessible on the intranet, and can be used for teaching purposes. Public display meters in Reception and other parts of the college allow the energy status to become readily visible. The school is delighted with its new energy system, and plans to do the same for the new school buildings it is designing.
- The Western Morning News re-assesses its strong anti position on wind turbines, announcing that its new position will be to be supportive of wind development, providing developments are not excessive in scale, and that some element of community ownership is involved". It runs an editorial praising the TRESOC application as demonstrating "best practice for wind".

ENERGY SECURITY

PATHWAYS ACRO

Strategic themes: • Renewable electricity generation • Energy efficiency measures

2011

Policy Makers & Service Providers

- The Department of Energy and Climate Change make available the new feed-in tariffs, which, for the first time, mean that homeowners generating electricity through micro-renewables (wind, solar) are paid more for that electricity than they pay the grid for energy. For householders across Totnes and District it becomes a more attractive investment to put money into installing photovoltaics than to put it into pensions.

- 50 photovoltaic systems are installed in Totnes within the first 9 months after feed-in tariffs are introduced.

- Local PV and micro-wind industry undergoes a period of intense strain, then rapid expansion providing plentiful skilled employment in Totnes (Beco) and throughout Devon. Support from RE4D helps industry through the strain and provides much training through expansion phase giving Devon micro-renewables industry massive advantage relative to other counties. Devon becomes an industry leader.

- SHDC agrees to reduce the number of streetlights by 30% and replace 25% of those remaining with PV lights as a phased in changeover for all lights.

- The Planning Inspectorate holds a planning appeal into SHDC's refusal of TRESOC's application for a wind turbine near Totnes. The inspector rules in favour of the application, over-ruling a small but high profile opposition campaign, arguing in his ruling that "at times of national insecurity, where ensuring future energy supply is the national priority, initiatives such as this, which has succeeded in raising £500,000 from the local community, and the benefits of which go back into the community, are desperately needed and absolutely vital".

Individuals

- Research by the Department of Communities and Local Government finds that of the 420 people who have taken part in TTT's Transition Together project, 85% have, as a result, cut their home energy use by over 40%. National government commissions a nationwide version of Transition Together.

- Totnes-based photovoltaics company Beco Solar report a 400% increase in orders, as feed-in tariffs mean that installing them is now a sound financial investment. On the back of a series of events promoting PV run by Transition Town Totnes, interest soars.

- Domestic Solar Hot Water installation in just about 10% of all households in T&D; with Solar PV just behind at 8%. Capital cost is clearly an issue but so are rising energy bills: grants or subsidized loans are needed.

- Electricians are getting trained in rewiring individual premises for Smart Metering. They recommend to all their customers to have these adjustments made for any small wiring job

Community

- Phase One of ATMOS adds 3 vertical axis wind turbines[17], which become a source of fascination to the town as well as generating reliable and silent wind energy in the urban context.

- Totnes Industrial Estate is clad in photovoltaics, as a demonstration project, funded in part by DECC.

SS THE TIMELINE

• Energy conservation measures • Sustaining grids and network

- The first wind turbine erected by TRESOC is put up. The Mayor of Totnes dedicates the 4.6MW turbine and many of the 1300 TRESOC shareholders are photographed in front of the turbine, waving their share certificates.

- Dartington Hall Trust installs a woodchip boiler to generate heat for the buildings on the Estate. They note that managing their own woodlands will only produce one-third of what they will need, the rest will come from elsewhere (e.g. Dartmoor Wood fuel Co-operative), but in the long term, their Agroforestry Farm initiative will add significantly to what they produce.

Policy Makers & Service Providers

- SHDC announces its 'Great Retrofit' initiative. The Council offers any homeowner or landlord funding to enable 4 aspects of energy efficiency, insulation (internal or cladding), new triple-glazed windows, solar thermal panels and energy efficient boilers. SHDC borrows long term at low interest rates on the open market for 25 years, and offers grants of up to £10,000 per property. The repayments are set so as to cover the interest repayments, and are added to the borrower's Council Tax bill. The repayments are less than the money saved, so it is a very attractive opportunity. The bulk of the loan is repayable if and when the house is resold, but sale value is increase by the efficiency of the property, providing the seller with the funds to repay the loan. SHDC invests in training local contractors to do the work to the highest standards, and from the day of its launch, there is a great deal of interest in the scheme.

- Totnes Hospital replaces its outside lights with PV and carries out a feasibility study into having an anaerobic digester on site to turn hospital waste and into heat and power while minimizing the need for sanitation by incineration, a process that emits dioxins and furans.

- The new Government sets out its plans for national offshore renewables that will equate to 50kWh per person per day by 2025. Local authorities are to be their local partners in rolling out the plan for capturing tidal, wave and wind energy. Tax payers heave a sigh of relief that urgent priorities are being addressed

- 'HotROCs' (Renewable Obligation Certificates for heat energy) programme begins.

- British Gas announces that its plans for Smart Metering, offering its customers a discount in electricity tariffs for a year plus an Energy Drop package that includes a PV panel, Solar HW system together with the Smart Meter installation. The other electricity supply companies quickly follow with similar offers.

2012

Individuals

- The carbon calculator built into Facebook, and automatically linked to one's online payment of energy bills, means that lowering one's carbon footprint becomes a matter of great personal pride. Research undertaken by the University of East Anglia shows that the lower one's carbon footprint, the more trustworthy people think you are as a friend. People with very high carbon footprints tend to receive more 'be my friend' rejections on Facebook than those with lower footprints. The Sun's alarmist take on this, suggesting that "'hello love, how big's your carbon footprint?" will become a widely used chat-up line, fails to materialise. The nation breathes a sigh of relief.

- Jumpers and thick socks are back in fashion as home heating costs rise.

ENERGY SECURITY
PATHWAYS ACRO

Strategic themes: • Renewable electricity generation • Energy efficiency measures

• Interest rises in domestic Micro hydro as rainfall increases and more generous feed-in tariffs make small mills more viable.

Community

• TRESOC's feasibility study on anaerobic digestion concludes that the commercial food waste generated by the hotels, restaurants and other outlets, as well as waste from larger scale food industries, would be sufficient, when put through an Anaerobic Digester, to create bio-methane to power 35 buses, or 200 cars[18]. They form a partnership with Stage Coach buses, and Bob the Bus, as well as with 2 local taxi firms, to explore the practicalities. Local biogas production and fuel refining creates much local skilled employment.

• A community woodland plan "30% Tree Cover", is drafted in conjunction with farmers and landowners to create additional woodlands and hedgerows for wood fuel, food production and biodiversity. SWW gets involved as a large landowner and funds the first phase of planting.

• KEVICC sets up an experimental Algae pond to see if they can produce diesel for the school bus.

Policy Makers & Service Providers

• Totnes Town Council puts together a plan to make Transition more visible to enhance tourism and benefit their budget; they install PV panels on all the bus shelters and streetlights in the area, and install more bicycle racks around the town.

• SWW announces new Anaerobic digesters will be installed at Moreleigh and South Brent to generate electricity from farm wastes. A combined heat and power scheme will be piloted in conjunction with 3 nearby houses at each plant.

• The Government offer a small grant as an incentive to bring in all premises not yet rewired for Smart metering, saying that legislation to make this compulsory may follow if needed.

2013-15

Individuals

• 100 KEVICC students take part in the Energy Drop Challenge, where they challenge and help their families to reduce their energy consumption by over 50%. The winner, Hannah Dove, reveals that she taught herself to use a sewing machine in order to be able to back her curtains with thick blankets.

• 80 households invest in 25 Electric cars, which come on stream at 6 new car pools in the district; they are part of an incentive scheme to support the grid in balancing the energy load.

• A survey shows that 25% of buildings are generating power. The frequent power cuts are stimulating major individual investment in PV and wood stoves.

• A heat wave in Devon causes problems for freezers closed down during a Smart Meter practice exercise in 2 adjoining streets. The householders hold a street Freezer Party to use the defrosted food. "I wouldn't usually serve fish-fingers at a party," says Henry James, "but actually they are quite nice with a chilli dip."

Community

• Supported by TRESOC, and with community investment, 3 new hydro schemes are put in across the area. The system at Staverton Mill is the largest, generating 68kW of electricity.

• TRESOC begins work on a large Anaerobic Digester on Totnes Industrial estate. Methane-powered trucks are brought in to collect food waste around town, and contracts are signed with major food manufacturers to guarantee that their waste will be fed into the digester.

SS THE TIMELINE

• Energy conservation measures • Sustaining grids and network

- The ATMOS Arts building becomes the first energy autonomous arts venue in the UK. It employs an innovative heat recovery system that stores the heat generated by the weekly big concerts, and the accompanying dancing, in a thermal store beneath the floor, and radiates heat at other times.

- Dartington establishes an algae pond on the flooded fields (near Swallowfields) to produce diesel for the vehicles and capture CO_2.

- A number of community hydro schemes are being explored in local villages to increase local renewable energy supplies. TRESOC is supporting these initiatives with advice and capital to groups setting up.

Policy Makers & Service Providers

- 15% of homes in the area have taken up SHDC's 'Great Retrofit' programme. SHDC feels it has probably attracted most of the 'low hanging fruit', i.e. those people who are already keen on energy efficiency. The rising energy prices of 2013 prove to be the incentive they have been waiting for, and soon, interest in the scheme is soaring again.

- The new fleet of public service vehicles at Devon PCT are all methane / electric hybrids and will run off locally produced renewable energy.

- National Government announces energy rationing to be administered locally to avoid supply cuts as fossil fuel imports become unreliable. Major national investment in off-shore wind and wave turbines meets with less objection as shipping has reduced

- Totnes Energy Company carries out a survey of locations identified for small water mills and offers incentives for development of micro hydro schemes. 5 old mills are identified for phase 1 and get the go ahead. They also assess potential (flooded) sites for algae to biodiesel production.

Individuals

- Due to a combination of retrofitting and reduced demand, and as a result of the Great Retrofit that began in 2011, domestic energy consumption in Totnes and District has now fallen 30% on 2009 levels. This fact is noted and celebrated at a 2 day 'Totnes: making the Transition real' festival in the new Civic Hall.

- More landowners identify land parcels for growing trees for wood fuel. New hedgerows are planted out with ash and hazel for coppicing. Local people sign up for their ration of wood fuel

- With the introduction of Carbon Rationing in 2016, a low-carbon lifestyle can actually become a part of one's income.

Community

- TRESOC apply for planning permission for a second 4.6MW wind turbine, on the same site as the one already successfully operating. This time, the planning process is much smoother, with no objections, and permission is approved within 16 weeks. A second share option raises £400,000.

- Woodland harvesting for fuel has become very popular as the new hedgerows are becoming productive. People work together to manage the woodland and dry and store the fuel.

Policy Makers & Service Providers

- SHDC's offices are clad with photovoltaics, and used to power a small fleet of electric vehicles for trips in and around Totnes. 3 smaller wind turbines are installed at Follaton House to maintain energy supplies for the new databanks and servers they have installed on site.

- Take up of the 'Great Retrofit' scheme passes 50%. Old boilers for new Heat pumps are SHDC's Christmas offer as they open a new recycling unit for complex materials.

2016-20

ENERGY SECURITY
PATHWAYS ACRO

Strategic themes: • Renewable electricity generation • Energy efficiency measures

2021-25

Individuals

- Farmers take up the carbon sequestration incentives offered by central government and plant out the new grasses that will draw more carbon into soils. The grasses have been shown to benefit both air emissions and grazing cattle.

- Micro wind turbines have become more acceptable and popular with most rural houses installing combined turbine and heat pump heating systems when their boilers need renewing. As a result of R&D coming to fruition, improved and worthwhile building mounted wind turbines become available, opening up options for urban and commercial situations.

- Solar PV roof slates are gaining in popularity on new builds and re-roofs as the prices have come down. Some of the 'Sunny Slates' are made from recycled plastics now being mined from landfill sites.

Community

- Zero Carbon Britain aim of 50% reduction in energy use has arrived in Totnes and district. The annual local energy assessments are showing that energy consumption has reduced to 50% of 2009 usage, and that 80% of this is all now generated by renewables.

- Local heat and power schemes have been set up in 6 housing groups drawing heat and gas supplies produced by on-site anaerobic digesters. The Dartington Abundant Life Community is part of one scheme being used as a model by Devon PCT to promote this system for all residential homes.

Policy Makers & Service Providers

- Wood rationing quotas increase as Follaton's arboretum coppice comes on stream. The wood chip boiler on site can now provide power and heat from the wastage for all SHDC offices on site.

- SWW brings its woodlands into local quotas for wood fuel.

- Offshore wave power comes on stream and supports the newly regionalised electricity grid. Electric cars are provided for community group car pools as decentralised energy stores.

- Totnes and District wins national award as first carbon neutral district in UK.

SS THE TIMELINE

• Energy conservation measures • Sustaining grids and network

2026-30

Individuals

- Garden lawns, which take up carbon from the atmosphere (through different grass varieties with deeper roots) come into fashion as concerns about climate change continue to rise. People 'adopt' foreign landholdings as stewards for carbon sequestration.

- Energy bills have declined with global warming and more spare energy is sold back to the grid than anticipated, taking advantage of the better tariffs for households.

Community

- Harberton's new Dance n' Disco floor at the Community hall harnesses feet power. The idea catches on at 5 more community halls in the district. Pedal power films arrive in the district to pilot work researched by People Power, who has already created a wave of interest in treadle power for household appliances including dishwashers.

- Algae ponds for bio-diesel production are established at ATMOS in the flooded gardens.

Policy Makers & Service Providers

- SHDC does a deal with Devon County Council to sell surplus national energy quotas. Council tax comes down as a result.

- New Local Authority housing at Old China Blue premises is a model of good planning and wins award for minimal embodied energy and systems.

- Totnes station gets a makeover in line with the Atmos Project. The refurbished waiting rooms, Whistle stop café and new footbridge reflect the strong artistic and energy aware designing. The giant carbon calculator on platform 2 now enables travellers to measure their carbon clean-up footprint while waiting.

Further Reading

Department of Energy & Climate Change.   www.decc.gov.uk/

Encraft (2009) Warwick Wind Trials Final Report. Downloaded from www.warwickwindtrials.org.uk/resources/Warwick+Wind+Trials+Final+Report+.pdf

Heinberg, R. (2009) Blackout: coal, climate and the last energy crisis. New Society Publishing.

Fleming, D. (2007) The Lean Guide to Nuclear Energy. Free download from http://www.theleaneconomyconnection.net/downloads.html#Nuclear.

Good Energy. (2009) A very useful website about microrenewables. http://www.generateyourown.co.uk

Johnson, D. (2009) Nuclear Power? No Point. www.greenparty.org.uk/assets/files/reports/Nuclear_Power_No_Point.pdf

MacKay, D.J.C. (2009) Sustainable Energy – without the hot air. UIT, Cambridge.

Tainter , J. (1990) The Collapse of Complex Societies. Cambridge University Press.

UK Government Renewable Energy Strategy 2009. www.decc.gov.uk/en/content/cms/what_we_do/uk_supply/energy_mix/renewable/res/res.aspx

UK Industry Task Force on Peak Oil and Energy Securities (2008) The Oil Crunch – Securing the UK's Energy Future – first report of the UK Industry Task Force on Peak Oil and Energy Securities (ITPOES). Downloaded from www.arup.com/_assets/_download/4D6FF5E5-19BB-316E-408B503DFB26ADDB.pdf

YouGen – Renewable Energy made Easy: http://www.yougen.co.uk. Online community (http://www.yougen.co.uk) for people who are interested in energy efficiency and renewable energy

Energy Action Devon (EAD) www.energyactiondevon.org.uk/

Grants for home insulation etc. www.cosydevon.co.uk/

Quiet revolution www.quietrevolution.co.uk innovative turbines

Wind Car by students at Grove School

The Old Mill at Dartington before renovations. © Lou Brown

© Rob Hopkins

The Totnes Renewable Energy Supply Company (TRESOC): empowering the community

A Transition Towns Energy Workshop in 2007 provided an opportunity to discuss community ownership of renewable energy, leading to the formation of TRESOC, the Totnes Renewable Energy Society. In 2008, TRESOC was registered as an Industrial and Provident Society to ensure the profitable development of renewable energy resources for the benefit of the community of Totnes and 15 neighbouring parishes. Following a protracted period identifying suitable projects, TRESOC is now preparing to launch its Prospectus, offering membership to everyone resident within Totnes and Environs.

There are technologies available to us now to develop commercial supplies of useful energy from renewable resources in the Totnes area, principally from wind, various forms of biomass including waste, and small-scale hydropower plant. To enable everyone to join, the minimum individual shareholding will be £20, up to a maximum of £20,000. Each member will have one vote, regardless of the size of their shareholding, ensuring democratic control of the Society. Shares can only be sold back to the company for their original value, providing protection against takeover or carpet bagging. TRESOC aims to become a locally owned renewable energy utility company, providing healthy, sustainable dividends to members as renewable energy plant comes on line.

All details of the Prospectus and share issue will be made available through the Transition Towns network – watch this space!

TRANSITION IN ACTION

TOTNES & DISTRICT RENEWABLE ENERGY BUDGET

Can Totnes and District Power Itself?

This is the question we will be exploring in this section. Is it feasible that Totnes and District might be able to meet its own energy needs through renewable sources of energy, to take the lead in demonstrating the hugely beneficial impact that localising energy generation would have? What even a cursory look at this question reveals is that if we look at meeting current energy demand the answer is no. Fossil fuels pack an energy punch unprecedented in human history, and they will be irreplaceable. If however, as the Centre for Alternative Technology argue in their 'Zero Carbon Britain' report[19], we are able to 'power down' (i.e. reduce demand) by 50%, then the remaining 50% could be met through renewables ("powering up"). So, let's look at the practicalities of that.

Before we start, there are a few caveats to be borne is mind. This energy budget will not be looking at addressing energy imported in the embodied energy of goods. As outlined in the Energy Security section, this is estimated to currently almost double our UK energy demand per capita. It may well be that to make a comprehensive energy budget, we should take this level of detail into consideration when we look at the capacity for producing the raw materials and industry for these goods in the UK. However for the benefit of simplicity, this EDAP limits any assessment to producing goods locally and quantifying the energy required to provide transport and services based on current usage. On the assumption of limited access to energy, we can assume that we will have considerably less consumer goods available to us in the near future.

Neither will we be looking at the seasonal impact of renewable energy production when assessing whether demand can be met. This is considerable and will be important to develop in further study when building a more detailed budget; when also weighing in the unknowns around climate change bringing in many meteorological variables which would be outside of the scope of this EDAP to bring any degree of accuracy to. We simply present the final assessments of estimated annual demand and renewable energy production to enable a rough estimate of what level of local energy demand could be met locally and weigh in the possible national large-scale production by per capita share.

Similarly this budget does not consider in detail the kinds of energy produced (i.e. fuel type) or the embodied energy of the technology, i.e. the inputs to technological devices such as turbines, before they return a net energy gain. These variables are likely to change considerably over the near future as energy concerns and needs increase and research and innovation in these important issues grows such that current information could be misleading.

3.23 Renewable energy choices in flower pots. © Jacqi Hodgson

We will not be going into extensive detail of possible energy efficiency and reduction in use of energy, except for a cursory exploration of the impact of insulation on space heating and reducing personal transport use. Again there are so many variables, we would get lost in the detail and could also be wildly inaccurate as there are likely to be many developments in societal behaviour and technology; instead we draw some basic conclusions to enable some useful comparisons to be made.

Establishing the Baseline Picture

In 2006, the Totnes Sustainability Group commissioned the Devon Association for Renewable Energy to write the "South Devon Renewable Energy Scoping Study" (hereinafter referred to as the DARE report). Its objective was "to quantify the available renewable energy resources within South Devon, to identify the constraints and opportunities for their implementation, to provide policy makers with the information they need in order to develop policies in this area and specifically to look at Totnes as a case study" [20]. The study focused on technologies then currently available or under development and linked up landscape considerations to the various technologies, so as to enable a realistic identification of the most suitable ones. Given that this excellent piece of work already exists, what we have done here is to adapt, update and add to the DARE report's findings for the Totnes and District area, rather than reinvent the wheel. We are hugely indebted to this detailed and visionary piece of work that was at least 5 years ahead of its time.

The DARE report covered the whole South Hams area, here we have adapted their findings for the Totnes and District area; i.e. the 16 parishes of T&D comprises about 25% of the number of households in the original study area. As it would not be feasible to gather individual household energy usage information, the data used here is based on UK national averages. The demand and consumption data has been updated to 2008 reference data based on Government statistics[21] for average UK energy supply and consumption data and Devon County Council 2008 population and household estimates.

Totnes and District has a considerable proportion of holiday homes and second homes, these have been included in the estimates and totals, as these houses may be part-time occupied and their consumption is probably lower than the average, but their energy production potential will be the same as other houses. Due to increasing scarcity of resources including housing over the next 21 years, we expect these houses may well also become occupied full-time during the timeline 2009 – 2030. If they remain as part time occupied, this would only lead to overestimates of energy needs (which is preferable) rather than underestimates.

In assessing energy demand for Totnes and District, estimates of both per capita and household annual demand are provided to enable a closer understanding of how we use energy. However only the household data is used to estimate the total baseline annual demand and to further calculate changing energy demand of rising projected population over the next 21 years and calculate in probable reductions in demand over the same period. The household data is also used in assessing the potential for annual renewable energy production, (as domestic buildings are an important structure for energy generation) along with landscape and spatial considerations. However non-domestic buildings (which are estimated to number approximately 1,838 in the Building and Housing section of this EDAP) are not included in these calculations as we do not have data for their energy demand and to assess this would be outside the scope of this EDAP. (It can be assumed however that non-domestic buildings will play an important role in energy production over the next 20 years, and this will further increase the ability of T & D to produce power to meet its own needs).

The Totnes and District area has a fairly low level of industrial activity, mostly small light commercial parks. However, the average UK figures take account of UK based industrial activity taking place that provides consumables and manufactured products brought into the South Hams for consumption.

Annual Energy Usage 2008 – Individual / per capita – by Sector

Sector	UK Average Usage Per capita MWh/y	UK Average Usage All persons T & D MWh/y
Electricity	5.75	137,212
Personal Transport	10.83	258,436
Heating, Cooling, Cooking	13.51	322,389
All else (services, goods etc)	0.47	11,216
Annual Total (est.)	30.56	729,253*

30.56 MWh/y equates to 82 kWh/d per capita, significantly less than Prof. David MacKay's figure of 125 kWh/d; however the former is a 2003 figure and would reflect energy consumption pre-installation of domestic renewables and insulation retrofits. To ascertain accurate average consumption in a local area is difficult and so for simplicity the former data is used.

3.24

Estimating Energy Demand in Totnes and District

So How Much Energy is Consumed in Totnes and District Today?

To estimate energy supply and demand, UK national statistics[22] for average consumption are used and calculated using the 2001 Devon County Council census and Family Health Service Estimates (FHSE) 2008 for populations and households in the parishes. Both per capita and household annual estimates are provided and calculated for the district to assist those who wish to understand and estimate individual usage (e.g. individual carbon footprint assessment) and by household (based on an average 3 bed semi).

It is also anticipated that household size is likely to change (from the current 3 bed semi current basis to perhaps larger extended family units of 6-7 persons sharing) during the 21 years of the EDAP timeline. As this is the functional system of domestic energy

use, we may need to revert to per capita estimates to make or adjust future evaluations. However as indicated in Table 3.26, estimates for increasing population based on DCC predictions are calculated as per capita increases, but calculations for increasing energy demand are scaled within limits of likely increases in households, in the context of increasing household size[23]. The DARE / BERR estimates also enable separation of the domestic, transportation, industrial and services usage, information which can further inform the EDAP across the timeline as the relative proportions of these uses are likely to change over the next 21 years

Per capita consumption

So how much energy do we, in Totnes and District each use every year? According to Devon County Council and **FHSE population estimates from 2008, there are 23,863 persons in the 16 parishes of Totnes & District.** If we multiply this by the national average energy consumption for different activities, we get the Table 3.24.

So each one of us, on average, uses around 30 MWh of energy every year. That's a lot of energy. As you can see, the highest use is domestic, cooking, heating and so on, but also our car dependency is also a substantial energy drain.

Per household consumption

It can also be useful to look at energy demand, based per average household. If we turn again to Devon County Council and FHSE, they estimate that there are 9,481 households in the 16 parishes of Totnes & District.

Annual Domestic Energy Consumption
by end use for an average
3 bed semi-detached house[24]

= 22.45* MWh

But what percentage of our total energy demand is used in other sectors? This is easy to establish. UK energy consumption statistics are divided into 4 categories, Domestic, Transport and Services (which includes agriculture) and Industry. Energy distribution is spread across these sectors in the following proportions (see Table 3.25) by DTI / BERR. From the estimation of average domestic use per household, we can calculate estimated sectoral and total consumption in Totnes & District - Table 3.25.

Increasing Population and Energy Efficiency

The population in South Hams is predicated to rise by almost 20% by 2030 from a 2006 baseline. This has substantial implications for energy demand. Similarly development plans are in place to build a number of new houses, to bring people off the current housing lists and to prepare for the increasing population, many of whom will be older people. It is difficult to estimate how all these changes will fit together, however since there is substantial embodied energy in the building of an average 3 bedroom semi[25] and we are entering energy declines, a very conservative (gu)estimate has been made in Table 3.26 of just 519 additional houses being built to cater for

Total Annual Energy Demand (2008) per Household in Totnes & District - by Sector

Sector	Energy use %	Annual demand all households T & D GWh/y	Annual demand all households T & D MWh/y	Annual demand per household MWh/y
Domestic	30%	212.8	212,848*	22.45
Transport	36%	255.4	255,418	26.94
Services	13%	92.3	92,250	9.73
Industry	21%	149.0	148,947	15.71
Total	100%	709.5	709,463*	74.83

See website only Appendix C1 for a break down of estimates of energy per capita and household by parish.
* Please note these totals vary slightly due to the different systems of calculating UK averages

3.25

In 2009 the current total
energy demand for T&D is
709,463 MWh/y (709.46 GWh/y)
based on an average annual usage of all energy of
74.83 MWh/y per household.

By 2030 we anticipate an increase of population
of around 19%
but expect to have achieved a 50%
reduction of total energy demand for T&D to
354,732 MWh/y (354.73 GWh/y)

based on an average annual usage
of all energy of
35.47 MWh/y per household.

these additional needs, since we are likely to be accessing empty 2nd homes and increasing the number of people sharing existing buildings. The estimates in Table 3.26 enable us to calculate the changes in energy demand over the timeline of this EDAP including a phased increase in energy efficiency.

So, in the next section, we will use the following baseline (from Tables 3.24, 3.25 and 3.26) when we try and answer the question, 'can Totnes and District power itself?'

Estimating annual Total Energy demand 2009 – 2030

by Household in Totnes & District in line with predicted increasing population, increasing energy efficiency & energy reduction measures (to achieve ZCB 50% of 2009 demand)

Year	Estimated % population increase[1]	Calculated population (based on estimated % increase)	Est. no. of persons per household[2]	Est. no. of households	Est. total energy demand based on 2008 usage per household 74.83 MWh)			
					Business as Usual Based on 100% usage in 2008 MWh/y	Drop in (2008) energy demand -towards ZCB 50%	Willing to Change Est. total demand T&D WITH % reduction MWh/y	Est. total demand per household with % reduction MWh/y
2008	Baseline	23,863	2.52	9,481	709,463	0%	709,463	74.83
2011	3%	24,579	2.55	9,631	720,688	15%	603,075	62.62
2016	7%	25,533	2.61	9,780	731,837	25%	532,125	54.41
2021	11%	26,488	2.69	9,850	737,076	35%	461,175	46.82
2026	15%	27,442	2.76	9,930	743,062	45%	390,225	39.30
2031	19%	28,397	2.84	10,000	748,300	50%	354,732	35.47 (52.6%)

1 Devon County Council data with TTT calculations of T&D as a percentage (based on 2008) of South Hams population
2 See Population estimates and discussion in 'Joined up Thinking' section

3.26

Estimating Potential for Renewable Energy Supplies in Totnes and District

Introducing the Technologies

The following information deals with the potential energy capture of each technology for T & D based mainly on the information provided in the DARE report. The reader is recommended to refer to the DARE report for the more detailed information about each technology, installation requirements, landscape impact, environmental impact, planning permission, scale and installation costs and pay-back period provided for each technology discussed. As in the DARE report, our focus here is not on what is politically achievable, nor on what is economic in the current economic picture, rather what is possible. Our assumptions, calculations and other details for the figures below appear in (on-line only) Appendix C.

The predicted increase in population is factored in by an estimated increase in the number of houses, i.e. buildings that can be used to generate power.

Large scale renewable technologies which are likely to come on stream are included here for information, and the potential capture which MacKay[26] calculates per capita of the UK population is recalculated for the quota for the population of Totnes & District. N.b. The later predicted increase in population is not factored in, as the general increase in UK population will reduce the per capita share in a similar value to the increase in local share; i.e. it is assumed to roughly balance out.

1. Harnessing Solar Energy

1a Photovoltaics (PV)

Photovoltaic cells convert sunlight into electricity. A large number of these cells, which are made from silicon, are made into panels or tiles, which can be mounted on south-facing roofs. This is a technology that is advancing technologically extremely quickly. The calculation below is based on PV panels.

Potential Annual energy capture from PV for T&D = 16,001 MWh/y in 2008 rising to 16,875 MWh/y by 2030

(Individual household potential gain where suitable = 3.38 MWh/y)

1b Solar Hot Water (SHW)

SHW collectors are either 'flat plate' or 'evacuated tubes'. Flat plate collectors consist of a black surface with water pipes enclosed within an insulated box. This fairly 'low tech.' system can be home made to produce efficiencies of 50-60%. Evacuated tubes collectors comprise a series of twin walled glass tubes enclosing a black collector tube which has a vacuum to reduce heat loss, these can reach efficiencies of 90% but would be impossible to construct at home. The hot water collected is transferred to the domestic hot water system by an additional coil in the hot water tank. They are the most cost-effective micro-renewable on the market at present.

Potential Annual Energy Capture from Solar Hot Water in T&D = 23,703 MWh/y in 2008 rising to 25,000 MWh/y by 2030

(Individual household potential gain = 2.50 MWh/y)

(n.b. All industrial and commercial premises could use SHW as could all the touring campsites and holiday parks. The output from SHW is directly proportional to the area of the collector. One constraint is therefore the area of the collector that can be accommodated, but the main constraint is the summer time demand and hot water storage, unlike electricity in PV, solar heated water is more difficult to move from place to place).

2. Hydropower

Hydropower is the capture of energy in flowing water and can be captured in the following ways:

◎ Micro-hydro – the capture of energy from rainwater runoff flowing in rivers

◎ Tidal lagoon – the capture of energy by the release of water impounded at high tide

◎ Marine current turbines – the capture of energy from tidal streams in the open sea

◎ Wave power – the capture of energy from the movement of water on the surface of the open sea.

N.b. under EU rules, energy generated from offshore resources such as wave and tidal current cannot count towards local RE targets.

2a Micro-Hydro

Turning moving water into energy is a very useful technology. Historically, this area had a number of mills that were used to power industries, mostly those to do with the production of fabrics or paper. The DARE report also speculated that as a consequence of climate change, there may be a need to construct additional reservoirs to retain excess winter rains to supply summer time water needs, this could provide additional micro-hydro potential, however no additional assumptions for power in the calculated capture were made on this basis at this stage. So what is the potential energy that could be generated from hydro?

In the mid 1980's a resource assessment was carried out for micro-hydro across the UK[27], known as the Salford Study. Part 2 of this study lists all sites identified as having a potential with an installed capacity of 25kW or greater (25kW was then considered the smallest size hydro that would be economic to develop). Part 3 lists the rejected sites (i.e. under 25kW). The DARE report researched this report and identified the following sites - Table 3.27.

Then there was another list of sites that were felt by the study to be unfeasible, for the reasons given - Table 3.28.

The DARE report did not investigate these sites, and since the power output is site specific, site flow data has not been calculated for each location. However, it concluded that "it would appear there could be merit in a further study of micro-hydro power at a number of sites" in the area.

We estimate that the annual potential energy capture from the T & D ETSU sites = 2,201 MWh/y

2b Domestic Micro-Hydro

On the basis that as energy shortages encourage householders to explore all possible sources of renewable energy that may be available to them, and taking into account the favourable topography in T & D with many small streams, a very rough estimation below is made on the basis that **0.1% of all households in T & D may be viable for micro-hydro** for electricity use on site. Potential Annual Energy Capture per domestic micro-hydro scheme = 10 MWh/y

Salford Study Results for Totnes and District
Potential hydro-electricity sites - feasible

ETSU No.	River	Site	Head (m)	Installed capacity kW	Annual Energy Capture MWh
046004	Dart	Staverton Mills	2.5	68	441
046005	Dart	Town Mills	2.4	90	430
046006	Dart	Swallowfields Weir	2.9	196	887
046007	Avon	Diptford Manor	3.2	43	221
046009	Avon	Lydia Bridge	6	(49)	25[1]
			Totals	**446**	**2,201**

1 Assessed by Salford Study as having an installed capacity of 49kW and an annual energy capture potential of 247 MWh; however the recently installed turbine has provided a lower actual capture of 25MWh/y

3.27 Source: DARE Report 2006

Salford Study Results for Totnes and District
Potential hydro-electricity sites - unfeasible

River	Site	Reason for rejection
Harbourne	Bow Mill	May be suitable for small scheme
Harbourne	Beenleigh Manor	Operational
Harbourne	Crowdy Mill	Operational
Harbourne	Old Mill	May be suitable for small scheme
Harbourne	Harbertonford	May be suitable for small scheme
Avon	Curtisknowle	Prior use
Garra	Garra Mill	Power under 50kW
Dart (trib.)	Stoke Gabriel	No potential

Source: DARE Report 2006   **3.28**

(DARE). In 2006 DARE conducted a feasibility study on the disused Rattery Corn Mill. They estimated a potential net output of 16MWh/y. Further small mills creating power for direct use in processes such as traditional flour mills, may also enjoy a renaissance, and while this may provide additional benefit in the future, there is no further speculation or assumption here.

Estimated potential
Annual Energy Capture in T&D
= 94.8 MWh/y

2c Tidal Lagoons

The DARE report suggests there may have been several old tidal mills sites in South Devon, however none still operate and all would only generate small amounts of power. A possible constraint is the availability of possible sites and the volume of water a lagoon may hold. A further possible site with a tidal lagoon identified by the DARE report is on the River Dart at Stoke Gabriel. There has been no investigation of this site, so no assumption of potential output is included here.

There may also be scope to capture energy from tidal barrages across all major rivers if climate change results in rising sea levels[28]. A Thames barrier style device to hold back tides and prevent flooding of low-lying areas would allow energy generation on falling tides. The DARE report makes no further assumptions or estimated energy potential from this speculative and uncertain long-term possible energy source in T & D. There is a potential of using Tidal Pools with Pumping as an energy storage system to moderate renewable energy supplies in the grid[29].

The River Dart at Sharpham, below Totnes

Many years ago the riverbank was canalised to create a narrow but deep stream suitable for boats to navigate up to Totnes. The bank created has recently breached and at high tide water inundates the reed beds to the side of this channel. Unless the breach is regulated, the entire length of riverbank may fail and this channel will silt up. However the flow in and out of the reed bed could offer an opportunity to generate power. An early assessment of the Sharpham site indicates that it may be possible to install a 64 kW turbine, which could produce up to **64,000 kWh** of energy annually.

The DARE report also suggests there may be potential for additional capture on the R. Dart at Stoke Gabriel.

Estimated potential
Annual Energy Capture in T & D
= 64 MWh/y

2d Marine Current Turbines

Marine current turbines are similar to wind turbines, but they function under water. Water is 700 times denser than air, so the energy contained in a moving body of water is far greater than air, against this, tidal currents move more slowly. Turbine blades need to withstand the pressure of water and algal growths. The constraints on marine current turbines is the availability of seabed with a high current flow and located close enough to land to allow a shore connection to the grid.

As this is an offshore technology, any energy capture would be fed directly into the grid and would not be included in any T & D local energy targets. The DARE report suggests that Start Point of South Devon could provide a suitable site with adequate current speeds and access to the shore, where 10 turbines together could produce a total of **3,570 MWh/y.** It is possible that once the technology is fully established, unit costs may come down, although in the first instance, other areas with a better energy density are likely to be developed. Once the infrastructure has been put in place, South Devon may benefit as installers seeks additional installations to give greater return on their investments. For more information about the potential for marine current in the South Hams area the DARE report should be referred to. The national potential for this technology is estimated at **9kWh/d** per person by Prof. Mackay[30] who goes on to review the greater possible resource, which could be tapped, based on bottom friction.

(For information only - assessed resource based on per capita share by population in Totnes):

T&D share of estimated national potential of
off-shore marine current farms
= 7,839 MWh/y

2e Wave Power

There are a wide variety of wave energy designs from the 'Pelamis', which comprises a string of sealed floating tubes with a pump at each joint to the oscillating column where water enters the bottom of the vertical tube and compresses trapped air to drive a turbine. The more recent Oyster designed for waters around 12m deep can produce 600kW; these devices may also be used to drive reverse-osmosis desalination plants[31]. Any marine device will need to be strong enough to cope with extreme weather and demonstrate an economic return. The constraints of wave energy are the availability of suitable locations to site devices and bring a power connection to the national grid. A suitable site might be an installation (in addition to marine current devices) at Start Point. There is scope for many devices off the North Cornish coast. Wave energy devices are still very much under development and costs remain high. This energy option is unlikely to contribute to T&D's renewable energy mix in the short term, and as an offshore technology, energy capture will not be countable towards local energy targets. . The national potential for this technology is estimated at **4kWh/ per capita/per day**[32]

(For information only - assessed resource based on per capita share by population in Totnes):

T&D share of estimated national potential for
off-shore wave power
= 3,484 MWh/y

3. Wind Power

Exploiting the power in the wind is an ancient technology and old windmills form part of a picturesque landscape in parts of the country where the absence of high ground eludes the possibility of hydropower. Modern materials and research has improved the design and efficiency of wind turbines offering scope for significant amounts of renewable energy generation. The technical resource is only limited by the size and number of turbines installed. Turbines work by slowing down the wind that passes through the swept area of the blades, but the wind soon recombines and a second turbine can be installed at a distance of about 20 rotor diameters. Wind energy can only be farmed where average wind speeds are high enough and will be confined to those areas with an average wind speed of over 7m/s.

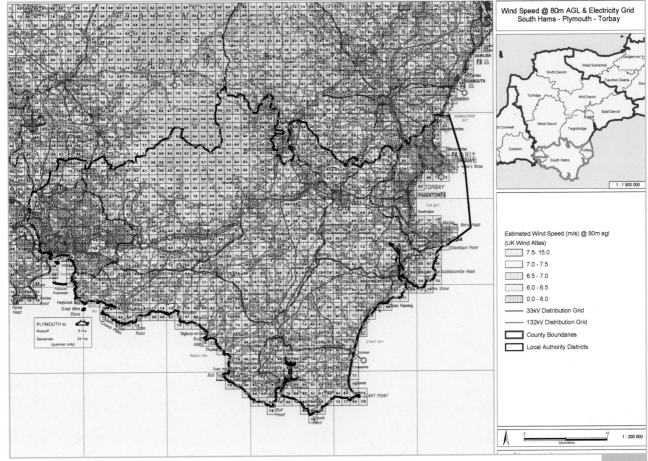

South Hams Wind Resource map. Source: Government Office for the South West   3.29

3a Small-Scale Wind

In South Devon, most of the suitable wind resource capture areas coincide with areas of outstanding natural beauty and Dartmoor National Park. Countryside Character Assessments indicate that South Devon has a moderate sensitivity to large-scale wind turbines and suggests that "for the purposes of this strategic setting exercise, large clusters of turbines have been discounted for reasons of landform scale. Because of the wide views across this incised plateau, consideration should be given to the spacing of turbine clusters to avoid inter-visibility or 'visual clutter'." Modern near silent wind turbines have been developed to be mounted like a TV aerial on rooftops, and there are also a wide range of intermediate sized ones for use on farmsteads and boats.

More realistic than roof mounted turbines for T&D, would be a small number of 5-6 kW machines on 12-15m poles for suitable farms and houses with adequate wind resource (of which there are several in S.Hams)[33].

The following estimate is based on around 1% of all current households being agreeable /suitable for this resource.

Potential Annual Energy Capture
from domestic micro wind in T &D
= 948.1 MWh/y

(Estimated Individual household
potential gain = 5 MWh/y)

3b Large-Scale Turbines / Wind farms

The thorny issue of wind farms is certain to appear and reappear as conventional energy supplies decline. Opinions are often polarised about the appropriateness of large-scale wind turbines. There is no doubt that these tall structures do have an impact on the landscape, they are however the one renewable energy technology that has been developed to the point where it can deliver energy at a comparable cost to current fossil derived energy. The UK has a good wind regime and South Devon a number of areas where, Landscape Designations apart, a significant wind resource could be harnessed. From a purely wind resource perspective, any site that has an average wind speed in excess of 7.5m/s will offer an economically viable site.

Sustainable South Brent has been assessing wind speeds in their area with a view to installing a community wind turbine. They hope to install a 50 kW windmill that would carry a 27meter diameter turbine on a 30m high hub. During 2008 their wind speed measurements indicated a potential yield of 488 MW/h/y. We use their figure below in one of the estimations.

To enable a rough idea of the potential capture of energy from large scale in Totnes & District, the following combination of large-scale wind turbines are assessed:

2 clusters of three 1.3.MW
wind turbines installed
= 17,202 MWh/y

2 single 460 kW
wind turbines installed
= 1,954 MWh/y

20 single 50 kW
wind turbines installed in T&D
= 2,440 MWh/y

Combined output
= 21,596 MWh/y

(For information only - assessed resource based on per capita share by population in Totnes):

National estimated potential
for on-shore wind farms is assessed at
20kWh/per capita/per day[34]

T&D share of estimated national potential for
on-shore wind farms
= 17,420 MWh/y

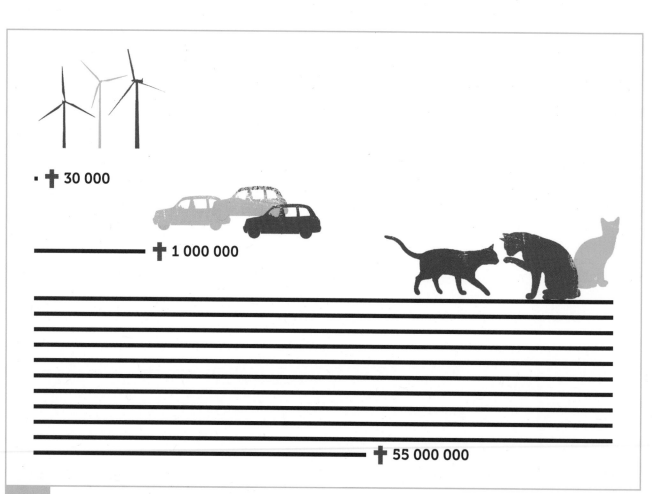

3.30   Birds lost in action. Source: Sustainable Energy Without the Hot Air

3c. Offshore Wind Resource

Totnes and District would not have direct access to benefit for its local energy budget from offshore wind, however such a resource could feed into the grid and benefit the area indirectly. The resource captured will be constrained by the number of turbines installed and the seabed conditions for installation.

(For information only - assessed resource based on per capita share by population in Totnes):

National estimated potential for
offshore wind farms is assessed at
48 kWh/per capita/per day

T&D share of estimated national potential for
off-shore wind farms
= 41,808 MWh/y

4. Biomass

Biomass refers to a wide range of organic material including timber, straw and energy crops. The DARE report looked at set aside land in 2006 as having the potential to produce energy crops, however since that report, the Government announced in 2008 a reduction in set aside to zero to allow that land to come back into full production. As conventional energy supplies decline, there are many competing issues that are likely to be hotly debated when considering land use for energy crops. More land will be brought under cultivation for food production, construction and clothing materials and these changes will also need to take into account local impacts on biodiversity in particular when bringing uncultivated areas back into more intensive productive use.

The enthusiastic interest in crops for biofuels for transport of a few years back has dwindled considerably in the recognition that land in a densely populated country like the UK will not be able to spare the large space this would require.

Biomass Capacity

As specific information about woodland cover and set aside for Totnes and District has not been obtainable, and the district as an area within South Hams is broadly similar, the agricultural statistics in the DARE report have been used and adjusted to scale proportionally. The total landholding area for South Hams is 90,650 hectares (ha.); the area of T & D is approximately (24%) 21,500 hectares.

This therefore indicates the following:

Total no of landholdings (est.) = 372
Landholding area (est.) = 15,549 ha.

52 landholdings with set aside covering (est.)
= 478 ha.

Total woodland cover
(incl. small woodlands of less than 2 ha.) est.
= 755 ha. (~3.5% of total area)

Of which:
181 ha. (est.) is ancient woodland
169 ha. (est.) is coniferous
586 ha. (est.) is deciduous

4a Woodlands

Wood fuel is probably the oldest known fuel to humans and is usually derived as a secondary product from other timber production processes. Anecdotal evidence suggests that on primary clearance, previously unmanaged, mixed woodland can yield 15 tonnes of timber per hectare and thereafter a sustainable 2.5 tonnes per ha per year.

Harvesting woodland

There are 4 primary ways of using timber: as slab wood, logs, woodchip and pellets (see Appx. C for details)

The estimation is that woodland in T &D can be exploited on a sustainable basis and provide in 2008:

1,465 d/tonnes of hardwood}
679 d/tonnes of softwood}
= 2,144 dt/y
= 8,934 MWh

(2008 Individual household potential share
= 0.94 MWh/y = 0.23 dry tonnes of timber/y)

The energy value of this yield will depend upon how the timber is processed. The more handling involved, the higher the cost of the resource and lower the energy balance. To maximise the benefit of harvesting existing woodlands, it will be necessary to develop local markets and timber handling processes that minimise the energy involved in getting timber to the user.

Increasing Woodland Cover by 2030

It is unlikely that much of the former set aside land will be available to plant new woodland. However in line with biodiversity considerations, 30% woodland cover by 2030 has been indicated as desirable and more hedgerow, amenity and garden woodland may be planted. This would mean increasing the current 3.5% current cover by a factor of almost 9. Rather than over assess the energy which may be available on the basis of woodland not yet in existence, this can be considered as a possible bonus at a later stage. However as agriculture reverts to a less intense and less mechanised system and more people are active on the land, and soil erosion may need to be addressed, fields and land areas may be reduced in size; if fields were to be reduced in size by a factor of 4 this could double the length of hedgerow and significantly increase the amount of timber available for wood fuel.

Assuming an increase of woodland cover by 2030 to 14% would quadruple the amount of timber becoming available. However as there is likely to be increased competition for its use for building, we will assume here that only 75% of this is available for fuel:

4,395 d/tonnes of hardwood }
2,037 d/tonnes of softwood }
= 6,432 dt/y
= 26,802 MWh

(2030 Individual household potential share
= 2,68 MWh/y = 0.64 dry tonnes of timber/y)

4b Short Rotation Coppice (SRC)

This term describes a system of harvesting a timber crop. Some tree species can be cut back to a ground level 'crown' and the re-growth of a large number of long thin stems harvested. Coppicing is a well-established method of tree management for fuel, charcoal and fencing. Several species can be used, but Willow (Salix sp) is the most commonly used for energy crops. Once established, stems can be cut back on a 3-year rotation.

SRC is normally harvested in winter when the moisture content is low and can be stored as long stems or chipped. The fuel can be used in 3 ways:

◎ Combustion to provide heat to boil water, produce steam for a turbine to generate electricity

◎ Gasification to produce a combustible gas for burning in an engine or turbine

◎ Pyrolysis to produce gas, oil or charcoal fuels.

(from 478 ha previously set aside) Estimated energy capture potential in T&D = 15,935 MWh/y

4c. Miscanthus

Miscanthus is a perennial grass, originating in the tropics but grows well in the UK climate. Once the rhizomes have been planted and become established, the crop requires minimal inputs, creates a strong root structure (tolerant to tractors) and typically grows to 3 meters high in season. At the end of the growing season, the chlorophyll retracts into the roots leaving just the cellulose stem above ground, this has two benefits; most of the soil nutrients stay in the ground and the stems have very low moisture content at the time of harvesting (Feb./Mar.), typically between 25-30%.

In line with the local topography, yields will vary considerably across the area. Growing over 3m in height, Miscanthus is susceptible to wind damage and is not suitable for areas with an average wind speed over 7m/s. While there are no areas of red (19 dt/ha/y), the more favourable areas are in yellow and green, it therefore reasonable to assume that T&D could sustainably support an average yield of 15 dt/ha/y.

(from 478ha previously set aside)

Estimated Resource in T & D = 29,636 MWh/y

Comparing Short Rotation Coppice and Miscanthus, the latter appears to be the better choice. Although planting costs are higher, the crop needs fewer inputs, converts solar energy more efficiently and has a low moisture level when harvested. Existing farm machinery can be used to harvest and it is not necessary to oven dry the crop to reduce its moisture content. Miscanthus can be left as long stalks, chopped or pelleted and has other uses such as animal bedding, so in some circumstances could be used twice and thereby adding value. It is possible to split areas between SRC and Miscanthus if soil circumstances dictate that one crop is better suited to a particular soil type.

5. Biofuels

The term biofuels refers to a wide range of products derived from organic material, but has generally come to mean liquid fuels intended for transport use. Bio-ethanol is the main replacement for petrol, whilst a variety of animal fats and vegetable oils can be processed into diesel replacement. Bio-ethanol can be produced by fermenting sugar or starch based material such as wheat and sugar beet. Lat-

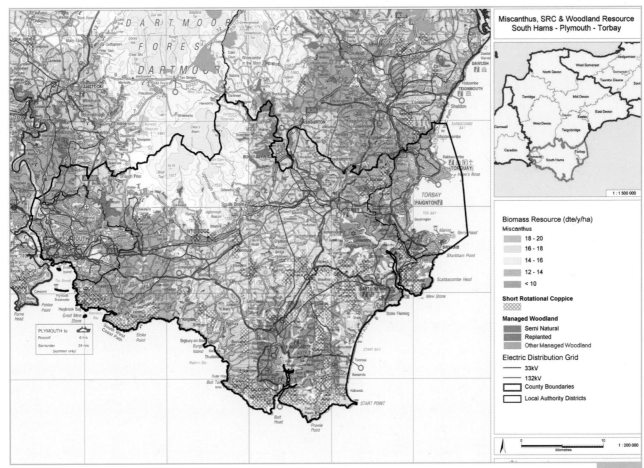

Miscanthus, SRC and Woodland Resource in South Hams. Source: Government Office for the South West   3.31

terly enzymes and other chemical processes have been used to break down cellulose found in plant material to produce alcohol, this opens up the possibility that a wide range of waste stalks and stems, and farming and forestry residues could become the feedstock for petrol replacements.

Bio-diesel can be produced by the trans-esterification of fatty acids from a wide range of plant oils and animal fats. This process is straightforward and the equipment can be purchased to allow small-scale local production. Some diesel engines can burn plant oil direct

5a Oil Seed Rape

Oil seed rape (OSR), which produces a distinctive bright yellow flower in spring, is usually grown for cooking oil. After the oil has been used for some time (e.g. in deep fat fryer), it degrades and is replaced. The old oil is collected and transported for re-processing into bio-diesel. There is a move to include 5% of bio-diesel in all mineral diesel sold at petrol stations. All diesel engines can accommodate

higher levels of biodiesel, some can run on 100% recovered vegetable oil. (N.b. take professional advice before switching fuels in your vehicle).

OSR is already grown in T&D as a commercial crop for use as cooking oil. It needs a number of inputs in terms of tractor operations to prepare the land and fertilizer. The balance between energy output and input is about 2:1. Although this is a positive energy balance, the question needs to be whether such a marginal benefit is the best use of land. It therefore seems likely that OSR will continue to be grown in T&D primarily as a food crop, not as an energy crop. After use as cooking oil, the waste vegetable oil (WVO) will be available for trans-esterification into biodiesel.

(from 478ha previously set aside)
Estimated Available resource in T & D
= 8,374 MWh/y

5b. Bio-Ethanol

Bio-ethanol is derived from fermenting either grain (wheat) or sugar beet into alcohol. This is a tried and tested technology in other parts of the world, particularly Brazil and USA. While there was a good amount of interest in bio-ethanol for vehicle fuel at the time of the DARE report (2006), this has largely been discounted due to the need for all available arable land and food crops to be used for food rather than fuel as the latter is of lower priority can be sourced through other processes. However for the benefit of providing a comprehensive summary of all possible fuel options and to enable considered comparison, the calculations for T&D are included here.

(from 478ha previously set aside)
Estimated Available resource in T & D
(wheat) = 7,287 MWh/y

(from 478ha previously set aside)
Estimated Available resource in T & D
(Sugar beet)= 17,399 MWh/y

It appears that Sugar beet will produce more than twice the energy yield of wheat per hectare.

5c. Energy from Algae

Experimentation is currently underway at Plymouth University. Information is included here for reference only as no data is currently available on the potential energy yield for their work. Algae to diesel energy has a number of steps including providing a CO_2 rich atmosphere and ponds for the algae to grow. Algae to hydrogen has a higher energy yield potential as it is a more direct process, however it requires high electricity inputs and a reactor for processing[35].

The algae to bio-diesel potential for energy production corresponds to a power unit pond area of 4W/m2 (similar to a Bavarian PV farm – 5W/m2).

The algae to hydrogen potential for energy production is 3.6 W/m2

Assuming some low-level development of this technology will take place in T&D during the next 21 years. For example on 5ha of flooded land no longer viable for food growing (e.g. at Dartington and ATMOS): Estimated Available resource in T & D from algae to biodiesel possibly 5 ha flooded land = 175.2 MWh/y

N.b. This technology may become important in0 carbon sequestration / removing carbon from the atmosphere.

Summarising Energy Crops

A straightforward comparison of the four main annual crops is difficult, whilst energy balance data is available for some crops, it is not for all. It seems reasonable to assume that all annual energy crops will need multiple tractor operations to plough, cultivate, sow, fertilise and harvest the crop so the energy balance for annual crops with a low yield may be marginal at best or negative. Further assessment should be undertaken to gain a more detailed breakdown of the energy inputs and outputs for bio-ethanol produced from annual energy crops[36].

Purely from an energy balance perspective using the set aside land, Miscanthus appears to be the crop of choice (and is therefore the data included in the energy totals in Table 3.32) as the other energy crops would be in competition for the same land. There will be multiple tractor operations in the first year to cultivate the ground, plant the crop and spraying to prevent weeds until the crop is established. But being a perennial crop, in subsequent years, the only input will be the single tractor operation to harvest the crop. Anecdotal evidence suggests Miscanthus can survive in the same plot of ground for 20+ years.

Algae to bio-diesel and algae to hydrogen are currently experimental but do offer productive use of flooded land, which is no longer viable for buildings or food growing or building.

Energy crops are generally regarded as 'carbon neutral', i.e. they only release the carbon absorbed when growing and therefore do not contribute new carbon to the atmosphere, but the energy capture per hectare is low. Energy from algae however utilises an enriched carbon atmosphere pumped into the pond and could be beneficial to carbon capture processes.

Comparing the energy capture from energy crops with other renewable technologies:

◎ One hectare of Miscanthus could produce 62,000 kWh/y

◎ One hectare of PV could produce 1,250,000 kWh/y (creating a significant 'heat island')

◎ One single 1.3 MW wind turbine could produce 2,867,400 kW/y (& most of the land remain available for planting)

6. Energy from Waste

The term 'waste' needs to be used with caution as nothing is wasted in nature. The by-products from one process are used as the raw material for the next. In this context waste is the collective name we call the organic material we no longer have a use for. It comprises the contents of our dustbins (after recyclables have been separated), kitchen waste, human faeces, animal slurries, animal by-products and food processing wastes. We also include here used waste cooking oil.

6a. Anaerobic Digestion (AD)

All organic material degrades quite naturally if oxygen is present, by what is known as an aerobic process and is familiar to us as composting. If oxygen is excluded, by enclosing the process in a sealed chamber, the process is known as anaerobic. The advantage of using an enclosed chamber is that the by-products of organic breakdown (methane) can be captured easily. The methane can then be used as a fuel. If the source material is predominantly wet, a process of anaerobic digestion can be used. If the source material is predominantly dry a process of gasification can be used.

The waste streams considered here are:

◎ Municipal solid waste (incl. commercial waste arisings)

◎ Animal slurries

◎ Sewage sludge

All anaerobic digestion processes rely on naturally occurring bacteria and enzymes to breakdown the source material. Some bacteria work better at 35 de-

grees C, others better at 56 degrees C. Lower temperature bacteria take about 7 weeks to work, the higher temperature bacteria take about 2 weeks, but are fussier about the consistency of the feedstock. There are a number of different systems based on variations on AD, each with advantages and disadvantages according to the different circumstances they may be required to operate within.

Anaerobic digestion produces both heat and power (CHP/Combined Heat & Power). Based on the DARE calculation for CHP plants (see 7) a 2:1 ratio of heat:power is delivered at CHP plants

6a(i). Municipal Waste

Statistics show 70% of waste arisings go to landfill and 30% is recycled or composted

**Estimated potential resource in T & D
= 23,886 MWh**

However this is the value for raw Municipal Solid Waste (MSW) that is made up of kitchen waste and other dry waste such as paper.

Using the **Ludlow Experience**[37] and translating their analysis to T&D

**Estimated Available resource in T & D 2008
= 5,316 MWh/y**

Rising by 2030 to 5,607 MWh/y

6a(ii). Animal slurries

Methane emissions from manures and slurry management make up 14% of the total methane emissions from livestock husbandry in the UK. The most promising option for the exploitation of manures and slurries to reduce greenhouse emissions is the controlled generation and recovery of methane from slurry systems through anaerobic digestion[38].

It is very difficult to assess accurately the available resource, as information is needed on the number of animals in the holdings, how the animals are housed (i.e. how the slurry may be collected). It has not been possible to quantify how much slurry would be available for AD. Instead a guide is taken from comparison with the Holsworthy Biogas Plant.

Holsworthy Biogas Ltd collects cattle slurry from 30 miles within a 20 km radius and food waste from food processing plants. This company has two 0.9 MW generators fuelled by the methane gas collected from the digesters. There is sufficient gas to maintain one engine working full time and the second engine part time. The AD process is very effective in killing pathogens and weeds; the liquid digestate is available to be returned to the farms as a liquid fertiliser. The electricity generator and its exhaust provide the heat needed for the plant, and the excess is piped to Holsworthy less than 2 miles away where it heats the hospital, the health centre, 2 schools, a sports hall, the council offices and 150 homes[39].

Scaled down to T&D, it is estimated that a similar plant could produce = 18,720 MWh/y

6a(iii). Sewage Sludge

Previously, the technical expertise required to maintain anaerobic digesters coupled with high capital costs and low process efficiencies had limited the level of its industrial application as a waste treatment technology. Anaerobic digestion facilities have, however, been recognised by the United Nations Development Programme as one of the most useful decentralised sources of energy supply, as they are less capital intensive than large power plants[40].

Sewage treatment is a significant user of energy requiring about 50kWh/y per person. An investigation in Queensland, Australia demonstrated that the dilute feedstock (compared with other bio solids stream normally used for AD) could convert the suspended organic solids by 66% to methane[41]. Sewage plants are capable of producing energy: electricity and fuel from sewage gas, and heat from wastewater and combined heat and power plants. The resulting digestate can be recycled back onto the agricultural land. The digestate can carry heavy metals according to the industrial component of the catchment area (agricultural land where the digestate is recycled is therefore monitored for heavy metals), however this is not a high risk in T & D.

Totnes Waste water and sewage treatment plant*. Production = 417 MWh/y electricity (used on site)[42].

Based on the DARE calculation for CHP plants (see 7) where a 2:1 ratio of heat: power is delivered at CHP plants.

Estimated Available resource in T & D 2008 = 1,251 MWh/y

Rising by 2030 to 1,388.61 MWh/y

*This plant also **produces heat** some of which is currently used on site. Currently this is used to heat the site offices and as these are then too hot in the summer months, energy is used to cool the offices. This could be used to heat water for nearby houses as a **CHP system**.

6b. Gasification & Pyrolysis

Gasification & Pyrolysis are advanced thermal processes for the disposal of any combustible material. Historically incineration has been used to dispose of waste, however there are concerns that this process can release highly toxic dioxins (carcinogens) into the atmosphere as well as not making best use of the heat generated. Feedstocks include: municipal solid waste, refuse derived fuel, miscanthus, clinical waste, old tyres, sewage sludge cake, animal litter, animal by-products (rendered) and various plant residues such as palm oil husks.

Gasification takes place when combustible material is heated up within a sealed chamber where most of the oxygen has been excluded. Incomplete combustion takes place so the gases given off still retain the ability to burn when they come into contact with a further supply of oxygen. The gases are piped away as a fuel.

Pyrolysis takes place where combustible material is heated up in the complete absence of oxygen. The heating breaks down the material into its basic components some of which form the basis of a fuel. Gasification and pyrolysis work best with dry materials. Wet material uses some of the energy to burn off moisture before the process can start.

It is highly unlikely that any kind of incineration plant would be acceptable in T&D, however for the benefit of completeness and to demonstrate the energy potential from current waste residues (which are expected to reduce as plastics – oil based - decline in the waste stream) potential energy generation based on this process is detailed.

Municipal Waste (MSW)
- Estimated potential energy capture T & D
= 18,466 MWh

Commercial Waste
- Estimated potential energy capture T & D
= 4,988 MWh

There would be other feedstocks available for the above energy from waste producing technologies such as construction industry waste, abattoir waste etc. but data is not currently available.

6c. Combined Heat & Power (CHP)

Combined heat and power is a generic term used to describe a process that produces energy in a more efficient way. CHP is not a renewable energy, it is a conversion technology able to make more efficient use of other renewable energy sources. When any combustible fuel is burned the primary energy given off is heat. The heat can either be used to drive a diesel generator or to heat water to make steam to drive a steam turbine. Approximately 1/3 of the energy in the primary fuel is converted into power whilst 2/3 remains as heat. The power can be transmitted many miles in the form of electricity along power lines. The further electricity is transmitted, the more power is lost. Energy as heat can be transmitted in the form of hot water in pipes, but however well insulated, heat is eventually lost. Unless there is a use for the heat close to the power generating station, this heat is frequently wasted via large cooling towers. As noted above in 6a, anaerobic digestion, Totnes Sewage Works produces CHP, but currently wastes a lot of the heat, as it does not have a suitable nearby use at present.

CHP seeks to overcome the inefficiencies inherent with centralised power generation by installing a smaller scale generating plant close to where both heat and power are needed. Any combustible fuel source can be used, so it is perfectly possible to have a logwood, woodchip or pellet boiler to heat water to drive a generator and the residual heat used in nearby properties. New CHP gas boilers are available for domestic properties, however current grid gas CHP is not renewable energy, simply a more efficient way of using fossil fuel. (This may change with Language coming on line at some point, natural gas could drive heat pumps; no data exists to assess this further at this stage)

The Bedzed project in South London uses waste timber from the construction industry and arboreal waste from trimming the city trees; the plant has been sized to supply all the local electricity needs so when demand is low, the surplus is sold to the grid[43].

Available resource in T & D: based on more efficient use of other renewable energy sources

Assuming the CHP plant is 90% efficient, **77,387 MWh could be delivered as an alternative** to the individual contribution from the various renewable energies listed (see Table 6c in - on-line only - Appendix C)

Of this:67% would be delivered as heat
= 51,784 MWh/y

33% as power
= 25,603 MWh/y

(N.b. NOT included in Table 3.32 - already accounted for under the separate sources)

6d. Recycled Waste Cooking oil

Totnes Rickshaw Company has made a rough assessment of 2,500 litres of waste cooking oil being available from local food commercial outlets each month for recycling into vehicle fuel. Some of this is already being processed and used in their 2 rickshaw taxis. Production is set to increase (2009) when they move into the woodshed at Sharpham as a pilot larger production system to supply fuel for more vehicles including agricultural vehicles.

Estimated Available resource in T & D
= 175.97 MWh/y

6e. Grape Seed Waste

This has also recently been considered in Totnes for its waste oil value. Sharpham Estate at Ashprington produces around 8,000 litres of wine each year with a high tonnage of residual grape seeds that are currently disposed of. Information about the energy inputs to crush the seeds and produce oil is not yet available. A preferred use of this high-grade oil may be for body therapy and cosmetic products. No estimation for this resource as an energy fuel is offered here.

Summary of Potential Renewable Energy Capture in Totnes & District

Energy Source	Technology	Potential Energy Capture				CO_2 saved @ 0.43 kg/ kWh (2009/2030)
		T&D 2009 MWh/y	T&D 2030 MWh/y	Nat. RE MWh/y	Int. RE MWh/y	
Solar	1a Photovoltaics (PV)	16,001	16,875			6.89 /7.12
	1b Solar Hot Water	23,703	25,000			10.19 /10.55
Rivers & streams	2a Micro-hydro -ETSU	2,201	2,201			0.96
	2b Micro-hydro domestic	94.8	94.8			0.04
Tidal	2c Tidal Lagoons	64	64			0.03
Marine	2d Marine Current			7,839		33.71
	2e Wave Energy			3,484		14.98
Wind	3a Small Scale (Micro)	948.1	948.1			0.40
	3b Large Scale On-shore	21,596	21,596	17,420		16.46
	3c Lg.Offshore Turbines			41,808		17.64
Solar-Bio-mass	4a Woodlands	8,934	26,802			3.84 /11.31
	4b Short Rotation Crop	15,935	15,935			6.85
	4c Miscanthus	29,636	29,636			12.74
	5a Oil Seed Rape	8,374	8,374			3.6
	5b Bio-ethanol - wheat	7,287	7,287			3.13
	5b Bio-ethanol – S. beet	17,399	17,399			7.48
	5c Algae to bio-diesel	0	175.2			0 /110.2
Anaerobic Digestion bio waste	6a AD Kitchen waste	5,316	5,607			2.24 /2.37
	6a AD Animal Slurry	18,720	18,720			7.9
	6a AD Sewage Sludge	1,251	1,388.61			0.53 /0.59
Waste plastics & organics	6b Gasification (MSW)	18,466				7.79
	6b Gasification (Comm.)	4,988				2.10
Waste Oil	6d Cooking oil - biodiesel	175.97	175.97			0.7
Solar	7 Heat Pumps	9,343	14,467			3.94 /6.10
	8. Solar from deserts				64,780.7	0 /27.33
Sub-Total (MWh/y)		137,983.87	163,750.68	70,551	64,780.7	133.19 / 281.13
Total (GWh/y)		138	163.8	70.6	64.8	

Not counted as feasible technologies in T & D
Not counted as would occupy land otherwise selected for biomass production

3.32

7. Heat Pumps

A heat pump works like a refrigerator, but in reverse, drawing heat in. A closed loop of pipe contains a liquid that evaporates and condenses at low temperature. One side of the pipe may be buried in the ground (ground sourced heat pump – GSHP), placed in a stream of flowing water (water sourced heat pump – WSHP) or be placed in a stream of moving air (air sourced heat pump – ASHP), where it collects a large quantity of low temperature energy from its surroundings. The pump that circulates the liquid around the loop compresses the liquid and delivers a smaller quantity of high temperature liquid where the heat is needed. The cycle is then repeated.

Depending on the level of temperature rise needed, it is possible for a 1 kW pump to absorb and deliver up to 4 kW of heat from a low grade temperature source to a heating system. Heat pumps are a renewable energy technology because although they need an external source of energy to power them, they collect solar energy from the ground, water or air.

Estimated Available resource (saving)
in T & D in 2009
= 9,343 MWh/y

Rising by 2030 to 14,467 MWh/y

(Individual household potential gain
= 19.71 MWh/y)

8. Solar Power from the Deserts

Importing renewable energy from other countries may be a future viable option for over-crowded countries like the UK. This type of technology and political arrangement is well beyond current options and is therefore reduced by a factor of 20 even for 2030. Solar power from the deserts is estimated by Mackay[44] to have the potential to provide 125k/day/per capita

(For information only - assessed resource based on per capita share by population in Totnes):

International estimated potential for solar power from deserts is assessed at 125kWh/per capita/per day[45]

T&D share of estimated
available resource by 2030
= 64,780.7 MWh/y

Summary

Totnes & District Baseline estimated total DEMAND of all energy
= 709.5 GWh/y in 2009

reducing to 354.7 GWh/y by 2030
(in line with ZCB 50%)

T & D Baseline estimated potential RENEWABLE ENERGY PRODUCTION
= 138 GWh/y in 2009

rising to 163.8 GWh/y by 2030

(2030 T&D estimated total renewable energy production
INCLUDING per capita share of National potential large scale renewable energy capture
= 234.4 GWh/y)

(2030 T&D estimated total renewable energy production
INCLUDING per capita share of National + International potential large scale renewable energy capture
= 299.2 GWh/y)

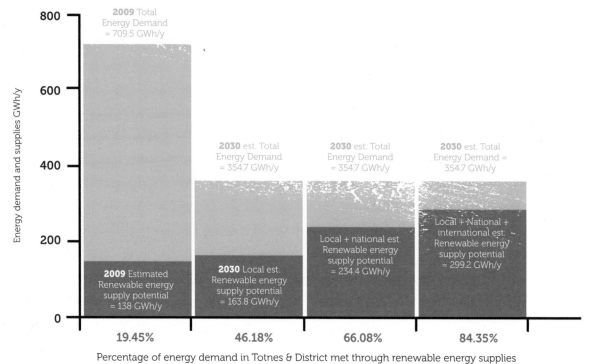

Meeting energy demand in Totnes and District from potential Renewable Energy Supplies

2009 Total Energy Demand = 709.5 GWh/y

2030 est. Total Energy Demand = 354.7 GWh/y

2030 est. Total Energy Demand = 354.7 GWh/y

2030 est. Total Energy Demand = 354.7 GWh/y

2009 Estimated Renewable energy supply potential = 138 GWh/y

2030 Local est. Renewable energy supply potential = 163.8 GWh/y

Local + national est. Renewable energy supply potential = 234.4 GWh/y

Local + National + international est. Renewable energy supply potential = 299.2 GWh/y

Energy demand and supplies GWh/y

19.45% 46.18% 66.08% 84.35%

Percentage of energy demand in Totnes & District met through renewable energy supplies

3.33   Meeting energy demand in Totnes and District from potential Renewable Energy Supplies

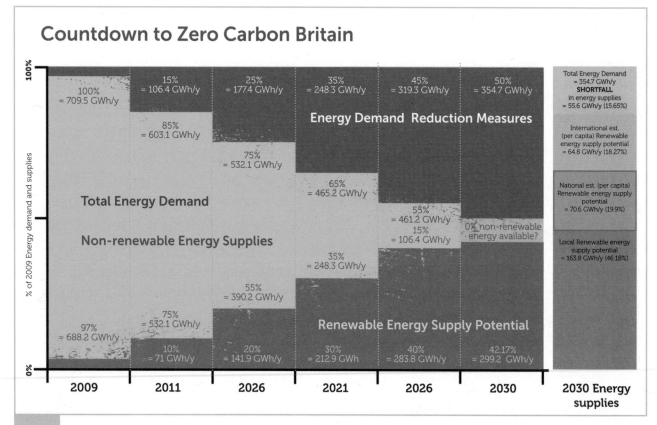

Countdown to Zero Carbon Britain

% of 2009 Energy demand and supplies

100% = 709.5 GWh/y

15% = 106.4 GWh/y
25% = 177.4 GWh/y
35% = 248.3 GWh/y
45% = 319.3 GWh/y
50% = 354.7 GWh/y

85% = 603.1 GWh/y

75% = 532.1 GWh/y

Energy Demand Reduction Measures

65% = 465.2 GWh/y

55% = 461.2 GWh/y
15% = 106.4 GWh/y

0% non-renewable energy available?

Total Energy Demand

Non-renewable Energy Supplies

35% = 248.3 GWh/y

55% = 390.2 GWh/y

97% = 688.2 GWh/y

75% = 532.1 GWh/y

Renewable Energy Supply Potential

10% = 71 GWh/y
20% = 141.9 GWh/y
30% = 212.9 GWh
40% = 283.8 GWh/y
42.17% = 299.2 GWh/y

2009 2011 2026 2021 2026 2030

2030 Energy supplies

Total Energy Demand = 354.7 GWh/y
SHORTFALL in energy supplies = 55.6 GWh/y (15.65%)

International est. (per capita) Renewable energy supply potential = 64.8 GWh/y (18.27%)

National est. (per capita) Renewable energy supply potential = 70.6 GWh/y (19.9%)

Local Renewable energy supply potential = 163.8 GWh/y (46.18%)

3.34   Meeting energy demand in Totnes and District across the timeline as demand decreases and renewable energy supplies increase

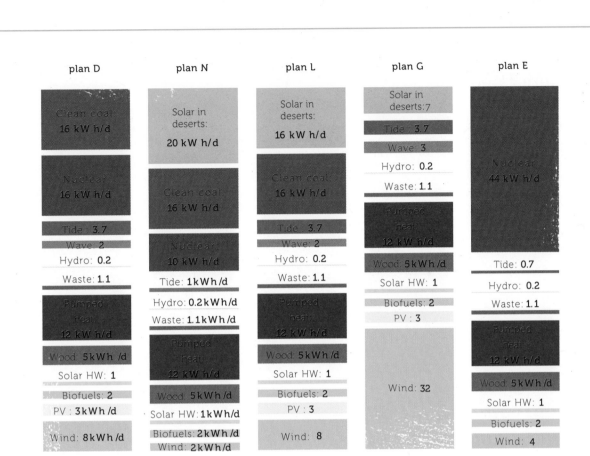

plan D	plan N	plan L	plan G	plan E
Clean coal: 16 kW h/d	Solar in deserts: 20 kW h/d	Solar in deserts: 16 kW h/d	Solar in deserts: 7	Nuclear 44 kW h/d
Nuclear: 16 kW h/d	Clean coal: 16 kW h/d	Clean coal: 16 kW h/d	Tide: 3.7	
Tide: 3.7	Nuclear: 10 kW h/d	Tide: 3.7	Wave: 3	
Wave: 2	Tide: 1kWh/d	Wave: 2	Hydro: 0.2	
Hydro: 0.2	Hydro: 0.2kWh/d	Hydro: 0.2	Waste: 1.1	
Waste: 1.1	Waste: 1.1kWh/d	Waste: 1.1	Pumped heat 12 kW h/d	Tide: 0.7
Pumped heat 12 kW h/d	Pumped heat 12 kW h/d	Pumped heat 12 kW h/d	Wood: 5kWh/d	Hydro: 0.2
Wood: 5kWh /d	Wood: 5kWh/d	Wood: 5kWh /d	Solar HW: 1	Waste: 1.1
Solar HW: 1	Solar HW: 1kWh/d	Solar HW: 1	Biofuels: 2	Pumped heat 12 kW h/d
Biofuels: 2	Biofuels: 2kWh/d	Biofuels: 2	PV : 3	Wood: 5kWh /d
PV : 3kWh/d	Wind: 2kWh/d	PV : 3	Wind: 32	Solar HW: 1
Wind: 8kWh/d		Wind: 8		Biofuels: 2
				Wind: 4

5 Possible Energy Budgets. Source: Sustainable Energy Without the Hot Air   3.35

Zero Carbon Britain?

Can we meet the challenge and by the year 2030 manage on 50% of current energy demand produced by renewable supplies[46]? As can be seen above there is a large shortfall of 53.82% of energy if we rely only on locally produced renewable energy and a smaller but very substantial shortfall of 33.92% if we rely on locally and nationally produced renewables. In other words it seems we may only get just about half way there with current renewable technologies in the UK. If we have access to international, less populated country's' surplus of renewable energy we may be able to get closer to meeting our estimated demand with a much lower shortfall of around 15.65%.

Generating local Renewable Energy to Meet Local Needs - Getting There

As has already been identified in the DARE report 2006 and also in this plan, reduction in demand and power supply will need to be achieved through gradual steps. This enables a timeline to be generated for renewable energies coming on stream against declining (fossil fuel) conventional supplies and rising carbon emissions.

Our estimates indicate that we may face a serious shortfall in energy supplies by 2030 as follows:

Supplying T & D with 50% of 2009 demand

Total energy required =   354.8 GWh/y

(50% of 2008 demand reduction measures
= 354.7 GWh/y)

(0%) conventional supplies = 0 GWh/y

(50%) Renewable supplies =   354.8 GWh/y

Short fall of 55.6 GWh/y

Can we Meet Local Domestic Demand from Power Generated on our own Houses?

Here we consider the potential for meeting local energy demand at the district and household level from power produced on individual houses. We have used the calculations from earlier in this section, which provide the potential energy generation from different types of domestic scale renewable energy generators and put these together to see what total amounts these arrive at.

The figures we have used can be further calculated to make assessments for farms, parishes etc.

District: Can we meet the total local domestic energy demand* for Totnes & District from power generated on all suitable houses?

**The highest amount we can calculate in is
58.95 GWh/y = 27.7% by 2030**

See diagram 3.34 (Calculated from 2008 T & D baseline Total Domestic Household demand* = 212.8 GWh/y)[47]

Individual Households: Can we meet individual household domestic demand* from power generated on our own houses?

**The most we can calculate is
25.59 MWh/y = 114% by 2030**

See diagram 3.34 (calculated from T & D 2008 average Domestic Household demand* = 22.45 MWh/y)

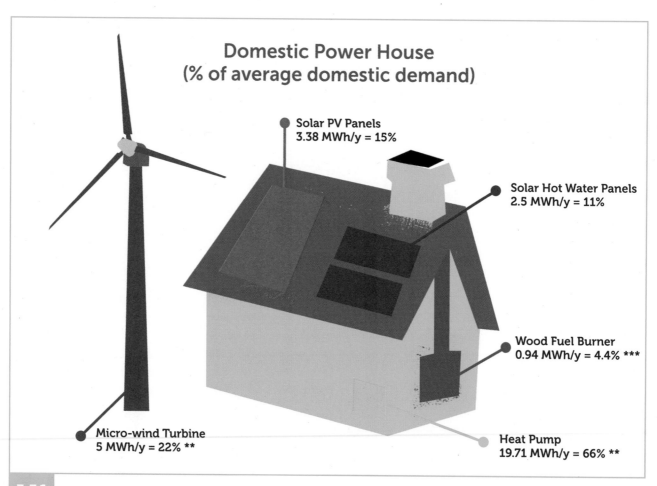

Domestic Power House
(% of average domestic demand)

Solar PV Panels
3.38 MWh/y = 15%

Solar Hot Water Panels
2.5 MWh/y = 11%

Wood Fuel Burner
0.94 MWh/y = 4.4% ***

Micro-wind Turbine
5 MWh/y = 22% **

Heat Pump
19.71 MWh/y = 66% **

3.36 Domestic Power House: Meeting Individual Domestic House Energy Demand Through Renewable Energy Production on Site.

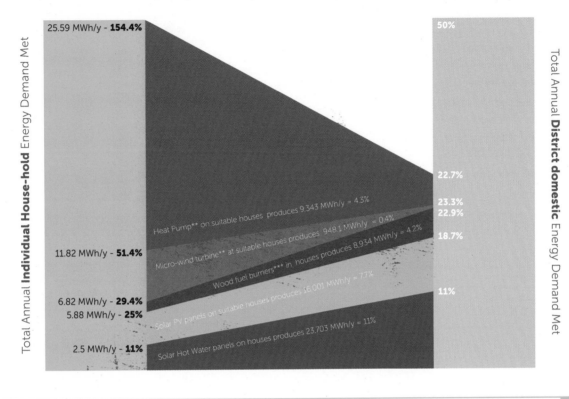

Producing Local Renewable Energy: Meeting domestic energy demands from power generated on our own houses?

*Total Annual **Individual House-hold** Energy Demand Met*

25.59 MWh/y - **154.4%**

11.82 MWh/y - **51.4%**

6.82 MWh/y - **29.4%**
5.88 MWh/y - **25%**

2.5 MWh/y - **11%**

Heat Pump** on suitable houses produces 9,343 MWh/y = 4.3%

Micro-wind turbine** at suitable houses produces 948.1 MWh/y = 0.4%

Wood fuel burners*** in houses produces 8,934 MWh/y = 4.2%

Solar PV panels on suitable houses produces 16,001 MWh/y = 7.7%

Solar Hot Water panels on houses produces 23,703 MWh/y = 11%

*Total Annual **District domestic** Energy Demand Met*

50%

22.7%

23.3%
22.9%

18.7%

11%

Calculated from T&D average household demand

3.37

Notes for these calculations and diagrams:

Seasonal and weather fluctuations as well as energy storage capacity will have a substantial impact on energy production and benefit at individual household level.

* per household use of electricity (appliances etc) + hot water + space heating ONLY = 30% of total energy demand

** not all houses in T & D are suitable for this technology

*** estimated share available in T & D (An average domestic wood burning stove installed in a fully insulated house is estimated to use between 6-7 tonnes of wood fuel a year).

Household Emergy – Embodied Energy

Embodied energy (or emergy) is defined as the available energy that was used in the work of making a product. Embodied energy is an accounting methodology which aims to find the sum total of the energy necessary for an entire product lifecycle. For any product, including a house, this lifecycle includes raw material extraction, transport, manufacture, assembly, installation, disassembly, deconstruction and/or decomposition.

Different methodologies produce different understandings of the scale and scope of application and the type of energy embodied. Some methodologies account for the energy embodied in terms of the oil that supports economic processes.

See Adam's Table of Household Emergy 3.39.

Breakdown of potential Renewable Energy Capture in T&D by 2030 by type of power / fuel

Energy Source & Technology	Approx power generation efficiency %	Potential total renewable energy capture T&D 2009 - 2030 MWh/y	Power / fuel type (at 100% efficiency)				National & International renewables supplied as power to grid
			Heat / hot water MWh/y	Methane MWh/y	Bio-diesel MWh/y	Electricity MWh/y	
Photovoltaics (PV)	18-25	16,001 16,875				16,001 16,875	
Solar Hot Water	50-60	23,703 25,000	23,703 25,000				
Micro-hydro -ETSU	V	2,201				2,201	
Micro-hydro domestic	V	95				95	
Tidal Lagoons	V	64				64	
Marine Current	V						7,839
Wave Energy	V						3,484
Wind: Small Scale	V	948				948	
Large Scale On-shore	V	21,596				21,596	17,420
Lg.Offshore Turbines	V						41,808
Woodlands	90	8,934 26,802	5,986 17,957			2,948 8,845	
Short Rotation Crop	90	15,935	10,676			5,259	
Miscanthus	90	29,636	19,856			9,780	
Oil Seed Rape	90	8,374			8,374		
Bio-ethanol - wheat	90	7,287			7,287		
Bio-ethanol – S. beet	90	17,399			17,399		
Algae to bio-diesel	90	0 175			0 175		
AD Kitchen waste	90	5,316 5,607	3,562 3,757	1,754 1,850			
AD Animal Slurry	90	18,720	12,542	6,178			
AD Sewage Sludge	90	1,251 1,389	838 931	413 458			
Gasification (MSW)	90	18,466	12,372	6,094			
Gasification (Comm.)	90	4,988	3,342	1,646			
Waste cooking oil	95	176			176		
Heat Pumps	75	9,343 14,467	9,343 14,467				
Solar from deserts	?						64,780.7
Sub-Total (MWh/y)		137,984 163,751	75,830 94,510	8,345 8,486	176 351	53,633 60,404	135,331.7
Total (GWh/y)		138 (2009) 163.8 (2030)					(2030) 135.3

Not counted as feasible technologies in T & D
Not counted as would occupy land otherwise selected for biomass production

3.38

Emergy Evaluation of Single Family Residential Unit

Note	Item	Data Units / year	Unit	Unit Solar Emergy (sej/unit)	Solar Emergy (E13 sej/yr)
		Renewable Inputs			
1	Sunlight	5.93E+13	J	1	6
2	Rain (chemical potential)	2.71E+10	J	3.02E+04	82
3	Wind (kinetic energy)	2.36E+11	J	9.83E+02	23
		Non-renewable Storages Used			
4	Net Topsoil Loss	4.52E+07	J	1.24E+05	1
		Purchased Units			
5	Natural Gas	3.29E+10	J	1.11E+05	365
6	Electricity	6.22E+06	J	2.69E+05	167
7	Water	3.61E+09	gal.	3.00E+05	108
8	Food	4.19E+07	J	3.36E+06	14
9	Goods	1.50E+04	$	1.10E+12	1650
10	Pesticides	1.59E+04	g	2.52E+10	40
11	Phosphate	8.44E+03	gP	3.70E+10	31
12	Nitrogen	2.26E+04	gN	4.05E+10	91
13	Construction materials	3.04E+07	g	1.55E+09	4712
Sum of Non-renewable & Purchased Inputs					7180 (1.5 units/ha = 10770)

Please see (on line only) Appendix C for details of notes and calculations

Emergy Evaluation of Single Family Residential Unit by Adam Dadeby

3.39

Reducing Energy Demand Through Energy Efficiency Measures

The Zero Carbon Britain (ZCB) report[48] estimates that by 2030 we need to have reduced our energy demand by 50% through energy efficiency measures.

To what extent can energy efficiency in the home reduce our domestic energy demand?

Space heating is by far the biggest use of domestic energy and this is where the best possibilities of energy efficiency occur. Through major retrofitting with insulation to existing buildings, and building all new houses to Transition Sustainable Homes code (see Building and Housing Section), we can save 53% of domestic energy demand. Applying additional energy efficiency measures such as behavioural changes (switching off the lights, TV etc when not in use) and changing to energy efficient lighting we can bring this saving to 58% of current demand[49].

Remaining total energy demand T&D
= 125.3 GWh   A total saving of 58%

The above estimates are based on a house heated to 21 degrees in the living room with other rooms correspondingly warm (World Health Organisation standards). For every degree we turn the home heating thermostat down, heat loss decreases by 10% and the savings in heating power will be even higher[50].

New Buildings

We can assume that all new housing built from 2009 on will have full insulation and energy efficiency standards. However new buildings carry high embodied energy (in 2006 housing consumed 52% of UK energy demand and contributed 25% of CO_2 emissions[51]. We have calculated that to build 519 standard[52] houses over the next 21 years would require 21.8 GWh of energy (i.e. 17% of total domestic energy demand). The energy to build these new houses would usually be included under services and industrial data and therefore will not be included in our local domestic demand calculations. It is included here to indicate the amount of embodied energy.

District Heating

Table 3.38 indicates that a high proportion of the local renewable energy is produced as heat or hot water.

Estimated potential of renewable energy produced in T & D as heat or hot water:

(75,830÷137,984=) 54.9% in 2009
rising to (94,510÷163,751=) 57.7% by 2030

While this heat can be converted to produce electricity, this process does lose some energy; it is therefore more efficient to use heat directly whenever possible. Where there are larger amounts of heat or hot water produced this can be used on site or piped to nearby buildings to provide district heating. The Holsworthy Biogas plant discussed under 6a(ii) demonstrates how effective this can be. However this relies on close proximity of power generation plants to buildings needing heat and well-insulated pipes. (This principle could also be applied to heated effluents from industrial units; this latter option has not been further explored in this EDAP, due to the low level of industrial activity in the area)

Estimating reduction in annual energy demand for transportation for Totnes & District as population increases but access to personal motorised transport decreases

Year	Estimated % population increase[1]	Calculated population with estimated % increase	Total Energy demand for Transport in T & D			
			Business as Usual Based on 2008 usage (100%) at 10.83 MWh/y	Est. % reduction in energy for all personal motorised transportation	Willing to Change Est. demand T&D WITH energy efficiency MWh/y	Average total demand per household MWh/y
2008	Baseline	23,863	258,436	Baseline 0%	258,436	27.26[2]
2011	3%	24,579	266,191	30%	186,333	19.35
2016	7%	25,533	276,522	50%	138,261	14.14
2021	11%	26,488	286,285	80%	57,373	5.82
2026	15%	27,442	297,197	Remains at 80%	59,439	5.99
2031	19%	28,397	307,540	Remains at 80%	61,508	6.15

1 Devon County Council data with TTT calculations of T&D as a % (based on 2008) of South Hams population
2 Varies slightly from All sectors table 2 as this is calculated from per capita figures in Table 1

3.40

To What Extent can Reducing Personal Transportation Reduce our Energy Demand in T&D?

Annual average personal transport use per capita in 2008 10.83MWh[53]

As discussed in depth in the Transportation section of this EDAP, personal transportation accounts for more than 1/3 of our total energy use, much of this is currently from individual short car journeys. The Table 3.40 sets out the estimated population increases in T&D and calculates the energy requirements for transportation over the next 21 years as we reduce our overall motorised transport use as fossil fuels become increasingly expensive and less available. Without attempting to suggest here how individual formulas for transportation might change over the next 21 years, it is reasonable to assume that out of necessity there will be a fundamental shift from personal car use to mass transit and that we will walk or cycle for more journeys.

The energy calculations in Table 3.40 are presented to provide rough data that we can then compare with the energy values of locally produced renewable forms of transport fuel. It is beyond the scope of this EDAP to suggest the numbers of, or individual access to bicycles or electric cars over the next 20 years. The latter is likely to have a role in individual transport as well as providing some off grid electricity storage.

Methane and bio-diesel are 2 fuels produced by renewable energy technologies, they can be further converted to produce electricity, but the most efficient use is use these fuels to run motors or in the case of gas, used for heating buildings. As fuels, they are suitable for transport. Excluding bio-diesel produced directly from energy crops (which would compete for other uses of land), Table 3.38 indicates the following potential estimated production of these fuels as follows:

Methane 8,345 MWh/y Rising to 8,486 MWh/y by 2030

Bio-diesel 176 MWh/y Rising to 351 MWh/y by 2030

Total combined = 8,521 MWh/y in 2009 Rising to 8,837 MWh/y by 2030

When these figures are compared with the estimated demand for transport as set out in Table 3.40, even when reduced to 80% of present demand, there is a substantial deficit in supply:

Locally produced renewable transport fuel meeting demand in T&D:

(8521 ÷ 258,436 =) 3.3% in 2009 rising to (8,837 ÷ 61,508 =) 14.4% by 2030

Further Reading

Details of grants and discount schemes for lofts and cavity wall insulations and all other aspects of energy efficiency can be found at the Devon Energy Efficiency Advice Centre[54]

http://en.wikipedia.org/wiki/Bioconversion_of_biomass_to_mixed_alcohol_fuels

http://oldweb.northampton.ac.uk/aps/env/Wasteresource/1997/Mar97/97mar38.htm

Report on Gas From Waste to power the grid.

Anaerobic Digestion Plant in Totnes. © Jacqi Hodgson

3.41

TRANSPORTATION

The Challenge

In 2009, about a third of our overall current consumption of energy is used on transportation that we use for personal mobility and distribution of goods and services. With around 95% of transport fuelled by oil, our systems are set to become increasingly vulnerable to the changes that the global peaking of oil production brings.

The climate change implications of our travel choices are clear. In the UK car use alone accounts for 13% of our total CO_2 emissions and (even ignoring aviation) the forecast around the world is for transport emissions to continue increasing. This contrasts with the emerging scientific view that targets for safe levels of greenhouse gases should be negative – i.e. we need not only to become carbon neutral, but also to remove some of the current concentrations of those gases from the atmosphere. How should we respond? Strangely, the default assumption appears to be that our reaction must somehow enable us to keep on travelling as far, and as fast, as we want - an approach that could turn a (soluble) problem into an (insoluble) predicament.

Dramatically cutting emissions while travelling further and faster demands a technological fix, but many technical "solutions" lead straight to new, worse problems. General embrace of agro-fuels as the substitute for oil based fuels has fallen as it became understood how they compete with food production or, via the rush to plant palm oil, cause rainforest destruction. Similarly visions of fleets of "clean" electric or hydrogen or hydrogen fuel cell powered cars raise a range of questions such as just how much extra energy will be needed to construct the necessary new infrastructure. A truly clean car would require all stages of its life to have been powered by renewable energy from the mining of raw materials, through its manufacture, shipping, sale and disposal, as well as for each and every electric charge used to power it.

Around the world, on average people make about 1000 trips (e.g. from home to work – that's one trip) per person per year. Travel behaviour research[55] from across Europe, the United States and Australia consistently shows that 10% of people's trips are shorter than 1km, 30% are shorter than 3km and 50% are shorter than 5km. This large number of small trips means that, even before relocalisation really starts to take hold, we have the potential to immediately intervene to support more cycling and walking trips - much more quickly than for any technological development and at a fraction of the cost.

Furthermore, if we can get people out of their cars and onto their feet or bikes, we get a long list of additional benefits. Increased health is just one of these – reduced traffic means cleaner, safer streets, more freedom for young people to roam and communities no longer divided by roads. This plan is

founded on moving away from our current unsustainable patterns of mobility towards enabling more people to walk, cycle and use public transport for all of their regular journeys, applying 3 basic guidelines:

◎ Make it quicker, safer and more attractive to walk, cycle or use public transport than to use the car

◎ Take road space away from cars

◎ Spend more on walking, cycling and public transport infrastructure and promotion: you get what you pay for.

Freight transport has increased since 1980 by 44% to 2 billion tonne kilometres, with 60% of this now travelling by road, 21% by water, 9% by rail and virtually all the rest by pipeline. The opening of the M6 Preston Bypass in 1958 and the first section of the M1 in 1959 marked the beginning of the motorway era, which changed dramatically the terms of competition between rail and road for goods traffic. In 2007 as part of its White Paper 'Delivering a Sustainable Railway,' the Government has set aside £200M of investment for the Strategic Freight Network[56].

The social implications of our transport system are huge. "Injustice is experienced by millions of people in the UK who do not have a car, or struggle to afford one in the 'must-have-car' society which we have created. These injustices include difficulties accessing work and other opportunities; enforced indebtedness; reduced opportunity to lead an active healthy life; and ironically, proportionately greater exposure than average to pollution, road danger and noise caused by those who do have a car"[57].

Local Mobility in Totnes & District

Cars are clearly the transport mode of choice for most of the 23,000+ residents living the district, and although 18% of households don't own a car, 45% have just one, while 2% have 4 or more. The central roads of Totnes and the villages were built before cars and driving through the middle and parking is as a result difficult, often making these busy roads dangerous. The rural hinterland is predominantly farmland and there is an extensive network of narrow lanes, with some passing places for cars; some of these are notoriously dangerous with poor visibility and no pavements. A Car share scheme has recently begun in Totnes, but has had problems finding a parking place. There are some off-road cycle and footpaths, including the extensive route which links Totnes station with the Steiner School at Staverton and (apart from a short stretch on the Plains where the cyclist has to take to the road) on to Ashprington. There are recommended cycle routes on quieter lanes which link up, and some plans for more off-road cycle and footpaths, for example at Littlehempston a short off road link is due to be developed later in 2009, and another at Berry Pomeroy is currently under consideration.

One key service is the excellent Community Bus service we know as Bob the Bus (whose passenger numbers trebled in the past 2 years). The Totnes Rickshaw Company has brought in 3 Indian (motorbike based) rickshaws that run on recycled biodiesel from the chip shops, bringing people up the steep rise of Fore street to the Market Square and the higher Narrows. These link in with expressway buses and local village services on the Plains, the Dart River boat services, the open top Round Robin summer buses and the mainline Totnes railway station.

The casual observer could be seduced into thinking a comprehensive public transport service has been taken care of. However, Bob the Bus is a private voluntary service, the drivers give their time for free to provide mobility, yet few of the buses run at capacity. The Rickshaw taxis, despite many attempts have yet to be granted a Hackney licence by the local council. Totnes town enjoys a good bus service, but access to and from the rural hinterland is very limited and fares can be prohibitive. There are no early or late services to the all the housing estates. Some of the surrounding villages have no service, Dipt-

ford for example has had no public transport since Beeching's disastrous transport plans of the 1950s took out the Primrose Railway which linked the village and its farming community with Totnes. The bus services to the other parishes are not all served by a daily service; Stoke Gabriel (pop. 1,349) for example only has a Friday bus service to Totnes. Many roads either are too dangerous for children to walk or cycle to school or are perceived to be too dangerous, which leads to the same result.

While Totnes station is conveniently close to the town with good services and a welcoming café, most commuters to Exeter and Plymouth travel by car along the busy A38. The train route from Exeter to Plymouth is one of the most scenic in the country; following the wide mouth of the Ex full of boats, the pretty town and rich red cliffs of Dawlish, clinging to the coast and diving into tunnels at Teignmouth, heading on to Dartmoor and Plymouth via Totnes and a beautiful and inviting rural landscape, but at busy times, the train itself is often over-

crowded. Little freight arrives or departs at Totnes Railway station, not even the mail. Freight arrives in juggernauts, which often get jammed in the middle of Totnes or clog the already busy A384 through road which links Torquay to the A38 and Dartmouth. Goods leaving the area take similar routes by lorry. The old Totnes to Buckfastleigh steam train operates in the summer months, essentially as a tourist attraction.

The majority of tourists visiting Totnes arrive by car using the Round Robin trips for pleasure. Caravanning, camping, walking and cycling holidays are all popular. Car parking is tight even in the winter and in the summer on a hot day, tempers can rise as cars circle the town and the villages looking for a parking space. Totnes' Christmas market draws shoppers and visitors in from a wide radius, car parking is free on those nights, and a Park and Ride scheme operates, but the number of parking spaces remains the same. The recent introduction of parking meters in Totnes has not been popular with everyone.

3.42 An Integrated Sustainable Transport System for Swindon

Promoting Modal Shift	Public Transport	Active Travel - Active Health
• Tailor-made support for every household, school & workplace • Meaningful incentives	• More buses. more often • Better facilities • Bus prioritisation • Cheaper Fares	• Safer walking & cycling • More routes • Combating obesity

What it will look like

Promoting Modal Shift	Public Transport	Active Travel - Active Health
Every person living or working in Swindon will be offered help and incentives to travel more sustainably • Individualised Travel Marketing Campaign • Car-Clubs in every neighbourhood • Car-Share at all workplaces • Working and shopping from home • Discount and rewards for green travel choices • Disincentives for polluting travel choices	It will be easy, pleasant and cheap to get around by bus • Bus every 10 minutes at peak hours and good evening, Sunday and rural services • New exchange, real-time information, harmonised ticketing • Bus priority on all main routes • Subsidised fares for all • Fuel poverty and social exclusion reduced	Health improves as cycling and walking replace most short car journeys • All streets have cycle lanes and pavements wide enough, well-maintained and signposted • Off-road cycle network extended and improved • Secure cycle parking at all amenities • Every child that can will cycle or walk to school • Obesity reduced

Getting started

Promoting Modal Shift	Public Transport	Active Travel - Active Health
• Travelsmart Marketing • Travelwise Businesses • School Travel Plans/Safe Routes to School • Bike It! Officer • CTC Community Cycling Development Officer	• SBC Management of Thamesdown Transport • SBC Local Transport Plan • Local Transport Bill (2008) regulation	• Cycle Demonstration Town • SBC Lifestyle Team • Active Swindon • NHS investment

Source: Swindon Borough Council

From our Survey

Our household survey[58] revealed the following about current transport trends in Totnes and District. Of those surveyed, 85% identified themselves as regular car users. The average distance travelled per year (39% of respondents) was between 5000 and 10000 miles, although 23% of people travel less than 2,000 miles per year. The most common reason for car trips is work, then leisure, and finally taking children to school. Of those surveyed that used their car to get to work, 44% said their work would be impossible without a car. 20% however said that it would be either possible or straightforward, although very few had discussed the possibility with their employer. Finally, those respondents who currently have no car were asked how they found life with no car. 45% said they found it easy, and 34% said they found it difficult or impossible.

Business as Usual or Willing to Change? - Emerging Trends - Where we are Now

In the short term, if we continue Business As Usual, we are heading for increased congestion on the main routes and traffic gridlock in the town and village centres. However, as oil inevitably becomes less available and the price per barrel becomes more and more volatile, private personal transport, delivery costs on goods and imports will become increasingly expensive and fragmented; transportation as we know it is heading for a grinding halt. In a rural area like this, the impact of this could be even more dramatic than in urban settings, which have far better public transport provision.

People living in Totnes and close to the more vibrant villages may be better prepared with easy walking access, bicycles and access to public transport, however those living in the rural hinterland and less well

---

Reducing carbon emissions, congestion, obesity and social exclusion
Promoting low carbon transport, health, environment and community

Public Realm	Environment	Transport Innovation
• Reduced congestion • Streets for People • 20 mph speed limit • Green Infrastructure	• CO_2 emissions reduced • Less road building • Air quality improved	• A UK exemplar • Redeploying funds • Levering government funding
What it will look like		
Public places and streets will be more attractive, safe and people-friendly • Traffic made less dominant by lowering traffic speeds • Amenity and well-being promoted through greening of streets • Residents help design and transform streets	The transport sector will play its part in tackling pollution and climate change • CO_2 emissions from • transport reduced by 20% by 2010 and • 80% by 2050 • Environmental impact of road • building reduced • Air quality improves and respiratory • problems decline	Investment will focus on creating and promoting an integrated and low-carbon transport system that is a national exemplar • Resources redirected from increasing road and parking capacity to sustainable transport • Major government transport funding levered • MPs and Councillors working together
Getting started		
• SBC Design Codes • Homezones • DIY Streets • DfT Manual for Streets • Streetscene	• SSP Climate Change Action Plan • SBC Sustainable Development Team • DfT Low Carbon Transport • Climate Change Bill	• SBC strategic direction, policy, planning and commissioning • Programme integration

served villages will not be so fortunate and are likely to become increasingly isolated unless real changes are made along the lines set out above, as soon as possible. The aging population in outlying villages will experience rapidly diminishing access to public transport, healthcare services and other people.

Businesses dependent on far-flung services, goods and distribution are likely to suffer rising costs and intermittent supplies. Goods with a short shelf life may not get to their destination in time. With over 30% of our food currently imported, the chances are we will experience severe shortages.

It is clear that there is very little in the way of good planning underway to prepare for the inevitable: a transport system that is not dependent on oil or other fossil fuels. For over 40 years, transportation has been at the mercy of top down privatised competing interests instead of the active provision of a comprehensive integrated service. The lack of forward strategic planning or strong leadership is leaving all sectors wide open to a collapse of our transport services and network. Public apathy is best symbolised perhaps by our general unwillingness to cut back on car use, walk, cycle or use public transport.

T&D Transport Plan B

If we are to be ready for a lower energy future, we will have to embrace a myriad of possibilities all of which can support a high quality lifestyle, protect the local economy and underpin a stable future for society. A sustainable transportation plan will need to be based on the following principles:

◎ Recognition of the urgent need to address car culture as a major user of fossil fuels

◎ Promotion of awareness and use of non-oil dependent transportation

◎ Provision of safe streets favouring walking and cycling

◎ Move towards to pedestrianised settlement hubs served by slow and safe mass transit

◎ Develop integrated services of fully affordable, accessible and convenient mass transport systems

◎ Integrated network of non-vehicular routes & mass transport access points

◎ Clear incentives favouring mass transit over individual car use

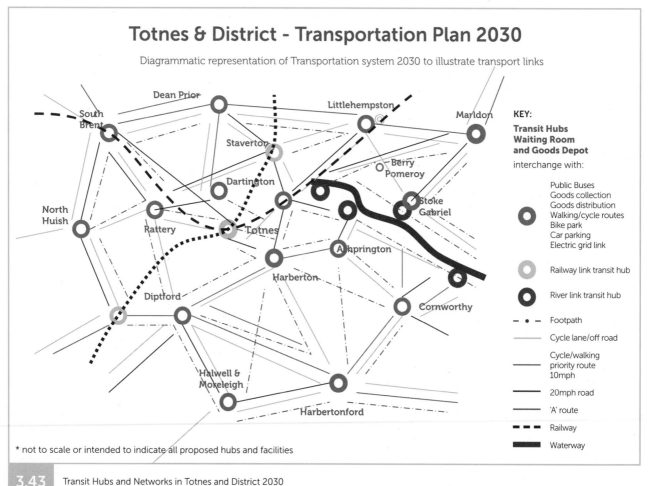

Totnes & District - Transportation Plan 2030

Diagrammatic representation of Transportation system 2030 to illustrate transport links

KEY:

Transit Hubs
Waiting Room
and Goods Depot

interchange with:

Public Buses
Goods collection
Goods distribution
Walking/cycle routes
Bike park
Car parking
Electric grid link

Railway link transit hub

River link transit hub

- • - Footpath

Cycle lane/off road

Cycle/walking priority route 10mph

20mph road

'A' route

Railway

Waterway

* not to scale or intended to indicate all proposed hubs and facilities

3.43 Transit Hubs and Networks in Totnes and District 2030

◎ Clear incentives encouraging freight to favour rail over road

◎ Provision of a local distribution service which links with wider networks

◎ Support localised distribution and consumption of locally produced goods

◎ Provision of energy (whether liquid fuel or other) for essential services and utilities

◎ Cross sectoral support and political will to implement policies which embrace these principles

From the climate change perspective, a Think piece commissioned by the Commission for Rural Communities[59] found that, even with optimistic assumptions about improved technologies, all of the following addition interventions will be needed to reduce rural transport carbon emissions as current science indicates is needed:

◎ Journeys foregone

◎ Increased tele-working, supported by the necessary facilities

◎ Remote tertiary, further and higher education

◎ Deliveries to the settlements replacing food and other shopping trips

◎ Leisure trips redistributed to the local area

◎ Mobile service provision, e.g. primary healthcare

◎ Tourist numbers capped at 2008 levels

◎ Mode shift to other forms of transport

◎ Smarter choices measures, primarily in the form of personalised travel planning

◎ Intensive measures to limit work journeys to destinations in the area, to 30% shared use of motor vehicles

◎ Small scale improvements to the local transit network, including flexi-routing

◎ (electrically assisted) Pedal cycle hire provision from strategic points

◎ Well maintained and improved public rights-of-way

◎ Car parking charges

◎ Road closures to improve walking and cycling conditions.

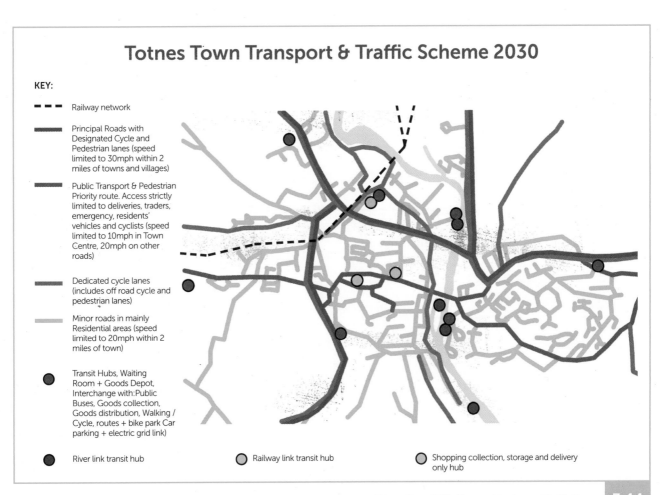

Totnes Town Transport & Traffic Scheme 2030

KEY:

- - - Railway network

▬▬▬ Principal Roads with Designated Cycle and Pedestrian lanes (speed limited to 30mph within 2 miles of towns and villages)

▬▬▬ Public Transport & Pedestrian Priority route. Access strictly limited to deliveries, traders, emergency, residents' vehicles and cyclists (speed limited to 10mph in Town Centre, 20mph on other roads)

▬▬▬ Dedicated cycle lanes (includes off road cycle and pedestrian lanes)

▬▬▬ Minor roads in mainly Residential areas (speed limited to 20mph within 2 miles of town)

● Transit Hubs, Waiting Room + Goods Depot, Interchange with:Public Buses, Goods collection, Goods distribution, Walking / Cycle, routes + bike park Car parking + electric grid link)

● River link transit hub   ● Railway link transit hub   ● Shopping collection, storage and delivery only hub

Totnes Town 2030: Transport Routes and Traffic Flows

3.44

A Model for Change - an Integrated Sustainable Transport System

In response to Swindon Borough Council Consultation on "A Vision for Transport 2030", a community vision was developed by a consortium of local groups. In this excellent plan they set out their strategies, their overall expectations of how this will evolve, and steps for getting started. There are a couple of things we in Totnes could add to this plan:

Freight:

◎ We need to address the travel miles of goods

◎ We need to reduce the volume of goods in transit (and thereby overall consumption)

◎ Shared mass transport for goods and passengers

Reduction Targets:

◎ We need to reduce our use of energy by 50% by 2030 (Zero Carbon Britain target) [60]

A tough call?

Budgeting our Energy for Transport Use

Personal transport use is currently 35.4% of all our energy use

Per capita energy use for transport in UK (2008) = 10.83 MWh/year

Total for Totnes & District (population 23,863) = 258,436 MWh/y

Including the movement of goods and services, our personal share looks more like this[61]:

Travel by car: 40KWh/day

Jet flights: 30kWh/day

Transporting goods: 12 kWh/day

total = 29.93 MWh/year each

(i.e. almost 3 times the personal use above)

In line with all our other energy budgeting we need to reduce our annual collective energy use for transport from 680 TWh to 151 TWh[62] i.e. a drop of 78% and this must run off renewable energy by 2030.

Transport Choices: Energy & Carbon Emissions [1]

Transport	kWh/person	kg CO_2 / Km person–km
Bicycle	0.02	0
Train	0.28	0.06
Bus	0.31	0.07
Car	0.50	0.11
Aeroplane	0.75	0.22
Boat	2.36	0.50

1 Travel Habits Now and Then. Ways of Transport – Aid 2. www.teachers4energy.eu/LangSpecPages/GB/PDF-GB/UK_transport/UK_transport/6t4_travel%20 habits%20now%20and%20then.pdf
2 www.climatefriendlybradfordonavon.co.uk

E.g. Journey London to Paris[2]:

Eurostar 2.75 hours. total CO_2 = 22kg / per person

Aeroplane 3.5 hours total CO_2 = 244kg / per person

3.45

What follows is one version of how transportation might become more localised and sustainable over the next 21 years.

Vision 2030

Nowhere in our transition to 2030 has the changing pace of life been more profound than in our mobility. Totnes and District has become an inspired model of localised integrated transportation. People's first thought when choosing how to travel is about walking or cycling and what vehicles there are, and to travel more slowly. Juggernauts are long gone; all goods are now delivered by rail or, to Totnes town, by boat up the river where they are offloaded at Baltic Wharf, and then distributed from there. Totnes station is a whirl of activity with passengers, goods and mail. The integrated transit systems carrying people and goods are popular and working out of the transit hub network that links in all the local travel routes and services. The choice of travel options is wide, an eclectic mix of the very modern, e.g. super sleek electric buses, with a revitalisation of our rural past in the form of Shire horses and Dapple Greys. Cars are used as a last resort – and the Totnes Car Club's vehicles are entirely fuelled by electricity generated locally from wind or hydro.

Our streets have reverted to being social spaces as well as being for travelling - they are much safer, with far less traffic and far more people, particularly in the morning when the children head off to school. The intermediate time of children needing to be protected by use of Cycle Trains and Walking Buses is now long gone, as any child aged 4 or older can travel safely without supervision. The walking/cycle route network has made cycling safer and it has roared back into popularity for leisure and commuting –and what's more it connects a whole series of pocket parks and community orchards and allotments. People travel together more than ever, walking together and sharing short lifts for shopping. Many streets have closed out the cars, children play and neighbours socialise there. The extensive river links are active all year and with the rise in tourism 'oiling the wheels', small boats have become more plentiful and busy.

All the wider roadways have been slimmed down into attractive and productive leafy boulevards with public walkways lined with fruit or nut trees and bushes. In the rural areas this space has been reclaimed for cycle lanes and growing fuel crops with narrow cycle lanes in between. Parking is no longer an issue and car parks have disappeared under bountiful allotments and gardens. The general consensus is that travel is more accessible, people friendly and relaxed. The air smells sweet and fresh.

Resilience Indicators

From the research that led to this Plan, we have identified a number of key indicators by which we can be sure that we we are moving forward. These include:

- % of people who walk for 10 minutes at least daily
- % of children who cycle or walk to school
- % of people who cycle or walk to work
- No of people with access to a local bus
- Distance driven each year
- Overall split of journeys between walking, cycling, public transport and car

These can be revisited regularly to see if the community is making progress in the right direction.

TRANSPORTATION

PATHWAYS ACRO

Strategic themes: • Creative and improved public & other mass transit systems
personal and commercial vehicle use • Creating safer streets and highways

2009

Individuals

- Walking is becoming more popular as fitness and obesity worries encourage people to walk the short trips. Car use declines as many people find the costs of keeping a car to be excessive. The Totnes – Dartington cycle & footpath use rises to more than 600 people on one sunny day in August.

- A new Car Share scheme in Totnes starts up and is instantly popular. Moor Cars plan more cars. Neighbours start to share cars and 2nd cars are dropped by many household. Very few SUVs new or used are being bought. Everyone is nervous about petrol prices rocketing again after the price spike of 2008. A new internet booking system is planned. Car insurance companies are offering 'non-commuter / social use only' deals

- UK holiday destinations are on the rise as budget airlines feel the brunt of the economic uncertainty and rising oil costs. Holidaying at home is found to be okay and the 10 Tors' visitors are 50% local people this year. Cornwall experiences a record year for tourism.

- Totnes Rickshaw Taxi Co. announces it has cost just £2.17 for 12 litres of recycled cooking oil to provide 645 rides from Steamer Quay to the top of town. The company identifies 1,000 potential passengers a day who need to travel from the Plains to the top of Totnes. The Way With Words Festival has the benefit of this Taxi Service and the Dartington route takes off with local people too. South Hams reconsiders the application for a Hackney Licence and gives the thumbs up.

Community

- Community groups are becoming more concerned about the lack of non-vehicular paths for pedestrians and cyclists. Many groups support TTT & Totnes Strategy Group's proposal under the Sustainable Community Act for an integrated system of non-vehicular routes in South Hams. The cycle route from Littlehempston is due to be completed this year and there are new plans for a new route at Berry Pomeroy to enable the children to walk and cycle to school.

- A Steiner School survey shows they have reached their school travel plan targets: Bus use rises to 15% (from 12% in 2007), car use falls to 70% (from 79%), and lift shares rise to 50% of car journeys (from 36%). The school are awaiting additional safe non-vehicular routes to be completed for their 40% walking and cycling targets to be achievable.

- Bob the Bus brings Bus no.3 into service and Car Free Day in September is celebrated in T&D with a major event involving 200 cyclists and 100 walkers

- Totnes Transport Forum's Parking Survey indicates introduction of parking meters has had little impact on parking habits.

Policy Makers & Service Providers

- As one of the first results of the Climate Change Bill, national road speeds are reduced by 10mph across the county. National Government invests significant investment in research and design for electric cars and other electrified transport, and £200m in rail for Strategic Freight Network up to 2014. The Government initiates a major public

SS THE TIMELINE

• Shared public transport for people, goods and services • Reducing individualised
• Getting freight onto rail • Encouraging walking and cycling for a healthier society

information campaign aimed at all levels to encourage people to understand the seriousness of carbon reduction and increase use of public transport systems. Town and Parish Councils in T&D arrange a meeting with DCC to discuss how they can take this forward locally.

- The Department for Energy and Climate Change reviews its 2006-2011 plan in line with the need for a transportation system that will tackle climate change and reduce energy consumption and convinces the Department for Transport to start taking real action to support this; severely reducing carbon dependence and move towards comprehensive local travel and distribution networks and services with measures to de-incentivise individual car use. More local buses are discussed with a view to a comprehensive daily local service being achieved within 3 years. They also debate a comprehensive cycle/walking network with transit hub / interconnections to public transport and the creation of safer streets and town and village centres. A number of surveys to assess use of fuel in PSVs, local travel movements and current use of public transport are undertaken. A mapping of local cycle routes reveals where cycling/walking routes are incomplete and where junctions with car users are dangerous. Steps are to be taken to improve safety and red/green pedestrian lights are prioritised for Ashburton Rd/ Western By-pass junction.

- Proposals to introduce a cash incentive for scrapping old cars and replacing with new, more energy efficient ones are seriously flawed, says sustainable transport charity Sustrans

- DCC reviews its staff travel energy budgets in line with voluntary reductions and reduces budgets by 25%. Incentives for staff to travel to work by public transport are under discussion. A budget for supplying staff with bicycles is a popular idea.

2010

Individuals

- Hundreds of people attend the "Future of Getting Around" travelling exhibition, where they get to road test a number of alternative vehicles, electric cars and bikes and a range of pedal powered vehicles. A rising interest in car pools and cutting back second car ownership is expressed. Many people sign up to talk to neighbours and start local lift shares and consider sharing their cars with other households. Standard car share contracts and website booking systems top the list for useful support.

- Use of public transport is up 15% on 2000 levels, exceeding the Government target of 12%. Bike shops are recording record sales.

Community

- In conjunction with the Carbon Neutral Schools Programme, Totnes and Dartington Safe Schools group offer teachers and parents from all schools across the district a day of free workshops to get practical advice on how to promote walking and cycling to school. The focus of the day will be to help boost healthy school travel across the region. 4 Walking Trains and 2 Cycling Trains are to be piloted.

- Community groups together with SHDC petition government under the Sustainable Communities Act to deregulate transportation to allow passengers, goods and mail to travel together on all public services to reduce costs and increase fuel efficiency. They look for more bike spaces on public transport to encourage commuters.

- A number of streets start their own Sustrans' inspired DIY Streets makeovers, and in particular focus on using arts to involve people like Roadwitch in Oxford.

TRANSPORTATION
PATHWAYS ACRO

Strategic themes: • Creative and improved public & other mass transit systems personal and commercial vehicle use • Creating safer streets and highways

- South Hams Small Farmers Association launch a scoping study based on Commonwork's ZEF (Zero fossil Energy Farming) project[63]. This includes looking at running farm machinery on biodiesel and reducing greenhouse gases from methane derived from animal waste.

Policy Makers & Service Providers

- The new section of traffic-free walking and cycling path at Berry Pomeroy is constructed and makes a difference to the way school children and local people travel, and has reduced parking in the village.

- In conjunction with Totnes Town Council, DCC agrees to implement a number of pedestrian safety measures including the 2009 traffic flow in town proposal in the EDAP: Reduce town centre speed limits to 10mph with pedestrian priority. Other villages in the district are likely to follow suit with lower speed limits. Speed bumps were going to be installed in Bridgetown but instead more imaginative interventions and used, on DIY Streets principles, and the pavements widened there and on the Plymouth road to Follaton. A number of new zebra crossings are to be installed.

- Local buses are to be fitted with bike racks to carry bikes, and buses on coastal routes will also have surfboard racks. The new look 'Beach Buses" with their distinctive paint work and racks are a hit with young people.

- DCC in conjunction with local district councils and Strategic Partnerships initiate an energy budget study of transport in the county to create a basis for change to a low carbon transport system. The outcomes indicate a potential 70% carbon saving just by switching fuels[64] devise a 10-year transport strategy to reduce individual car journeys by 80%. In recognition of the "lack of time before oil scarcity begins to

impact local mobility", a number of incentives to support car pools and lift share systems are to be implemented and a local transport forum are established in each LA district to drive changes. An application is made to the national Transport Innovation Fund for additional local buses and services.

- DCC in conjunction with local consultation identifies locations for Transit Hubs to create service access and links for a local district network across T & D (as a pilot for Devon) to integrate all public and private transport services and networks. These hubs will encourage use of public services for passengers and goods (including mail). Information about cycle lanes and walkways is made widely available on line and at all visitor centres in the area.

- Network Rail start investigating how locally generated wind, hydro and tidal electricity could be used to electrify lines from Exeter down into and through Devon and Cornwall.

Individuals

- Local entrepreneur Andy Markham opens for business retrofitting bicycles with electric motors, 'EcoPimp my Bike'. His bikes are popular with residents with hilly journeys. A number of new bicycle retail outlets and service centres open.

- School children celebrate the opening of a new local section of the National Cycle Network in Berry Pomeroy, which encourages hundreds of people to walk and cycle their way to a healthier lifestyle.

- A survey shows 20% of people have changed their travel habits in 3 years. More people now walk, cycle or take public transport.

SS THE TIMELINE

• Shared public transport for people, goods and services • Reducing individualised
• Getting freight onto rail • Encouraging walking and cycling for a healthier society

2011

Community

- With the new dedicated cycle/walkway from Dartington to Buckfastleigh, Cycle Trains and Walking Buses are established for all routes leading to the Steiner School at Dartington. The Walking Buses have been catching on at other primary schools in the area and the Steiner School training for all parents and teachers has encouraged this. The completing of phase 2 of the cycle/walking network will open up these options for the other schools to bring in these changes. A new generation of children start to understand the meaning of horse-power as school travel plans supported by parents, teachers and local bus companies, include Cycle Trains, Walking Buses, Rickshaw Taxis and public transport to the bus stop.

- Groups representing the elders, people with disabilities and youth welcome the plans for transit hubs and increased public transport, saying this will increase safety and access to travel for a much wider group.

- Car pools are very popular but finding it difficult to get enough electric cars due to a surge in demand nationally. Streets link up to increase access to vehicles. Underused bicycles are added to some local pools.

- A community pace car scheme is introduced through a children led "Traffic Tamers" project. Once it gets going, speeds rapidly fall.

- The DIY Streets schemes start to link up, forming DIY Neighbourhoods.

Policy Makers & Service Providers

- Government announces a Transport Framework that will support local plans. A public campaign is initiated at all levels to encourage people to understand the seriousness of carbon reduction and increase use of public transport systems. Road tax based on carbon emissions is introduced. The newly appointed Secretary of State for Transport tells the public that politicians at all levels will no longer be claiming car allowances, instead they will be using public transport to set a good example. There are a few rumblings in the backbenches, but their free travel passes quieten discontent. The scene for a cash incentive for scrapping old cars and replacing with new, more energy efficient ones is itself scrapped, and replaced by incentives to give up car ownership entirely or to retrofit existing cars, so saving on embodied energy. At the same time there is a move towards investment in car pools to reduce cars on the road, and incentives to make mass transit more affordable and accessible, and where possible free to local people.

- National Rail creates a local cooperation consortium to bring freight back to rail, harmonise services and pricing and work with local travel providers and distribution services to increase access and integrate services. National Government injects freight and passenger supplement to rail companies to incentivise additional services and bring down ticket costs. In line with increasing leisure access and use of train services, Sunday and public holiday services are to be increased to Saturday services and extensive weekend maintenance is to reviewed, with most maintenance to be carried out at night. No maintenance will be carried out on public holiday weekends to ensure all services are running. Totnes Railway Station gets an artistic

TRANSPORTATION
PATHWAYS ACRO

Strategic themes: • Creative and improved public & other mass transit systems
personal and commercial vehicle use • Creating safer streets and highways

face-lift; a brightly painted footbridge, new cycle rack and the old freight depots are brought back to life. The Government signs a new deal with Royal Mail, which will travel by train.

- Based on DCC's highly successful staff travel plan and incentives, SHDC initiates a '50% less Carbon" travel plan for Follaton House with incentives for staff to travel to work without the car, showers and lockers are installed for cyclists.. Staff at DCC and SHDC are to be offered discount bicycles which they can buy over a 2 year period out of their wages; the scheme is met with an enthusiastic response from staff and large sections of the staff car parks are to be changed to covered cycle parks. 50 car parking spaces are removed from the smaller car park at Heath's in Totnes in response to lack of use and need for growing space. The new allotments are quickly spoken for.

- The new DCC/SHDC Totnes & District pilot transportation strategy assigns a substantial budget to invest in the new hybrid methane/electric buses to cover a comprehensive network, and a number of new bus routes and stops are designated filling in the gaps in present services. 25% of PSVs[65] will use fuel from the local AD[66] supplies now coming on stream. A night bus service is established connecting Totnes and the surrounding villages and supporting local evening social and cultural activities. A pilot study is commissioned, looking at how the Smart Jitney or Wiggly Bus concept could be introduced.

- DCC open a new cycle path between Stoke Gabriel and Totnes along the route of an old green lane called Fleet Mill Lane. This hill-free, scenic route quickly becomes popular with both commuter cyclists and leisure cyclists.

Individuals

- Virtual travel to meetings is widely used for people working from home and international business people for whom the cost of air travel has become prohibitive. Public monies can no longer be claimed for international travel except by special application. People have more access to public representatives who become more locally based. A number of business people make use of the new fast SKYPE Across the Miles centres at post offices to have virtual meetings on camcorder and others have virtual family get to-gethers to save travel.

- 'Lessening the Load' car pimping is initiated by a local entrepreneur whose company will retrofit vehicles to reduce fuel consumption. Heavy doors and other parts can be replaced with lighter materials or removed altogether and turned into beach buggies. Brian Keener, who runs the company, plans to bring on stream his conversions of fuel cars to electric motoring in the next 2 years.

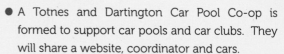

Community

- A Totnes and Dartington Car Pool Co-op is formed to support car pools and car clubs. They will share a website, coordinator and cars.

- Totnes Chamber of Commerce organises a meeting for all producers and retailers in the district to create a local good distribution network based on the new PSV + Goods transport being initiated by DCC & SHDC. The comprehensive plan is found to be very cost effective for all users who are delighted with the new services and a Goods Distribution Co-op is set up by the Chamber to work with the LA to help with tuning the services and timetables. The mail and other deliveries will also be distributed via new local Transit Hubs using this service

SS THE TIMELINE

• Shared public transport for people, goods and services • Reducing individualised
• Getting freight onto rail • Encouraging walking and cycling for a healthier society

Policy Makers & Service Providers

- Work is underway on the first 8 travel hubs in the outer ring and the walking and cycling networks for everyday journeys across the district. The waiting rooms with cycle parks for transport at the new hubs are to be designed to provide comfortable waiting space and where new building is required, will be built using local building materials and incorporate solar heating and lighting. All waiting rooms will carry local transport and visitor information.

- Car parking at the rear of Civic Hall is reduced to 10 spaces to make way for the new covered market space being built. The Civic Square will become pedestrianised and no longer be open for vehicles to drive across. New bike parking facilities to accommodate 4 lots of 25 bikes are to be placed at the front and rear of the civic square.

- SHDC creates a Local Bus Consortium to link local buses companies and harmonise services and charging. Bus services are extended to cover social and commuter hours as part of a national initiative to provide more comprehensive transport services. PSVs are hybrids running on methane fuel from South West Water's Totnes AD unit. Free local bus passes are issued to all local residents to get people using the new buses. The public respond with gusto.

- DCC agrees to set 10 mph speed limits on roads adjacent to schools for 60m each side of the school entrance, and rumble strips, road markings and traffic calming measures are to be installed this year. DCC adopts 50% plan initiated by SHDC to get its staff out of cars; measures and incentives are rolled out across the county including free travel passes for all public transport.

- Totnes is now linked to the national cycle route with links to the rest of the country, by an extension of the Totnes - Dartington route up the Dart Valley on to Buckfastleigh.

2013-15

Individuals

- Train Tours for holidays regain popularity and National Rail offer good Train Package deals for 2-week holidays both in UK and into Europe via Eurostar. Couchettes are improved and cycle facilities extended. They sell out very quickly. Flying has dropped in popularity with high prices and uncertainty, companies folding and taking holidays with them.

- Horses and donkeys are making a comeback, as the streets are now quieter. A call for more bridle paths is being considered by DCC and local landowners.

Community

- Totnes Chamber of Commerce agrees to pedestrianisation of the lower portion of Fore Street as the Electric Town Hopper road train service starts up services (entering Fore St. from Station Rd). The Town Council are the first passengers, although there is a minor furore when the Mayor, as she leans on the vehicle for a press photo, accidentally scratches the paintwork with her chain of office. The 14-seater vehicle has a large low backspace to make access easy for wheelchair users, and to carry local deliveries and luggage. Hailed as a fun ride, the stylish open vehicle is due to come on stream in Harberton

2012

TRANSPORTATION

PATHWAYS ACRO

Strategic themes: • Creative and improved public & other mass transit systems
personal and commercial vehicle use • Creating safer streets and highways

and South Brent too and has already taken bookings for 2 weddings. Totnes Rickshaw Taxi services have become more popular for taking shoppers home from the top of town and will link departures with the Hopper Time Table. The mid portion of Fore Street becomes buses and taxi access only and cars must go off via South Street or enter at Castle St. to access the higher part of the town. Pavements in Fore Street are widened across the defunct parking spaces.

Policy Makers & Service Providers

- DCC & the Dart Harbour Authority open discussions on increasing riverboat services to create a regular round trip service which carries goods as well as passengers and visitors between Totnes Babbage Rd, Totnes Plains, Baltic Wharf, Tuckenhay, Dittisham and Stoke Gabriel travel hubs. A feasibility plan running the service on locally produced AD methane finds this proposal workable and that it would supplement local bus services.

- A comprehensive and attractive walking and cycling network of routes is a step closer as DCC rethinks plans for major roadway maintenance and decides to reallocate its budgets to narrowing many roads, creating avenues of trees and walkways in the urban areas and broader hedgerows for fuel crops and cycle lanes in the rural roads. Cyclists are given priority over cars at junctions. The final phase of Travel Hubs is completed and a further wave of new bus services is brought on stream. A survey to assess annual usage and satisfaction is set up; initial finds indicate a 30% change in travel by local people and 20% change in goods distribution over the period 2010-13. The new walking /cycling links between Totnes Littlehempston station, Totnes Town station and Castle Street are completed.

- SHDC removes a further 50 car parking spaces from the smaller car park at Heath's in response

to lack of use and need for growing space. The entire car park is turned back into a small horticulture area in conjunction with the new anaerobic digester. A further 25% of PSVs are to be switched over to hybrid methane / electric. Local businesses are offered council tax incentives to provide employees with car-less commuting and initiate car pools

- In conjunction with local Parish Councils, DCC agrees to implement the 2009 pedestrian priority plan in the villages, improve pavement quality and reduce village centre speed limits to 10mph. A review of spatial strategies in view of carbon reduction needs acknowledges the urgent need to align more intensified developments with public transport access and discourage car use.

- To reduce fuel consumption and increase road safety, national road speeds are reduced to 50mph on motorways, 40mph on A roads, and 30mph elsewhere unless other restrictions apply. High speed trains make good journey times, efficiency has increased; they are becoming very popular. National Government adopts the Storkey coach hub plan, promoted by George Monbiot.

Individuals

- Children playing on the side streets have become a familiar sight again. Ball games and windows don't mix well, but people are very tolerant as it is good to see the children outside. Many streets have benches on the pavements and have become social meeting places. Some streets have designated one side for skate boarders who impress with their acrobatics. Contrary to many peoples' expectations, a study shows that having more children playing in the streets has led to a fall in reported crime.

- More producers in the district are bringing their products to market by horse and cart. Hitching

SS THE TIMELINE

• Shared public transport for people, goods and services • Reducing individualised
• Getting freight onto rail • Encouraging walking and cycling for a healthier society

posts and water troughs have been set up at the back of Civic Square and under the shade of the new orchard at the old market in Cistern Street.

- Bicycle delivery schemes are popular with local shops and shoppers, saving people carrying their shopping around with them and they can phone in orders to be delivered locally. People travel less; more are working from home and commute less; 20% of all journeys are now by bicycle. 30% of locally owned cars and 80% of taxis are electric & plug into the grid.

- More horses and donkeys are visible on the streets that are much quieter now. Farmers are using more horses and donkeys on the land and looking into some of the old horse drawn machinery.

Community

- Local towpaths in Totnes, Stoke Gabriel and Tuckenhay get a makeover by local community groups who want to improve local walks from the riverboat links.

- CVS initiates Health trip taxis as part of a local health forum with LINK initiative to help people access health and care services. Taxi drivers take a special training to learn how to assist passengers using their vehicles, which also get special fittings and can carry wheelchairs. Visitors to patients can also use these services, which are subsidised by the PCT.

- The Community Late Nite Bus service adds more journeys to the public services setting off at 10pm and working during the night until 7am to collect and deliver goods in the cool of the night. Late night revellers and early starters can catch this bus too.

2016-20

Policy Makers & Service Providers

- In response to the major drop in car use and need for more growing space, SHDC closes the Old Market Car Park to cars and 50 car spaces are taken out from the main car park at Heath's. Both areas have their tarmac broken up and are planted up for community orchards.

- Totnes Riverboat Connection comes on stream and is found to be popular for local distribution of goods and travel by school children. The new service links Dartmouth's transport services bringing imports directly into T&D. The Travel hubs are proving very popular and attractive horse troughs and hitching posts are installed to increase access to all local transport options. Older bus shelters are given a retrofit to make them more comfortable and provide better shelter in line with the waiting rooms at Travel Hubs.

- Local government agencies and service providers get together on a major retrofit of all 'outdated' PSVs and their own fleets. These vehicles will be adapted for methane or methane /electric hybrid. Interest in joining the emergency services increases 5 fold when the new fleets of sleek electric vehicles come into use. Mountain bicycles replace 50% of police cars, and ambulances carry a full range of home birth delivery equipment.

- National Government introduces a Private Owners' Car Licence requiring individual owners to pay an annual fee. Disabled drivers are excluded.

- In 2016, the Totnes - Stoke Gabriel cycle path is now extended right down to the coast, completing the final leg of the Dart Valley Cycle Path, this now extends from Buckfastleigh where it meets up with the National cycle route down to the coast. The Dart Valley Cycle Path following the course of the river Dart is voted the country's most scenic cycle way and becomes a major tourist attraction, bringing in holidaymakers from all over the country.

TRANSPORTATION

PATHWAYS ACRO

Strategic themes: • Creative and improved public & other mass transit systems
personal and commercial vehicle use • Creating safer streets and highways

2021-25

Individuals

- A survey shows asthma levels are down and people feel healthier due to the reduction in traffic noise, stress and congested roads.

- A flourishing of use of horses and donkeys by farmers is creating a revival of interest in breeding, riding and animal handling

Community

- Totnes & District Cycle hire scheme is established. The small group started off recycling and repairing unused bikes, based at Totnes Station, they now have enough bikes and staff to service all the transit nodes.

- Residents groups take advantage of the bollards being offered by DCC to create filtered permeability[67] of transport access to their street. Emergency services can still gain access.

- T&D Equine Association is formed to promote breeding and use of horses and donkeys on the land. A stud festival is held on the Plains with special exhibitions of horse drawn farm machinery. The rural regeneration horse breeding and handling course Dartington continues to be oversubscribed.

Policy Makers & Service Providers

- SHDC turns the rest of the parking spaces at Heath's Car park back to a growing space, becoming small allotment spaces for the town residents. Parking in Totnes is restricted to North St and the old Somerfield car parks, most spaces are taken up by local car pools and for disabled drivers. All local authority vehicles and PSVs are methane / electric hybrids to utilise fully all the AD fuels and local electric generation. Hitching posts are installed in all the local village squares with horse troughs

- 50% of UK Motorways are decommissioned to provide additional rail routes for high-speed services and deliveries. National Rail services get a makeover as all trains are retrofitted for electricity only with PV generation on roofs, grid storage and faster speeds. New matting under the rails reabsorbs energy generated from vibration and reduces maintenance work

- The Totnes & District Travel Model has been implemented in most parts of Devon and is catching on much further a-field.

SS THE TIMELINE

• Shared public transport for people, goods and services • Reducing individualised
• Getting freight onto rail • Encouraging walking and cycling for a healthier society

Individuals

- People enjoy their car free neighbourhoods and quiet streets. Car ownership is down by 80% on 2009 figures. 100% of local cars are all electric & plug into the grid. A survey shows that car use continues to reduce as cycling has become a national pastime. Per capita energy use of energy for all transportation is down by 80% on 2008 statistics.

- More young people have taken up skateboarding and roller skating Road traffic accidents have diminished as the main cause of death or injury for under 14 year olds.

Community

- Jogging and Cycling clubs numbers continue to grow and members can join from age 7. The new tandem club has bicycles that can carry families of four people and tow a trailer. The Tour de UK stops over in Totnes and links with the Tour de France via Plymouth.

- Totnes Chamber of Commerce agrees to Totnes High St being completely pedestrianised (delivery only) as cars are few and far between anyway. Shoppers and visitors use the popular Hopper Road train; this has increased access and enjoyment of the town.

- European Car free day bike is renamed European Walking day; over 500 people join the carnival procession around the T&D walkers' 20-mile loop.

Policy Makers & Service Providers

- DCC upgrades a number of bike priority lanes to "Class A" where commuters and racers can travel at top speed. Some cycle/walking routes have been widened and marked out with lanes to increase safety. More transit hubs for out of village locations to accommodate extra needs.

- National Rail is expanding the rail network to reduce distances on some journeys. At the request of Totnes Travel group, they are to consider extending the Totnes - Buckfastleigh Train line to Paignton via Berry Pomeroy. The re-opening of the Primrose line to Diptford and Kingsbridge is also under discussion. Gladys Davies of Diptford travelled on the last train in 1968; she hopes to be the first on the new train service. The refurbished trains are likely to run on electricity rather than steam.

2026-30

Further Reading

Dept. for Transport's Carbon Pathways Analysis: http://www.dft.gov.uk/pgr/sustainable/analysis.pdf

Thinking about rural transport: Rural life without carbon: http://www.ruralcommunities.gov.uk/files/CRC%20Rural%20Life.pdf

Regional Transport information www.devon.gov.uk/transport

Dept. for Transport's 2004 White Paper "The Future for Transport: A Network for 2030"

Measuring carbon emissions of transport: www.adb.org/Documents/Information/Knowledge-Showcase/Measuring-Road-Transport-Emissions.pdf

Transport Energy Consumption. A discussion paper. Roger Kemp, Lancaster University. 2004 www.engineering.lancs.ac.uk/research/download/Transport%20Energy%20Consumption%20Discussion%

Community Energy: Planning for a Low Carbon Future. Combined Heat & Power Assocn.

Smarter Travel Planning: http://www.smartertravelplanning.com

http://www.explorethesouthwestcoastpath.co.uk/sthdevonpt.html

Dart Harbour Authority. www.dartharbour.org/harbour-authority

Transport Energy Descent Plan for Oxford. Steve Melia 2009 http://www.stevemelia.co.uk/research.htm

Devon Local Transport Plan 2006-2011. Devon County Council. 2006

David Engwicht and Pace Cars: http://www.lesstraffic.com/Programs/Pace%20Car/Pace%20Car.htm

Smart Jitneys: http://www.communitysolution.org/rideshare.htmlCombined Heat & Power Association. (2008) Community Energy: Urban Planning for a Low Carbon Future. http://tinyurl.com/y9zh847

Dept. of Transport (2004) The Future for Transport: A Network for 2030. A White Paper. http://tinyurl.com/y8fnhgg

Kemp, R. (2004) Transport Energy Consumption. A discussion paper. Lancaster University. http://tinyurl.com/y8n87hw

Schipper, L. (2008) Measuring carbon emissions of transport. http://tinyurl.com/y873nwm

Useful Websites

www.smartertravelplanning.com. Helps in the design of journeys within the UK.

www.seat61.com. The Man in Seat 61. A wonderful tool for planning train journeys on the Continent.

www.explorethesouthwestcoastpath.co.uk/sthdevonpt.html. Exploring Devon.

www.dartharbour.org/harbour-authority. The Dart Harbour Authority

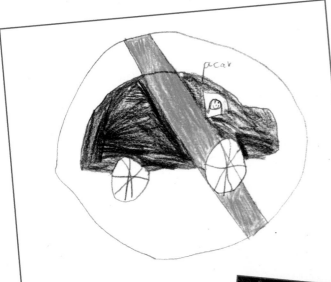

Cars and Bikes by students at Grove School

Cycleway in Totnes. © Lou Brown

Rickshaws do Weddings. © Totnes Rickshaw Company CIC

Totnes Rickshaw Company

Totnes residents and visitors now have the opportunity to avoid the uphill walk from the River Dart through Fore Street into High Street by taking a ride in what must be one of the most eco friendly vehicles in Britain today. Two Indian rickshaws have been imported. Their engines have been converted in the UK to run on bio fuel produced from the recycling of locally collected waste cooking oil. The rickshaws are now becoming a familiar sight around town, they drop people at the Rotherfold in the ancient Narrows; visitors can then enjoy a leisurely downhill stroll through Totnes' High Street and Fore Street. A further development has been the novelty interest generated in hiring the rickshaws for weddings and other special events and occasions.

The vehicles are very fuel-efficient. They can achieve 80 kilometres to the litre with a top speed of 50 km per hour. (Way in excess of what will actually be needed!). The project was the brainchild of local businessman Pete Ryeland. It was initially supported by means of interest free loans from local traders who are now the directors/shareholders of the company. Additionally, following registration of the Company as a CIC (Community Interest Company), grant assistance from South Hams District Council has been secured.

A number of local restaurants, fast food outlets and businesses throughout Totnes have already been signed up to provide the used cooking oil. They are now on the way to expanding the waste oil bio-fuel business with a new company, Totnes Bio-fuel Co. being set up at Sharpham to supply not only the Rickshaws, but also the farm vehicles on Sharpham Estate and eventually to supply community transport and the local public with bio-fuel.

Totnes Rickshaw Company and Bio-Fuels Totnes plan to use the profits from their enterprises for the benefit of the local community – starting with the regeneration of the Rotherfold area.

**For more information visit
www.totnes.transitionnetwork.org/transport/
rickshaws**

THE TOTNES RICKSHAW
COMPANY CIC

BUILDING AND HOUSING

When we build, let us think that we build forever. Let it not be for present delight, nor for present use alone, let it be such work, as our descendants will thank us for. And let us think, as we lay stone on stone, that a time is to come when those stones will be held sacred, because our hands have touched them, and that men will say as they look upon the labour and wrought substance of them, "see, this our fathers did for us".
John Ruskin

The Challenge

Around 30% of the energy currently consumed in Totnes and District is accounted for by the domestic sector. Apart from a handful of buildings in the town that are exemplars of sustainable construction and retrofit (see below), most of the housing in Totnes is of a low standard of energy efficiency. As our survey reveals, 58% of households don't even know how much insulation they have in their loft. To put it simply, the challenge in terms of building and housing in Totnes and District is threefold.

Firstly, it will be important to ensure that all new building meets the very highest standards in terms of energy efficiency, as well as using the healthiest materials with the lowest environmental impact and carbon emissions? Secondly, how can the existing 9,481 residential properties be retrofitted, so as to maximise their energy performance? Although the first is more attractive, it is the second where the greater challenge lies, but also where the greatest impact can be had. Then thirdly, and perhaps most importantly, how can the previous two be done within the very short period of time available to us, whilst also ensuring social equity and access to affordable housing?

Although Totnes and District is in a rural area, it has a fairly high density of housing and this will have serious implications if there is a need to accommodate

more diverse use of land, such as food and fuel production for local people. Future planning is subject to the Local Development Framework (LDF) which, while very restrictive in terms of individuals who may wish to live in the rural hinterland, does anticipate a considerable programme of new building to accommodate those on current housing lists in response to a predicted housing shortage over the next decade. The new planning system is intended to speed up planning decisions, having opened up community consultation at the earlier local strategic planning stages to outline Core Strategies and agree local Development Plan Documents (DPD).

In the 21 years up to 2030, there is also a need to plan for less familiar structures and designs in a rapidly changing landscape. We need to plan for more renewable power systems, some very close to home, and some indeed mounted on our roofs. We need to plan for more people growing their own food, more agricultural workers, more affordable homes and developments, which cater for an ageing community. Our landscape is likely to be more pressured by a growing need to provide local food, wood-fuel and building supplies, while maintaining the natural biodiversity within local habitats and without exceeding the natural environmental limits.

Where we Find Ourselves: a Snapshot from 2009[68]

The town of Totnes evolved within, and around, an early 10th c. Saxon defended burgh, though the find by archaeologists, of a Roman Hypocaust tile suggests much earlier significant occupation. The Saxon town was subsequently altered and extended following the Norman Conquest; the ford and bridge, crossing the River Dart, and the quays and water powered mills becoming a focus of development. The Saxon/medieval enclosed town followed a classic plan with property boundaries, the burghage plots, extending from the main street to the walls. Early building materials were principally from local sources; random quarried stone, clay/loam for cob, oak, reed, straw and slate for the area's vernacular buildings.

Lead copper and iron would have been mined and processed on, and around, Dartmoor. Traded materials brought to the town, by boat, included more exotic stone, red sandstone and trap, granite, Bere stone, Portland stone, Purbeck marble, high quality brick and culm/coal for local kilns. Cut stone was expensive and only used on higher status buildings. Lime, for mortar and plaster, was made in nearby kilns (limestone is well distributed throughout the area). Local clay was used for ridge tiles and coarse domestic wares. Early foreign trade included bricks from the Low Countries and timbers from the Baltic.

The nineteenth century saw the arrival of the railway in 1847 and with it the easier sourcing of materials such as York-stone paving, pig iron and machine made bricks. The Elizabethan core of the town was built with timber frame and wattle-and-daub, and later brick, infill. This was followed in turn by brick-built Victorian and 1930s semi-detached properties, and, in the 1960s, by widespread use of concrete-block and panel construction. Although the more recent properties were drier and lighter, they weren't necessarily warmer, as Part One of this Plan has revealed. Much the same pattern can be found in the adjacent parishes. **Totnes and District contains around 9,481 houses houses**[69] and with 0.5% of those houses being replaced annually, the houses of the future are, to all intents and purposes, already here.

Although we do not currently have accurate survey data for the number of non-domestic buildings in the district, many are large and probably consume a lot of energy. The following is a rough estimate of these buildings in T&D (Appendix C2 in the web-based version of this document carries the details):

◎ 10 very large buildings (multiple connected buildings, e.g., Follaton House)

◎ 515 large buildings (essentially single large building, e.g., a church, school)

◎ 1,248 medium buildings (about the size of a three-roomed flat, e.g., a restaurant)

◎ 65 small buildings (e.g., a pair of public toilets).

Non-domestic buildings vary widely in their construction and energy efficiency requirements as some are used for human occupation (e.g. schools), others for animal use, storage or operating machinery. But adding the total of **1,838 non-domestic buildings** to the rest, results in an estimated total of **11,284 buildings** in Totnes and District[70].

Totnes, like most other parts of the country, is under enormous pressures from the Spatial Strategy, to find space for hundreds of new houses, based on forecasts which are in turn based on assumptions which contradict those of this Plan (i.e. continual economic growth and the perpetual availability of cheap energy). The community response to the proposals set out in South Hams District Council's (SHDC) Totnes and Dartington Development Plan Document (which identified over 30 potential development sites) was comprehensive and, under the co-ordination of the Totnes & District Community Strategy Group, unprecedented in its depth and professionalism. However, local consultation came to an unexpected impasse when the Community response[71] was shelved (in June 2008) until 2011[72]. The subsequent process of Enquiry by Design (EbD) in June 2009 under the Prince's Foundation attempted to bring clarity to these issues, but, at the time of writing, the jury is still out on the success or otherwise of this process to consult widely and agree suitable development sites.

The area suffers from lower than the national average wages and high house prices, exacerbated by the failure to provide much in the way of affordable housing. A recent Oil Vulnerability Audit carried out by TTT for a commercial business in the town found that all but one of their staff were unable to afford to live in Totnes, and that if the rising price of oil made it unaffordable to drive, they could lose most of their key staff. The lack of affordable housing in the area is not only a housing issue, but also key to the vulnerability of the area's economy, particularly that of the town itself.

There is little assistance (apart from small discounts) for homeowners who want to insulate their homes, unless they are elderly or in receipt of benefits. Across the area, hundreds of thousands of pounds a year are spent heating the sky above our homes, as expensively-generated heat pours out of windows, roofs, walls and draughty doors. At the same time, new buildings are still built using high embodied energy materials such as concrete, steel, PVC (a toxic product already banned in some European countries due to its health impacts[73]) and a wealth of other industrial building materials. The complex web of well managed woodlands, slate quarries, craftspeople, artists and builders that produced the older buildings we so treasure, has been all but entirely dismantled. Most modern building materials are manufactured elsewhere, and most of the money generated by their sale, like the heat from the buildings, pours out of Totnes.

Business as Usual or Willing to Change?

If the current trends in construction continue, with SHDC taking no inspired leadership when it comes to construction standards, and adopting a position of letting the market lead rather than the community, the prospects for Totnes are decidedly unattractive. Within 10-15 years, one can envisage another 800-1000 houses having been added to the Totnes and Dartington parishes, with perhaps half as many again added to the rest of the Totnes and District area, all built to the minimum standards permitted at the time. We are fortunate therefore that the Government is taking a proactive stand when it comes to energy performance standards of new buildings.

By 2016, all buildings are expected be built to Code for Sustainable Homes Level 6, an enormous improvement on present-day standards (see table below for the timetable of implementation). However, this may be a very optimistic goal under current practices, and while these standards will tackle energy performance, they do little to deal with the energy embodied in the materials themselves. Cement production, for example, is responsible for 5% of global carbon emissions[74], and materials like PVC, use large amounts of energy and petrochemicals. Before the residents even move in, the carbon footprint generated by the materials is already substantial, yet avoidable. The Code for Sustainable Homes ignores the potential benefits that a change of materials could bring, in terms of the health of the residents, and the health of the local economy.

Under this 'Business as Usual' scenario, most developments will continue to be built by large developers, using materials brought in from wherever in the world they can be sourced most cheaply. The financial gain generated by the developments will be accrued to investors and speculators outside the town, and the community is left with a legacy of poor development, the design of which they had no influence over, and few of the financial benefits. Affordable housing will continue to be the exception rather than the rule. Totnes could end up like so much of the rest of the UK, a bland, faceless sprawl, with little open space, and far less character than it has at present. Visitors would have fewer, rather than more, reasons to come to Totnes.

The houses added over that time will have been designed and built on the prevailing assumptions that everyone will own a car, need to travel to work, have no time to grow food, be able to service a large mortgage and desire very little interaction with their neighbours. As this Plan has identified, these are all highly questionable, especially in the current economic situation, where very little is being built, and even the new buildings in the town's Southern Area are unfinished, and locked up, waiting for an economic 'bounce-back' which may or may not happen. It may be that community-led and resourced developments will soon be the only viable model for new housing.

SHDC have set the following goals for building and housing over the next 20 years:

◎ Affordable homes

◎ Competitive local economy

◎ Community vibrancy

◎ Quality build and natural environment

◎ Social inclusion (access to services and facilities)

◎ Climate change (addressing its causes and impacts across the South Hams).

In light of an unpredictable economic situation, the impacts of volatile energy prices, the energy demanding nature of modern construction materials, the amount of money that current development practices leach from the local economy, and the different demands people may make of buildings in the near future, we would argue that SHDC will find it impossible to meet these objectives through current practices.

There is, however, another way of considering housing that is more relevant and appropriate to a lower-energy, more localised and self-reliant Totnes. It would be based on the principle of buildings causing the minimum possible harm to the users and to the environment, as well as using any building project as a way to stimulate, diversify and re-skill the local economy.

TTT estimates (see below) that if 50% of materials in all new buildings in the area were locally sourced (timber, clay, straw, hemp, etc) it would bring almost £5 million per year into the economy. The multiple spin-offs from a more localised approach to construction are as much economic as they are ethical. The principles underpinning this new approach can be seen in the proposed Transition Zero Carbon Homes Code (see below).

What Could our Buildings be Like?

by Chris Bird, TTT Building & Housing Group

What do we Want from our Buildings?

◎ Energy efficient houses (new and old) close to where people work and socialise

◎ Homes that are part of communities, smaller and closer together, and making efficient use of energy and materials

◎ Existing houses fitted with effective methods of insulation and energy generation wherever feasible

◎ Example: Terraced houses with communal gardens and associated work unit.

What do we Build with?

◎ Local and sustainable materials with the minimum of embodied energy – cob, timber, straw, etc.

◎ Used and recycled materials wherever feasible, especially those on sourced on site

◎ Alternatives wherever possible to oil-based materials which will be at a premium

◎ Example: Sheep's wool insulation, a local material with around one-tenth the embodied energy of rockwool.

How do we Build?

◎ Decreased reliance on oil-driven machinery such as diggers and bulldozers will dictate different building systems that are achievable with human energy

◎ Developments and buildings designed to a human scale.

◎ Use of brownfield rather than greenfield sites, keeping the latter for growing food, biodiversity and open space

◎ Example: Replacement of reinforced concrete structures which require a lot of mechanical energy and unsustainable use of cement with timber framed structures built on pile foundations.

Co-housing?

Co-housing is the name for a type of housing started in Denmark in the early 1970's. There are now over 150 co-housing sites worldwide, in both town and country, as either new build or conversions, incorporating private, rent-buy and social housing.

Why Co-housing? Contemporary living now includes more single parents, women working, and high numbers of elderly and single people. Many of us face social isolation and a chronic shortage of time/money.

How does Co-housing work? All Co-housing has some element of communal facilities, such as dining & cooking as well as each dwelling still having its own basic equivalent. Ecological co-housing provides a more 'green' life, with sustainable building methods, sharing of utilities like freezers and washing machines, a common heating system and/or solar panels[75] to reduce bills. It creates car free, more people friendly 'streets' and strongly encourages car sharing and other alternative forms of transport.

With shared land use it becomes possible to be more self-sustaining, producing our own fruit and vegetables.

The Proposed Transition Zero Carbon Homes Code

This Plan proposes that by 2014, SHDC takes a proactive position on the creation of low-carbon homes, pushing Government guidance as far as it can, and becoming a leader nationally in the creation of low-energy, affordable buildings. It does so via implementation of the Transition Zero Carbon Homes Code developed in conjunction with the Association of Environmentally Conscious Builders, approved in 2011, and enforced from the beginning of 2014. A Transition Zero Carbon Homes Code would be based on the following requirements:

◎ Meet the current highest standard for sustainable buildings (i.e. Passivhaus / exceeds level 6)

◎ Be designed so as to maximise natural lighting and solar space heating

◎ Eliminate toxic or highly-engineered materials and energy-intensive processes

◎ Be independent of fossil-fuel based heating systems

◎ Be designed for adaptability and dismantling: so as to allow the building to be subsequently adapted for a range of other uses

◎ Where appropriate, integrate working and living

◎ Ensure outdoor spaces are south facing with the minimum of overshadowing, so as to maximise the potential of the property/development to grow food

◎ Maximise grey water recycling and rain water capture

◎ Be built to address needs not speculation

◎ Adhere to good spatial planning to benefit communal interaction and shared open space

◎ Maximum use of locally produced materials: (defined as clay, straw, hemp, lime, timber, reed, stone)

◎ Maximum use of used and recycled building materials, particularly those on site

◎ The inclusion of water-permeable surfaces rather than hard paving, etc.

Transportation in Totnes in 2009 © Lou Brown

Hunter's Moon from Dartington. © Lou Brown

Vision 2030

By 2030, the appearance of the existing building stock would not differ very much from how it looks now. Those properties that could be insulated internally with cavity wall and loft insulation, look largely unchanged. Apart from solar panels and photovoltaic slates shimmering on roofs in the sun and the triple glazed windows many of them now have; it is mainly the homes built with a single skin wall that had to be externally clad and then re-rendered that look different. There are also noticeably more people occupying buildings, and greater attention given to detail in the gardens, many of which are used for growing food. But it is in the areas of new housing that the main differences can be seen.

In spite of the move towards zero carbon building standards, the sharp hike in energy prices after the first oil shock in 2012 made much modern construction practice no longer viable. With thousands of builders in the area trained only to build with materials and techniques that were no longer sustainable, there was a new urgency to move rapidly towards building with re-used and recycled building materials and to switch from new-build to the refurbishment of old and existing buildings and the subdivision of larger buildings into a number of smaller units.

A walk around the ATMOS development, on the old Dairy Crest site, takes one past offices and workspaces, light industrial units, and then houses, all built to the highest levels of energy efficiency, with predominantly local materials. The place buzzes with people and activity. The lower KEVICC site has

also been partially developed, again with houses built to the highest standards, with south-facing shared gardens and also with gardens on their roofs. Over at Baltic Wharf, a scaled down development on the waterfront has been designed to allow the wharf to continue to be used as a working dock for bringing goods into the town as an increasingly viable alternative to road freight, while also integrating housing, work units, and the town's first co-housing development.

All three are designed to minimise car use, fleets of shared electric vehicles being available to residents. The new buildings at KEVICC are a celebration of local materials, and feature the first food-producing roof garden in the county. The buildings are heated entirely by the body heat of the students. Dartington Estate is now home to two eco-village developments, providing affordable housing for key workers employed by the Agroforestry Farm project. Almost all (93%) of the building materials are from on the estate itself, and provide an important research opportunity into how to house the many thousands of people who will be required to move into rural areas to help with food production as the oil required to run conventional agriculture becomes unaffordable.

These new 'quarters' of Totnes, and the beautiful, quirky and iconic buildings they contain, are now as much of an attraction for tourists as the historic merchants' houses at the heart of the town. Their creation was also the opportunity for a huge programme of retraining of local builders, and to the establishment of many new businesses to supply the materials that are now needed for sustainable construction.

Resilience Indicators

- Percentage of houses that have been retrofitted to maximum possible standard.
- Number of second homes that have been let though the 'Homes for All' scheme.
- Number of houses with solar hot water panels installed.
- Number of builders that have undertaken the 'Construction in Transition' training course,

which introduces them to a range of natural building materials and techniques.

- Heat emitted from buildings – as measured by an infrared scan from the sky.
- Trends in fuel poverty.
- Average amount of energy produced by buildings in Totnes and District.

These can be revisited regularly to see if the community is making progress in the right direction.

BUILDING AND HOUSING
PATHWAYS ACRO

Strategic themes: • Access to locally produced building materials
• Good planning and best practice in new-builds with

2009

Individuals

- TTT promotes its 'Transition Together' home study programme extensively around Totnes. Ten teams are set up; one of the first things they do is assess the energy efficiency of their houses

- 'Retrofit your Home' evening class at the Mansion House is oversubscribed

- Work at Devon's first Zero carbon school, Dartington Primary is finished. Head teacher Jill Mahon is thrilled and agrees to an open day for visits by local residents and other schools.

Community

- The Totnes Sustainable Construction Company is incorporated, emerging from the TTT Building and Construction group

- The former Dairy Crest site is bought into community ownership. A detailed prospectus[76] gains widespread interest and a planning application for the first phase is prepared.

- Dartington Hall Trust agree to release land for an affordable ecological building development, called 'Transition Homes'

- 'Baltic Wharf Co-housing Company' is established. The proposed Baltic Wharf development is discussed at a public meeting hosted by the town council and opens up public debate about the importance of balanced building developments and maintenance of transport and commercial options for the town's future

- The local Warm Zones initiative to support home insulation gets underway with a well-attended workshop.

- Steward Community Woodland hosts Off-Grid Renewable Energy Course for DIY[77]

Policy Makers & Service Providers

- The Enquiry by Design (EbD) process succeeds in bringing all interested parties together to agree on the future of development for Totnes. This EDAP, as well as the community's DPD response and the work of TOTSOC through its Public Realm initiatives, all feed into the revised DPD, which sees ATMOS as one of the key developments that will do a great deal to unlock the transition of Totnes and District

- SHDC reviews its options for the new Housing and Communities budget line for new local authority housing under the National Affordable Housing Programme. It puts in a bid for the ATMOS project[78]

- The Government announces a scaling-down of its plans for 10 eco-towns due to local opposition

- A group in Totnes petition national Government to allow local authorities to revert to being the governing body in the provision of affordable homes, rather than the onus being on private developments which distort the planning process.

2010

Individuals

- Inspired by their involvement in the Transition Together scheme, six streets in Totnes bulk-buy insulation and have a 'Street Makeover' day, when they help insulate each other's lofts, and then celebrate together at the end of the day. The BBC makes a documentary about the day and the preparations for it, which inspires many hundreds of other streets across the country to do the same. Many Local Authorities across the UK offer the scheme to their local Transition groups

SS THE TIMELINE

• Energy-efficient buildings • Reused and recycled materials
social, affordable and community housing.

- TTT's annual tour of ecological buildings in Totnes attracts over 200 people (up from 70 in 2009)
- 200 people sign up for the Warm Zones initiative, helping themselves to discounts and home insulation; TTT also raise some funds.

Community

- Work on Phase 1 at ATMOS commences. It consists of approximately 16 office units, and 3 workshop spaces as well as a renovation of the Brunel building which is converted into ATMOS Arts, a centre for music, community, youth, and the arts. These are to be built in a variety of materials, so as to showcase, in miniature, the potential of those materials for the site as a whole. They include straw-bale, hemp, cob and other more experimental approaches and reused materials where available. The development is co-ordinated by the Totnes Sustainable Construction Company
- 'Construction in Transition' training begins, in partnership with Dartington, the Devon Earth Building Association, the Building Limes Forum, Totnes Sustainable Construction Company and South Devon College. The nationally recognised training runs one day a week for 30 weeks, and building companies in the area send key staff for the training. It is designed as a hands-on immersion in natural building techniques and materials and is designed around the first phase of construction at the ATMOS development
- T & D Local & Natural Building Materials Cooperative is formed. They open a trading post at Totnes market selling sheep's wool for insulation and set up a website with information about locally available building materials, how to produce them and where to buy them.

Policy Makers & Service Providers

- Intrigued by the number of applications coming through their Planning Department specifying local materials, SHDC commissions a major piece of research into the potential stimulus that the local sourcing of building materials could bring to the flagging local economy. The report, "From the Ground Up: the case for local materials", takes six months, and concludes that a requirement by the Council for any new buildings to contain at least 50% of local materials, could bring over £36 million into the local economy, as well as promoting opportunities for new businesses, skills, research and product development[79].
- SHDC review the potential of recommending reused and recycled building materials and decide to improve their recycling centres to support recycling of all building materials, recognising that large-scale reuse and recycling needs to be carried out on building sites. They commission an information brochure 'The reuse and recycling of building materials' which is to be issued with every granting of planning permission; planning conditions will indicate where used materials may be appropriate
- SHDC, in partnership with TTT, launch 'Homes For Totnes'[80], a scheme that offers owners of second homes the opportunity to let their homes to local key workers. Although the rents are slightly lower, they are secure and guaranteed, and the 'feel good' factor of the scheme means that within the first year, 40 homes are made available
- Planning permission is fast-tracked on the first phase of ATMOS, and building work starts on this and the Dartington Transition Homes project
- Central Government announces zero rate VAT for locally-sourced natural building materials
- SHDC revise their policy on grants for roof insulation to allow sloping roofs (i.e., as in dormer bungalows and roof extensions) to qualify for these grants.

BUILDING AND HOUSING
PATHWAYS ACRO

Strategic themes: • Access to locally produced building materials
• Good planning and best practice in new-builds with

2011

Individuals

- The Totnes Retrofit Street Challenge begins. With part funding available from the Department of Energy and Climate Change, six streets in Totnes do battle with each other to see which can lower its carbon footprint in the most imaginative ways possible (the event is promoted as "It's a Carbon Knockout!"). Many of those involved have been previously been involved in Transition Together groups. The Challenge runs for a week during July, as part of the Village Repair Festival, which brings hundreds of people to Totnes for intensive bursts of sustainability activity. The street makeover becomes an annual event, like the Festival itself

- The new cob house on Staple Hill in Dartington, which was completed in 2009, wins the prestigious Innovative House of the Year Award, reflecting the growing interest in local materials and natural building among the architecture profession.

Community

- The first businesses move into the straw-bale section of the ATMOS office centre. The building proves a huge hit with tourists, and Network Rail finds it has to make repairs to the station's bridge more frequently, as most people who get off the train and walk into town want to see the ATMOS buildings en route. Their iconic design is soon picked up by postcard manufacturers, and within a year they appear on postcards of the town alongside the Clocktower and the Castle, displacing Vire Island as a local landmark people most want to see

- The South Devon Hemp Farmers Co-operative is formed. Eight farmers from within 10 miles of Totnes set themselves up to produce the hemp that will be needed as part of the forthcoming Zero Carbon Homes Code. They travel first to Northern Ireland, and then to France, to see hemp building in practice. With a loan from the Triodos Bank, they buy a mineraliser/decorticator, which will allow them to process the hemp they grow. They apply to DEFRA for a licence to grow hemp.

Policy Makers & Service Providers

- SHDC unanimously approve the new Transition Zero Carbon Homes Code, developed in the wake of the previous year's local materials report and also as part of its new commitment to the 'Transition' branding of the town. The Council funds a 'Totnes, a town in Transition' sign to be fixed to all the 'Totnes' signs on the entrances to the town. The code will be enforceable from the start of 2014. Despite initial opposition from developers, the Council holds that the opportunities for innovation and being 'ahead of the curve' far outweigh any inconvenience caused

- Following on from the successful review and renewal of Landmatters' planning permission in Allerleigh, SHDC begins a review to look at the role of low-impact dwellings in the countryside

- SHDC begins producing a range of leaflets and information packs for builders and homeowners about the implications of the new building code and drops its proposals for new development on greenfield sites, apart from rare examples where the need for access to uncontaminated growing land can be shown to be integral to the development

- SHDC decide to re-evaluate how they intend to deliver their core objectives. Although the Council still aspires to promoting enterprise, building skills, affordable housing, entrepreneurship, new

SS THE TIMELINE

• Energy-efficient buildings • Reused and recycled materials
social, affordable and community housing.

businesses, and so on, it changes the aspiration of 'promoting the economic growth of the region' to 'promoting economic resilience and diversity'. It states in a new position paper on the local economy, that it sees the low carbon/Transition agenda of promoting local food production and procurement, energy efficiency and strengthening local economies as being far more likely to deliver its core aims than a continued belief in 'business as usual'

- The Government reverses its policy on VAT exemptions for new buildings. Instead VAT exemptions will apply to building goods and services for refurbishments.

another new business 'South Hams Eco-Prefab'starts up in partnership with the Totnes Sustainable Construction Company, specialising in off-site construction. Their straw-bale panels, in effect a pre-tensioned straw-bale wall, with its lime render base coat already in place[81], rapidly becomes one of their best-selling products. Their straw-bale kit homes also sell very well, and within 12 months they have a waiting list. This success inspires other local entrepreneurs to start similar business ventures

- New planning applications to SHDC reflect the concern about a hotter, wetter climate, with proposed buildings incorporating features such as external shading, high-capacity guttering, shutters for heat retention and cooling in the summer

2012

Individuals

- The quarter of the houses in the Transition Homes development on the Dartington Estate that are to be self-built get underway. Seven families from the Dartington housing list come forward, and receive a low, but manageable, income during the 14 months when they are trained in construction and learn how to build their own houses. While most use timber frame, two families build in cob. Jennifer Dade, a single mother who is part of the scheme, tells the Totnes Times, "This really is a dream come true. I am actually building a house for my family. The training has been fantastic, and we have built such a strong community, long before we actually will be living together! I don't think I have ever seen my kids happier than when they were clay plastering the house last weekend"

- The rest of the houses are manufactured off-site. Based at Greyfields Timber Yard at Dartington,

Community

- Dave Hampton, a 21 year-old former KEVICC student, buys the rights to extract from a rich clay seam near Rattery, and sets up the Clay Plaster Company with a small business loan from the Totnes Pound Community Start-up Fund, run from a workshop within the first phase of ATMOS. He makes easy-to-use clay plasters[82] and offers training in their use. His first six months of trading are brisk, and by the end of the year he has expanded into making cob bricks as well

- The South Devon Hemp Farmers Co-operative harvests their first crop of hemp. It proves a sharp learning curve, but they are pleased with the first year's harvest, which is to be used the following year to retrofit Totnes Museum

- Greyfield Sawmill, on the Dartington Estate, who in 2009 built Devon's largest straw-bale structure, loses its position to the Dartington Fungus Factory, a climate-controlled building set up to grow a variety of mushrooms for medicinal uses, to be both sold as gourmet foods, as well as being processed into health tinctures[83]. A huge work

BUILDING AND HOUSING
PATHWAYS ACRO

Strategic themes: • Access to locally produced building materials
• Good planning and best practice in new-builds with

party from the town raises the building's walls in three days

• Suppliers' yards for used and recycled building materials open up around the area, many re-using empty farm buildings. The 'Builders Barns' open up employment opportunities and interest in building crafts

Policy Makers & Service Providers

• Emboldened by the success of the first phase of ATMOS, SHDC grant planning permission for Phase 2 which features live-work units and some retail and light-industrial units

• SHDC announce that from March 1st, all lights and non-essential appliances in its buildings will be switched off at night. They also announce sweeping energy conservation measures across the authority, and the building of 12 timber framed straw-bale houses in an under-utilised part of their car park, to provide overnight accommodation for staff who live far from Totnes to reduce the amount of travelling they have to do

• SHDC publishes its 'Low Impact Development in the South Hams' report, which sets out criteria by which such development would be allowed. In its opening preamble, it states that the sharply rising price of oil, and the grave impacts this is having on local farmers' ability to continue to farm, means that innovative measures need to be taken in terms of providing reliable and committed extra labour[84]. With a significant movement from the cities of people needing to be gainfully employed[85], the Council promotes small clusters of energy-efficient houses, built with local and recycled materials, with certain restrictions and caveats, as a way of enabling this

• Insulation made from recycled plastic fleece is free by SHDC as part of their local energy efficiency scheme

• SHDC commence the review of its Development Plan and agree to start from scratch as "the entire nature of building as we knew it 10 years ago has turned upside down". They open consultation on their next 10-year plan and are astonished by the active interest and informed nature of the initial response that is for minimal new development. They discover widespread interest in making good use of the existing building stock, and that people are generally more content with smaller living space and enthusiastic about maintaining open space for growing food. They decide to look at the possibility of fitting taller buildings into the landscape to minimise the area of land used, and to review options for linking semi-detached buildings into small terraces, adjoined by first-floor flats. SHDC also receive many requests for co-housing and other communal living arrangements, which can be accommodated in existing buildings. With the trend towards a generally older population, they investigate innovative living arrangements working elsewhere which have a good age mix.

Individuals

• Local energy companies introduce the '2030 Tariff' as part of the national Government's push to reduce carbon emissions. Under the scheme, householders commit to keeping their electricity consumption below an agreed number of units per person and in return get put on a lower tariff. This encourages energy efficiency, and by helping reduce demand, makes the Government's renewable plan for the UK more realistic. Janet Staplehead, who, along with her husband Mike, recently bought a house in Diptford, tells the Totnes Times "this new tariff has been amazing

SS THE TIMELINE

• Energy-efficient buildings • Reused and recycled materials
social, affordable and community housing.

2013-15

for us. We've never been huge users of electricity, but for the first time we feel actually encouraged to use less"

• The new wave of strong interest in natural building materials is extending to the paints and finishes being used within buildings. Now that many buildings are far more airtight, builders and building occupants are sourcing non-toxic paints and furnishings.

Community

• Totnes Museum becomes the first listed building to be retrofitted, to make it more energy efficient. After detailed discussion with English Heritage, the building is plastered internally with locally grown hemp mixed with lime, with sheepswool insulation. Curator Alan Langmaid tells the Totnes Times "it's been quite a juggle, trying to keep the Museum open for visitors while at the same time the team have been in doing the work. For a while I was worried about the fact that most visitors found the hemp and the work the lads were doing more interesting than the exhibits, but the increase in visitor numbers has been due, I think, largely to the work happening here. It also looks beautiful, everyone comments on it. Also, it's the first time since I started working here that I have been warm in February"

• One of the workshops in the first phase of ATMOS is used by Michael Ricketts to start manufacturing triple-glazed high performance windows with local timber, as 'The Zero Carbon Window Company'. Given the amount of windows that will be required by the next two phases of ATMOS,

the ATMOS developers become 49% partners in the business, having negotiated a good price for windows, and Ricketts also secures a start-up grant of £100,000 from the South West RDA. The deal suits both himself and ATMOS, and Michael is able to employ six people in the workshop. The company also refurbishes old window for re-use

• Work commences on the second phase of ATMOS. This will provide 1,730m2 of commercial space, 1,380m2 of retail space and 1,100m2 of cultural space. The issues that had to be resolved to enable this phase to be built on the flood zone were challenging, but resulted in innovative solutions

• Prince Charles visits ATMOS and hails it as 'an architectural gem of the South West, one that embodies the great ambition of the Transition movement'. Hundreds turn out to see him. He arrives by train, part of his new image as the 'Post-Oil Royal'

• The same model is used to establish a second enterprise at ATMOS, 'Lofty Ideals', which processes waste paper, particularly newspapers, to produce loft insulation

• Building inspectors receive training in natural building materials, so as to enable them to act as advisors as much as enforcers. They train people in how to make clay plasters, and offer guidance as to what is a good plaster

• Many community groups have expanded the Builders' Barn idea and separate out old building tools, screws, nails as well as many building parts, making good income to provide local employment. They have set up a website where they all log their current stocks and 'opening' prices (to barter).

BUILDING AND HOUSING
PATHWAYS ACRO

Strategic themes: • Access to locally produced building materials
• Good planning and best practice in new-builds with

Policy Makers & Service Providers

- SHDC become the key delivery agent for national Government's 'Great Retrofit' project. The aim is to retrofit all homes in the country by 2025, a key output of the Climate Bill. Totnes, given its status as a Transition Town, is selected to be in the first phase. The Council train 70 local builders to carry out the work, and start with the least efficient housing stock, in Bridgetown. For those on benefits the service is free; for those more able to afford it, the cost of the retrofit takes the form of a 20-year, interest-free loan, which is tied to the house itself, not the owner. This makes the repayments far smaller and more manageable, avoiding the need for up-front capital

- The new SHDC Local Development Plan for Totnes and District comes on stream and is remarkable for the minimal amount of proposed new housing. By contrast, the review of existing buildings which led up to the plan has identified a number of buildings, domestic and commercial, to be redeveloped on site (to Transition Zero Carbon Homes Code), increasing the height of the buildings, making them more suitable for the hotter and wetter climate, and re-using existing materials on site and local building materials otherwise. Many allotment and horticulture sites are identified in the area and there are interesting proposals for mixed domestic and commercial developments, in particular on the Babbage Road site where flooding has encroached, and for local power generation. The notion is that development will not be so market-led, and SHDC state their intention to use compulsory purchase to provide buildings and land for affordable housing. Local people feel very engaged with the innovative and interesting proposals in this development plan

- The Transition Zero Carbon Homes Code becomes law for all new planning applications across the county

- After refusing several planning applications for re-opening slate quarries (the largest being near Brooking) which had all been closed for over 100 years, as well as for new lime kilns, SHDC issues new guidance on the re-opening of such local small scale operations. After deliberating the nature conservation issues around such operations, the Council recommends that unless the impacts on neighbours are completely unacceptable, and where they can prove commercial viability, modest-output operations should be approved

- DCC Senior Officer for Children's Services unit invites schools to submit applications for retrofitting in schools to "try and match the zero energy levels at Dartington". Their energy audits indicate that most schools have marked improvements in efficiency and behaviour but lack capital investment for insulation and renewable energy supplies

- In response to the 2009 petitioning which led to a national debate on the issue, the Government announces a roll-back of the role of local authorities to provide affordable housing stating, "local authorities are the bodies best-placed to access needs and implement social and affordable housing. Let's put them back in the centre to deliver on this vital need". With the revisions to tax collection, Local Authorities are well placed to purchase property to accommodate housing needs

SS THE TIMELINE

• Energy-efficient buildings • Reused and recycled materials
social, affordable and community housing.

2016-20

Individuals

● The 'Re-inhabit Your House' movement gathers momentum in Totnes and surrounding parishes. With no space left for building new houses, and with people struggling to afford to keep their homes, architects begin to specialise in looking at how to enable more people to share and divide up houses. Innovative design approaches mean that aged relatives move back with their families, and some streets begin to resemble co-housing developments

● The dramatic and very noticeable decline in traffic on the roads has meant that communities are able to re-inhabit their streets. During the summer, street parties and games become a regular occurrence

● Many people are retrofitting their homes with heat wave add-ons; pergolas with vines, porches and shutters are giving the area a Mediterranean appearance. Larger gutters and huge water butts are also very visible

● People are generally much fitter; hod carriers, carpenters and builders all prefer the natural and often lighter materials they are using for new builds and retrofits.

Community

● Totnes and District now features five working slate quarries and 10 small lime kilns, as well as eight new sawmills. Oak and sweet chestnut shingles are now commonplace

● As the local building materials infrastructure grows, with more sawmills, well-managed woods, and so on, building becomes a more seasonal process. Timber has to be ordered in advance, and materials such as cob, clay plasters and lime can only be used during the spring and summer months.

● The wealth of experience that has been amassed over the previous six years in all aspects of natural building, and the innovation that has been unleashed by the many new businesses that have emerged, culminate in the redevelopment of the Civic Hall in Totnes. The iconic building, hardly recognisable from the old one; has been refurbished using timber frame, straw-bale walls, and solar heating. It features a partial food garden on its roof, and also offers an innovative outdoor space to provide cover for the markets and functions in the Civic Square. The building is lime rendered, and the pargeting (relief limework) on the front depicts scenes from the town's history. The new hall is light, spacious, and was rapturously received by the town. At the official opening, Sir Kevin McCloud, told the audience "this Civic Hall is not only a wonderful new resource for the town, but also a celebration of the wealth of imaginative ideas, the wide variety of local building materials and traditional skills revived over the past decade"

● Applications for the new retail and commercial units at the newly completed Phase 2 at ATMOS outnumber the number of units available. Many are re-siting their business operations to be close to the railway station and a couple of the commercial units, which directly serve the growing, exports of local food products to City

BUILDING AND HOUSING
PATHWAYS ACRO

Strategic themes: • Access to locally produced building materials
• Good planning and best practice in new-builds with

markets. Transport operators, including Totnes Rickshaws, Bike deliveries, and bicycle hire companies, are all interested in relocating to ATMOS

- Financial and planning considerations sorted out, ATMOS Phase 3 gets underway. Many of the live-work units have already been purchased off-plan and there is considerable enthusiasm for this new and very interesting development.

Policy Makers & Service Providers

- The site of the former Morrisons supermarket, which closed the previous year, is given planning permission for a mixture of live-work units and light industrial units. Two-thirds of the car park is taken up and converted into an intensive market garden. A weekly fruit and veg. market takes place every Monday

- Totnes emergency services co-locate with Totnes Police Station and give the station and Magistrates Court a full retrofit. "No more chilly shifts" says Constable Waring, who is delighted with the new under-floor heating in the reception area. The old fire station is, retrofitted, refurbished and turned into a new residential home for Elders.

2021-25

Individuals

- All 18 year-olds complete their education feeling confident that they could help build a house. They have been trained, during their school years, in the range of natural building techniques, and much life and beauty has been breathed into their sterile classrooms through their practical workshops

- Many people now live in the landscape rather than in more formal homes, often occupying yurts, bothies and small cabins which dot the countryside, give the land a more lived-in look and enable more people to work in agriculture.

Community

- Over 50% of development that now takes place in Totnes is done through community-owned businesses. The return that this generates is used to initiate and support more development, and the virtuous cycle is by now well established

- Sophisticated tree houses have become popular as student accommodation in Dartington. Summer school studies are extended to include craft, bush-craft and forest-gardening skills. Award-winning 'Totnes Tree Residences' win a competition to construct a two-bedroom solar apartment in Harberton's largest oak tree

- All residences and commercial units are now completed and fully occupied at ATMOS, "a wonderful regeneration of the old Dairy Crest site" says the new Town Mayor as she cuts the ribbon at the official launch of the edible water gardens.

SS THE TIMELINE

• Energy-efficient buildings • Reused and recycled materials
social, affordable and community housing.

Individuals

- All existing houses in Totnes have now been retrofitted to a high standard
- Roof surfaces have become a valuable commodity, with businesses selling the rights to put photo-voltaic on the roofs of their properties for as much as £10,000
- A survey shows that 100% of householders can tell a casual enquirer the depth of the insulation in their loft, walls and under the floor. Many of them put it there too
- The survey also reveals that 30% of the local community live in buildings with some shared or communal space occupied by people to whom they are not directly related. Most agree they prefer to live this way.

2026-30

Policy Makers & Service Providers

- Totnes Hospital is given a full retrofit by Devon PCT. As part of its new in-house energy systems, photovoltaic cells are fitted across the entire area of the roof space not already occupied by solar hot water panels. The PCT also provides funding for solar-powered water heating to be installed in all the community halls where rotating family services and dental clinics are now held
- Follaton House opens a new Home Construction Model Suite, which provides an in-house demonstration model and advises on all aspects of eco-design based on locally sourced and reused materials. All sixth-form students have trips to visit this new resource
- SHDC purchases properties at ATMOS for those remaining on its housing list.

Community

- Many young people spend their gap year staying in the area, but getting involved in a natural house building process. They volunteer, and live and work as part of a team for nine months, during which time they build a house or shelter and learn all the relevant skills by doing so. Employers particularly seek out young people with this experience, as research has shown that young people who have done this tend to be able team workers who excel in any team situation
- Alan Sugar's new series ' The Baleprentice', puts 10 novice natural builders onto a building site with the brief to build him a straw bale retirement cottage. Each week he weeds out the member of the team who is pulling their weight the least, and throws them off the site.

Policy Makers & Service Providers

- SHDC publish their latest guidance on building and planning, and for the first time, barely mention the word 'cement', as this has become a very expensive and rare material. They also publish guidelines on what they call 'Filling in the Gaps', which is the filling in of spaces between existing houses. In streets with semi-detached houses, there is a growing demand to join more houses together, so as to make the existing houses more energy efficient, create space for new people, and to transform streets of isolated residents into co-housing developments. Although such developments take a lot of facilitating at the community level, the first two pilots prove highly successful and look rather Venetian
- South Hams Green Bonds, which have been issued since 2014, are found to have made a substantial return for investors and a major contribution towards the development, building and retrofitting of Totnes and District.

© Richard Hodgson

Transition Homes

Emerging from the TTT Building and Housing Group, Transition Homes is a development of low-impact, low-cost homes for local people that centres on the close integration of housing and sustainable food production and features high energy efficiency and the use of local natural materials. The development will have a small carbon footprint and be self sufficient in energy and power, which will be generated by the use of renewable energy technologies and locally available fuel sources.

Some features of the development will include:

◎ Housing integrated with gardens and shared growing areas to enable residents to produce their own food, herbs and medicines

◎ Fruit and nut trees will be incorporated into the landscaping of the scheme,

◎ Minimal parking on site and a community car share scheme designed to discourage car use and encourage walking, cycling and the use of public transport

◎ High levels of natural insulation and air tightness

◎ All flooring, walls and cladding will be constructed from and coated with natural, non-fossil fuel materials

◎ Wood-burning stoves will provide for heating, cooking and hot water in the winter with the addition of solar hot water systems and the potential use of biogas

◎ The installation of compost loos will reduce water use and eliminate the need for a sewage system

◎ Grey water will be diverted for irrigation and rainwater will be harvested from the roofs.

This will be a conscious experiment in sustainable living; the lessons learnt and the research data collected will be documented and shared for the benefit of the community at large. A Community Land Trust has been set up in the form of a company limited by guarantee, to provide a benefit to the local community and ensure that the houses remain affordable in perpetuity, along with a not-for-profit development and construction company. Discussions are underway with a number of landowners in the area.

For further information, visit www.totnes.transitionnetwork.org/buildingandhousing/home

Building Transition Homes. © Jim Carefrae

Totnes Sustainable Construction Company

Members of the Transition Town Totnes (TTT) Building & Housing Group have founded Totnes Sustainable Construction Ltd (TSC Ltd) as a not for profit company limited by guarantee. The aims of the company are sustainable design, construction and refurbishment with an emphasis on real affordability. Although the company has no formal link with the Transition movement the close association is signified by the fact that all of the directors are longstanding TTT activists. As a company limited by guarantee any profit must be ploughed back into development and growth and cannot be paid as dividends.

The directors have over a hundred years of building experience between them and are determined to work according to ecologically sound and sustainable principles and methods. Company Chair, Chris Noakes, said, "We will prioritize the use of local and sustainable materials and want to build in an aesthetically pleasing as well as environmentally friendly way. We want to pioneer building in a way that meets the challenges of climate change, peak oil and people's aspirations for a different way of life."

Projects currently under consideration range from retrofitting existing housing to small developments of new build 'eco-homes'. Good employment practice is another objective listed in the company's memorandum of association and TSC Ltd undertakes to promote the wellbeing of employees and subcontractors through work that is satisfying, safe and useful. TSC Ltd is compiling a register of local building trades people who may wish to work with them. Registration forms will be available soon.

More information: Operations Manager, Chris Noakes: cknoakes@hotmail.com.

TRANSITION IN ACTION

TRANSITION IN ACTION

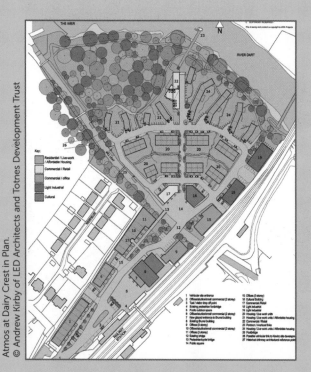

Atmos at Dairy Crest in Plan.
© Andrew Kirby of LED Architects and Totnes Development Trust

Further Reading

Totnes & Dartington Development Plan Document: Community Focus Report Document. May 2008 Coordinated by Totnes Town Council and The Totnes and District Community Strategy Group

A Pattern Language, by Christopher Alexander et al., New York OUP (1977) www.patternlanguage.com

The Natural House Book 1990 by David Pearson

South Hams District Council Sustainable Development & Building related documents:

- Totnes and Dartington Development Plan Document (DPD). October 2007
    - Local Development Framework (LDF)
    - Statement of Community Involvement
- Affordable Housing Development Plan Document (Sept. 2008)
- Consultation & Participation Strategy
- Prosperity Strategy gp meme AONB Management Plan
- Housing Strategy
- South Hams Local Development Plan

The ATMOS Project

The Atmos Project is being developed with the intention of bringing into community ownership and developing the former Dairy Crest milk processing plant, which closed in 2006 with the loss of 160 jobs. It is a partnership of Totnes Town Council, Totnes Chamber & District of Commerce, Totnes Development Trust, Totnes & District Community Strategy Group and Transition Town Totnes.

The project has been developed to meet many of the economic and social requirements of Totnes and its parishes. It is striving to create a vibrant place for businesses, visitors and the whole community. Its Vision for the Atmos Project is:

- To be a unique, contemporary, globally significant, carbon neutral site development
- To be an inspiring place to live, work, learn and relax
- To be partially owned and managed as a community enterprise closely aligned to the emerging response to peak oil
- To complement and improve the prosperity of other organisations in the area by attracting new investment, new talent and new customers
- To establish a meaningful connection with this historic town; selecting environmentally responsible materials and building forms.

You can download a detailed prospectus for the development at http://tinyurl.com/yb7489o

The Guildhall at Totnes, parts of which date back to 1088AD.
© Jacqi Hodgson

The Cob House at Cott.
© Jacqi Hodgson

Richard & Heidi's House with PV and SHW at Dartington.
© Jacqi Hodgson

Straw bale House in Totnes.
© Jacqi Hodgson

NOTES & IDEAS

Resourcing
Localisation

Totnes Friday Market. © Lou Brown

ECONOMICS AND LIVELIHOODS

"...does not mean walling off the outside world. It means nurturing locally owned businesses that use local resources sustainably, employ local workers at decent wages and serve primarily local consumers. It means becoming more self-sufficient, and less dependent on imports. Control moves from the boardrooms of distant corporations and back to the community where it belongs."
Michael Shuman[1]

The Challenge

Our present economic system is based on wealth creation from trading commodities, rather than meeting needs. Economic growth based on GDP is linear (exponential) and profit-based, requiring increasing consumption rather than a cyclic system which would trade resources more sustainably, returning more fairly shared benefits to all of society. The credit bubble has burst causing a major recession. Unemployment stands at 2.2 million having risen 100,000 per month for four consecutive months. There are worries of a 'lost generation' of young people (under 25s) entering the work market with no hope of ever having work. The tax base has collapsed and income tax rises are predicted to pay for the problem[2].

Petroleum oil has been the main economic driver since WWII, creating an opportunity for fiscal credit based on an assumption of the availability of an endless supply of cheap energy to fuel the economy, repaying the debt as profits roll in. Global oil production is now peaking and can no longer be relied upon as an economic staple; as predicted[3] we are on the cusp of a growing gap between production and demand. The age of cheap oil and speculation is closing in and with it the forecasts for growth of the economies at all levels need to be re-evaluated.

Growth-based global economics has resulted in money pouring out of local economies, while the lion's share of trading profits have been pouring into millionaires' pockets, international banks and trans-national corporations (TNCs). The World Trade Organisation (WTO) has developed a set of rules that prevent impacts on local economies, environment or social consequences being a barrier to trade, while protectionism of the local economy is touted as being bad for international development. Major international players have played havoc with small traders and local employment, sucking dry local economies across the UK and further afield. As Colin Hines (who spoke at a TTT event in February 2009[4]) puts it in his book Localisation – A Global Manifesto[5].

"Globalisation - the ever-increasing integration of national economies into the global economy through trade and investment rules and privatization, aided by technological advances. These reduce barriers to trade and investment and in the process reduce democratic controls by nation states and their communities over their domestic affairs. The process is driven by the theory of comparative advantage, the goal of international competitiveness and the growth model. It is occurring increasingly at the expense of social, environmental and labour improvements and rising inequality for most of the world."

Unfortunately key decision and policy-makers are trying to continue with the same system. The Turner Review, set up on behalf of the UK Financial Services Agency reported back in March 2009[6]. Amongst its key proposals were the following:

◎ The quality and quantity of overall capital in the global banking system should be increased, resulting in minimum regulatory requirements significantly above Basel rules. The transition to future rule should be carefully phased given the importance of maintaining bank lending in the current macroeconomic climate.

◎ Additional powers to the IMF to challenge conventional intellectual wisdoms and national policies.

2009 Global Economic Crisis hits the UK

The UK finds itself in an increasingly bewildering and alarming economic situation. The news gets worse every day, and keeping a sense of the bigger picture is difficult. Some of the key trends include:

◎ The UK's deficit on trade in goods and services was £3.6 billion in January 2009, compared with the deficit of £3.2 billion in December 2008. Exports fell by £0.8 billion, and imports fell by £0.3 billion.

◎ The national unemployment rate has risen to 6.5% for the three months to January 2009. The unemployment level and rate have not been higher since 1997.

◎ The number of people out of work and claiming benefits was 1.39 million in February 2009, up 138,400 over the previous month and up 595,600 over the year. This is the largest monthly increase in the claimant count since comparable records began in 1971.

◎ The redundancies level for the three months to January 2009 was 266,000, up 86,000 over the (previous) quarter and up 154,000 over the year. This is the highest figure since comparable records began in 1995.

◎ There were 482,000 job vacancies in the three months to February 2009, down 74,000 over the previous quarter and down 203,000 over the year. This is the lowest figure since comparable records began in 2001.

Source: Office for National Statistics.
www.statistics.gov.uk/CCI/

Totnes & District – a Traditional Local Market Town Economy

Local market town economies have been evolving since human settlements began and were thriving, relatively self-contained local systems until cheap energy stepped in, initially with coal and the steam engine fuelling the 18thcentury Industrial Revolution, and latterly the age of oil fuelling the industrialisation of agriculture, and the rise of consumerism, which has been made possible by the evolution of vast, sprawling, global distribution networks, since the 1960's. Local trading networks have been decimated as large supermarket chains operating across national and international markets set up deals with local producers, selling through large retail outlets which could out-price local shops. Subsidies to compensate farmers for reduced farm gate prices and tax incentives to encourage companies to bring employment to regions needing jobs have simply complicated matters further as they do not generally relate to the geographic resource base and have distorted farming practices away from responding to local needs.

The economy of Totnes and District was, in effect, a market town trading with its rural hinterland. For centuries the local economy was labour-intensive and based on a wide diversity of small local producers, craft workers and consumers trading and bartering local products and services. Devon's traditional resource base has been its highly productive farmland, more recently this has also become a popular tourist attraction. Local farms, skilled workers and producers successfully managed local resources, a relatively resilient local economy, historically trading outside of the area and supplementing local products with imports of luxury goods. By the 17th century, Totnes was one of the wealthiest towns in England, such that royal visits were commonplace. As Dewi Lewis puts it in 'Shutting Up Shop - The Decline of the Traditional Small Shop', "all the shops were incredibly well cared for and cherished and there was a real connection between the shop's identity and the people who ran them."

As with other local market economies in the UK, Totnes has seen dramatic changes in the past fifty years, globalisation has had its impact locally; of the seventeen villages in Totnes' rural hinterland, just nine currently have a local shop or post office. Many small businesses are operating on very small profit margins; just six months into the current recession, Totnes' farmers market closed and several small and medium sized businesses have since followed.

Business in the South Hams – Emerging Trends - Where are we Now?

The South Hams has strength in its diverse base of very small to medium size enterprises. There are over 5,000 businesses in the district, more than half of which employ fewer than five people. 'Land based industries' are most likely to employ the fewest people per business while 'manufacturing' and 'ICT' businesses tend to employ the most. This can be seen in the table below. In 2004 local businesses employed 7.5% more paid workers than in 2003.

Business as Usual or Willing to Change?

If we continue business as usual we will find ourselves in a steadily worsening situation. At the national level the over-reliance on global markets and debt-based wealth will continue the downward trend of a worsening economic crisis affecting local economies at home and abroad, unemployment will continue to rise, bringing immense hardship and undermining local vibrancy. The global economic downturn and disintegration of financial pillars already witnessed in the banking systems will be exacerbated by rising costs of energy and declining availability of oil-based fuel and products, leaving national and local economies extremely vulnerable and the least well-off in society exposed to poverty. Locally, over-reliance on a narrow base of growth sectors such as transportation, communications, distribution and construction[7] as well as low energy costs is risky as all of these are currently oil-dependent.

On the other hand if we collectively adopt the approach set out in this Plan, if we bring some sectors of the economy back into local ownership and rebuild local trading networks, we can rekindle a more resilient localised economy based on local resources being used to provide for many local needs. Alongside our current dependence on IT services and tourism for employment, we can begin to strengthen and build a more locally focused economy based on small-scale intensive agriculture, food processing, local provision of services and skills with less dependence on tourism (yet which may, ironically, become an attraction for increases in tourism!). We can stimulate local business and investment through encouraging people to buy local goods and keep money local by using local currencies, such as the Totnes Pound, bartering and local banks such as the Credit Union and the Post Office.

Employees and Business Activity (numbers) in major South Hams Business Sectors 2004

Sector	% OF EMPLOYEES	% OF ACTIVITY
Land-Based and Fishing	3.1	12.8
Tourism and Leisure	15.2	14.7
Manufacturing	17.1	8.0
Retail and Wholesale	16.5	21.2
ICT	6.2	4.0

3.46   Source: South Hams Business Survey 2001

We can take these changes even further and re-consider the fundamental basis of our economy, moving towards the principals of natural capital to underpin our values and redirect investment of time and other resources:

Checking the balance - Principals of Natural Capital / Holistic Economics:

◎ Community, Friends, Family (nurture our soul – valuing the heart)

◎ Biodiversity (provide sustenance for food & air, recreation, relaxation. Gaia, / valuing the head & the heart)

◎ Education & Skills (potential for our future & understanding of the world – valuing the hands & the head)

◎ Mineral Resources (inc. petroleum oil) (current economy based on this principal only – distorted with credit)

We can use this system to develop and check the natural economy in terms of overall balance, needs and assets

What follows is one version of how economics might become more localised and sustainable over the next 21 years.

Vision 2030

By 2030, Totnes and District has a robust localised economy linking local producers, traders, services providers and consumers. The traditional agricultural resources, seasonal products, tourism, IT, some manufacturing and local skills are the basis of the revitalised localised economy. The system is flexible, active and diverse, providing local markets with locally based goods and local people with a broad range of services and skilled employment.

The local economic currency is an interchangeable mix of Totnes Pounds, Sterling, LETS[8] credits and bartering which local businesses trade through the Totnes Bank. 80% of money now stays within the local community. Investment in the Totnes Bank and Totnes Pound has enabled many projects for local benefit to be supported and these have returned a modest interest, which has been reinvested locally. Investment in people and social enterprises, enabling them to changes people's lives and build community cohesion, has increased the social capital. Investment in education and skills for power down and the more localised community life has supported and prepared the community through difficult times.

Investment in local resources, primarily renewable energy systems (through the TRESOC[9] share option), IT, waste recycling, farming systems and research has opened many new horizons and increased local capital. The majority of local businesses operate co-operatively through local trading networks and co-operatives in mutual support. Most are modest in size and trade primarily in local products and services with sales focused on local demand. Many have scaled down their enterprises and tuned into meeting local needs rather than extravagance or luxury goods which carry risk. They co-operate on local procurement, delivery and marketing of goods and products, sharing local public transport systems and stores. In-house energy auditing and trimming waste led to a general business environmental charter[10] being adopted; this has helped guide other resilience measures.

Resilience Indicators

◎ The percentage of economic leakage out of the community

◎ The percentage the local community spend on locally procured business, goods and services.

◎ Percentage of major employers in the community that are locally owned

◎ Niche markets (in which unique opportunities exist) that take advantage of community strengths.

◎ The relative value by percentage of community owned major assets for the economic and social benefit of the community.

◎ The number of Totnes Pounds in circulation.

◎ Degree to which people perceive an openness to alternative forms of earning a living

These can be revisited regularly to see if the community is making progress in the right direction.

Employment Opportunities for a Post-Peak Oil Totnes and District

Employment Sector	Industry Type	Opportunities for Economic Development
Food Production/ Land Use	Organic Farming	Farm workers, research and innovation, value adding and processing, retail, Community Supported Agriculture initiatives
	Textile Production	Farming, processing, manufacturing
	Organic Food Production	Training, freshwater aquaculture, organic gourmet mushroom production for food and medicines, intensive market gardening, food preservation
	Forestry	Timber for construction and a variety of uses, sawdust for mushroom cultivation, charcoal, wood gasification, coppice products, saps, tannin, bark mulch, education, training, food crops, fibre
	Urban Agriculture	Co-ordination, land access provision, edible landscaping consultancy, online tools for linking growers and consumers, large potential for commercial production, plant nurseries and propagation
	Gleaning	Apple harvesting and pressing, hedgerow drinks and other products, education
	Agroforestry systems	Design consultancy, planting and ongoing management, selling of wide range of produce, long term enhanced timber value, courses, publications, research
	Schools	Edible landscaping, teaching, Education for Sustainable Development, food growing training, apprenticeships, bespoke Transition training programmes
Manufacturing and Processing	Recycling	Salvaging building materials, processing and reclaiming materials (bricks, timber etc), making insulation from waste paper, glass bottles into insulation
	Sustainable Industry	Renewable energy technologies manufacturing and installing, technology systems,
	Repair	Extending the life of machinery, building for durability
	Fabric	Processing of locally produced fabric, hemp, flax etc, making a range of clothing for retail, and repairs
	Scavenging	Materials reuse, refurbishing, resale to low-income families
Services	Healthcare	Holistic healthcare, research into effective herbal medicines, local herb growing and processing, training for doctors, apothecaries, nutritional advice
	Energy	Home insulation advice, energy monitoring, energy efficient devices, investment co-ordinators, sale of energy to grid or decentralised energy systems, producing wood chip/pellets for boilers, Energy Resilience Analyses for businesses
	Compost Management	Collecting, Managing, Training, Distribution, Education, potential links to urban food production
	Information Technology	Creation of effective software systems for energy management, carbon foot printing and much more
	Hospice services / bereavement	Hospice services, supporting families who keep relatives at home, green burials
	Financial Investment	Credit Unions, local currencies, mechanisms whereby people can invest with confidence into their community, Green Bonds, crowd funding

3.47

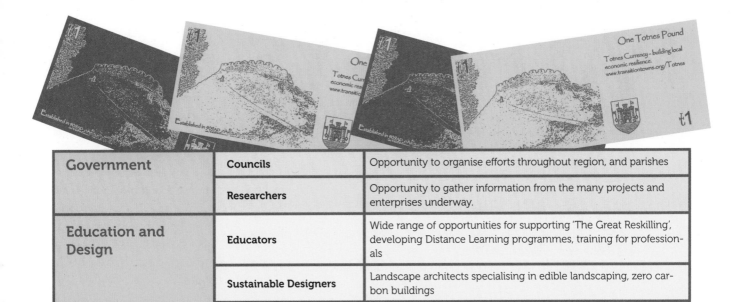

Government	Councils	Opportunity to organise efforts throughout region, and parishes
	Researchers	Opportunity to gather information from the many projects and enterprises underway.
Education and Design	Educators	Wide range of opportunities for supporting 'The Great Reskilling', developing Distance Learning programmes, training for professionals
	Sustainable Designers	Landscape architects specialising in edible landscaping, zero carbon buildings
	The Arts	Art projects documenting the Transition, installations, exhibitions, public art workshops, local recording studios, storytelling
	Transition Consulting	Working with businesses on energy audits, resilience plans, a range of future-proofing strategies
Personal / Group Support	Counselling	Personal 'Transition Counselling', group support, community processes
	Citizens Advice	Debt advice, housing advice, financial management skills, debt scheduling
	Outplacement/ Redundancy Support	Support, retraining, ongoing support and training
Media	Print media	Local newspapers, small print run books on different aspects of the Transition
	Internet	Online retailing systems for local markets
	Film media	Online TV channels documenting inspiring examples of Transition in Action
Construction	Reskilling	Retraining builders to use local materials and green building techniques, improving awareness around energy efficiency in building, setting up local construction companies, rainwater harvesting systems, design and installation
	Materials	Creating local natural building materials, clay plasters, timber, lime, straw, hemp etc. Growing, processing, distribution, retail etc. Locally made wallpaper.
	Architects	Specialists in passiv haus building, local materials, retrofit advice
Transportation	Low energy vehicle fleets	Marketing, maintaining, renting, chauffeuring
	Bicycles	Selling, servicing, maintenance training, rental
	Rickshaws	Importing, servicing, taxi service, weddings etc.
	Biodiesel	Sourcing, processing, selling, training and advice
	Biomethane/Electric vehicles	Fleet management, sales, leasing, car clubs

This chart is based on and expanded from Chen, Y., Deines, M., Fleischmann,H., Reed, S. & Swick, I. (2007) Transforming Urban Environments for a Post-Peak Oil Future: a vision plan for the city of San Buenaventura. City of San Buenaventura.

ECONOMICS AND LIVELIHOODS

PATHWAYS ACRO

Strategic themes: • Reducing energy consumption and dependence of local resources • Inspiring innovation in localised economics • Supporting small scale

2009

Individuals

- Many people grow increasingly worried about the further deterioration of the global economy and decide to not be so reliant on their paid jobs. Many sell their cars and reduce energy consumption at home, investing the savings in solar energy devices and insulation around the home. Where possible, edible plants are squeezed into gardens and patio pots

- Internet-based eco-business is growing. Moor Cars car-pool scheme opens for business. Totnes (on-line) Swap Shop Forum goes live

- More businesses in Totnes carry out Energy Resilience Assessments and introduce a range of energy-saving measures, making great savings and protecting themselves from rising bills and reducing risk.

Community

- Totnes Chamber of Commerce looks for ways to improve trading for local businesses as the national economy deteriorates further and local sales drop. They consider how social enterprise and offering training could stimulate local trading and their sales. Attracting more visitors through local package tours which include accommodation, outings and evening meals is actively explored.

- TTT launches its Totnes Pound loan scheme for local projects[11]. The number of applications for funding far outstrips grants available; the number of Totnes Pounds in circulation increases by 20%

- Refurnish recycling store takes the advice of the

Sustainable Design project[12] and has a makeover, setting up sitting-room displays and bedrooms to dream for with help from local charity shops who supply curtains and bedcovers. Its new marketing strategy reaps rewards and enables it to create more paid jobs

- TRESOC (Totnes Renewable Energy Supplies Company) launches its sale of shares for investment in local renewable energy schemes. Local support and enthusiasm enables this company to make huge strides in its first year

- Totnes Christmas Festival is extended to four Tuesdays and will include a number of street performances and story telling events in local pubs and restaurants

Policy Makers & Service Providers

- A flurry of new politicians emerges from the local and European elections with commitment to better local governance of finances, budgets and investments. Local surveys to assess the local impact of major unemployment and opportunities to create local community work and green jobs are undertaken. The new SHDC £1K community grants are a first step in a number of new measures to support local projects. DCC and SHDC agree to issuing green bonds to encourage local investment and provide money for local programmes

- G20 London Summit agrees to refinance International Monetary Fund (IMF) with $750bn plus an additional $1.1 trillion programme to restore credit, growth and jobs in the world economy. It agrees to prevent and report on protectionism of currency flows. An open letter on email to Gordon Brown suggests that the total liabilities from the vast majority of UK PFIs[13] from 2006-07 – 2032-33 is likely to be £157.9bn[14] People are shocked and demand that finances stay in the UK

SS THE TIMELINE

businesses • Keeping money in local control • More energy efficient use of production and supply chains • Localising provision of products and services

Individuals

- 5 new retail businesses open in Totnes main street; Ernie's repair services for electrical appliances, EcoAware eco-gadgets with wind-up radios, solar torches and smart meters (also an outlet for Beco's solar panels), Grappling with Grapes (requisites for home brewers), Computer Exchange & Retrofit and Totnes Natural Building Supplies

- Totnes Times runs a series of articles on how local society can benefit from supporting local businesses, they benefit too from increased advertising.

- Local tradesmen and women are adding energy saving retrofitting to their skills and getting a lot of work as plumbers installing solar hot water systems, electricians fitting PV units and builders improving internal and external insulation on walls and filling cavity walls. Many are so confident of the instant benefits that they invite their customers to pay them over six months. Some tradespersons are helping people to complete their grant applications to encourage work.

- Farmers and individuals are investing in land to let for allotments and smallholdings. Some are offering greenhouse space for rental too. The average return is about 25% and the market for people wanting allotments is growing.

Community

- Totnes becomes a Fair Trade Town – Local and Global. Most of the businesses in Fore St and High St agree to sell only goods that have been bought at fair prices from the producers.

- The new Totnes Pound is launched, in £T1, 5, 10 and 20 denominations[15]. The new launch is supported by Totnes Chamber of Commerce, and by South Hams District Council, as a way of supporting a local economy that is starting to struggle as the recession deepens. The notes are printed on DeLaRue Bank paper, and feature prominent historical local people on the notes, Leonard and Dorothy Elmhirst gracing the £5 note. Many hundreds are snapped up by collectors within the first few days of the launch. The new notes stimulate pride in the Totnes Pound, with many taxi drivers accepting them, and a surge in trading across the area.

- TTT hosts another business swap shop to help businesses save money and reuse unwanted or spoilt goods. The event identifies a much wider wide range of interests and items to exchange than before and decides to link in with Totnes Online Swap Shop Forum

Policy Makers & Service Providers

- South Hams DC and Devon County Council issue the first Green Bonds to private investors to the value of £250k. The funds generated are to be invested in local projects to reduce energy consumption and support renewable energy production in the area.

- National election manifestos of political parties set out broad economic policies aimed specifically at delivering well-being for people and demonstrate how this can also deliver high employment and public services. A carbon army

ECONOMICS AND LIVELIHOODS
PATHWAYS ACRO

Strategic themes: • Reducing energy consumption and dependence of local resources • Inspiring innovation in localised economics • Supporting small scale

of jobs of high and low-skilled workers is to be established to revitalise the UK economy and prepare the country for a low-carbon economy, as part of the Green New Deal introduced by Government. Green procurement policies for all public spending are to be initiated.

- The global economy fails to reach IMF estimates of 2% growth, used as a benchmark at G20 London Summit in 2009. IMF request for additional funding for its 2011 quotas meets with concerns about global mismanagement. "The US economy needs a rethink, we have come to the end of the line with economic growth, the time has come to look to the national and possibly the local economies to create a circle of investment and market stimulation" says President Obama. Revisiting its agreement on protectionism, the G20 summit agrees to some measures to support local economies and local trading.

2011

Individuals

- Several shops in Totnes are selling a number of energy-saving devices in response to public interest. Shopkeepers have taken to downloading energy and carbon savings about products they sell off the internet and making 'display briefs' to assist customers' understanding of the benefits.

- Christina's Designs 4 Change in Totnes opens a clothes alteration service with a special offer to revamp an old suit into a new look. Mending is coming back into fashion.

- The levels of unemployment continue to grow and an Unemployment Forum based in Totnes Connexions is established to link people with

local work paid and unpaid. A website and regular local radio slot helps stimulate local work. A number of hours work with local growers and small farmers benefits local food production and provides work. Many shops are employing people to do local deliveries as an incentive to buy local.

Community

- Fore Street and High Street in Totnes win the Carbon Trust's national competition for the High Street with the Lowest Carbon footprint in the UK. Receiving the award, the Mayor of Totnes tells The Daily Telegraph "The lesson for me from today is what a remarkable place this is, and what remarkable traders we have here. There are many awards a town can win, but surely this is the one our grandchildren will thank us for the most."

- Local co-operatives of shared-interest trades people begin to form, looking for ways to increase business as a group and stimulate local business based on local resources. One group is to carry out a feasibility study into setting up a local recycled glass business

- The first businesses open up in the business units that comprise Phase One of the ATMOS project. There is huge demand for spaces, and the units are all allocated before they are completed. Many of the businesses are new start-ups, and they find working in proximity to other green-minded enterprises to be inspiring. Many business collaborations take place, and partnerships are formed. Riverford Comes to Town's Café building with its edible rooftop garden that covers the whole building complex wins an Ethical Observer Award, Riverford's fifth. Many of the businesses based at ATMOS use the garden in some way in their logos and on their headed notepaper.

- Tibetan paper makers set up a recycling project at Dartington to recycle business waste and cardboard back into cardboard using water

SS THE TIMELINE

businesses • Keeping money in local control • More energy efficient use of production and supply chains • Localising provision of products and services

and energy from the Dart. This £10m scheme arranged by Totnes Indian Connection is funded by American grants to enable the Tibetan refugee workers (from India) to share their skills and gain a degree at Schumacher, leaving a legacy of new jobs and a business to run.

- Totnes Pounds are accepted in 30% of businesses in Totnes & District. Some discounts are offered for locally produced goods. Totnes Pound goes electronic with the launch of the 'TotCard', a debit card that incentivises the support of local shops.

- Timebanks are being developed by community groups wishing to encourage local unemployed, retired and those with spare time to involve themselves in social projects[16].

Policy Makers & Service Providers

- The new crèche at SHDC opens the way for a more flexible approach to enable staff to reduce their hours and job-share.

- SHDC announce a grant scheme for people wanting to set up new businesses in Totnes and District that play an active part in bringing the 2009 EDAP into reality. The criteria are strict, but such is the enthusiasm for business start-ups that accompanied by TTT's 'Transition Social Entrepreneur Training', there is a huge take-up for the scheme.

- Totnes Recycling Centre is to be enlarged to provide increased facilities for a re-use centre and allow for more employment based on the recyclables. Five more jobs will be created in the first instance

- SHDC proposes to invest in a broad range of environmental services to support development of local resources, as part of its 'Green New Deal' programme. Jobs will be created in recycling, tree and hedgerow planting, and home insulation and renewable energy supplies. In line with national initiatives, local green procurement policies are to be implemented

2012

Individuals

- With rising unemployment, the Connexions office has become a more open employment exchange with unemployed people waiting around for people with work to offer to turn up with a job. Many people are looking for just three or four-day working weeks and job-shares.

- Enterprising individuals find creative ways to self-employment, offering services on the doorstep: mower and knife sharpening, window cleaners, eco-cleaning services, upholstery cleaning, grass cutting, filling window baskets and herbaceous borders with edible plants.

- More people are working from home, many using the spare room(s) vacated by grown-up children as an office, beauty salon or to take in a lodger.

- Mechanics are retraining to apply their skills to electric and biofuel vehicles.

- Resource taxes including land-use taxes are to be applied to empty premises and holiday homes to reduce waste of premises, waste disposal taxes to encourage more recycling and reuse, and quarrying tax to reduce the use of virgin materials. The revenue raised from these taxes will be administered by local authorities to create green jobs. Spending on the military on overseas manoeuvres is to be reduced to allow increased investment in national contingency plans to combat climate emergencies

- National government agrees an Energy Rebate on income tax to encourage taxpayers to invest in renewable energy on their homes. Investments are tied to trained personnel carrying out the installations, and are expected to create at least 20 new jobs in Totnes and District.

ECONOMICS AND LIVELIHOODS
PATHWAYS ACRO

Strategic themes: • Reducing energy consumption and dependence of local resources • Inspiring innovation in localised economics • Supporting small scale

Community

- Fairtrade status extends out to the entire district as outcomes of the Totnes Retail Audit find this has had a positive impact on sales and increased interest in local products.

- Tourism enterprises have expanded to build on the local low-energy travel systems. A number of small café enterprises serving predominantly local food have appeared at the new Travel Hubs and Well-being Gardens. Tourists get a T&D travel pass which includes bike hire and safety bands for walkers together with a map of walks, bike lanes, buses timetables, café opening times, public toilets and facilities for children and nappy changing.

- The ATMOS development's Light Industrial units open for business. Immediately they are all leased, to some innovative businesses, a waste oil processing/biodiesel plant, a business turning waste paper into an insulation material, a garage for servicing electric vehicles, and a 'local food station', which gathers food from local small producers and distributes it around the town. They all say they are attracted to the development by its profile and the potential interactions with other green businesspeople.

amount to cover needs at affordable prices. All Government subsidies for fossil fuels are to be redirected to producing renewable energy supplies.

- UK Post Office Services make a deal with E-bay to deliver their goods to local post offices (and a collection card to the customer) for a lower fee. Courier services are disgruntled but many buyers are delighted.

- DCC & SHDC announce a number of budget reallocations to support local job creation and reduction in fossil fuels. There is to be greater investment in recycling and waste to create employment, and highways budgets are to be reduced and reallocated to providing public transport.

- National Government bows to public pressure to support local communities by conducting a major overhaul of the income tax system. This is to move towards simplification and a greater proportion of budgets being administered locally. National insurance will be included within income taxation, VAT will be combined with resource taxation

- Credit Unions announce major increases in local membership and investment.

Policy Makers & Service Providers

- The newly expanded Totnes Post Office is employing more people and has a range of services for local shops and businesses. With a new suite of telecommunication services to support small businesses and individuals, it offers full internet access facilities, virtual conferencing portals and hot desks.

- Rationing is to be introduced to help people access lower-price electricity, fuel and food staples. Energy quotas are likely to vary and people will be assisted in accessing a certain

Individuals

- A general move away from full-time work is happening and many people job-share or work a four-day week. Salaries at the lower end of the scale have improved to enable changes as hierarchies have flattened since large earnings have become embarrassing

- A major increase in jobs and services comes on-stream as the energy business is identified as the fastest growing industry. A number of local commercial companies are changing their operations in this direction

SS THE TIMELINE

businesses • Keeping money in local control • More energy efficient use of production and supply chains • Localising provision of products and services

- Horse breeding is making a comeback and many farmers, having been unable to afford to replace their tractors have invested in single horsepower for transport and carrying on the farms. Many people are supplementing their income with home kitchen enterprises; home knitted slippers from Dartmoor wool, home-made preserves and bottled foods from local produce, and home-produced natural beauty treatments are becoming a very familiar sight on market stalls

- UK holidaymaking has grown and Devon is the no. 1 UK destination. Eco-holidays are expanding with many new small operators in the area who offer on-site yurt accommodation, soup kitchens with music and board games for holidaymakers. Many people thinking about moving out of the city try out these holiday adventures. The new Green Hotel at Dartington boasts ground source heat pumps, solar hot water and smart energy lighting with motion sensors. The gym captures pedal power and food waste is recycled via their chickens

Community

- Totnes and District Local & Natural Building Co-operative open three Trading Posts at Dartington, Marldon and South Brent. They are a wide network of local suppliers, builders and fitters. In response to popular demand they carry on selling sheepswool insulation at Totnes market adding Draughty Corners Insulation mini-packs to their 'Easy and Natural' home improvements range.

- Under the T&D Chamber of Commerce, a Post-Office consortium is formed for T&D to implement the recent Government proposals and supports for new rural Post Offices in all the villages in the district. They help network potential traders with local suppliers, the local distribution network, and apply for post-office workers' training days.

- Use of the Totnes Pound within more official systems, Post Offices and credit unions is under consideration.

- Totnes Glass is established as a Community share company making standard utility glassware out of recycled glass. The plant to be sited at Babbage Road Industrial Estate alongside the recycling depot will employ eight people. They plan to set up a more comprehensive glass collection system to avoid glass being broken unnecessarily and wasting energy; wine bottles, jam jars etc. will be checked for cracks and washed ready for reuse and resale. They have been awarded the contract for milk bottles for the new T & D Dairy Co-operative.

- Totnes Pounds are accepted in 50% of businesses in Totnes & District. Credit Unions are taking this currency. The loans scheme has expanded to underwrite £25k for local projects and has attracted £75k of match funds.

Policy Makers & Service Providers

- Community jobs are being created by SHDC and the Parish Councils under a Community Employment Scheme established to create jobs and support local transition activities. Parish Councils can apply for one part time employee per 100 residents to support local initiatives under the Sustainable Communities Act and energy reduction programmes in their parishes. Some of the initiatives involve community research and local plans and are anticipated to appeal to GAP-year students, who it is hoped will gain interest in their local areas.

- A package of changes is announced by national government to allow localisation and support community led initiatives. These include 50% of income tax and 50% of business tax being collected and administered by local authorities

2013-15

ECONOMICS AND LIVELIHOODS
PATHWAYS ACRO

Strategic themes: • Reducing energy consumption and dependence of local resources • Inspiring innovation in localised economics • Supporting small scale

2016-20

Individuals

- Totnes Travel has pioneered 'Exchange is as Good as a Rest Holidays' web-booked house exchanges. Initially targeted at the UK markets, it has now spread to northern France. Families book other people's houses via a web pool. Local businesses also profit from the package of days out, cycle hire and dinner deals etc. that go with the house.

- Farmers are offering a wide range of local work opportunities, many including simple accommodation. The work includes training in food growing, hedgerow management and animal husbandry skills. People with these skills are highly sought after. Reimbursement is part paid in food.

Community

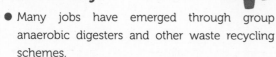

- Many jobs have emerged through group anaerobic digesters and other waste recycling schemes.

Policy Makers & Service Providers

- The restructuring of Income Tax is revisited and it is agreed that 70% will be collected directly by local authorities for them to administer, the other 30% will be paid to National Government.

- Under a ruling of the UN, the Global Agreement on Trades and Tariffs (GATT) is to be replaced with the Global Agreement on Sustainable Trade (GAST), which will strengthen democratic control of trade, stimulate industries and services that benefit local communities and re-diversify local economies.

2021-25

Individuals

- Ebay is estimated to have more turnover than any other trading company. It is widely used for people to buy foreign goods such as tea and coffee directly from the growers. Most national post office services have agreed a similar reduced tariff model to the UK.

- Stoke Gabriel Tanners finally opens the new tannery (using digestate from the anaerobic digesters and local hides) with strict planning conditions. The leather will be used locally at the expanded Conkers Shoe and Leather works. Two new cobblers and leather repairs shops have opened in Diptford and Cornworthy.

- Most people now work just four days for paid work, using the additional time for food growing, community activity and supports and family time. This has released a lot more jobs to be shared around.

Community

- Totnes Pounds are accepted in all businesses in Totnes & District. Totnes & District Bank is under discussion. A feasibility study has indicated a strong chance of success provided 80% of trade is local.

SS THE TIMELINE

businesses • Keeping money in local control • More energy efficient use of production and supply chains • Localising provision of products and services

Policy Makers & Service Providers

- DCC and SHDC invite proposals for co-operative and community-based commercial ventures that would diversify local production and light manufacturing further. A key objective is ideas that support local needs and increase local vibrancy. Clothing made from nettles is an early success from this scheme. T & D also wins the national tender to produce portable waste oil conversion kits and components.

Individuals

- Tourism in the area has changed. Fewer rooms and apartments are available, as the local population has swelled. Boarding houses and campsites have made a comeback and restaurants have declined. Some farmers offer traditional farm work and skills holidays; families from the city enjoy getting their hands dirty and working the horse-drawn carts to collect wood.

- Vibrant and busy local shops and post offices are now well established in all the villages in the district. Post Offices are well used; in particular the local business communications and poste restante service for newcomers and foreign migrants. Notice boards and other information exchange services have sprung up around these shops. Some businesses have opened a combined food shop with another business such as a bar, tearooms, nappy laundry, alteration service, etc.

- Car mechanics at 'Modern Vintage' are refitting some of the old petrol vehicles with modern electric motors.

- Employment is almost 95% although very few work a five-day week. Most people have enough time and enough money to lead happy fulfilling lives

Community

- Art groups have emerged as an important marketing element for many local businesses and hand-painted signs over shops and on hoardings are producing attractive and colourful streetscapes.

- Community work parties to induct and support foreign migrants are creating jobs in waste services and craft work

Policy Makers & Service Providers

- The restructuring of income tax is revisited and it is agreed that 80% will be collected directly by local authorities for them to administer, the other 20% will be paid to National Government. 60% of business tax will remain local and 40% will go to national government. Pensions and other state benefits will now be paid out of the local tax budget. Town and parish councils are to get a greater share of finance and their responsibilities will also increase to managing a number of open spaces, community halls and recreational facilities.

- Through the passing of the Green Bank bill, National Government sanctions a federation of local banks that can exchange funds and local currencies electronically within the UK.

2026-30

The Totnes Pound

The Totnes Pound was launched as an initiative of Transition Town Totnes Economics and Livelihoods group in March 2007. Economic localisation is considered to be a key aspect of the transition process, and local currency systems provide the opportunity to strengthen the local economy whilst preventing money from leaking out.

The benefits of the Totnes Pound are:

◎ To build resilience in the local economy by keeping money circulating in the community and building new relationships

◎ To get people thinking and talking about how they spend their money

◎ To encourage more local trade and thus reduce food and trade miles

◎ To encourage tourists to use local businesses

There are around 70 local businesses that now accept the Totnes Pound. The Totnes Pound has had three phases so far, the most recent being a One Pound note which is exchanged for a pound sterling. Every pound bought into circulation leads to £1 sterling being banked, and the Totnes Currency team recently announced that they would use their bank balance to provide interest-free loans to 'green' projects in Totnes. There are plans for an extension of the currency, drawing from other local currencies, which have themselves been inspired by the Totnes Pound experiment. Lewes in Sussex, Stroud in Gloucestershire and Brixton in London now have their own more widely denominated currencies, with £1, £5, £10 and £20 notes. In Brixton, the Chief Executive of the local Council has even indicated that it would be happy to accept payment for Council Tax in Brixton Pounds, a national first! What started as an experiment here is rapidly taking off in other towns.

For a list of issuing points and businesses that accept the Totnes Pound see www.totnes.transitionnetwork.org/totnespound/home

Totnes Market © Lou Brown

Landscope at Dartington

Our vision is a vibrant landscape of interconnected business and enterprise, of healthy and productive soils and woodland, and an abundant and fulfilling quality of life for all.

We attract, support and promote small-scale, innovative and financially-viable ventures that put people and enterprise back on the land, build resilience into the local economy and provide prosperity for the long term. Operating from the Dartington Estate, the experimental heart of generating and applying new ideas, in Devon, England, we have scope to host a range of small scale sustainable businesses and experimental or demonstration projects. We also work with a growing network of landowner partners across the country, through which new sustainable business models can be promoted in order to proliferate and have maximum impact.

Our approach to pioneering sustainable land use is bringing the countryside back to life with a richness of innovation and enterprise. Among the projects we currently have underway are:

◎ Greyfield Timber

◎ School Farm / Foxhole Organics

◎ Forest School at On Track

◎ Rural Business School, Duchy College

www.dartington.org/landscope

Engaging the Totnes Business Community - Some Emerging Thoughts

By the TTT Economics & Livelihoods Group

This section aims to set some context around which we can start to engage with more local businesses and organisations in order to begin the Energy Descent Planning work for this area. We need to work together to produce a collective vision of how our local economy could survive and indeed thrive, in a low-energy, volatile oil-price future, and then plan the pathways that could best take us there. Please note that from here on when the term 'organisation' is used it includes private, public and voluntary sectors.

Our community's needs

The community of Totnes & District creates demand for a wide range of goods and services to meet its needs, both essential and non-essential items, including food, water, transport, education, homes, household items, clothing, leisure, energy and so on. Organisations exist to meet these needs and in turn create needs of their own. Of course they also provide employment so that we can earn money to buy the goods and services. These organisations from which we buy things may be local, regional, national, European and global. Even if we are buying goods from a small independent local shop, they may well have been sourced from a major corporation and manufactured on the other side of the world. In fact most of the goods we buy are imported to the UK and created using long, complex supply-distribution chains. For example, 80% of the UK's annual consumption (by weight) of clothing and textile products is imported[17].

The challenges

Obviously businesses and organisations are a key component of our community. For our community (and our nation) to build resilience, our local organisations must also work to reduce carbon emissions and fossil fuel dependence. As the pressures from peak oil and climate change become more apparent, organisations of all types and sizes will need to assess their own risk exposure and understand what mitigating action could be taken short-term, as well as exploring how their own business strategy and operations may need to fundamentally change to succeed in the future, where the economic playing field and its rules will likely be drastically different.

The opportunities

For our own community then, this raises one key question - how can organisations continue to meet our community's needs (including provision of employment) in an increasingly energy, resource and financially constrained world?

To answer this question we need to further understand our needs, and how they could be met:

◎ What are our essential, important and luxury needs? How are they being met today?

◎ What must be or could be substituted? With what? From where? (Of course, not everything can be provided locally and some trade will always exist, as it always has done, across the region, the country or the globe for those items that we can't provide here).

◎ Of this, what could be provided locally that isn't at the moment? What local resources and assets do we have (energy, material, human etc.)?

◎ What skills and labour will we need that's different from today? How might we best re-train, re-skill?

◎ How can this major shift in our local economy and livelihoods be financed? What options exist besides global banks/financial markets?

Peak oil and climate change-related issues are providing a fantastic opportunity for our local economy to provide an increasing percentage of our community's goods and services, particularly as the resource/energy constraints and true prices come into play, and it is no longer always cheaper to make things out of plastic in China.

Supporting our transition to the new economy

Once this kind of mapping work has helped to highlight the best economic opportunities, support needs to be offered to existing businesses and organisations to help them to make a well-planned and proactive shift. The Transition Network is building a set of services specifically aimed at the organisations already operating in our communities. These services will help the management and employees to understand how peak oil and climate change will likely affect their operations and their profit margins, and help them to explore potentially more viable, sustainable operational models that make the most of the opportunities, while minimising the risks. These services are being offered by Transition Training & Consulting. For example, the Energy Resilience Assessment service helps a business or organisation to understand and quantify its own risk to rising oil/energy prices, and starts to identify possible solutions.

At the same time new business start-ups and entrepreneurs will need to be nurtured and supported. Within the TTT E&L group a sub-group called 'Growing New Businesses' has been identifying what these needs might be. The aims of the sub-group are to (1) foster and support transition-related commercial opportunities and businesses and (2) encourage resilient, sustainable business operations in line with the transition ethos. – see link for more info www.totnes.transitionnetwork.org/economic-sandlivelihoods/growingbusiness/home

Having great working examples is also important to help provide further incentive to act. Dartington's Landscope project is already providing tangible evidence of how businesses (commercial and not-for-profit) can successfully and sustainably add value to local resources and rural assets, while at the same time working together in a mutually supportive relationship.

Where do we go from here?

This section aims to provide some context to the work of the TTT E&L group and share our initial thinking about how we might transition successfully, and as smoothly as possible, to a new economy here in Totnes & District. We believe there are great opportunities that go hand in hand with the challenges and uncertainty that peak oil and climate change bring.

To do this it's essential that we form an effective, representative working group made up of people who run local businesses and organisations here in Totnes & District, and which can build on the TTT projects already undertaken with the local Chamber of Commerce and other partners. Together we can plan the activities that will give us all the best chance of surviving and thriving in these times of change, and helping contribute to the resilience of our entire community. This will form the basis of our Economics & Livelihoods Energy Descent Action Plan and initial activities are likely to include:

- ◎ Build a 'Transition Action Group' of local businesses and organisations
- ◎ Mapping the local community's needs for products and services
- ◎ Import substitution analysis
- ◎ Inventory of all local assets and resources – create database so all can see what is available locally already
- ◎ Identify skill gaps
- ◎ Explore alternative financing systems e.g. mutual credit clearing, alternative currencies, localisation of savings and investments, local banks and bond issues, community ownership,

If you run or can represent a business or organisation locally, and would like to find out more about our group then please contact us at **economicsandlivelihoods.totnes @transitionnetwork.org**

Further Reading

Daly, H.A. (1991) Steady-State Economics. Island Press.

Devon County Council (2008) State of the Devon Economy. Download from www.devon.gov.uk/ stateofdevoneconomy-2007.pdf

Hines, C. (2000) Localisation, A Global Manifesto ISBN 978-1-85383-612-1

G20. (2009) Report of G20 London Summit 02.04.1009. http://www.londonsummit.gov.uk/en/summit-aims/ summit-communique/

Jackson, T. (2009) Prosperity without growth? The transition to a sustainable economy. Sustainable Development Commission.

New Economics Foundation (2008) A Green New Deal.

Victor, P.A. (2008) Managing without Growth, Slower by Design, Not Disaster. Edward Elgar Publishing.

South West Regional Development Agency www.futurefootprints.org.uk

Devon Rural Network www.drn.org.uk.

Totnes Street © Lou Brown

CONSUMPTION AND WASTE

IN BRIEF

*"Infinite Growth of material consumption
in a finite world is an impossibility."*
E.F. Schumacher

Business as Usual or Willing to Change? - Emerging Trends - Where we are Now

A 'Business as Usual' approach to consumption and waste assumes that economics will guide consumption levels such that common sense and carrot-and-stick pricing and waste charges will affect our habits. However since UK society is hooked on over consumption this is unlikely to change without some severe interventions. Similarly, while Totnes is recapturing some of the energy potential of some sewerage waste, there is a vast amount of organic matter and other animal effluents that are simply going to waste and causing pollution.

If we are willing to change our practices, we can very quickly improve matters. The 'Polluter Pays' principle, embodied in waste charges, creates a strong deterrent to excess consumption. Reduction in consumption leads to a reduction in energy use, and leaves us better prepared for coming changes. Reclaiming energy from organic waste and sewerage effluents through anaerobic digestion reduces greenhouse gases and produces vehicle fuels, piped heat for local district heating and agricultural materials to return to the land.

Minimising and localising our consumption and waste and increasing resource efficiency will create more jobs, increase innovation and competitiveness, change values towards better quality goods, reduce our impact on the environment and increase global equity whilst saving money and energy, and we can enjoy being creative and resourceful with less. Rather than seeing Totnes and District as a linear system, one which imports goods, uses them, and throws the waste away, this Plan advocates a more cyclical approach, creating as many cycles as possible.

What follows is one version of how consumption and waste might become more localised and sustainable over the next 21 years.

Strategic Themes Across the Timeline

◎ Waste minimising resource management, infrastructure and policies

◎ Comprehensive range of recycling services and facilities

◎ Reducing consumption patterns – awareness & information; meeting needs not wants

The detailed timeline developing the themes on this topic are available in the web version of this publication at www.totnesedap.org.uk

Vision 2030

By 2030, Totnes and District has achieved almost zero waste and almost 100% resource recovery. Everything is valued and reused and recycled in ways that minimise impact on the environment. Few people have money to spend on luxuries, nor the space to accommodate a lot of clutter, as home space is used for all the tools, materials and books needed being more creative to meet own needs, such as cooking, sewing, DIY, gardening. In place of excess money, most people have created more time to live more diverse lives to enable them provide for more of their own basic needs. Through this change, values around resources and waste have moved on and reflect respect, an ethical approach and prudence, and recognition of the connection between resources and the planet, viewing with astonishment the brief but severe mass-consumerism and the throw away society at the turn of the 21st century.

Resilience Indicators

From the research that led to this Plan, we have identified a number of key indicators by which we can be sure that we we are moving forward. These include:

◎ Overall waste volumes.

◎ % Of agricultural and sewerage waste to anaerobic digestion

◎ Reduction in packaging on goods

These can be revisited regularly to see if the community is making progress in the right direction.

Modern Consumption. © Jenny Band

3.48

NOTES & IDEAS

Nurturing Transition

Community garden event: © Lou Brown

ARTS, CULTURE, MEDIA & INNOVATION

"Art does not lie down on the bed that is made for it; it runs away as soon as one calls its name; it loves to be incognito. Its best moments are when it forgets what it is called."
Jean Dubuffet

The Challenge

Totnes and its surroundings have, since the arrival of the Elmhirsts in the 1920s, been a vibrant centre for the arts. Many who attended Dartington Art College have chosen to remain in the area, and events like Dartington's Summer School, Totnes Festival and Ways With Words are major cultural events. Dartington has also formed local creative partnerships, through Dartington Plus, which has led to KEVICC being a Centre of Excellence for the Performing Arts. Totnes has an Arts and Design Foundation course at KEVICCS. Outside of Dartington, Totnes and District is home to many artists and creative craft workers, who regularly exhibit in the town, as well as a strong amateur dramatics community. For a town of its size, Totnes hosts an amazing array of musical, artistic and other media events. The challenges that these times of transition present to the arts are many. How will many of the larger arts events that take place in the area finance themselves as central government funding for the arts starts to dry up? The recent Design Our Space (DOS) initiative recommended many public art works throughout the town, yet they mostly remain unfunded. For events that rely on cars to get people to them, how will they adapt to falling audience numbers? Finally, but perhaps most importantly, how might the arts, in all their forms, reflect, inform, document and inspire the changes taking place?

A Snapshot of the Arts in Totnes and District

Totnes and District are home to a wide array of arts initiatives and projects in addition to those set out above. These include:

- ◎ Ways with Words Literary & Theatre Festival
- ◎ The Barn Theatre
- ◎ KEVICC Arts Department
- ◎ Venues encouraging exhibitions and cultural events
- ◎ Totnes Art & Design Foundation post 6th form course at KEVICCS
- ◎ All the local schools
- ◎ Soundart Radio
- ◎ Transition Tales (a TTT project working with Year 7 KEVICC students)
- ◎ The Wondermentalist Cabaret
- ◎ Mirror Mirror Playback theatre company
- ◎ The Totnes Times and other local print media
- ◎ Totnes Festival
- ◎ Devon Open Studios
- ◎ Totnes Library
- ◎ Local publishers, printers, picture framers, film production companies...

3.49 Mosaic Dog sculpture and photo by Jynja Claderon.

Business as Usual in 2030

If we continue Business as Usual, by 2030 Totnes and District may have a fragmented art and cultural community due to severe under-funding and problems with transportation. Dartington Art College students may be long gone and resident artists based in the rural hinterland may no longer be able to bring their art to the public eye or acquire art materials to create their works. High-energy prices will mean that sculptors and ceramicists are likely to experience difficulties firing their kilns or moving their larger art pieces. Public art will remain minimal and continue to suffer from low investment. The deficit of people with knowledge about making paints, handmade papers and the lack of producers in place is likely to create a gap in supplies and some of these skills.

Performance art is likely to remain strong although there is likely to be less variety of visiting performers and musicians etc. as travel costs may be prohibitive. The lack of late public transport services will also affect audience size. The rising cost of energy and raw materials will impact the arts just as it impacts all other areas of life. A new genre of writing, celebrating the positive aspects of Transition, starts in Totnes and takes the publishing world by storm.

The local media will continue to compete for a smaller pool of buyers and advertisers, but with rising energy costs it is likely that most printed media will not survive to 2030. Bookshops selling new books are unlikely to have available such a wide choice of books to sell and with paper, printing and distribution becoming more expensive their bookshelves may be carrying more used books than new ones. Some of the larger bookshops start their own local imprints, small print runs by local authors, which become very popular.

There is, however, little reason to believe that in a more energy-constrained future the community's artistic impulse will simply evaporate. There is every reason to believe that actually a slower, more local, less energy- and carbon-intensive world would actually be a more creative and artistic time, with people rediscovering the role of beauty in everyday life.

Such a future may be based on the following principles:

◎ Creative thinking and methods will need to be more widely shared and placed at the centre of how we think about our lives, our education system, and how we plan for our future

◎ Visual and performance art is fully resourced both at the national level and the local level through education, adult education, art, drama, creative writing and music schools and investment in public art works to nurture society's creative talent

◎ Visual and performance art should be used to influence our understanding of how the community can respond to peak oil and climate change

◎ TV, radio, the internet and printed media use and support, through their stories, documentaries and programmes, the visionary story of transition, helping people understand and enter the new paradigm with a positive approach.

◎ Printed media will need to consolidate to reduce the excess of paper and its high energy-dependence. New ways of recording and dispersing the writings of journalists, creative writers etc.; perhaps through libraries, electronic billboards or more use of the internet (if it can continue to exist).

What follows is one version of how our arts and culture might become more localised and sustainable over the next 21 years.

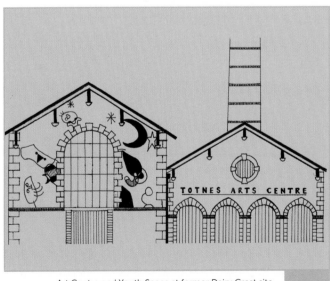

Art Centre and Youth Space at former Dairy Crest site.
© Richard Hodgson

3.50

Totnes Times Classifieds of 2030

OFFERED:
An ancient policeman's helmet.

WANTED:
A potting shed

OFFERED:
A dozen eggs

OFFERED:
Thermal underwear

OFFERED:
CDs of celestial music

WANTED:
Set of sharp knives

OFFERED:
Brace of pheasants

WANTED:
Roll of paper

OFFERED:
A pig

WANTED:
A goat

WANTED:
Bi-curious couple seek amorous couple to generate heat for cold Ashburton flat

WANTED:
Electric footspa.
I just wondered what one was.

WANTED:
Car to keep chickens in. Must have opening glove box / nesting box.

OFFERED:
for the post-liquid-fossil-fuel enthusiast who is seeking an unusual structure up which to grow his legumes, this wonderful 'pea coil'.

OFFERED:
Potato jewellery, carrot combs, beetroot

WANTED:
Creative recycler seeks spare vegetables

OFFERED:
Top hats sown with mustard cress for mobile snacks. £30 each

OFFERED:
Entire back collection of 'Thimbles of the World', collected over 2 years into a full collection in its own binder, because I recently got a life.

OFFERED:
Outdated computer, made 2029, still functions, with retro old-fashioned design. Slow, compared to what's hot today. Give-away price only one bale of hay.

WANTED:
Marmalade.

OFFERED:
All the bread in my cupboard

WANTED:
Full scuba-diving kit

OFFERED:
Shoelaces

WANTED:
Socks

OFFERED:
Will trade anything

From Wondermentalist
Transition Cabaret workshop
January 2009

Arts, Culture, Media and Innovation

Vision 2030

By 2030, Totnes and District has successfully retained its creative, artistic edge, and the arts are more an element of people's everyday experience of life in the area. The 'Transition years' have brought together people in exciting and imaginative ways to enjoy and express their feelings and talents through creative community-based activities and developments. The Dartington Estate continues to benefit local society through its nurturing presence supporting new ideas and ways of being creative. Localisation has expanded creative talent at a more practical level and artistic expression is to be seen in almost every product, building and view.

Artists, writers, singers, poets, actors have all found more local support as people want their local areas where they spend more time to be enriched with local culture, and with little electricity available for TV, people spend more time enjoying live performance, and everyone now has a 'turn' to perform at parties and social events, a song, a story, a magic trick. One of the most profound changes has been how what was, thirty years previously, a community that largely saw art as something to be bought/consumed, now sees it as part of everyday life, with locally-made crockery, furniture and other household essentials being more commonplace than the long-travelled, high carbon, Ikea-style products of twenty years previously.

Resilience Indicators

From the research that led to this Plan, we have identified a number of key indicators by which we can be sure that wewe are moving forward. These include:

◎ The number of public art works commissioned each year

◎ The amount of funding allocated to art initiatives with a Transition theme

◎ The number of new business start-ups that are about making everyday household objects, at affordable prices, yet which incorporate art

◎ The % of local society engaged in transition projects and activities

These can be revisited regularly to see if the community is making progress in the right direction.

ARTS, CULTURE, MEDIA & INNOVATION

PATHWAYS ACRO

Strategic themes: • Arts in Society • Culture & Entertainments

2009

Individuals

- Open Mike nights are very popular this year, pubs and their clients are using this form of performance for entertainment and creative soap-box

- Individual exhibitions reflect the broad interests of the surrounding area in their shows

- Individuals at the Wondermentalists' Transition workshop and subsequent evening cabaret[1] produce tales and thoughts of hope and fun

- Totnes Festival's Lantern Procession is a huge success

- Students at Totnes Art & Design Foundation Course develop their vision for 2030.

Community

- Mirror Mirror Playback Company astonish the audience at the 2030 Cabaret night with their reflection of how the transition had felt to those who had experienced it

- The TOSCA's, run by Totnes Allotments Association to raise awareness about the need for new land for food growing, brings Billy Bragg to the town and hundreds of people make scarecrows. Hundreds of people turn out for this huge event. The scarecrows remain on the allotments for months afterwards

- TTT brings out its Energy Descent Action Plan (EDAP) to wide acclaim and interest. There is a lot of interest in Transition both locally and from afar from individuals and students as Totnes is seen as the centre which can inform about this new movement

- 'In Transition', a film about Transition[2] premieres in Totnes and sells out the Barn Cinema, before taking the world by storm. The film documents the emerging movement by inviting Transition initiatives to film themselves and send in the tapes. It is called 'Version 1.0' as the process will be repeated each year, to capture and reflect the growing spread of the concept. Plans are also unveiled for 'Transition Media', where the footage from the film will be made available so that people can 'remix' it, and make their own locally appropriate versions of the film

- Transforming the Future – a design perspective[3], recommends creating mobile art and re-skilling units for shared workshop and studio space for Totnes' Sustainable Makers.

Policy Makers & Service Providers

- The Prince's Foundation conducts an Enquiry by Design (EbD) series of workshop with the support of SHDC and local stakeholders. One of its findings is that the town needs much more in the way of public artworks, and that the proposed ATMOS development should also act as an arts incubator

- The Totnes Festival continues to grow in scale and popularity, offering a spectacular range of events

- Local festivals begin to grow in smaller parishes organised by their Parish Councils

SS THE TIMELINE

• Media – telling a new story • Innovation & Design

2010

Individuals

- Local artists produce an astonishing exhibition *Postcards from 2030*, which opens a wide debate on how the area will look in twenty years time

- TTT and Dartington Arts present an event in Totnes called '2030 Day'. During the night, the Plains in Totnes are made-over, so as to look as they might in a powered-down 2030. The road is narrowed to one lane, raised beds are installed on the open spaces, hanging baskets containing edible species are installed, and trees in pots are put in place. The event took weeks of planning, with a team of 60 volunteers and support from South Hams District Council. People awake the next morning to an experience of a powered down future. The installation becomes a major talking point, and when it is removed after 2 weeks, the Totnes Times is filled with letters from people asking for it to be put back as it was, but on a permanent basis. It becomes a regular event each year, with the initiative having to work very hard to ensure secrecy each year, as the town is rife with rumours as to where might get 'made over' this year.

Community

- Over 10% of the local community are engaged in transition activities hosted in all sixteen parishes, a ten-fold increase in two years

- 2 empty shops in Totnes High Street become artists' shared studios

- A sense of Totnes being at the heart of the new transition culture is reflected in local news and stories

- Totnes Sustainable Makers initiate their first mobile re-skilling unit to bring people, arts and crafts closer together. The series of workshops at six roadside venues are popular with all ages

- TTT Arts group together with KEVICC students initiate the 'Sea Level Rise in our Streets' project. 'High tide marks', showing where a five-metre sea level rise would reach are created around the town. It becomes a major talking point

- Discussions around the impacts of consumer culture on both mental and physical health are increasingly aired in the media.

Policy Makers & Service Providers

- Many meetings are now held virtually and through Skype, and SHDC staff have been encouraged to car-share

- The culture of using public transport rather than the car is beginning to gain popularity

- Artists are invited to shadow leading members of SHDC for two weeks in order to create artworks that encapsulate the difficulties and opportunities that those in positions of power are experiencing as the oil price starts to rise once again. One of the outputs by Dartington-based performance artist Glen Rider, is a performance art piece called 'The Slippery Ladder', where he tries to climb a ladder covered in oil and keeps slipping backwards.

ARTS, CULTURE, MEDIA & INNOVATION
PATHWAYS ACRO

Strategic themes: • Arts in Society • Culture & Entertainments

Individuals

- A sense of pride about how Totnes has taken a lead on many of these issues begins to be palpably felt. 'Transition Tours' are now offered to cater for the number of people who want to visit the area to learn about sustainability

- A new wave of interest in writing emerges in Totnes. Many established and new writers are feeling inspired to write about solutions to the issues of Peak Oil and Climate Change. The Totnes Reader, a quarterly publication, emerges as a showcase of local writers.

2011

Community

- A major surge of community amateur dramatics is witnessed, with plays being chosen that resonate with the tightening economic situation and also the exciting new emerging thinking

- The EDAP goes through its first review and finds a strong response from local people in all the parishes; people want to share their ideas and successes. The second version of the EDAP draws from that, and its launch is celebrated across the area

- Transition ideas are becoming more apparent in the media and clothing made from recycled clothes stitched together becomes increasingly fashionable.

Policy Makers & Service Providers

- As part of the Totnes Town Repair Festival, which is focussed on the community pulling together, and building resilience, Totnes Town Council hosts a local exhibition of Ideas for Change to further the outcomes of the Prince's Foundation work started in 2009. It provides a celebration of the diversity of work happening across the town, and an acknowledgement of its importance

- The 'Late Nite Bus' service enables more people from around Totnes to attend evening social and cultural activities and is very popular.

SS THE TIMELINE

• Media – telling a new story • Innovation & Design

2012

Individuals

- Take-up of evening classes in practical and craft skills starts to rise

- The 'Totnes Got Talent' event in Totnes gets hundreds of people across the town practising their acts, learning songs, practising dance routines. The final show, in the Totnes Civic Hall, is a complete sell-out, and generates huge interest. The winners, a dance act called 'Massive', become local heroes and go on to become well known nationally.

Community

- A wave of café culture and buskers hits the streets as more people have time on their hands with unemployment affecting all age groups. Cafés are becoming more of a central aspect of local life, with the board game evenings and community dinners started in the Red Wizard in Totnes really catching on elsewhere. The 2012 Totnes Monopoly Championships is declared a draw, when, in order to reflect the changes taking place around them in the world, they decide to form a co-operative and work collectively for each other's benefit. The judges and organisers are not happy with the outcome, but Brian Lawson, one of the finalists, tells the Totnes Times, "it occurred to us during the first tea-break of the final that actually Monopoly reflects the thinking in the world that is partly to blame for the economic situation we

now see, the crash that began in 2008. We felt, given the profile we have here, that we wanted to model a different way of approaching economics. It makes Monopoly more boring to play, but it has certainly got people talking."

- The media is reporting a lot of stories about local innovation, as people seek to accommodate solar panels in odd places, and in some cases engage local artists to help them design the most striking and eye-catching way to install them. Local photovoltaics company BecoSolar engage local designers to create a range of limited-edition 'designer' solar panels, which help to make photovoltaics the 'must-have' additions to houses. To talk of 'payback periods' for photovoltaics becomes as ridiculous as to talk of 'payback periods' for cars or holidays

- The Totnes Pottery opens in one of the new light-industrial units on the ATMOS development. The rising oil price has meant that what had been cheap imports of crockery from China and elsewhere are now very expensive, and the Totnes Pottery opens as a social enterprise based on the idea of making plates, bowls, cups and so on, not as highly priced artisan items, but as affordable, mass-market everyday items. The designs are modern and colourful, and the imprint on the underside, "Thrown in Totnes", becomes iconic

- Totnes Art & Design Foundation course at KEVICCS expands and is to include a full three year degree course. Director Bruce Timson is delighted, telling Art Quarterly[4], "this course is so different from others in the UK as it is so personal and students engage at very deep and meaningful level; they bond and work together. The holistic and eco-artwork opens all our eyes to what is happening below the surface."

ARTS, CULTURE, MEDIA & INNOVATION
PATHWAYS ACRO

Strategic themes: • Arts in Society • Culture & Entertainments

Policy Makers & Service Providers

- Devon County Council's Arts officer makes a range of grants available for community arts in response to the growing unemployment figures. This year's projects will be displayed during the Totnes Festival

- Totnes Library gets a new home on the Civic Square, and a major expansion with a discussion café. Smaller reading rooms are set up in outlying villages in conjunction with the new biodiesel-powered mobile library. The Transition section, begun in 2007, continues to expand, and is by now a major resource for the area to find out about all aspects of sustainable living.

2013-15

Individuals

- A new exhibition, 'Scorched Earth', features artists depicting strong visual scenes in the wake of two major heat waves (2011 and 2012)

- The change towards a more Mediterranean climate is being reflected in warm pastel shades that many people are painting their houses (prompted by the move to more locally made paints) and the fig trees and grape-vines planted in gardens

- Many urban spaces are looking very different with edible plants and scented herbs growing in every small space. In some cases, artists are collaborating with landscape designers to create striking edible landscapes.

Community

- TTT's 'Eco Art 012' workshop weekend attracts over 500 attendees and the astonishing array of artworks produced are set up in the refurbished Civic Square as a permanent public art display

- The Totnes Pottery is soon joined by the Totnes Furniture Company, based on the same ethic of creating affordable household objects. Described in the local media as a 'local IKEA', they make simple, but beautiful furniture at affordable prices using local timber. They are one of the first places for many years to offer apprenticeships to local young people, who are promised that at the end of the two-year apprenticeship, they will have a broad range of skills. Ten young people are taken on in the first year, alongside five professional furniture-makers

- Newspapers producers are finding it increasingly difficult to keep going and many local papers have linked up to reduce costs; some have reduced their papers down to just a few sheets with starter stories that people can then go and finish reading on-line

- TV advertising is falling away as commerce feels the burden of rising costs; the fewer 'coffee break' slots benefit power grid managers

- By now, some of the '2030 Day' installations are kept through popular demand, with local residents taking ownership of them and even adding to and enhancing the original installation.

SS THE TIMELINE

• Media – telling a new story • Innovation & Design

Policy Makers & Service Providers

- The culture of reuse and recycling has become popular and local authorities are keen to support communities in a number of innovative ways, including opening workshop facilities at the reuse centres on weekends for students to make arts and crafts pieces from some of the unwanted items brought in. A trip to the recycling centre is now an artistic, as well as a practical, experience

- Radio reception goes completely digital in 2015. Designers are still busy trying to improve reception in cars and create conversion units for analogue radios.

2016-20

Individuals

- Colour is coming back strongly in society and people are wearing very bright clothes and a home-made look is gaining popularity with teenagers

- There has been a rise in people wanting to learn crafts and a revival of interest in textiles and knitting using local wool. Sheep farmers on Dartmoor find the increase in demand for wool to be making a huge difference to their viability

- Songs about the area and its people are becoming more popular and many new songs are reflecting the sense of being local and valuing friends and family. A drum and bass remix of a song by Jenny Bird, an eighteen-year-old KEVICC student's song, called "So in love with my sprouts", becomes one of the most downloaded songs of 2017

- A strong sense of local pride and good citizenship is bringing people closer together.

Community

- A sense of austerity is being felt at all levels but the benefit is an increased sense of equality and friendliness. People are becoming very locally minded and community-spirited and 'Our Street' is a popular sense of identity for many small community groups who are creating very clearly individualised streetscapes with shared community spaces and artistic additions to railings etc.

ARTS, CULTURE, MEDIA & INNOVATION
PATHWAYS ACRO

Strategic themes: • Arts in Society • Culture & Entertainments

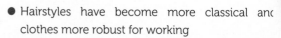
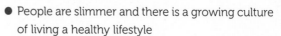

- A lot of performance theatre takes place in public places and with the warmer temperatures street life is more of a central part of daily life during the summer months. Sales of local ice cream soar

- Wallpaper makes a comeback. Another new business at ATMOS is 'Wonderful Wallpaper', which uses local inks and recycled paper to make a range of vibrant wall coverings.

Policy Makers & Service Providers

- Local colour and distinctiveness is being supported by most local service providers who are willing to accommodate local variations in needs and preferences over harmonisation of styles

- All local agencies are working more closely together to reduce costs and there is a general culture of co-operation, especially given that the Councillors themselves now model a more frugal lifestyle as part of the Council's decision to 'lead by example.'

Individuals

- Hairstyles have become more classical and clothes more robust for working

- People are slimmer and there is a growing culture of living a healthy lifestyle

- The enthusiasm for painting al fresco rural scenes is matched by the rising numbers of people buying art pieces, reflecting a desire to distil, through artworks, what it is that has felt so historic and extraordinary about the previous five years, and the sense of pride people feel in the area's achievements

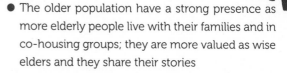

Community

- The older population have a strong presence as more elderly people live with their families and in co-housing groups; they are more valued as wise elders and they share their stories

- The art of storytelling is reviving interest in old books and many more are collector's items on the internet

- Bookbinding has become a popular pastime and many people have been mending their old books

- Day trips on the train and picnics have revived in popularity with villages and towns within the UK forming local twinning partners and paying each other visits

- Public transit and 'chatting on the bus' has, by this stage, replaced individual car culture.

2021-25

SS THE TIMELINE

• Media – telling a new story   • Innovation & Design

Policy Makers & Service Providers

- Communal public spaces in every town and village are being given special priority by local authorities and LA workers are being made available for community groups to create pleasant open public spaces with plenty of edible plants and natural local building materials

- Local artists are being engaged by service providers to design and create attractive and individual street furniture, railings, sub-power stations, buses, turbines etc., resulting in a blossoming of imaginative shapes, styles and colour in neighbourhoods

Community

- Community halls are very much at the centre of community life and talent shows, festivals, music hall events are popular and singing competitions, inter-village events and candlelit story nights are regular events that most people support. Local and national media cover many of these events and while the age of celebrity may have passed, local stars can attract a wide audience from long distances

- TV and radio have very few channels, most countries have one TV channel at most but local radio is very much more popular as people listen to this in their gardens and allotments and programmes are full of handy tips and seasonal recipes

- A monument to waste is built on the plains in Totnes. The tall column is marked with rising water heights.

Individuals

- Good drawing technique is very valued and used to set out unusual plans for all kinds of developments from new power harnessing products to new housing

- People have become very willing to share ideas and collaborate on projects. Conspicuous consumption is in the past and replaced with conspicuous resilience. People are more skilled and creative and happy in discovering and sharing their talents.

2026-30

Policy Makers & Service Providers

- The new National Arts Forum has grant-aided a number of local artists to reflect on 'Our Changing Times'. A wave of local exhibitions has been very popular and encouraged by local authorities

- Art spaces have evolved out of the regular gallery, and the many covered walkways where cafés have spilt out on to pavements and pedestrianised roadways and public buildings are filled with local artworks

- A number of regional film companies have emerged and are making films that celebrate the extraordinary work that has taken place over the past twenty years

- A beautiful and extraordinary Eco-Art centre is developed in the Brunel building at the ATMOS project. Opening with an evocative exhibition of life in 2009, it depicts images of folly as its central theme.

INNER TRANSITION

"No longer a dead rock we live upon, the Earth is a living process in which we participate."
Joanna Macy

Introduction
– Why Inner Transition?

The challenge of our times is one of responding well to continuing far-reaching change. The Transition movement presents information about the scale of change that is coming and invites a choice – plan for the change and ride its waves, or be caught unprepared and possibly knocked sideways by its force.

At the core of the work developed in the Heart and Soul group of the Transition Town Totnes project is the understanding that our outer actions, and therefore the external systems for living that we create, are shaped by our inner worldview and belief system. Likewise our inner world is affected by the outer world, which creates in particular our physical experience and shapes our relationships.

So we might consider our challenge as a question like this: if we see the need for changes to our outer systems – food production, technologies for building, heating, transport and so on – what does

Planet Earth from the Cosmos. © Richard Hodgson

the inner transition look like that supports, reflects or initiates that outer change? And in designing a community process, what can we do to help create a healthy inner transition to a sane, stable and enjoyable world in the same way that re-localising food production helps to make a healthy sustainable physical world for the future?

Fortunately we live in a time when we have unprecedented understandings of our inner workings, and access to many traditions that have been exploring these questions. These include relatively new western psychological and social models for enabling and supporting change, responding to difficulty or crisis. In addition there are many spiritual and religious practices and philosophies to which we can turn for insight and support.

The "Heart and Soul" group of Transition Town Totnes was the first to form in the project, launching just after the main project unleashed. It quickly gained a large membership including those with professional interest and experience in inner change – social workers, therapists, psychologists, workshop leaders, spiritual teachers and leaders; and those with a personal interest in the inner aspects of transition. Early on it defined its area of interest as the psychological, spiritual and consciousness aspects of transition – the inner world of the individual and the community. This section has been written by the Heart and Soul group using material from open meetings as well as workshops run as part of the EDAP project.

The Current Situation

Totnes offers a wealth of healing and psychological therapies, and groups, providing a wonderful diversity of approach and focus. The Heart and Soul group has drawn on the skills, commitment to the Transition process, and contacts, of many of those practitioners.

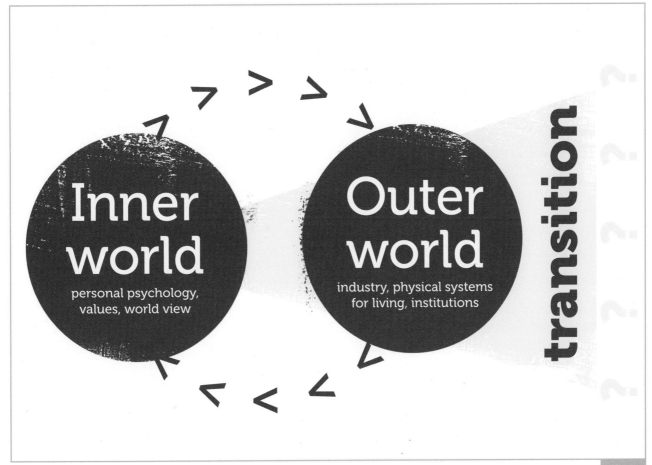

Inner and outer world transition | 3.52

◎ We have been able to invite talks from international and local writers, teachers and poets to challenge and inspire us, people such as Marianne Williamson, Joanna Macy, Drew Dellinger, Tim Macartney, Alistair Mackintosh, Starhawk, Peter Russell, to name but a few

◎ We run experiential workshops, along the lines of Joanna Macy's Work That Reconnects, to explore and express some of the range of feelings that come up when we fully allow ourselves to face the reality of climate chaos and oil depletion.

◎ We continue to hold meetings to explore what needs to be done and to examine how we work together (and how we might make meetings as effective and enjoyable as possible)

◎ We hold outdoor celebrations to mark the seasons and festivals

◎ We have explored different ways of structuring discussions of controversial subjects to widen the voices that are heard – including "Fishbowl"

discussions, forms of indigenous council and representing future beings and non-human life forms in the debate.

◎ Some people have formed into small, self-facilitating "Home Groups" – where ideas, information or skills may be shared and support, of an emotional or practical kind.

◎ A "Mentoring service" to build resilience is offered to Transition activists by trained counsellors. One to one sessions provide the opportunity for a non-judgemental and confidential space in which to express and explore issues within the work they do, and its relationship within the rest of their lives.

◎ A Heart and Soul meditation group has met regularly for more than a year.

Issues and Challenges

Some of the issues and challenges that members of the Heart and Soul group have identified are:

◎ To work with people's reactions to deep or rapid change such as decreasing energy supply, job loss, migration; and dealing with the unknown

◎ To heal and support those (many of us) who have been conditioned and hurt by the current materialist and isolated lifestyle

◎ Promoting understanding of what builds – and harms – healthy, strong, lasting relationships

◎ To embody qualities that deepen our connection and help us stay present, to hold a timeless wisdom whilst bringing in practical projects which have a timescale

◎ To acknowledge our interdependence with all other humans and living beings that allows us to develop ways of acting that embody Justice, Equality and Care for the Earth

◎ To sustain ourselves emotionally, and develop ways to support ourselves and others when we are overstretched, or overwhelmed

◎ To learn to work in groups so that we can cooperate more effectively

◎ To learn to value and respect all members of the community, young and old, and those whose background or beliefs are very different from our own

◎ To build a safe and supporting environment for all especially children and vulnerable people.

The Territory of Inner Transition - Psychological Awareness

Many people from environmental activists to governments are currently researching and exploring how individuals and groups respond to change, and engage with the need for change. Within the Transition movement and the Heart and Soul groups, are many models for understanding this process; what follows is an example of one, described in some detail to show how such a model helps to bring clarity and compassion to the process of change.

Responding to change we can't control

One aspect of Transition is that external factors will force change upon us. In 2008 we started to see impacts of high oil prices and major recession starting to bite. How do people react when major change hits their lives? Or smaller changes – social pressure to "go green"; the need to recycle?

One model that has proved useful and relevant is that of Elizabeth Kubler Ross, a doctor who worked with terminally ill patients, and their bereaved relatives and friends. She observed the process of coming to terms with approaching death – of the patient, or of a loved one, and noticed there were clear stages that people went through. In some ways we are going through a similar process as we come to terms with the end of a world view and a way of life – a belief that we can have unlimited growth, that in every year or generation there will be more

A thousand years of healing

With this turning we put a broken age to rest.
We who are alive at such a cusp
now usher in a thousand years of healing.

From whence my hope, I cannot say,
but it grows in the cells of my skin,
my envelope of mysteries.
In this sheath so akin to the surface of earth
I sense the faint song.

Beneath the wail and dissonance
this singing rises.
Winged ones and four-leggeds,
grasses, and mountains and each tree,
all the swimming creatures.
Even we, wary two-leggeds,
hum, and call, and create
the changes. We remake our relations, mend
our minds, convert our minds to the earth.
We practice blending our voices,
living with the vision
Of the Great Magic we move within.

We begin the new habit, getting up glad
For a thousand years of healing.

material wealth for more people. This is a response to change, which is out of our control.

The stages that Kubler Ross observed are:

◎ **Denial or shock**

◎ **Despair**

◎ **Rage**

◎ **Bargaining**

◎ **Acceptance**

It is possible to see the stages expressed in the behaviour of individuals, organisations and institutions, and understanding what is happening gives a more compassionate and grounded response to those who are at a different stage. Insight into this process also leads to ways of working which are appropriate and helpful, rather than dismissing or judgemental attitudes.

Denial or Shock

The denial response "It can't be true" is a familiar reaction to any shock. **This inner protective mechanism allows a distressing truth to be assimilated gradually.** The underlying belief expressed is that business as usual is the best or only way, and we must get back to it as soon as possible. In the Industrial Growth Society (IGS) this means we believe and behave as if the world offers unlimited resources including energy, and a limitless sink for our waste.

The evidence of reaching limits to resources (e.g. peak oil, drinking water, fish), and the wide reaching effects of human waste (climate change, pollution) is clear, yet there are still many people in denial about both. This is not a rational position, there is a psychological process going on. And there are many other complex reasons why we do not change – ranging from our relationship to the media, the demands and inherent beliefs of an economic system based on perpetual growth, and the stranglehold of power elites. We can feel ill equipped to deal with the arguments and powerless to have any effect.

Despair

Once information about coming change is understood a first reaction for many is a feeling of despair. This can take many forms. For some there is a feeling that it's too late to do anything. For others that we are powerless to make the scale of changes needed. Feelings of fear – for the future, especially for children and grandchildren – are common.

The danger of despair is that it leads to paralysis. The idea that we are powerless to make changes becomes reality when we believe it. As Vandana Shiva said **"The uncertainty of our times is no reason to be certain about hopelessness".**

Isolation and continuing negative information feeds the state of despair. Being with others and hearing about actions that are already underway, seeing the motivation and courage of others to hear the news and take steps all help people to move through this stage.

Rage

How is it to find out that the basis on which we have been living our lives is flawed, and that the future is not being taken care of by those with power? If our jobs and pensions disappear, do our plans for the future and children change dramatically? Who will we be angry with, whom will we blame? One strategy is to put all the blame onto others – the government; rich people; the person who brought the information. A common scene is for anger to be taken out on those who are accessible and not necessarily responsible.

In the longer term we need to express anger and move on to a more complete view, for some understanding our own part in creating the situation; for others developing compassion for the complex system that makes us all part of itself. Without this the heat of anger can become destructive – to others or to ourselves.

Bargaining

In relation to terminal illness this takes the form of making deals with death. "If I live a clean life perhaps I can get well. If I think only positive thoughts and eat well maybe I can live another 10 years, long enough to see my children grown, long enough to achieve my goals..."

In the face of peak oil and climate change we do other deals with the future. "If I change my light bulbs and recycle everything it's ok to fly to the sun this winter, treat myself to some new clothes, keep the hot tub..."

Another version of this is to take a survivalist route – "I can't save everyone but I can look after me and my own." This head for the hills is a common reaction – and many do live this out, moving to the country and aiming for self-sufficiency. This has produced lots of useful projects, skills and outcomes. In the end however we are all interconnected, and if runaway climate change takes hold no part of the earth will be unaffected.

In the bargaining stage more measured action is happening as the powerful emotions of despair and rage ease. Once we start to take action something transformative happens – we start to see that even as an individual I can have an effect – and when one becomes part of a group committed to change perhaps something wonderful can happen.

Acceptance

The final stage of coming to terms with change is acceptance. Here it is understood that life goes on with the change integrated. We can make a good life for all with much less energy, and face and overcome the challenges. The overwhelming despair, fear or rage recedes; the bargaining is no longer needed as we can look at what is without having to change it - calm returns, and from this calm comes the possibility of realistic positive action.

Understanding Response to Change as a Process

Someone who has been told that their illness is terminal often goes through the five stages listed above – denial, despair, rage, bargaining and acceptance. The process is not linear or predictable. The stages can happen repeatedly, simultaneously and in any order. This seems to be a useful analogy

for what happens both to individuals and to groups and organisations as they awaken to the need for Transition.

Thus I may have recognised the need to dramatically reduce my energy bill, have switched to green energy and started buying local organic produce (acceptance) but because I'm driving less I'm still flying twice a year for that much needed summer break and winter sunshine (bargaining). I am looking for places where my savings can earn good interest and putting money into a pension that invests in the stock market (business as usual). I've seen the film An Inconvenient Truth and sometimes lie awake remembering the image of Holland disappearing under the sea wondering whether there will be anything left of London, Totnes, East Anglia, and Bangladesh. (despair). I want to shout at my neighbour who doesn't even bother to recycle and leaves the outdoor lights on all night (anger).

For the Christian scholar Thomas Berry
"The world is not a collection of objects
but a communion of subjects"

Other Feelings and Responses

Of course there are many more feelings that come up as we wake up to the situation. Guilt, blaming others, grief, hope, not knowing. What is useful is to know that any of these feelings or states pass – none is the whole truth – and that we can create places and processes that help people to move through them with grace and love.

What Helps Healthy Change?

There are many tools and practices that help us to respond to change in good ways, even welcome it. In the section on Tools and Practices below we list some of these tools – many already in existence and many that have already been offered by the Heart and Soul group in Totnes. A group looking at support for healthy inner change might offer any or all of these – and the list is certainly not exhaustive – depending on what skills are available locally, what facilities, and what the local needs are. For some celebrating nature's abundance with an outdoor ritual will be very uncomfortable but fine as a harvest festival in a church. Some will feel OK about joining a support group; for others having one to one support is more acceptable.

One of the important aspects of inner transition is that our culture has taboos about expressing our true emotions, especially in front of others; that vulnerability is often judged as weakness, getting support is self indulgent and celebrating our successes is showing off. The very processes that we need most to get us through challenging times are likely to feel deeply uncomfortable at first. Can we even use words like Heart and Soul in a community process without alienating local government, the business community, others? And yet if we can't talk about what we love and what we long for, what kind of process will we create?

The Zen master Thich Nhat Hanh tells us "We are here to awaken from the illusion of our separateness"

The Spiritual Dimension of Transition

Whenever questions are asked about how we come to be here, why are we here, what is the purpose of living, we enter a line of inquiry commonly called 'spiritual'. Children in their fresh innocence often ask very big questions with their persistent "why's".

In recent years science and scientists have been much more transparent in meeting that edge of spiritual inquiry. Fields such as quantum physics, Gaia theory or neuroscience, have shattered our long-held belief in a solid reality made of inert stuff. Two particular beliefs - our sense of each being as a very separate self, and the collective notion of the supremacy of the human species, have both been found to be deeply flawed in the face of evidence of the profound interconnectedness of systems of life on the planet.

Alistair McIntosh, one of our speakers in Totnes last year, says "there is a danger when we speak about 'spirituality' that we enter a never-never land of fantasy which, as the existence of religious cults suggests, can be both delusory and deeply harmful". Yet he says: "...it is not sufficient to think of spirituality – that which gives life – as being a mere optional 'dimension' or 'element'. If activism is not grounded in spirituality it cannot be sustained in the long run: we either burn out or sell out as the oil of life runs low."

There are many who believe that taking time and "being present" – i.e. intimate with life as it unfolds rather than stuck in mental constructions – allows wisdom and love to flourish and healing to take place. Through this state of sustained awareness, the pain and numbness of our ordinary busy-ness, which fuels insatiable wants, can be transformed and our consciousness expanded. We can start opening our heart to the grief of the world as we commune with it and allow wholesome responses to emerge.

The challenges of peak oil, climate change – the need for energy descent –could provide a unifying catalyst for us to embrace a new way of seeing the future –as something that we create, rather than wait for. This will involve changes to the way we live our lives and the beliefs on which that is based. To transform our lives takes time, a sense of purpose, belief, imagination and courage, and in the process we may become more rounded, resilient, happier human beings.

Vision 2030

What follows is taken from a number of visioning sessions: public workshops covering Society and Values, Community, Education, Government, Biodiversity (none were run that specifically addressed inner transition). A gathering of the Heart and Soul group did a guided visualisation imagining walking through Totnes in 2030, meeting friends in the market square and reflecting on the years that have passed since 2009.

One person's vision

This comes from a visualising exercise done with the Heart and Soul group in October 2008, imagining walking through Totnes in 2030 to meet a friend for a drink in the market square.

Visit to Totnes in 2030

I will have travelled down from Staverton - how? Horse and cart? Tricycle? Train? Golf trolley/ our community of 9 houses + pub now much more communal.

Countryside will be different- more orchards- forest garden style- more trees.

I think of all tough things we have gone through in the world - 2008 when capitalism first obviously threatened - then disintegration of financial system, more frugality - little travel. Houses poorer inside, all intensively lived in. enormous variety of styles

Weather extremes- hard to cope with- today quite mild and pleasant

Communication worldwide still working, hearing of islands washed away, whole coast and inland seas: tsunamis and volcanoes frequent, wars over territory and death of millions of people. A lot of incomers in Devon, usually coming with few goods.

Town government now run by an open council, with voting by show of hands.

Animals and bird mix much better freely with human population less distinction town and country

My sister still in Australia she did come over by boat and stayed a couple of years, but went back because of her children and grandchildren. I have shortly returned from seeing her -great effort- sea voyage but pirates a danger worth it because we closer than ever we've been.

Instead of knowing many people in Totnes as I did 20 years ago I now feel I know everyone. Great feeling of friendship: reliant on each other as our pensions have disappeared.

Groups, colleges, talks story telling still continue as ever - education, music, still very important. Very aware we're in the midst of a great change not only in way of life, but also in consciousness: close to the earth. Life and death seen as close together, all part of the spirit of the earth in which we live.

(From a member of the Heart and Soul group)

Tools and Practices That Support Inner Transition

It is a remarkable feature of our time that at exactly the moment in history when we need a diverse range of tools to understand and transform our inner worlds there is a vast array of methods that offer exactly that. From meditation techniques and personal exploration of the psyche to ways of exploring highly charged issues with groups of several hundred the range is enormous.

In the Totnes area we are very fortunate to have many people who are already competent both in personal practices and in leading workshops and training others and many of these people are already engaged in Transition in some way.

What follows is a summary of some of the tools that are available, and how they might be used to meet the issues and challenges outline above.

Workshops on Change

Workshops on embracing change are held in many settings (schools, local groups and organisations, workplaces and people's homes). These help people to move through their reactions to change in healthy ways, and to find the positive side of what's happening.

Support groups

Modelled on the women's movement, peace movement, and a host of self-facilitated support groups, home groups were launched in Totnes in 2007, based on the understanding that there will not be the resources – funded or voluntary – to provide a support "service" to everyone needing it in times of change. With a basic resource pack including carbon saving and group facilitation ideas a group sets its own agreements for having meetings and gatherings, follows its own interest – practical, emotional, intellectual in any mix.

The Work That Reconnects

Originally called Despair and Empowerment work this was developed in response to the threat of nuclear war and destruction by Joanna Macy, and adapted with others to work with our relationship to the natural world, and particularly its destruction or degradation. Some of the key elements are:

◎ We need to come together to open our eyes to what is happening to our planet and our society. Together what seems overwhelming can become manageable

◎ When we express our own feelings and hear those of others something in us can come back to life, as if our emotions are a way of telling and hearing truth.

◎ If we can truly express how we feel and hear others we reconnect with our true nature, our love of life, the will to act, and with others around us, unleashing a great energy for compassionate action

Outdoor activities, reconnecting with nature

Much of our lives are lived separate from the natural world, reinforcing the illusion that humans are separate from nature. To go outside and reconnect with the living breathing environment of which we are part can be deeply nourishing, healing and transformative. Again there are many practices that use this, from business leadership training in wild places to deep ecology.

Storytelling

Woven through the whole Transition process, storytelling is a powerful tool for looking at what is hard, frightening or monstrous; for inspiring ourselves with courage, love and wisdom; for opening and exploring what is and what could be. Telling stories round a fire, sharing with the children, hearing about how things used to be when humans lived well with far less energy, and visioning a healthy future world are all ways in which story telling has been used already in Transition.

Celebrations and ceremonies

It is often said that "Transition should feel more like a party than a protest march".   It is vital that we remember to celebrate our successes, to honour and appreciate those who have given a lot and to have fun!

Constellations – exploring our place in the systems we belong to

Using the work of Bert Hellinger and others to explore relationships, including within our family, ecosystem and community.

Changing the Dream workshop

Originated by the Pachamama Alliance through their work with indigenous Ecuadorean people, these workshops offer a wake up call to the plight of our natural world and a call to change the way we see our place in the world.

Body / movement work

Dancing for joy, peace, expressing through our body, using the wisdom of the body to connect with earth and life. This could also include yoga and gentle martial arts – Tai Chi, Chi Gung which includes physical movements that keep the body healthy with meditative and spiritual aspects.

World Work, "Fishbowls" and other ways of holding discussions and meetings

Meetings for discussing issues, dilemmas and challenges (e.g. inequalities, how to share resources, death, disabilities etc.) can take many different forms. These can help to enquire into different aspects of complex issues rather than trying to get to the "right" answer; can encourage different viewpoints to be heard and encourage cooperation rather than competition. There are also very useful methods for going into (rather than avoiding) charged issues – bringing peace and resolution rather than stalemate or continuing conflict.

Communication Skills and Conflict Resolution

Non-violent communication, mediation and conflict resolution will all be useful skills to help us deal with difficult issues and conflicting perceptions or needs – skills that can be learnt and practised, and used in personal as well as professional settings.

Counselling

One to one and facilitated group counselling has been widely used both to support people through change – such as loss of work or relationship, or traumatic events. This could be provided through job centres, social services, and doctor's surgeries as well as privately or voluntarily.

Co-counselling is another form where two people work together taking it in turns to be speaker and listener, avoiding the need for professional training or payment.

Heart and Soul's Mentoring service is one example already in place where qualified people are offering support and supervision for those who give a lot to the Transition Movement, often voluntarily.

Trauma Training

It is widely recognised that trauma work is invaluable for those who have experienced severely disturbing events – as victims or witnesses. This may be a vital part the response where climate events cause displacement, or other shocks to our system leave people scarred.

Supporting parenting

"It takes a village to raise a child" is a well know phrase from the Dagara people of West Africa – and many parents trying to do the job on their own might well agree.

Faith Groups and Interfaith practices

Many faith groups are already actively engaging their members in thinking about environmental issues as well as how to support those in crisis or need. Finding ways to cooperate through coalitions and finding our common ground to meet the challenges ahead is already being modelled by many in established religions.

Meditation

Taking the space to "be" rather than "do", to listen within and to sit – alone, with others or in nature – is known to be deeply relaxing and beneficial to health. Many types of meditation are practised and taught in the area.

Prayer, Worship and Contemplation

Each religious or spiritual tradition has its own method and words to describe the process of invoking or contemplating the divine, or what is beyond the human.

From our Survey

Respondents were asked whether they would describe their outlook on the future of the community as being optimistic. 79.5% of people said they felt optimistic. When asked whether they considered themselves "a religious or spiritual person", 52.6% agreed that they did, 47.4% stated that they didn't. The next few questions explored consumerism and respondents' relationship to it. 55.7% of respondents disagreed that they felt the things they own say a lot about them, and the minority of people, 46.9% of people feel that buying things gives them pleasure.

The next question explored the degree of dissatisfaction that consumerism brings. Respondents were asked whether they felt their lives would be better if they were able to acquire certain consumer durables that at the moment they don't have. Only 25.6% of respondents felt that to be the case. In the same vein, respondents were asked whether they agreed or disagreed with the statement "I consider myself to be a frugal person?" 59.3% of respondents either strongly agreed or agreed, only 5% strongly disagreeing.

When asked whether they felt that spending time with friends and family was important to them, the response was overwhelming, 95.3% either agreed or strongly agreed. There was also a strong rejection of the idea that keeping up with fashions is important. 85.9% of people felt it wasn't of great importance. When asked whether they agreed or disagreed with the statement "in general I would say that I am satisfied with my life", the question used in the World Values Survey and in other international surveys measuring happiness, 94.3% agreed or strongly agreed.

Resilience Indicators

What might an emotionally resilient human community look like and how might we measure this? Below we suggest two areas to explore – first how are people doing, measuring feelings of well-being, security and connection. And secondly whether there are adequate support services available. From within the Heart and soul group we might also survey what needs there are, and whether we are meeting them.

Personal well-being

◎ In general I am satisfied with my life (Footnote: This is the question used in the World Values Survey and in other international surveys measuring happiness, also used in Rob's survey with 94% agreeing or agreeing strongly).

◎ Questions from the "Your recent feelings" section of the Happy Planet Index could be used to assess personal well being (see reference below)

◎ I feel confident that in the future my needs and those of my loved ones will be met (Agree strongly to disagree strongly)

◎ On the whole I feel safe in my community

◎ Connections with other people, nature and spiritual life:

◎ I feel included and welcome in my community

◎ I know most/all of my neighbours

◎ How often do you spend time outside in natural or green spaces?

◎ Do you consider yourself to be a spiritual person?

◎ Availability of Support

◎ I can find support that is appropriate when I need it (from family, friends, community services or other organisations)

A fuller version of this chapter can be found in the web-version of this document; this includes an extensive list of further reading and references. For further information on the Happy Planet Index and the questions in Our Householder Survey, please refer to (on-line only) Appendix Q. www.totnesedap.org.uk

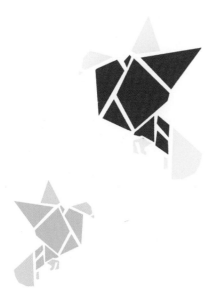

Snapshots Along the Path of Inner Transition to 2030

"How can we create a timeline for inner transition?" was a question we spent some time pondering when we came to write this section of EDAP. Each person's journey of inner transition is unique and probably at some level indescribable. Many have found that engaging with Transition takes them on a profound and continuing journey of deepening connection, grief, joy, companionship, release of hope, hopelessness – from bliss to despair – often in the same day! (For others it's a calm journey of practical action... how different we are!)

In the end we've bypassed trying to suggest pathways of psychological and spiritual awakening or shifts in consciousness, and offer some snapshots of events that might – or might not – happen, which reflect some of the changes we have envisioned. They are given below in a chronological order that you are welcome to imagine very differently...

INNER TRANSITION

PATHWAYS ACRO

Strategic themes: • Foster sharing, equity, citizenship & community
• Inner change

2010

A new course aimed to equip us in dealing with the changes arising from falling energy availability, climate change, and credit crunch, is being offered by Transition Town Totnes in association with the Mansion House and various church groups.

"Living Well in Times of Change will help you understand the changes that are happening, and think about how you can live well through challenging times ahead. It includes ideas for saving money and energy – something we all need as oil and gas prices go up sharply yet again."

2011

A survey has found more and more Totnes groups and organisations using silence or meditation as part of their meetings. The technique has become more widespread since a group of Quakers offered training in the practice they use and call "worship".

Whenever a difficult situation is encountered, instead of everyone pitching in with their point of view and trying to "win" the argument the chairperson calls for silence, and the group sits for a few minutes until someone feels "able to speak from a different place, offering a new way forward". Just repeating the previous points of view isn't allowed...

Connecting elders in our community with young children was the aim of the 'Local Life, Local Stories' project set up in the Bridgetown Youth Centre last year. Now the scheme has spread to schools, three Totnes primary schools inviting local elders to come in for an extended lunch twice a week – eating locally grown food and sitting at tables with school children telling them tales of how local life used to be.

"It's a real win-win-win" enthused Lydia Overbury from Totnes social services. "Elders get some company; the children get to hear some really interesting stories, and everyone gets a good meal."

2012

A new service is to be offered to people losing their jobs in the recession following a government initiative to widen the availability of counselling and support for those affected by the continuing downturn in economic activity. Anyone who has become unemployed, or suffered a significant loss in income can have up to 12 sessions of one to one counselling. Similar services are already running in Torbay, Plymouth and Exeter. Smaller communities are looking at offering the service through doctor's surgeries and local information offices.

2014

At the annual Transition Together Teams festival, this year hosted by the upper Bridgetown team, prizes were awarded as follows:

Biggest group carbon reduction – St Mary Street

Most innovative Transition invention – the bicycle pump (bicycle powered pumping of rainwater from the off-roof tub up the garden)

Community service award – Transition Team Rotherfold made lined curtains for several elderly residents on Leechwell Street following energy audits of their homes.

There are now over 30 Transition Teams in Totnes and we've lost count of what's happening in nearby villages.

SS THE TIMELINE

- Develop respect & sense of connection with others & nature
- Personal development & empowerment

2018

The latest town survey has found that 92% of Totnesians say they know all or nearly all their neighbours, and the feeling of safety and trust in the community is at an all time high. Our reporter asked a Totnes Home Group why they thought this was. One member told us;

"I think it's because of all the things we do together these days – it seems like we do loads of stuff in groups which used to be done alone or in the family – shared meals, taking it in turns to plant gardens and sometimes even doing the spring cleaning together".

2019

Totnes Town Council has agreed to the formation of an Elders' Council for the Town. The Elders will advise the Town Council, and be available for other local groups to go to for advice, help with resolving problems, and support for new projects.

They are looking for elders who really know how the town works and have been involved for a long time – but also who bring the wisdom and experience of having seen a lot of change, and got beyond personality issues.

2020

A joint harvest festival celebrating the season's produce will take place in Totnes Town Hall this September 23rd and all are welcome. Organised by several of the town's faith groups – churches, Quakers and Buddhist groups, and assisted by the Townswomen's guild, the event is expected to bring together several hundred people including growers from the community allotments and Dartington community supported agriculture. Now a major fixture in the growers' calendar – as well as a great celebration – the harvest festival shows the enormous range and abundance of local produce.

2023

A gathering of parents, friends and supporters welcomed home the group of 25 teenagers who completed their "Wilderness Wandering" time on Dartmoor yesterday. Accompanied by the team of Wilderness Wanderers that ensured their safe completion of the four-week adventure outdoors they looked jubilant, healthy – and weathered.

The culmination of a year's training in making fires, living from wild food, creating shelters and living cooperatively and alone outdoors, the month in the open had clearly made a big impact on the youngsters.

"It was awesome!" said Annette Dawson of Bridgetown, "I've never felt so alive! I'm glad I did it, and I'm glad it's over. I feel like I know how to take care of myself outdoors, maybe not in really bad weather, but all the basics. It was great to learn so much more about how it all connects up – water, soil, life, weather and the landscape. And I'm looking forward to a hot shower & sleeping in a bed!!"

2030

The 2030 Lantern procession up Totnes Fore Street and High Street will be a commemoration and celebration of the years of Transition in the local area. Starting back in 2006 at the plains, there will be reminders of how life used to be – cars and the noise of traffic, food flown in from Africa covered in packaging, electronic gadgets and the old fashions.

As the procession makes its way up it will travel through the years of transition remembering some of the key events on the way, and ending in the castle with a celebration of South Hams life in 2030.

EDUCATION, AWARENESS & SKILLS FOR TRANSITION

"To have any chance of making the transition to a sustainable, low-carbon economy, the UK workforce urgently requires new skills. And although useful, new technical skills will not by themselves be sufficient. Some of the most important capabilities we need to foster are critical thinking, systems thinking, and the ability to envision a brighter, more sustainable future, and lead others towards that goal."
Commission for Sustainable Development

The Challenge

The 2003 Government White Paper 'The Skills Strategy' aimed to "ensure that employers have the right skills to support the success of their businesses and individuals have the skills they need to be both employable and personally fulfilled". This leaves many gaps in personal development, building relationships, creative thinking, community engagement, awareness and understanding of broader issues and development of compassion, good citizenship, wisdom and enlightened thinkers. Transition Town Totnes

A Walking Bus on the Way to School. © Richard Hodgson

uses the term The Great Reskilling to capture the immense scale of retraining that is needed in order for a society as oil dependent and unskilled as ours to be ready in time for a world that needs more skilled market gardeners and less website designers, more builders familiar with hemp, lime and clay, and less familiar with plywood, concrete and steel, and more solar installers and less oil fired central heating installers.

While third level education institutes in the UK have developed considerably in the last 25 years to embrace sustainable development and environmental sciences, there are very few courses and learning opportunities to prepare society for the major challenges we face. Many agricultural colleges and research institutes have closed and few farmers have sons and daughters prepared to fill their shoes or take on trainees to learn their trade. Few adult education courses offer the opportunity to learn about the issues around peak oil or climate change or skills for power-down such as retrofitting your home, urban food growing or getting involved with your local community. Apprenticeships, once the pride of many firms and businesses are now few and far between as inflation and economic instability have undermined long-term planning. Never before has education had such a vital role to play in preparing communities and the nation as a whole for profound change, and also in modelling, as institutions, the practicalities of that change.

Business as Usual or Willing to Change? Emerging Trends - Where we are Now

If we continue on our current path, by 2030 Totnes and District will have probably made more educational progress than other areas around the UK as it has the benefit of some very progressive educational institutions in the area, however few of the adult population of the area are taking full advantage of this to be adequately prepared and skilled for a resilient response to the coming challenges. Teaching about sustainability and transition subjects will continue to be a bolt-on at all levels of the state education provision, rather than the underlying ethos. Most young people and older students will still be leaving education programmes without a sense of holistic development, without a clear understanding of their role and responsibility in local and global sustainable development, and without the practical skills required by the emerging, more localised, economy.

The alternative is making a determined effort to bring awareness and education about transition to local society. We can take full advantage of and build on the inspirational and educational opportunities already here in Totnes and District, and the huge amount of experience among those within education. Our future depends on all of us, young people and adults being excited and inspired by the challenges of transition, and acquiring skills such as the ability to think long-term and critically about situations, recognise the value and limits of natural systems, apply systems thinking to their work, and have a creative vision of what a brighter, more sustainable future might be so that we develop good leaders and strong citizenship. We might identify the following principles as those that must underpin education in coming years:

◎ A broader provision of many educational and personal development opportunities for all sectors of local society, promoting awareness and understanding about the challenges of peak oil and climate change and the role of transition

◎ An ethos of sustainability has to be central to all our educational institutions in terms of what they teach as well as what they do as institutions

◎ Our local schools could work more closely together and with the local community: in order to: share ideas, programmes and projects: develop new ones

◎ More agricultural and horticultural training and research

◎ More apprenticeships and practical training for the diverse range of power-down skills

◎ More time for reflection, at all ages.

What kinds of things might we do to support the current system to move towards resilience? Steps to change:

◎ Continue to develop Transition Tales as a project for KS3

◎ Children become the main teachers and leaders of the education project

◎ As part of ongoing research into how people best learn ask those who attend TTT events over 6-12 months to fill in a very small slip of paper which asks them to reflect on what helps them to learn best: e.g. I learn best through reading/listening/talking/group work/individually (on the shelf ones do exist)

◎ Establish the concept of "Transition Schools";

◎ Make use of the current opportunities such as the "new" work with parents: spot all such opportunities for making the most of the available resources

◎ Actively link school and community projects to the story of Transition e.g. intergeneration work.

What follows is one version of how education, awareness and skills development might become more localised and sustainable over the next 21 years.

Doing the Sums. © Jenny Band

3.54

Education in Preparation for Transition Opportunities in Totnes & District

Educational Establishment	Already doing...	Some Next Steps?
Primary Schools (there are 12 within Totnes and District)	Some have gardens, grow vegetables, plants trees, have bird tables, teach outside, learn about climate change and the environment, separate waste, make compost, actively encourage children to walk or cycle to school, organise Walking Buses, involving parents in activities. Some have the healthy school award and focus on provision of nutritious local food as part of food provision. Some have worked on the Eco Schools and Sustainable Schools award. Some are involved in the global curriculum. Some are involved with TTT's Transition Tales.	Retrofitting of classrooms, visits to sustainability initiatives, gardening training for every student, installation of renewables, following the food cycle from sowing seeds to eating meals, involve more parents, more personal development and reflection, smaller classes. Establish a Transition Team within and across Totnes schools to develop ideas and projects that they then manage. Link up all current sustainability projects and initiatives into the story of transition.
South Devon Steiner School	Excellent vegetable garden, food production and other land-based skills central to the curriculum, cooking taught, transport plan encouraging cycling, walking and shared community transport. Story telling tradition.	
King Edward VI Community College, (KEVICC) Totnes	Has a sustainability committee (staff + students), teaches about climate change, have a vegetable garden and Forest School area, have hosted lectures about transition and TTT, Transition Tales sessions run for all Year 7 students. Are involved in H.S.A and Sustainable schools award.	A food production plan for the whole site, zero carbon energy systems, high level of specification for local materials in new classroom buildings, agroforestry plantings, a GCSE in Transition studies. Work with primary schools as part of the Transition Team. Link up all relevant educational activities into a holistic approach.
The Mansion House, Totnes.	Courses for some practical skills for transition such as crafts (sewing, basket-making, weaving).	Could host a range of evening classes and daytime trainings on all practical aspects of Transition e.g. repair, maintenance, simple design & construction as well as developing awareness and understanding of the broader issues [see TTT below]. Could start using an outdoor classroom. Could create a model urban food garden and teach others how to do the same.
Dartington Schumacher College	Has a global reputation, hosts lectures and runs a wide selection of courses offering transformative learning for deep and holistic engagement with sustainable living. Residential students at the college spend time working in the forest garden as well as cooking and studying together. Very few students are drawn from the local community.	Schumacher TV, an online TV station, courses within the town, open evenings for local organisations. Develop an online forum for discussion and ideas sharing. Initiate practical courses and continue to develop site as exemplar agroforestry/permaculture site.

3.55

TTT's Transition Together	Teams of neighbours learn about issues and take a series of practical actions to make the transition in their own homes.	Could be delivered far more widely across the community, be promoted by workplaces and institutions. Link Transition together with schools and establish a family in transition offshoot.
A thriving community sector, with individuals and groups organising and promoting their own courses or programmes	Many opportunities for all age groups to learn and get involved, however most rely on volunteers to support newcomers and activities. Examples include: Wildwise, Sharpham Estate, Friends of the Earth, Dartington Trust, Moor Trees, Landmatters, RAISE, DARE, Eden Project etc.[1]	Groups link up from time to time to discuss long term objectives that they can be involved in working towards as separate groups and collectively. They look at the strategic educational needs of society that can be addressed through practical and conceptual projects.
Transition Town Totnes	Talks, trainings, the Beginners Gardening course, Skilling Up for Powerdown evening class, offers trainings such as the 'Weaving Magic' course for those involved in Transition.	Link with Mansion House to establish a menu of options Link with all other groups that are offering educational courses and training to promote power-down thinking and objectives in their programmes.
Totnes Library	Has a Transition section with a group set of the Transition Handbook and hosts book groups.	Likely to be relocated to a larger premises; could host adult creative writers groups on the theme of transition.
3rd Level Courses; e.g. Plymouth University, Exeter University, Open University	Offer a wide range of 3rd level and post-graduate study courses that are directly relevant to understanding and contributing to the debate about Peak Oil and Climate Change. Bringing this into the public domain via television (e.g. Prof. Iain Stewart's series about the evidence for Climate Change in Autumn 2008). Also in-house conferences on Sustainable Development.	In-house development of Universities in Transition. The ethos of the University as an identifiable community taking on the challenge of transition. More links with local (50 mile radius) community and key players to nurture transition in the wider community through both shorter 3rd level courses and public events on transition topics.
Devon County Education Dept. & Devon Education for Sustainability Working Group (DESWG)	Various programmes, seminars and conferences targeted at various groups e.g. Education for Sustainable Development South West Conference. Nov '08.	More of the same, in particular looking at peak oil and concepts of local resilience.
BBC Educational programmes	A wide range of excellent programmes and screening of films e.g. The Future of farming by Rebecca Hoskins.	More of the same especially programmes & films about peak oil and local resilience. Also programmes targeted at younger audiences that schools could use as discussion points.

1 See contact details lists in (on line only) Appendix G www.totnesedap.org.uk

From Our Survey

One key aspect of establishing the resilience of a settlement is getting a picture of the level of skills that people in the community have. When asked whether they agreed or disagreed with the statement "I am adaptable and can turn my hand to new skills fairly easily", 82.2% of people agreed or strongly agreed. We then asked respondents which of a list of skills they felt a reasonable level of competence in. The affirmative answers were as follows, in descending order;

- ◎ Cooking 91.3%
- ◎ Painting and decorating 72.2%
- ◎ Making basic house repairs 62.7%
- ◎ Repairing clothes 52.2%
- ◎ Growing food 45%
- ◎ Storing garden produce (i.e. Food) 24.5%
- ◎ Keeping small livestock 21.1%

The Role of Education in EDAP

Many people feel that the sense of community in our society has weakened over recent decades, and that consumerism, with advertising pressures in the media and in mail, has encouraged people to be more self-indulgent and self-centred. For an "action plan" to succeed, it is not sufficient to teach relevant skills: it is important to strengthen the sense of local community, and the sense of social responsibility. This needs to be given more priority because of the economic pressures.

There are known methods of education which will contribute substantially to this, and they can be started as soon as children begin school. (Children now aged 5 will be adults by 2030!) The government and others who influence schooling now talk about "Social and Emotional Aspects of Learning" (SEAL), but the activities they suggest are not in practice given the same emphasis as that given to literacy and numeracy, and do not necessarily involve as much listening to children, or sharing responsibility with children, as would make them really effective. A priority given to good education in personal relationships can result in more efficient learning of facts and skills. Teachers may need time, and access to training, to achieve this.

Bureaucracy, too, has increased, in many social contexts, and is a major barrier to constructive social education. It would be good if a "transition" community, as a whole, could explore ways of minimising bureaucracy, including the reduction of the pressures, which it puts on schools and teachers.

Arthur French, TTT Education for Transition Group

Vision 2030

By 2030, Totnes and District has evolved into a community that is underpinned by principles of sustainability and resilience in all aspects of life. These are deeply integrated in local society and underpin all educational institutions in the district. Teaching and learning embrace a wide liberal system whereby students of all ages learn through exploration and interest and share their learning as part of the broader teaching process. Learning about transition, and skills for power-down skills are available to all through a diversity of opportunities, alongside the other core curriculum subjects. Young people are keen to learn, understand and develop deeply rooted values about sustainability and social justice, eventually leaving formal learning highly motivated with a broad toolkit of creative thinking, knowledge, practical skills and enthusiasm for learning. Older people have many opportunities for learning and reskilling. Elders and good teachers enjoy a central place in a community, which respects and uses their knowledge and wisdom. All have opportunities to study further, train and retrain for interesting work and practical tasks and most people enjoy a good story.

Resilience Indicators

From the research that led to this Plan, we have identified a number of key indicators by which we can be sure that we we are moving forward. These include:

◎ Percentage of population who have trained in specific transition skills; academic, practical, personal development.

◎ Percentage of people whom, when asked, state that they feel confident in a range of skills (see above).

◎ Percentage of adults registered in post secondary education.

◎ Percentage of children who walk or cycle to school.

◎ Percentage of students who reach 16 with a firm understanding of climate change and other environmental issues, as well as being familiar with practical solutions.

These can be revisited regularly to see if the community is making progress in the right direction.

A list of references and further reading can be found at www.totnesedap.org.uk

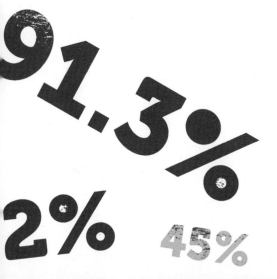

EDUCATION, AWARENESS & SKILLS FOR TRANSITION
PATHWAYS ACRO

Strategic themes: • More learning choices • Integrated learning about relationships

2009

Individuals

- TTT initiates new courses: Transition Together runs 2 pilot programmes to support individuals and households through transition. 50 new people sign up for courses. 3 new transition gardening courses are over subscribed. More gardening trainers are needed, says Lou Brown of TTT.

- Local people learn about and get involved in new ways of visioning and planning for the future through EDAP public workshops. Many attend the TTT public events and bring friends and family to become more informed about the issues. Over 350 people attend the public launch of the EDAP.

- 3 primary schools sign up for Transition Tales sessions with TTT. "The children are really enthusiastic," says Steph Bradley, co-ordinator of the project.

- Leading Head teacher and political commentator Anthony Seldon, along with the majority of educational leaders, major assessment bodies, teachers associations and politicians condemn the current emphasis on league tables and national tests. Seldon comments, "soulless schools cursed by league tables and dominated by 'formulaic' exams are squeezing the lifeblood out of education. A system that stifles imagination, individuality and flair." He advocates a severe cut back of external testing and examinations. He argues for smaller schools, playing fields, placing orchestras and music at the heart of the curriculum and offering dance, physical exercise, outdoor adventure and challenge to everyone. "We should not ask how intelligent a child is, but how are they intelligent"[5].

- Dartington Eco-School, Devon's first zero carbon school opens. They invite teachers from all the other schools in Totnes and District to an open day to encourage them to make changes. "We really want to share the terrific ideas and encourage other schools to make even some small changes," said thrilled head teacher Jill Mahon. "We will be paying visits to other local schools for some ideas for our school garden project."

Community

- Transition Tales schools' project expands to more students at KEVICCS. 8 new volunteers train to deliver the sessions. KEVICCS starts a Buddy scheme between yr 7 and yr 12 students to share transition ideas and promote links between students. Parents at the school form a Transition Together group.

- Transition Tales initiates a transition teacher training programme including inset days, Community & Personal Development (CPD) courses as well as tailor made courses for specific schools' needs including skills and activities for teaching about transition, working with inner development, both at a personal level and with the students, and starts working with Embercombe, Bowden & Sharpham offering residential camps for schools and away weekends for teachers.

- A field is purchased by Transition Tales using crowd funding from parents, teachers, and local philanthropists to transform into a Transition Tales Wild Garden where children and their significant adults will be able to help create a forest garden, forage for, cook and eat wild foods, and tell transition tales in the storytelling barn.

- St John's School opens talks with the Healthy Futures group and the Allotments Association regarding an intergeneration learning, growing and sharing project.

SS THE TIMELINE

& feelings • Awareness of transition & developing empowerment

- Totnes primary schools establish a children's Transition Team to weave together transition stories and create new ideas.
- TTT Education for Transition project commences. Members of TTT's Education group make links with local schools and offer 'Teaching for Change' sessions about transition. They discuss ways to reduce the weight of bureaucracy on schools and teachers.

Policy Makers & Service Providers

- The Mansion House Courses include Powerdown training. They are immediately oversubscribed.
- DCC & RE4D (Renewable Energy 4 Devon) offer advice and information about installing renewable energy.
- Through their Friends' groups, Library services have been looking at ways to support people through the economic downturn and promote their services to the wider community and in particular young people[6].
- DCC funds a presentation of Localeyes web voting in Devon to key officers involved in young person's wellbeing, educational officers and others involved in the Children's and Young Person's Plan. They also invite elected representatives from the Youth Parliament and members of the Young People's Scrutiny Committee.
- SHDC runs staff training sessions to increase energy efficiency and reduce wastage. The staff enjoys the training and agree to carry out some energy measures at home. A short leaflet will be issued to all households and business premises based on the key parts of the training most people enjoyed.

2010

Individuals

- Transition Together goes from strength to strength and a part-time coordinator is employed. Some of the trainers join together for a training and mentoring course to help new teams coming together.
- Local bookshops set up transition sections covering information about energy issues and climate change, practical skills and personal development topics. Old books about local resilience are making a comeback.
- School groups arrange visits to local allotments and the local Steiner School to learn about growing food.
- 'Construction in Transition' training commences at Dartington. A number of local builders sign up.
- Arthur French shares his experiences of 'Circle Time' and 'Active Tutorial Work' as proven method for children to achieve self-discipline and personal development at the TTT Education for Transition evening. The idea catches on rapidly in local schools.

EDUCATION, AWARENESS & SKILLS FOR TRANSITION

PATHWAYS ACRO

Strategic themes: • More learning choices • Integrated learning about relationships

Community

- An evening for local teachers is hosted by TTT. Teachers are introduced to a number of resources including films and a Transition Tales taster available to their schools. The Schools in Transition (SIT) network is initiated.

- TTT go out to visit all local schools offering a taster of Transition Tales workshops for teachers & students. The Schools in Transition network links in with the National Transition Schools (initiated by Transition Tales in 2009 with collaboration from Forest Row, Scotland & Bristol).

- Sustainable Makers group offer classes (weaving, woodcraft etc.) at their temporary Craft Hub. They are oversubscribed.

- TTT seasons of events are becoming very popular and public talks are attended by large numbers of people. They host some film evenings with discussions in outlying village halls, which prove popular.

- Local women's groups get together for a seasonal cooking session at the Civic Hall. They share recipes and tasters of dishes cooked entirely from local food and share tips about low energy cooking.

- Students and staff at KEVICCs have become much more aware of energy issues with the help of Global Action Plan, running a campaign within the college and planning to directly influence the 2000+ households of those who work and study at KEVICC. Having some renewable energy now installed at the college has given the group leading this work a mandate to encourage everyone not to waste a precious resource.

Policy Makers & Service Providers

- In the wake of the Copenhagen Summit, the new Government plans a complete review of teaching and schools with a view to implementing a phased change towards "an underlying ethos of sustainable development". The UK CSD[7] will advise on how to implement the change in as short a time scale as possible. DCC plan to follow up with an in-service training for teachers and ask TTT to assist.

- Teacher training is to include modules for implementing sustainable development in schools and teaching about climate change. These topics are to be compulsory in all schools.

- A number of teaching unions join the clamour for the abolition of SATS tests across the board. They are looking for more time in the school day to be spent on personal development, relationships and creativity.

- DCC's Joint Commissioning Team recommends a significant increase of National Government funding to the Dedicated Schools Grant from the Department of Children, Schools and Families (DCSF), claiming that currently Devon's share enables barely 70% of assessed needs to be met, leaving risk of gaps in services for young people. They are also looking for additional funds to recruit additional staff to enable smaller class sizes. Information on Devon's Extended Services (ESS) is available or signposted at all schools in the area[8].

- NICEIC and CORGI are funded by the Dept of Trade to extend apprenticeship schemes and offer retraining for registered electricians and plumbers in design and installation of renewable energy systems.

SS THE TIMELINE

& feelings • Awareness of transition & developing empowerment

2011

Individuals

- The more skilled gardeners at the local allotments offer training sessions for local people and school children to learn about growing food and herbs for health and wellbeing.

- School groups set up visits to local farms to learn about growing food and other farm practices. Popular visits include Velwell Biodynamic Orchard where the students can help pick the autumn fruit, Beenleigh Meadow where they can try their hand at building with cob, Landmatters where they learn about community living and growing and the Transition Tales Wild Garden where they can get involved in forest gardening, cooking together, and storytelling.

- Primary schoolchildren write to local natural builders and request a demonstration on building with straw bales. 3 schools build a straw bale outdoor shelter with a sod roof for bicycles. Diptford Primary School uses their shelter for an outdoor theatre production at the end of summer term.

- Sharpham Trust hosts a month long tree planting marathon for all schools in Totnes and District to link together in planting a community woodland, orchard and hedgerow. The schools are to raise money for the trees; one will be planted by every pupil.

- KEVICC and the Steiner school hook up and inaugurate an annual transition storytelling and music festival, which is broadcast live on the web.

Community

- Totnes Townswomen's Guild and Dartington and Diptford WI attend an open evening at Schumacher College. They are very interested in the talk about local food and are invited back for a supper which they help cook.

- All 13 primary schools in Totnes and District join the Schools in Transition (SIT) Network and participate in creating a Schools Transition Day, which is to become an annual event. Gaia is a popular theme for students.

- KEVICCS school garden expands and students pick salad leaves and potatoes for the school lunch across the summer term. The pumpkin competition is won by Angie Hartwell in yr 8 with a whopping 25kg specimen, which is later sculpted and goes on show at the library for Halloween.

- Mobilising your Street is a popular training course for people trying to get their neighbours together for shared activities. TTT organise the sessions and participants share ideas about building local actions. Buying solar panels in bulk and having street parties are still the most popular themes.

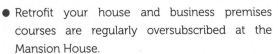

Policy Makers & Service Providers

- Retrofit your house and business premises courses are regularly oversubscribed at the Mansion House.

- The Department of Education is to fund a new Schools' Sustainability Officer post in all counties, to assist schools to implement the new sustainability thinking. Devon Learning and Development Partnership issues new school policies on sustainable development in schools, reducing energy, green procurement and school travel.

EDUCATION, AWARENESS & SKILLS FOR TRANSITION
PATHWAYS ACRO

Strategic themes: • More learning choices • Integrated learning about relationships

- The new Government initiates a smaller classroom model and agrees to invest funding for all schools to gain (pro rata) two additional part-time teachers per 100 students to enable the process to commence.

- DCC invests in cycling training for all schools. 5 new officers are to provide week-long training in schools for both pupils and staff. Bowing to popular demand the scheme is extended to include parents and teachers too.

who are animal enthusiasts. Most schools have a small garden - some with vegetables, some with herbs and trees.

- Interest grows in relaxation and self help for self-awareness and personal development. Local organisers note a steady rise in people of all ages and backgrounds signing up for yoga classes as people are generally working fewer hours.

- Following on from Sharpham's very popular School Tree-athon the previous year, The Duke of Somerset initiates a similar event at Berry Pomeroy. Parents at the schools are delighted when they are offered locally grown saplings for the children to plant. Later the school parties make a trip to Sharpham to see how their other trees are growing. Nigel Flaws, age 10, observes rather dryly that trees grow much faster than his dog.

2012

Individuals

- The Devon interschool Design a Board Game challenge is won by KEVICC for their game of Energy Challenges. Year 11 spokesperson Anthony Knewell said the game had been "inspired by all that talk of transition when he was younger." Adding that he "plans to go into the games business as this can really show people what is happening out there." KEVICC is awarded a pedal powered LED light system for the student theatre.

- Spindletop Farm at Cornworthy invites local schools to a hedge day. Pupils learn about hedgerows and coppicing, forage for some edible foods and try their hand at planting a hedge and dry stonewalling.

- All schools in Totnes and District have a space they use as an outdoor classroom. Some have created a tree house, others a small theatre structure for the students to decorate and use as part of their studies. Bird tables, bat boxes and small animal watching hides are popular with many students

Community

- Totnes Art & Design Foundation course at KEVICC expands to include a full 3 year degree course. An energy awareness component will look at low energy impact medium and materials.

- Education for Powerdown training commences at village halls in Diptford, Rattery, Stoke Gabriel and South Brent. Registering for one course is 85-year-old Arnold Brewer who wants to learn to spin wool.

- South Brent Primary School in conjunction with Sustainable South Brent wins the Chop Energy Challenge. The school has planted a crop of carbon absorbing plants on the turf roof of its straw bale bike shelter. The entire shelter has been built from local recycled wood and straw and turf brought on site by pony and cart.

- Members of TTT's Cycle group offer local schools cycling training to encourage use of the new cycle ways. Students and parents are invited to join up for outings along local greenways.

SS THE TIMELINE

& feelings • Awareness of transition & developing empowerment

- TTT offers training on Energy Descent Planning; helping other groups and sectors to work with assumptions, visualisation and back-casting techniques. A number of community and development planners sign-up.

- University of the 3rd Age courses on Climate Change and Peak Oil come on stream.

- Dartington Abundant Life Community opens to its first residents. All rooms are zero carbon heating and the new residents are very interest in their new concept living. Within a month they have organised a bookshelf of literature about transition they can share; some have old wartime resilience books to add to this collection.

Policy Makers & Service Providers

- In line with many Local Authorities including Devon CC, SHDC has taken the decision to support transition initiatives and has funded Transition Training, access to resources, as well as offering some core funding. TTT will provide some training to key LA officers and Councillors.

- Totnes Library opens at its new enlarged premises and starts junior reading and adult creative writers groups.

- Totnes Town Council invites groups of year 10 students from KEVICCS to an in-house session on running a local town council. The students are invited to create an agenda and discuss how to spend a budget on local facilities. Enjoying the first session, Town Mayor Tom Whitty says he "learnt a lot too as the students had been full of good ideas"; though he says "growing vegetables in the church yard might not be very popular with the Rector".

- South Devon College offers a new range of natural building courses including 'Construction in Transition' courses for trainee builders and 'Renewable Energy Systems design & installation

for plumbers and electricians'. The course includes a series of one-hour sessions for personal development related to transition.

- The SATS for under 14s are finally abolished after the majority of schools return empty test papers in protest.

2013-15

Individuals

- Local plumbers and electricians offer local apprenticeships in installing renewable energy systems and retrofitting.

- Totnes Museum becomes a model example of retrofitting an old building with sensitivity. Local church representatives attend a guided tour and talk by the builders on site and consider ideas for similar retrofits.

- The Consciousness Café group meeting at the Barrel House starts a monthly virtual discussion group using video conferencing technology with other international consciousness raising groups. Their first night links with members of an Eco-Village in Ohio and they discuss deepening the links between people and ecology.

EDUCATION, AWARENESS & SKILLS FOR TRANSITION
PATHWAYS ACRO

Strategic themes: • More learning choices • Integrated learning about relationships

Community

- Schools in Transition Week organised by the SIT network has become an extended annual event with themes ranging from pedal power, zero energy planning, singing for change and telling imaginary tales of transition.

- Totnes Chamber of Commerce organises a seminar in business training for new local producers and school leavers. Local business people share their expertise and knowledge about running a successful enterprise. Paul Wesley chairs the Meet the Apprentice open forum session for students' question time saying afterwards, "it wasn't exactly the Dragon's Den, but I think some of the experts were surprised by the new ideas from the newcomers and young people. We all learnt a lot".

- The annual open day at Leechwell Community Garden offers an introduction to herbs for general well-being and medicinal use. By popular demand it opens a weekly course across the summer.

- Registration & welcome classes open from 9.00 to 9.50am are made up of the entire age range of the school.

Policy Makers & Service Providers

- DCC decides that while school intake size has reduced with the smaller population of children, staff levels are to remain the same to provide better quality teaching and more integrated activities such as gardening, crafts and cooking with the students, many of whom are now choosing to stay on at school into the 6th form. More visits and excursions are planned to broaden the children's education.

- Further to national training being given to local Authority Engineers, SHDC initiates a series of training session in flood management and contingency planning for local people. The sessions are well attended and people learn about staying safe, helping vulnerable people and looking after wildlife areas when there are storm surges. They plan to extend the sessions to ensure that 25% of the adult population has been trained to respond to emergencies. A short booklet is provided to all homes and businesses with advice on contingency procedures.

- The Mansion House instigates Community training, this is to be provided to community based groups who wish to explore communication skills, how to listen, conflict resolution, self-awareness, personal development and working with others at a feeling level. Students of all ages are to be encouraged to participate in this one-year pilot project.

SS THE TIMELINE

& feelings • Awareness of transition & developing empowerment

2016-20

Individuals

- Making and repairing your own clothes has become a key part of school life, and shoes and other garments are now designed for durability rather than disposability. People with skills in handicrafts, sewing knitting, quilting etc. give some lessons in schools.

- Many people register with St. John's for their First Aid Courses to help people suffering from heat exhaustion. St. John's are also training additional ambulance drivers.

- The Elders sharing stories with younger people has gained in popularity, as the younger children enjoy stories about the crazy years of extravagance. Some children make pictures of the stories.

Community

- With school numbers reducing, adult education expands into KEVICCS and some courses are held during the day. Students are interested in the novelty of having older people around the school and suggest some combined classes. The school orchestra and choir benefits from the mix of skills and experience.

- Small allotment spaces are being offered at some schools to local parents in exchange for giving surplus vegetables to the school kitchen and training to students in gardening. A number of the parents take it in turns to help provide school luncheon, the children are allowed to take turns in help cook.

- Community training has developed into a wide choice of opportunities for young people doing their community gap year. They can gain community credits at the end of the year that reflects well on their CVs.

- In groups roughly the size of yearly intake, some members meet to discuss and vote on what changes they would like to see in the school and how any agreed changes can best be realised.

Policy Makers & Service Providers

- The Department of Education agrees to reduce the school week to 4 days in places where a local community day has become established. This is to enable children to participate in local food growing and other community based and 'extended classroom' activities.

- Schools from pre-school to 6th form have more autonomy and much less prescriptive national curriculum to adhere to. Teachers use their unions and networks to exchange ideas and many have taken additional training in 'Teaching through Play and conversations', which has become a popular part of general studies for all age groups.

- In the wake of the unpopularity of the loans system, 3rd level education is diversified to include people from the community, business and academia who can build education credits by offering lectures, research and supports into the system.

- The Mansion House's Community Training proves a very popular course that leads onto clear community benefits. Community groups are being encouraged to share the teaching with members of local groups and organisations.

EDUCATION, AWARENESS & SKILLS FOR TRANSITION
PATHWAYS ACRO

Strategic themes: • More learning choices • Integrated learning about relationships

2021-25

Individuals

- A survey by the teaching unions finds that despite the austerity of the times, teachers are enjoying their work more and find students much more responsive. The smaller classes are said to have reduced pressure and children have increased self-esteem. Disciplinary issues are much less of a problem.

- Climate migrants arriving from displaced communities share skills about growing different foods and other practical skills.

- Schumacher College commences a pilot virtual course for overseas students unable to travel to their courses and to include speakers who would otherwise need to travel a long way.

- 6th class Pupils can decide by majority vote which subject areas they would like to drop or include

Community

- English conversation courses are being offered by some local groups to help new migrants learn some useful language and meet people. The lessons are extended to a shared meal.

- Community groups have formed an introductory group and offer an orientation week to help new arrivals adjust and find their way around the area and facilities etc.

- The Steiner School opens an in-service training for teachers wishing to introduce some of their techniques in other local schools. The SITs schools' network supports this with organising some teacher exchanges in local schools.

Policy Makers & Service Providers

- Biodiversity research and management courses are offered by Defra in an attempt to draw in comprehensive monitoring of species at most risk from increasing temperatures and flooding. Children have been drawn into a broader understanding of nature and interdependency and are enthusiastic bird and invertebrate counters.

- DCC initiates a 'Sharing our experiences and knowledge' programme for newcomers, new foreign migrants and local people to broaden understanding and build relationships for mutual support within local society.

SS THE TIMELINE

& feelings • Awareness of transition & developing empowerment

Individuals

- Climate migrant children share stories about the floods and heat waves to enthralled audiences at local schools. Embellishing the stories with tales of sharks and dinosaurs eating their houses is frowned upon by teachers who initially thought the students had just made errors in translation.

- Children and elders share many stories under the new creative tales work every morning. Head teacher Irene Mellor from Diptford said the reflective quiet time opened up the children's ideas and imaginations, followed by an avalanche of thoughts that feed into their stories, they really enjoy this and are very expressive.

Community

- Parents and other members of local communities are getting involved in the sports and PE with the schools and youth groups. Opportunities for a wide choice of activities have expanded with the new facilities in Totnes and the outer parishes. The Community website carries the listings of activities.

- Transition initiatives continue despite the sense that 'we have arrived', and the difficult times, there is an awareness that there are many more changes and challenges to come. The groups and projects within TTT have found a working balance that supports the community. With travel being less frequent for most people, the wide screen virtual talks and discussions with other transition groups around the world provides opportunities to share information, ideas and sympathy for difficulties.

Policy Makers & Service Providers

- DCC's Children, youth and education and supports units are simplified into one team to assist more directly with school and educational needs. They have become a one-stop shop for information about local education and provide more local in-service training for teachers. In response to requests from local schools, they provide a series of creative studies short courses as refresher courses for teachers.

- DCC agrees to a pilot project to extend the mobile library service to provide books for and service Reading Rooms in all the Community Halls in Totnes & District. A volunteer librarian will be appointed for each reading room and s/he will exchange and select books for the local sub-library. Janet Young from Harberton who has been pushing the idea for 5 years told the Totnes Times "The extensive use of community halls for many healthcare services as well as community events and suppers etc. means this service will be widely used."

2026-30

© Transition Town Totnes

Transition Together

Transition Together is a very local programme designed specifically for anyone living here in Totnes and its surrounding villages. It is a simple workbook that enables you to take a number of effective, practical, money and energy-saving steps together with a group of neighbours, your friends or your family. The workbook shows you the easiest ways to:

◎ Take control of your daily costs

◎ Understand better these times of change and uncertainty

◎ Reduce your impact on the environment

◎ Act together with your friends, family and community

◎ Have fun, make friends and save money at a pace and schedule that suits you

It also explores easy, practical ways to take advantage of cheaper transport options and the great value, healthy, local food available in our town. It also helps you understand what's behind the rising oil prices and climate change, and what this means for you, your family and your local community.

The programme is very flexible. Together with your group, you arrange dates and venues where you'll make your way through the workbook together.

◎ The ideal size for a group is 5 - 8 households

◎ You'll meet about 7 times, usually once every 2-3 weeks

◎ Group members generally take turns to host a meeting at their homes, but other places can be used

◎ There's a new chapter for each session which you'll discuss together, but you'll each develop your own plans specific to your home and family

◎ At each session you have space and time to catch up with the rest of your group, share trials and tribulations, exchange ideas and offer support and generally, consume a lot of cake!

As well as the workbook itself, you will also have access to a range of other resources and offers.

Two pilot groups in Totnes have now completed the programme, with others set to start. Anyone who lives in Totnes and District can sign up for Transition Together, and it's really easy to get started – just call us on 05601 538658 or email us at info@transition-together.org.uk.

Find more information on the web, including stories from current groups at www.transitionnetwork.org

Transition Tales at King Edward VI Community School, Totnes.
© Jacqi Hodgson

Transition Tales

Transition Tales" are visions of a positive future world. In a sense the whole transition movement is a story we are telling ourselves as we step into it. Transition Tales are the more specifically located stories, told of a time and place and of people. They help us to collectively envision a future in which we are meeting the challenge and also to negotiate our feelings from the present day. They can entice us to take the next step and affirm that however small step might feel its part of the interweaving of a larger whole, which we have glimpsed in these stories from the future.

Transition Tales are an especially effective way of introducing young people to these issues and of engaging their creativity and imagination in what future we would like to create together.

Check out our Transition Tales in Schools page for our recent education projects: www.totnes.transitionnetwork.org/transitiontales/schoolswork

TRANSITION IN ACTION

NOTES & IDEAS

Empowering People

Fields at KEVICCS © Lou Brown

LOCAL GOVERNANCE

In this section we look briefly at local authority plans as these are charged with providing local leadership, supporting and guiding the implementation of sustainable development; i.e. development that meets the needs of the present without compromising the ability of future generations to meet their own needs[1].

Sustainable Development is achieved through a balance of social, environmental and economic development, which is underpinned by all sectors working together in co-operation and partnership. Supported community engagement, consultation at all stages of local, regional and national development is essential to ensuring local development is appropriate to meeting the needs of society, and that people are actively encouraged and empowered to be involved as responsible citizens.

The current overriding development plan for Totnes is the Devon County Council's Community Strategy[2]; this embraces the following key goals (which are common to most local authority strategic plans):

◎ Homes for all: building for the future

◎ Improving the life-chances of children and young people

◎ Protecting and improving our outstanding environment

◎ Working for sustainable wealth creation

◎ Making Devon an even safer place to live

◎ A County for everyone

◎ Promoting a healthy and caring Devon

"By 2015 we want Devon to be: A County with safe, healthy and inclusive communities, a strong and diverse economy, and a cherished environment"

Local Governance in Transition

In seeking support for Transition from all levels of local administration, we need to be able to understand what a **Local Authority adopting Transition** might look like. A useful model is provided by the key recommendations in Descending the Oil Peak: The Report of the City of Portland (US) Peak Oil Task Force 2007

Recommendations: Act Big, Act Now

While all the recommendations are important, **achieving a significant reduction in oil and natural gas use** is a necessity for easing the transition to an energy-constrained future.

1. Reduce total oil and natural gas consumption by 50% over the next 25 years

Leadership builds the public will, community spirit and institutional capacity needed to implement the ambitious changes. Leadership is needed to build partnerships to address these issues at a regional and statewide level.

2. Inform citizens about peak oil and foster community and community-based solutions

3. Engage business, government and community leaders to initiate planning and policy change

Urban Design addresses the challenge at a community scale.

4. Support land use patterns that reduce transportation needs, promote walkability and provide easy access to services and transport options.

5. Design infrastructure to promote transportation options and facilitate efficient movement of freight and prevent infrastructure investments that would not be prudent given fuel shortages and higher prices.

Expanded efficiency and conservation programmes shape the many choices made by individual households and businesses.

6. Encourage energy-efficient and renewable transportation choices

7. Expand building energy-efficient programmes and incentives for all new and existing structures

Sustainable economic development fosters the growth of businesses that can supply energy-efficient solutions and provide employment and wealth creation in a new economic context

8. Preserve farmland and expand local food production and processing

9. Identify and promote sustainable business opportunities

Social and economic support systems will be needed to help (Devonians, Totnesians etc) dislocated by the effects of fuel price increases

10. Redesign the safety net and protect vulnerable and marginalised populations

Emergency plans should be in place to respond to sudden price increases or supply interruptions.

11. Prepare emergency plans for sudden and severe shortages

In Totnes and District, we offer this Energy Descent Action Plan as a source for building Transition through bottom-up planning which can be adopted by all sectors wishing to create a future development plan. We have had the benefit and had access to a number of parish plans that have been developed for this district, and hope we have done justice to the ideas and local knowledge they carry. One such plan is The Totnes and District Community Plan

In Totnes, the Totnes and District Strategy Group co-ordinated the development of a Community Plan for the area in 2003, which was subsequently reviewed and revised in 2005. Through in-depth consultation with local people and organisations, a broad range of desirable projects was identified. The Totnes & District Community Plan can be viewed on the Town Council website www.totnestowncouncil.gov.uk

Where are we Now?

Traditional governance, essentially a mix of bureaucratic structures and political ideology, which evolves in response to the population of the day, is a very mobile force. The present dominance of essentially a two political party system in the UK means that every decade we swing from the right to the left of politics, each often undoing and changing their predecessors' changes in education, health, social services, privatisation, nationalisation policies etc. As these policies trickle down through to local administration, extra layers of bureaucracy are created to support the implementation of the changes. This results in a very top-heavy administration, employing many people working on our behalf, drafting and redrafting policies and plans and working on implementation.

The plans and procedures used in our present bureaucracy have created a highly sophisticated system and the language used matches this. There is a need for plain English and availability of support to understand the system for all parties involved in decision-making. This applies to those within the system as well as communities and citizens seeking to be involved in the democratic process. This is clear from who does and more importantly who doesn't get involved in public consultation exercises.

Totnes & District Community Plan 2005.
Source: Totnes Town Council

3.56

These issues frequently lead to a lot of frustration and a sense of 'us and them' from both local authority and citizen perspectives.

We have become a very risk conscious society, with health and safety rules established to protect us from a range of potential dangers; from accidents in the workplace, waste movements to our own DIY. Many of these rules are difficult to follow and expensive to implement, especially for small businesses. Many citizens feel suffocated and feel their commonsense and personal responsibility is being fundamentally challenged.

While sustainable development has been in common parlance for over 30 years and understood as a balanced approach which embraces social, environmental and economic needs; economic development is perceived as the dominant sector and need for profit the driving force supported by public authorities.

As traced in Jared Diamond's extensive study of societal rise and fall in his book Collapse[3], we do make choices as individuals and society; the way in which we govern ourselves, cooperate with each other and maintain our environment is paramount to survival of society. Diamond traces the rise and fall of ancient and more recent societies and illustrates the trends towards failure and the role of governance and leadership; he wants us to learn from history. Using Diamond's assessments, nationally and globally we are well within a dangerous zone; we need to take strong remedial action.

An agenda for change

A process for implementing sustainable development called Local Agenda 21 (LA21) was unilaterally agreed in 1992 by nations in Rio de Janerio at the United Nations World Summit on Environment and Development. Renamed Local Action 21 at Johannesburg a decade later, this (Agenda / Action for the 21st Century) agreement recognised that the highest quality environment care under the umbrella of sustainable development takes place at the most local level, and that people and communities need and are entitled to support from their governments to make this happen. Local Authorities were identified as the structure for supports and resources to be channelled to local people. To be effective, Local Agenda/Action 21 must be enshrined in all sustainable development based plans and procedures, from Town and parish plans to national legislation. To some extent this has happened through social partnerships etc. However the sheer volume of plans and procedures can make it prohibitive for ordinary citizens and community groups to engage in these processes, unless pro-active support is initiated by the local authority. ICLEI[4] a highly effective network of local authorities around the world has made some very good progress with LA21, particularly in other countries such as Canada and Germany.

Business as Usual or Willing to Change?

Re-doing, re-inventing and tightening bureaucratic structures, processes, procedures, legislation and services is on-going. The goal-posts frequently change. Those in governance can loose a lot of ground and waste a lot of resources just moving the deckchairs around; the population it is intended to serve can experience problems understanding and being able to use the system. There are SO MANY plans and layers of plans.

While this EDAP has looked at many different actions to contribute towards local resilience, much of this can only take place effectively and in the timescale needed, if supported through good governance and strong leadership. If those in power are willing to change, local governance could support the following priorities as outlined in Lester Brown's Plan B 3.0 Mobilizing to Save Civilisation[5]:

"Implementing Plan B means undertaking several actions simultaneously, including eradicating poverty, stabilizing population, and restoring the earth's natural systems. It also involves cutting carbon dioxide emissions 80% by 2020, largely through a mobiliza-tion to raise energy efficiency and harness renewable sources of energy. Brown's book talks about a great mobilization, on the scale and speed of preparations of wartime Britain. While issues such as global population may be outside the remit of local governance (indeed this is a challenge at national level), there are many aspects of these 3 fundamental issues that local authorities can address; essentially if local government departments are willing to open up to the challenges outlined in the Joined up Thinking section (see box below)

To mobilize and implement these changes on a scale that will affect adequate progress, local initiatives will need to be supported all the way up from local authorities right up to UN level. Many of the laws and plans already exist that could make these changes happen. We simply and urgently need the willpower and strong, visionary leadership to take this forward.

Further Reading

Plain English Campaign www.plainenglish.co.uk

Local Agenda 21- UN Dept. of Economic & Social Affairs; Division for Sustainable Development www.un.org/esa/dsd/agenda21/

Challenges & Possible Solutions

Challenges	Possible Solutions
Peak Oil; power down from 9 barrels pp/y in 2009	Local food production; public transport; fewer journeys etc
Climate Change: getting carbon below 350ppm	Local energy efficiency & conservation measures
Carbon sequestration:removing some carbon	Planting schemes to absorb carbon
Stabilising Population growth to around 7 billion	Public education and youth opportunities
Renewable energy supplies at 50% of current use	Local provision of renewable energy
Reducing consumption and waste to zero	Local taxation on imported goods, zero waste policies
Repairing biodiversity	Replanting hedgerows, protection of green space & wildlife
Maintaining adequate clean water supplies	Water rationing, re-open old aquifers, protection of waterways
Society making an inner transition and taking responsibility	Provide a good example, promote & support communities and good citizenship

COMMUNITY MATTERS

"Communities in the UK are facing a number of challenges: from the impact of globalisation, economic recession and climate change to concerns about street crime, anti-social behaviour and the threat of terrorism. At the same time society is more diverse and more polarised in terms of wealth (and power) than it has been for many years."[6]

The Challenge

Since the 1950's and the rapid rise of a consumer driven culture, people are spending less and less time with family, friends and neighbours, but more time working, commuting and shopping. Writing about the generation brought up in the 1980's, psychologist Oliver James has said: ' They were soaked in the values of the winner-loser culture and brought up to believe that the pursuit of status and wealth was the root to fulfilment. This has turned out to be manifestly not true[7].

The modern UK lifestyle is generally one that aspires to living comfortably within one's means. Having family, friends, access to good education, transport and health services, a pleasant social life and having an income that provides for today and puts some savings away for holidays and retirement. For many people long-term security of this future has been seriously undermined by the recent economic collapse. For others there is a question about whether this was the life they were actually leading, or the life they would like to be leading, the life they were working towards, but had little time to nurture. For others this is the lifestyle they exist on the periphery of, being excluded through a lack of local acceptance of diversity, poverty, illiteracy or social difficulties. Good citizenship is apparently going out of fashion, replaced by self-focused consumerism.

Totnes and District is not a homogenous community. As noted elsewhere in this EDAP it contains, for historical reasons, a larger than usual proportion of residents who are artists, psychotherapists, spiritual seekers and "ex-hippies". Partly due to early GM crop trials it has also attracted a number of committed environmental activists. The area has a large number of affluent incomers attracted by the beauty and tranquillity of the area, and the low crime rate. This may account for the results of a survey a few years ago, which found that, of all the Magistrates Courts in the area, Totnes magistrates handed out the harshest sentences. At the same time, rising house prices and falling manual employment opportunities contribute to a section of the local population living in deprivation, to the extent that the Bridgetown area of Totnes was deemed in need of a "Mini Surestart" project (a calculation based on various indices of deprivation) when other surrounding market towns were not.

The number of community groups and interest based organisations and social clubs in Totnes and District runs into the hundreds. Many are very active and engage their members in activities that benefit the local area and support community cohesion. However very few are actively preparing their members and local society for the coming challenges of peak oil and climate change. Many of those who do understand that there may be a problem with these issues, are unsure how to tackle it and the relevance of strengthening community to be a meaningful response.

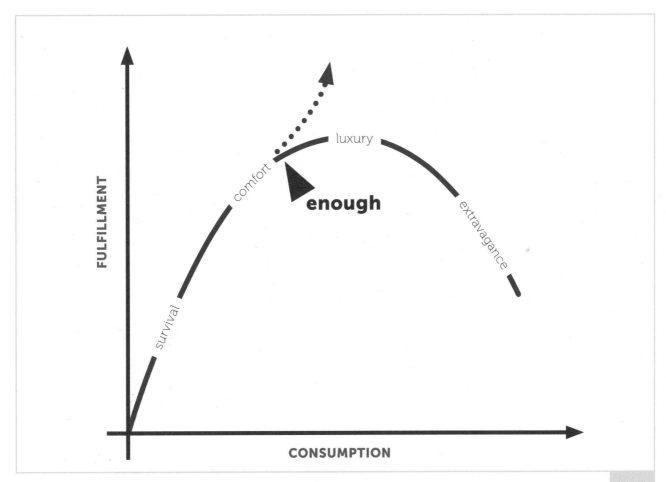

FULFILLMENT

survival

comfort

luxury

enough

extravagance

CONSUMPTION

Happiness and Fullfillment Curve. Copyright: Tellus Institute. The Great Transition. Based on Dominguez and Robin (1992)

3.57

Business as Usual or Willing to Change? – Emerging Trends - Where we are Now

A Business as Usual or Plan A's approach to community is to assume that it functions as well now as it did 60 years ago just after WWII and 'that wartime pulling together' will re-emerge when an urgent need arises. Currently people have very little time to spare outside of their working hours such that widespread community cohesion along with active citizenship has declined and become fragmented in recent years.

If we are willing to change or make a Plan B on the other hand, a resilient localised community would need to be based on the following principles:

◎ Closer working relationships and interdependency between family, neighbours, friends.

◎ People having more time outside of regular working and commuting.

◎ Better publicly funded facilities where people share transport, amenities, recreation.

◎ Support and investment in community led initiatives from policy makers and service providers.

◎ Inclusive educational facilities for all ages.

◎ A full flexible range of public health and social support services.

◎ Publicly funded support for diversity, fairness, equality and eradication of poverty.

◎ Supports for older people to remain active and contribute to society.

◎ A localised economy that meets people's needs.

What follows is one version of how our community might become more localised and sustainable over the next 21 years.

From Wondermentalist Transition Cabaret workshop January 2009

Luxury Wedding Travel Service

Lonely? Desperate? Celibate?

Looking for an indulgent celebration with a difference?

Wait no longer!!

Be transported to your perfect future by simply coming along to our Totnes office for a painless and relaxing aromatherapy aura-recognition scan (100% organic)

After just 2 hours, we guarantee to have matched you with your perfect trans-global partner.

For only 100 Totnes pounds, and a llama, we will then transport you to your perfect mate on one of our custom-design love vehicles.

Choose from:

- The air balloon of hot desire [a pesticide free willow weaved basket, hand crafted with love by the Dartington WI]
- The chauffeur driven pedalo of passion
- Or the best-selling charismatic carrot-driven pumpkin carriage.

Now! You don't even have to leave your home with our vibrant Venus virtual encounter – our new inclusive package for agoraphobics or paranoid reclusives and those with bad hair.

Book your appointment now – and specify our popular lifetime model or, at a giveaway price upgrade your subscription to our polyamory package which entitles you to regular swaps.

Live happily ever after or your money back!

In the unlikely circumstance of misalignment we offer a free aura rescan or your Totnes pounds refunded [NB llamas will be kept as a deposit]

Read the small print.

3.58   A Pumpkin Built for Two. © Jenny Band

Vision 2030

By 2030, Totnes and district has become a shining light for a sustainable, localised and resilient community. People feel close to each other, they know their neighbours and do many things together. Most people are involved in some activity outside of their household that benefits other people and through this young people, older people, those with special needs and newcomers are involved and included and their needs supported through the local community. People are happy living and working together. There is a strong sense of common purpose.

The difficulties of peak oil and climate change have bonded local society through a common purpose which has evolved into strong networks of people linked together in a mutually beneficial system of producers, service providers and consumers contributing towards and meeting local needs. Local people have a strong voice in how their community is developed. Participatory democracy is strong and well developed. Educational systems support all ages and confer a strong sense of citizenship and understanding about sustaining community and the wider global issues affecting society. Crime has remained almost non-existent. Local people are ac-

tively involved with policy makers and service providers in development planning and decision making processes. There are strong mechanisms and contingency plans in place for difficulties that may arise from time to time, and local problem solving has opened up empowerment for local society who enjoy a good debate.

The community enjoy good access to public services and facilities. Adequate clean water, health care, education, transport, housing, and energy needs are usually met. There are many open public spaces where local people meet and do things together, the community hall is a special place, which is widely used and valued. The local environment is respected, valued and cared for in a shared stewardship by all sectors, mitigation of the damage done by previous carelessness is being repaired. People understand the need to live within the carrying capacity of the earth and that resources must be shared and sustained for future generations, in this they are content with less and share what they can. There is no waste or glut, when resources are low, people understand that all must have a lower share and that everyone else is experiencing the same.

People are happy, well-adjusted and live meaningful lives within the carrying capacity of the local area.

Resilience Indicators

Some indicators of a more resilient community would be:

◎ Decrease in the recorded rate of acquisitive crime (burglary, shoplifting).

◎ Decrease in alcohol-fuelled aggression and violence.

◎ Decrease in the number of children placed in the care of the Local Authority.

◎ Decrease in reported incidents of domestic abuse.

These can be revisited regularly to see if the community is making progress in the right direction.

Strategic Themes

◎ Vibrant Local Communities

◎ Sharing Tasks and food

◎ Friendships & Family

◎ Transition Lifestyle

The detailed timeline developing the themes on this topic is available in the web version of this publication at www.totnesedap.org.uk

YOUTH ISSUES IN BRIEF

© Richard Hodgson

"If you can trust yourself when all men doubt you, but make allowance for their doubting too."[8]
Rudyard Kipling, poet & writer

"How would the realization that we are responsible for a coming 7-metre rise in sea level and hundreds of millions of refugees from rising seas affect us? How will we respond to our children when they ask, 'how could you do this to us?' How could you leave us facing such chaos?"[9]

Business as Usual or Willing to Change? – Emerging Trends - Where we are Now

A Business as Usual or Plan A approach to youth is to assume that good education, training and law enforcement are the key to young people becoming responsible citizens. However with the enormous pressures on society and families which is likely to increase with the difficulties of peak oil and climate change, young people need many additional direct and indirect supports for personal development, creativity and self confidence building as well as supports for their families, schools and additional youth facilities.

3.59 Changes to Totnes and environs by 2030 .Photos: Jacqi Hodgson. Post-its: Art & Foundation Students at KEVICS Totnes.

We can assume that if current trends continue, by 2030 young people will display more despair and anger with a society that they feel misled them and has let them down, and reflect the fear and despondency of their parents and grandparents as unrest in society evolves and life becomes more unpredictable and difficult.

If we are willing to change or develop a Plan B on the other hand, this would need to be based on the following principles underpinned by intergenerational justice:

◎ Children should grow up in healthy and sustainable environments, free from noise, pollution and danger from roads, and within easy reach of green and natural spaces for play and learning.

◎ An education system which prepares children and young people for a bright sustainable future, not a failing consumption economy. That means understanding the roots of climate change, poverty, insecurity and obesity, and looking at our values.

◎ The services that children and young people encounter as they grow up – their schools, doctors surgeries, youth centres, children's homes, playgrounds, hospitals and transport services – should be examples of sustainable operation so it becomes the norm.

◎ Children don't stop learning when they become adults. Whether it's in the workplace or in communities, now or in the future, being skilled at sustainable development is essential for our national success.

◎ Children and young people feel ready to stand up for what they know is right and prepared to take responsibility for their own future.

What follows is one version of how Youth might become more empowered, prepared and involved in the transition to a more resilient and localised society over the next 21 years.

World Without Oil by students at Grove School.   3.60

Vision 2030

By 2030, the young people of Totnes and District are an integral part of the happy and healthy local society within which they take a lot of responsibility. Children and young people are very visible in the streets which are very safe for playing, walking, cycling, working and sharing together. Young people emerge from the educational system well prepared for adult life, they are less concerned with logos and watching TV reality shows and more concerned with doing interesting activities than the previous generation. They are well versed in sustainability based solutions, skilled and resourceful, well informed and with well balanced self-esteem and a sense of pur-

pose and place in society. Low self-esteem, binge-drinking and bullying are past problems, addressed through children being engaged in personal development, social and community building activities in school, improved supports for families through local community activities and parents needing to work less hours away from home. Young people leaving school have many opportunities open to them to continue learning or take up interesting and worthwhile employment opportunities. Young couples needing a home are supported locally. Young people understand and recognise the problems created by peak oil and climate change faced by society and are keen to bring their enthusiasm, imagination and energy to address these problems in their local area.

Resilience Indicators

From the research that led to this Plan, we have identified a number of key indicators by which we can be sure that we we are moving forward. These include:

◎ Rates of smoking, substance abuse and alcohol consumption by mothers during pregnancy

◎ Breastfeeding rates at 6-8 weeks after birth

◎ Size of the poverty gap (the links to shorter life expectancy, accident rates and lack of qualifications are well established)

◎ The number of children and young people killed or seriously injured on the roads

◎ No. of families with children under 18 where a parent is home outside of school hours and during school holidays

These can be revisited regularly to see if the community is making progress in the right direction.

More detailed discussion developing the themes on this topic is available in the web version of this publication at www.totnesedap.org.uk

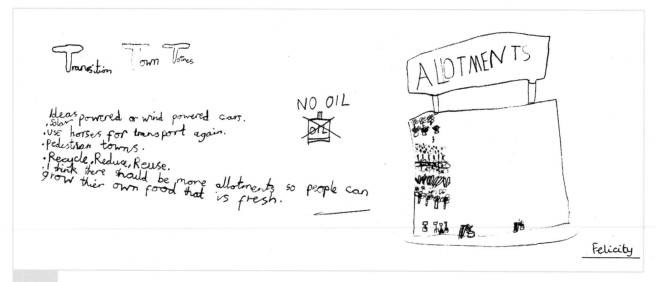

Allotments by students at Grove School.

Youth Issues

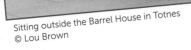

Sitting outside the Barrel House in Totnes
© Lou Brown

Inviting shop window in Totnes
© Lou Brown

Skulling on the River Dart in Totnes
© Lou Brown

NOTES & IDEAS

APPENDICES

*   Edited version - full text appears in web version

**   Included only in web version: www.totnesedap.org.uk

APPENDIX I: INSPIRATION

Some references for inspiration & useful information

A Green New Deal (2008) New Economics Foundation. www.neweconomics.org/

A Pattern Language (1977) Christopher Alexander et al., New York OUP www.patternlanguage.com A structured method of describing good design practices within a field of expertise.

Atmos Prospectus for Totnes Dairy Crest Site download at http://transitionculture. org/2009/07/21/the-atmos-project-transition-in-action/

Bedzed www.bedzed.org.uk South London project uses waste timber from the construction industry and arboreal waste from trimming the city trees; the plant has been sized to supply all the local electricity needs so when demand is low, the surplus is sold to the grid.

Can Britain feed itself? The Land 4 (Winter 2007-08) Fairlie, S.

Climate Safety: in case of emergency (2008), Public Interest Research Centre. www.climatesafety.org

Collapse: How Societies Choose to Fail or Succeed (2005) Jared M. Diamond Deals with societal collapses involving an environmental component, and in some cases also contributions of climate change, hostile neighbours, and trade partners, plus questions of societal responses.

Commonwork's ZEF (Zero fossil Energy Farming) project. Download at www.commonwork.org/Downloads/ZEF_Roadmap.pdf.

Community Resilence Manual. A Resource for Rural Recovery and Renewal (2000), The Centre for Community Enterprise, British Columbia. Free download from www.cedworks.com/communityresilience01.html

Continuous Productive Urban Landscapes (2005) Vijoen, Andre, et al. Architectural Press, Burlington MA

DARE report (2006) Devon Association for Renewable Energy www.devondare.org/

Going Local (1998) Michael Shuman

Homes for Wells scheme running successfully in Wells in North Norfolk. www.homesforwells.co.uk/index.html

Living Through the Energy Crisis (2008) C.J. Campbell and Graham Strouts http://zone5.org/

Localisation, A Global Manifesto (2000) Colin Hines Earthscan. Economics and trading that underpin a local economy

Kinsale 2021 An Energy Descent Action Plan (2005) Kinsale (Ireland) FEC'Students & Rob Hopkins download at http://transitionculture.org/2005/11/24/kinsale-energy-descent-action-plan/ Probably the first attempt by a community to design an EDAP

Making the Invisible Visible: the real value of park assets (2007) Commission for Architecture and the Built Environment download from http://www.cabe.org.uk/publications/making-the-invisible-visible

Managing without Growth, Slower by Design, Not Disaster (2008) Victor, P.A. Edward Elgar Publishing

One Planet Agriculture: the Case for Action Edited by Rob Hopkins and Patrick Holden. Soil Association. www.transitionculture.org/wp-content/uploads/2007/thecaseforaction.pdf

Plan B 3.0 Mobilizing to save Civilization (2008) Lester R. Brown. Free download from The Earth Policy Institute website. http://www.earthpolicy.org/ Concise yet very informative and readable summaries of the key issues facing civilization as a consequence of the stress we put on our environment. Problems and very practical solutions are laid out.

Plan B 4.0 Mobilizing to save Civilization by the Numbers (Oct. 2009) Lester R. Brown Plan B goals for eradicating poverty and stabilizing population. Behind the scenes are a number of datasets and graphs that delve deeper into the trends discussed.

Prosperity without growth? The transition to a sustainable economy (2009) Jackson, T. Sustainable Development Commission. www.sd-commission.org.uk/publications.php

Real England - The battle Against the Bland (2008) Paul Kingsnorth Portobello Books

Resilience Thinking: Sustaining Ecosystems and People in a Changing World (2006) Walker, B. And Salt, D. Island Press

Small is Beautiful, a study of economics as if people mattered (1973), E.F.Schumacher A remarkable book, as relevant today and its themes as pertinent and thought provoking as when it was published over thirty years ago

Sustainable Communities: the potential for eco neighbourhoods (2009) Barton, H. (ed) Earthscan Books

Sustainable Energy - Without the Hot Air (2009), David Mackay. Cambridge University Press. Focused on the UK, brilliant reference for the serious study of energy issues and how to budget for a post-peak and carbon reducing world. Plenty of facts, figures and wry humour. Free download.

The Collapse of Complex Societies (1988), Joseph Tainter. Tainter argues that societies collapse when their investments in social complexity reach a point of diminishing marginal returns.

The Earth Care Manual: A Permaculture Handbook for Britain and Other Temperate Countries (2004) Whitefield, Permanent Publications.

The Energy Challenge (2007) Geoffrey Haggis Troubador Publishing Ltd.

The Party's Over (2003), The Essential Relocalisation of Food Production.(2007) Blackout (2009) Heinberg, R.

Towards Transport Justice: Transport and Social Justice in an Oil-Scarce Future (April 2008), Sustrans, http://tinyurl.com/5kfjfn

Transforming Urban Environments for a Post Peak Oil Future: A Vision Plan for the City of Buenaventura (2009) The City of Buenaventura (2009) Available at www.cityofventura.net/files/public_works/maintenance_services/environmental_services/resources/post-peakoil.pdf

The Transition Handbook: from oil dependency to local resilience (2008) by Rob Hopkins (Green Books). The 12 steps of Transition +.

The Transition Timeline (2009) Chamberlin, S. Green Books/Transition Network UK perspectives and scenarios and timelines for a post-oil future

Transforming the Future: a design perspective April 2009. Case studies and sharing ideas with 2 projects in Totnes, Sustainable Makers and ReFurnish. Partners: Transition Town Totnes (TTT), Dartington College of Arts, & others www.transformingthefuture.wordpress.com

What should tomorrow's world energy production look like? A GreenFacts summary of the IEA's global energy scenarios to 2050

Global energy scenarios & strategies to 2050 are explored by the International Energy Agency (IEA) in their 'Energy Technology Perspectives 2008' report. Published and accessible free of charge at www.greenfacts.org/en/energy-technologies/

Why Your World is About to Get a Whole Lot Smaller: What the Price of Oil Means for the Way We Live Rubin, J. (2009) Virgin Books

Wondermentalist's Cabaret on Tradio (transition radio) Tradio www.traydio.com/UserConsole/ViewArticle.aspx?Title=The_Wondermentalist_%26_Transition_Tales_Cabaret_(full_show)_-_17th_January%2c_2009&ArticleID=1758

Zero Carbon Britain (2008), Centre for Alternative Technology (CAT) commissioned study. Free download www.zerocarbonbritain.com/

Inspirational websites

Agroforestry Research Trust

www.agroforestryco.uk

Has a research forest garden at Dartington

Association for the Study of Peak Oil ASPO International

www.peakoil.net

Produce monthly newsletter

Canadian Centre for Community Renewal

www.cedworks.com

Expertise and resources for Community Economic Development

Change4Life, NHS

www.nhs.uk/Change4life/Pages/Default.aspx

Climate Friendly Bradford on Avon

www.climatefriendlybradfordonavon.co.uk

Energy Bulletin

www.energybulletin.net

Upbeat daily updates and articles for a post-peak world

Growing Communities

www.growingcommunities.org

"Improving the food we eat, the community we live in and the environment"

Low Carbon Communities Network

low.communitycarbon.net

New Economics Foundation

www.neweconomics.org

Economics as if people and the planet mattered

Post Carbon Institute

www.postcarbon.org

Highly informative and covers a wide spectrum of related topics

Richard Heinberg

www.richardheinberg.com

Regarded as one of the world's most effective communicators of the urgent need for transition.

Riverford's assessment of its carbon footprint

www.riverfordenvironment.co.uk/Rivercarbfoot.aspx

Stroud Food Hubs

transitiontowns.org/Stroud/Food

Sustainable Development Commission

www.sd-commission.org.uk

Sustrans

www.sustrans.org.uk

UK's leading sustainable transport charity.

The Oil Drum

www.theoildrum.com

On-line daily discussions about Energy and our Future

The International Council for Local Environmental Initiatives

www.iclei.org

Drafted Local Agenda 21

The Work That Reconnects

www.joannamacy.net

www.ecopsychology.org

www.greatturningtimes.org

YouGen – Renewable Energy made Easy

www.yougen.co.uk.

Online community

Transition Websites

Transition in Action, Totnes and District, An Energy Descent Plan

www.totnesedap.org.uk

Extra material, the updates, reviews and blogs to this plan can be found

Transition Culture

transitionculture.org

An evolving exploration into the head, heart and hands of energy descent.

Transition Network

www.transitiontowns.org

(wikipage) General background and outline of Transition movement.

Transition Town Totnes

totnes.transitionnetwork.org

Where transition really started to lift off and the transition network was founded

APPENDIX V: VISIONS

A selection of visions of 2030 collected at workshops and public events

Clearer smoother lives   Less animals in the fields   Happy faces
A self-sufficient community with pollution free very small vehicles
Transport system to link to nearby communities   Sound of chickens
More people on the streets (less people as a whole)   More small scale
farming   People working from home or very locally   Perhaps less
interested in work but more in community   It's hot   Windmills,
hydroelectric power and cycle lanes   An improved village centre
Windmills   Closer Community   Natural history being introduced
at primary level   Harmony   No traffic noise – all cars are electric
Local power and heat generation   Sound of wood being chopped
Fields of vegetables   Photovoltaic panels everywhere   Working
from home   People working together   No waste collection service!
Locally based economy   Warm family togetherness   Technology
Having greater control of energy use   Smelling gloriously of
woodsmoke   Regained sense of community   Fly with electronic
planes   Cooking over a wood burning stove   Using herbs and
preserving foods   There will be a local energy supply company – both
heat and power   A supportive (rather than debt based) money supply
encourages economic co-operation in place of frantic competition
Not much oil   Food waste – very different attitudes & practices
Climate Change stopped   Prisoners made to cycle to produce
electricity   TV's turned off when not watched   Much co-housing in
existence   Living in a community   Well insulated buildings   Feeling
of usefulness even though I'm 90   The next level of human culture

APPENDIX W: WONDERMENTALISTS

A poem created at the Wondermentalist's Cabaret by the audience December 2008

2030 what are you like?

Like 1930 but 100 years older

Free vegetable gardens on every roadside ditch

More communal meals – let's eat the rich

Upside down and back to front

You're beautifully seedy, much less greedy – not needy

2030, the outlook is bleak

But will it mean I'll be more of a freak?

Will there still be seven days in the week?

Or are we on a winning streak?

Totnes Castle, covered in grass,

Your-round salads, rather than grass

Pavilions potatoes, Civic Hall spuds

Bridgetown bananas, not Follaton Floods

2030 – Happy and dirty, gardening madly, hair-drying badly,

Shivering or baking, digging and co-operating,

Alive and connected or ill and dejected.

Water mills, windmills, tank traps, mines,

Get off this land, it's all mine

More toil, less toiletries

More bluebells, less consols

More 'we', less 'wii' !!

No salad dressing? Oil live without.

For oil and gas we really won't care

Our energy will come from what we share

72 and 11/12, canning, jamming, baking, making wonder woman

Voluptuous vegetables

Windmills, hydroelectric power and cycle lanes

The year is 2030, I'm 66, old and dirty, and the planet isn't far behind,

the filthiness raging through my senile mind

2030, I'll be 74 then! We'll walk everywhere.

And maybe, we'll smile more.

Age 60, you and me, 2030, flirty, fungus-munching, down'n'dirty

Smelling gloriously of woodsmoke

You warmed to Totnes and didn't peak too early

2030 – Jerri's bird has had a son

Who's left the trifle for an organic bun...

Like 2029, but just a little bit older

Older, wiser, with the wry smile of a Bodhisattva

But that's another chapter

Re-open the old railway lines

2030, when all done and said, I might be peaceful, possibly dead

Six foot under, in a biodegradable box,

Pushing up daisies, generating organic compost!

The new solar-powered Tate Totnes opens to rave reviews

With Damien Hirst's piece "Scrotum Pole" polarizing views

Hopefully we'll have invented teleportation...

REFERENCES

INTRODUCTION

1. Plan B 3.0 Mobilizing to save Civilization. (2008) Lester R. Brown. p.287

PART ONE

1. Oil Drum, The (2009) World Oil Production Forecast - Update May 2009. May 19th 2009. Retrieved from www.theoildrum.com/node/5395

2. Rubin, J. (2009) Why Your World is About to Get a Whole Lot Smaller: What the Price of Oil Means for the Way We Live. Virgin Books.

3. Birol, F. (2008) Outside View: We can't cling to crude: we should leave oil before it leaves us. The Independent on Sunday. 2nd March 2008. Retrieved from www.independent.co.uk/news/business/comment/outside-view-we-cant-cling-to-crude-we-should-leave-oil-before-it-leaves-us-790178.html

4. Jenkins, G, Perry, M & Prior, J. (2008) The Climate of the United Kingdom and Recent Trends. Met Office, Exeter, 2008.

5. Public Interest Research Centre. (2008) Climate Safety: in case of emergency: www.climatesafety.org

6. Pilkington, E. (2008) Climate target is not radical enough – study: Nasa scientist warns the world must urgently make huge CO_2 reductions. The Guardian. 7th April 2008. http://www.guardian.co.uk/environment/2008/apr/07/climatechange.carbonemissions

7. CNBC. The World's Biggest Debtor Nations. www.cnbc.com/id/30308959/

8. EMAS The EU Eco-Management and Audit Scheme. http://ec.europa.eu/environment/emas/index_en.htm

9. You can read a detailed analysis of this from a Transition perspective at http://tinyurl.com/llmpn9

PART TWO

1. Walter King (2008) The Long Slow Death of a Working Town. Totnes Review No. 3.

2. Edited version, see EDAP website www.totnesedap.org.uk for longer text.

3. You can see a film about this at www.tinyurl.com/l8usrg

4. More detail about some of these can be found in 'The Transition Handbook: from oil dependency to local resilience' by Rob Hopkins (Green Books).

PART THREE

JOINED UP THINKING

1. Small is Beautiful, a Study of Economics as if People Mattered. (1973), E.F.Schumacher

2. Plan B 3.0 Mobilizing to Save Civilisation (2008), Lester R. Brown. p285

3. Sustainable Development Commission website, June 2009: http://www.sd-commission.org.uk/

4. Plan B 3.0 Mobilizing to Save Civilisation (2008), Lester R. Brown p136

5. Data source: Base – Registrar General – Projections – Devon County Council: www.devon.gov.uk

6. Data source; Devon PCT. Devon County Council website: www.devon.gov.uk

7. Collapse: How Societies Choose to Fail or Succeed. (2005) Jared M. Diamond

8. Community Resilence Manual. A Resource for Rural Recovery and Renewal (2000), The Centre for Community Enterprise, CCE Publications, Port Alberi, B.C. V9Y 7H2

9. Ipsos MORI The Big Energy Shift Report from Citizen's Forums 2009

10. guardian.co.uk, Friday 29 May 2009, John Vidal, Environment Editor

WORKING WITH NATURE

1. www.transitionnetwork.org

2. Seeley, T. (2008) U.S. Regulator `Closely Monitoring' Nymex Oil Prices (Update1). Bloomberg.com. Oil touched a record $147.27 a barrel on July 11 2008.

3. An argument also made in more depth in Public Interest Research Centre. (2008) Climate Safety: in case of emergency. www.climatesafety.org

4. www.ukclimateprojections.defra.gov.uk/content/view/1334/543/index.html

5. The concept of 'food deserts' is explored in, for example, Cummins, J. & Macintyre,S. (2002) "Food deserts": evidence and assumption in health policy making. BMJ 2002;325:436-438 (24 August).

6. See, for example, Drescher et al. 2000. Urban Food Security: Urban agriculture, a response to crisis? UA Magazine (2000) and Vijoen, Andre, et al. (2005), Continuous Productive Urban Landscapes. Architectural Press, Burlington MA

7. This concept is set out at more length in Hopkins, R. (2008) The Transition Handbook: from oil dependency to local resilience. Green Books.

8. For more information on the methodology for calculating food footprints, please go to:www.geofutures.com/2009/07/food-fooprints-re-localising-uk-food-supply/

9. This paper defines Totnes as being the area defined in the Census as MSOA E02004191 or 'South Hams 003'

10. Heinberg, R. (2007) The Essential Relocalisation of Food Production. In "One Planet Agriculture: the Case for Action". Edited by Rob Hopkins and Patrick Holden. Soil Association. Retrieved from www.transitionculture.org/wp-content/uploads/2007/thecaseforaction.pdf

11. Hernandez-Reguant, A. (2009) Cuba in the Special Period: Culture and Ideology in the 1990s. Palgrave Macmillan

12. Also explored in a talk by Heinberg entitled 'The Implication for Peak Oil on Agriculture', available at www.podcastdirectory.com/podshows/1119264. For a more detailed account, see Wright, J. (2008) Earthscan Books.

13. The Defra Agricultural Land Classification divides farm land into five grades according to climate, site and soil characteristics. These can be summarised as:
Grade 1: excellent quality agricultural land, suitable for a wide range of crops including top fruit, soft fruit, salad crops and winter vegetables
Grade 2: very good quality agricultural land, suitable for all but the most demanding crops, with yields possibly lower and more variable than Grade 1
Subgrade 3a: good quality agricultural land, capable of producing moderate/high yields of a narrower range of arable crops including cereals, grass, rape, potatoes etc
Subgrade 3b: moderate quality, capable of growing moderate yields of cereals or high yields of grazing grass
Grade 4: poor quality agricultural land, with severely restricted crop range or yield, mainly suited to grass or occasional forage crops; also includes droughty arable land

Grade 5: very poor quality agricultural land, only usable for permanent pasture or rough grazing. Full definitions and grading methodology can be found at www.defra.gov.uk/farm/environment/land-use

14. Fallow land is here referred to as cropland that is not seeded for a season; it may or may not be ploughed. The land may be cultivated or chemically treated for control of weeds and other pests or may be left unaltered. (http://www.infoplease.com/ce6/sci/A0818206.html)

15. Clearly this would need a change in the current legislation relating to feeding food wastes to livestock.

16. www.growingcommunities.org

17. Major organic grower close to Totnes. www.riverford.co.uk.

18. Personal interview, January 2009.

19. 40% of a hectare (www.britannica.com/EBchecked/topic/4100/acre)

20. This will be published as part of the Totnes Energy Descent Plan.

21. Vijoen, Andre, et al. (2005) Continuous Productive Urban Landscapes. Architectural Press, Burlington MA

22. Little is written about the foggage system. Developed (and still flourishing) at Fordhall Farm in Shropshire by the late Arthur Hollins, it is a system of permanent grass-based livestock farming, using a broad diversity of grass species. See Whitefield, P. (2004) The Earth Care Manual: A Permaculture Handbook for Britain and Other Temperate Countries. Permanent Publications.

23. From personal communication with John Watson, founder of Riverford Farm, 24th June 2009.

24. Ibid.

25. For one example of this from Sweden, see Schonning, C. (2001) Urine Diversion: hygienic risks and microbial guidelines. www.who.int/water_sanitation_health/wastewater/urineguidelines.pdf.

26. A point made most cogently in Hirsch, R.L.Bezdek, R, Wendling, R. (2005) Peaking of World Oil Production: impacts, mitigatation and risk management. US Department of Energy. Retrieved from www.netl.doe.gov/publications/others/pdf/Oil_Peaking_NETL.pdf

27. For one summary of some of the potential models, see Hopkins, R. (2000) The Food Producing Neighbourhood. In Barton, H. (ed) (2000) Sustainable Communities: the potential for eco neighbourhoods. Earthscan Books (2000)

28. www.agroforestry.co.uk

29. Based on Richard Heinberg's assessment of 7.3 calories of energy required to produce I calorie of food in USA. (The UK imports more of its food than the USA) Food & Farming in Transition. Toward a Post Carbon Food System. http://www.postcarbon.org/food

30. www.southwestid.org.uk/download/4149492c18325edd0118329c40690001/family%20spending.pdf

31. Matthew Beard Families 'spending less on fresh food than on takeaways. The Independent, Friday, 19 January 2007. www.independent.co.uk/news/uk/this-britain/families-spending-less-on-fresh-food-than-on-takeaways-432765.html

32. Devon County Council (2006) Totnes: Devon Town Baseline Profile. http://www.devon.gov.uk/totnesbaselineprofile.pdf

33. Jenny Gallatly. Regional Co-ordinator in the South West. Mapping Local Food Webs. Campaign to Protect Rural England. Contact jennyg@cpre.org.uk / 07833 250136

34. This list is taken from the excellent The City of Buenaventura (2009) Transforming Urban Environments for a Post Peak Oil Future: A Vision Plan for the City of Buenaventura. Available at www.cityofventura.net/files/public_works/maintenance_services/environmental_services/resources/post-peakoil.pdf

35. A natural rainwater catchment which can supply water to a distinct geographical area.

36. www.thesun.co.uk/sol/homepage/news/special_events/green_week/article2388213.ece

37. http://transitiontowns.org/Stroud/Food

38. Medicine at the Crossroads of Energy and Global Warming, Synthesis/Regeneration, Winter 2008, http://tinyurl.com/5mbjy7

39. Foresight Tackling Obesities: Future Choices – Project Report. 2nd Edition. Dr B. Butland et al. Government Office for Science

40. http://www.bumblebeeconservation.org.uk/bumblebees_id.htm

41. http://www.rspb.org.uk/wildlife/birdguide/name/s/skylark/index.asp

42. Strategic Environmental Assessment of Draft Water Resources Plan 2008. Environmental Report. Blackler et al. South West Water Ltd.

CREATIVE ENERGY SYSTEMS

1. Sustainable Energy-Without the Hot Air (2009), David Mackay

2. ERoEI - Energy Return on Energy Invested

3. DARE report. (2006) Devon Association for Renewable Energy www.devondare.org/

4. Sustainable Energy – without the hot air (2009) p.166 David Mackay

5. Dr Colin Campbell, Then Chairman of the Association for the Study of Peak Oil (ASPO). 2004.

6. Alastair Gill of RWE Innogy given at a presentation to the 2008 Renewable Futures conference in Bristol; primary energy from renewables was only 1.5%

7. BERR website: www.berr.gov.uk/energy/sources/renewables/index

8. BERR-DUKES (2008), www.berr.gov.uk/energy/sources/renewables/index

9. Devon Affordable Warmth Strategy – working together for warmer homes 2004. Devon Local Authorities & Partners

10. See Riverford's assessment of its carbon footprint http://www.riverfordenvironment.co.uk/Rivercarbfoot.aspx

11. Sustainable Energy – without the hot air (2009) p.322 David Mackay

12. Zero Carbon Britain, (2008), p9 Centre for Alternative Technology (CAT) commissioned study

13. DARE Report 2006

14. Zero Carbon Britain, (2008), p71 Centre for Alternative Technology (CAT) commissioned study

15. These figures are forecasts taken from Chamberlin, S. (2009) The Transition Timeline. Green Books/Transition Network.

16. www.becosolar.com

17. For example, have a look at those produced by www.quietrevolution.co.uk

18. This already happens in Lille in France, where over 100 buses are powered using bio-methane made from waste food and sewage from the town.

19. www.zerocarbonbritain.org.uk

20. The Dare Report. South Devon Renewable Energy Scoping Study, DARE (2006) p4

21. BERR website: www.berr.gov.uk/energy/sources/renewables/index & Boyle, G (2004) Renewable Energy, Power for a sustainable future, Oxford University Press. Boyle G. et al, (2003) Energy Systems and Sustainability, Oxford Press.

22. Dept. of Trade and Industry on line data. www.berr.gov.uk

23. Transition Town Totnes / Jacqi Hodgson calculations loosely based on current SHDC Development Plans and the South Hams District Council Local Development Framework to 2016

24. DARE report / Domestic Energy Fact File 2003

25. See Appendix C Calculation which includes amounts of embodied energy in buildings

26. Sustainable Energy - Without the Hot Air (2009), David Mackay

27. Results in a document entitled "Small-scale hydro-electric generation potential in the UK" Published by the Energy Technical Support Unit (ETSU) as report ETSU SSH 4063, parts 1,2,&3 (no longer in print)

28. DARE report p.18

29. Sustainable Energy – without hot air, David Mackay 2008. P321

30. Sustainable Energy – without hot air, David Mackay 2008. P317

31. Sustainable Energy – without hot air, David Mackay 2008. P310

32. Sustainable Energy – without hot air, David Mackay 2008. P317

33. Dr Joddy Chapman, Sustainable South Brent 2009 www.sustainablesouthbrent.org.uk/

34. Sustainable Energy Without the Hot Air, (2009) p33 David Mackay also British Wind Energy Association www.bwea.com/

35. Technical information from Sustainable Energy Without the Hot Air (2009) p285-6 David Mackay

36. Useful reference for detailed breakdown for wheat based bio-ethanol www.cropgen.soton.ac.uk/Agro-%20energetic.htm

37. See DARE report for details p 39

38. Assessment of Methane Management and Recovery Options for Livestock Manures & Slurries. Report for: Sustainable Agriculture Strategy Division, DEFRA. 2005

39. The Energy Challenge (2007) p81, Geoffrey Haggis 2007

40. http://en.wikipedia.org/wiki/Anaerobic_digestion

41. Making Sewage Treatment Plants Energy Self-sufficient. Aquatec-Maxcon Pty Ltd. University of Queensland. www.epa.qld.gov.au/sustainable_industries

42. South West Water officer 11.05.09

43. www.bedzed.org.uk/main.html

44. Sustainable Energy - without the hot air (2008) p19, David Mackay

45. Sustainable Energy - without the hot air (2008) p19, David Mackay

46. See EDAP Section:Energy Security for more information about ZCB 2008 report

47. See Appendix C for calculations

48. See Energy Security Section for details of this report and reference etc

49. See appendix C – Calculations for calculations to explain this information

50. Sustainable Energy without the Hot air. (2009) p21, David Mackay

51. DARE report 2006 pg. 50

52. This may change, ie more wooden or locally sourced building materials could be utilised and reduce the embodied energy of the new buildings

53. DARE Report / Domestic Energy Fact File 2003

54. Householders can phone 0900512012, www.devon-energy-advice.co.uk

55. www.sustrans.org.uk/what-we-do/travelsmart/travel-behaviour-research-and-evaluation

56. www.dft.gov.uk/about/strategy/whitepapers/whitepapercm7176/multideliversustainrailway?page=26

57. Towards Transport Justice: Transport and Social Justice in an Oil-Scarce Future, Sustrans, Ian Taylor and Lynn Sloman, April 2008 http://tinyurl.com/5kfjfn,p4

58. See previous discussion in Part 1 – Introducing Our Survey

59. www.ruralcommunities.gov.uk/events/itstimefornewsolutionsforruraltransport

60. Zero Carbon Britain (2008) Centre for Alternative Technology Commissioned study

61. Sustainable Energy - without the hot air. (2008) Prof. David Mackay

62. Zero Carbon Britain Report (2008) p62, Centre for Alternative Technology

63. www.commonwork.org/Downloads/ZEF_Roadmap.pdf.

64. Mendips Partnership Survey 2009

65. Public Service Vehicles (public buses etc.)

66. Anaerobic Digestion (of organic matter to produce methane gas)

67. Coarse grain for motorised vehicles, fine grain for cyclists

68. Thanks to James Bellchambers, Totnes for his potted history of the town and ancient burgh.

69. Based on DCC 2008 estimates of 9,481 households in the 16 parishes of Totnes and District

70. Information about whether these buildings are listed is not included or within the current scope of this EDAP.

71. Totnes & Dartington Development Plan Document: Community Focus Report Document. May 2008 Coordinated by Totnes Town Council, Totnes and District Community Strategy Group and Transition Town Totnes, Building & Housing, DPD Working Group. May 2008

72. SHDC Press Release 25th June 2008 'Statement to the Herald Express regarding the Totnes and Darlington Development Plan'

73. www.independent.co.uk/news/three-countries-ban-chemicals-at-centre-of-baby-milk-alert-1349639.html

74. www.nytimes.com/2007/10/26/business/worldbusiness/26cement.html

75. And other suitable sustainable heat and energy sources as they become available.

76. You can download this prospectus at http://transitionculture.org/2009/07/21/the-atmos-project-transition-in-action/

77. www.stewardwood.org/intro.ghtml

78. Homes & Communities Agency information http://www.homesandcommunities.co.uk/bidding_for_new_build.htm

79. This is a back-of-an-envelope calculation created as follows: By 2026, the Spatial Strategy suggests that Totnes and District might have around 1,200 new houses. The cost of materials for a house built today is around 30% of the total cost. If the cost of building a new house is, on average, around £200,000, one could put a speculative figure of £60,000 on the amount spent on materials; and 1,200 multiplied by £60,000 produces a total of £72million. If we assume that 50% of materials in new buildings are locally sourced, the total spend on them would be £36million, which over the 20-year period covered by this Plan, is £1.8million per year. This doesn't take into account the additional benefits of employing local construction companies that employ local people, or the economic benefits of retrofitting with locally sourced materials.

80. Modelled on the 'Homes for Wells' scheme running successfully in Wells in North Norfolk which does exactly this. www.homesforwells.co.uk/index.html

81. See www.modcell.co.uk/page/modcell-overview for a UK company already making these

82. At present, one can buy clay plasters, but they are mostly made overseas, usually Germany, and imported. See, for example, www.constructionresources.com/products/interiors/claytec_plaster.asp

83. Modelled on Fruiting Bodies in Wales: www.fruiting-bodies.co.uk

84. A template for such guidelines already exists, see Chapter 7's 'Defining Rural Sustainability' document, www.tlio.org.uk/chapter7/defining.html

85. This is already happening in Japan. See www.nytimes.com/2009/04/16/business/global/16farmer.html?_r=3&em=&pagewanted=all

RESOURCING LOCALISATION

1. Going Local. (1998) Michael Shuman

2. BBC2 Newsnight programme (21.05.09) Stephen Timms MP Treasury Minster

3. ASPO, The Oil Drum etc.

4. www.transitionculture.org/2009/02/11/the-perils-of-an-economy-based-on-bricks-and-boutiques-colin-hines-speaks-in-totnes/

5. Localisation, A Global Manifesto (2000) Colin Hines ISBN 978-1-85383-612-1

6. The Turner Review on behalf of the FSA March 2009 (available as download) http://www.fsa.gov.uk/pages/Library/Corporate/turner/index.shtml

7. South Hams Economy 1992-2002, p9 (2004) Owen Nankivel MA (Econ)

8. LETS Local Economic Trading System

9. TRESOC Totnes Renewable Energy Society

10. Eg ISO 14001

11. This already exists. Contact the Totnes Pound group if you wish to apply.

12. Transforming the Future: a design perspective (see Arts & media section p...) www.transformingthefuture.wordpress.com <http://www.transformingthefuture.wordpress.com>
Partners: Transition Town Totnes (TTT), Glasgow School of Art, HDK Gothenburg, Les Atelier Paris, University of Plymouth, Dartington College of Arts, Sustainable Makers and ReFurnish

13. Public Funded Institutions

14. Steven@katirai.com

15. This recently happened in Lewes (www.thelewe-spound.org), Stroud (www.stroudcurrency.org) and Brixton (www.brixtonpound.org) inspired by the Totnes Pound experiment.

16. www.timebanking.org.uk

17. From Well Dressed, p16 (2006) University of Cambridge, Institute for Manufacturing

NURTURING TRANSITION

1. Can be heard at www.traydio.com/UserConsole/ViewArticle.aspx?Title=The_Wondermental-ist_%26_Transition_Tales_Cabaret_(full_show)_-_17th_January%2c_2009&ArticleID=1758

2. To find out more see http://transitionculture.org/in-transition/

3. Transforming the Future: a design perspective. April 2009. Case studies and sharing ideas with 2 projects in Totnes, Sustainable Makers and ReFurnish. Partners: Transition Town Totnes (TTT), Glasgow School of Art, HDK Gothenburg, Les Atelier Paris, University of Plymouth, Dartington College of Arts, Sustainable Makers and ReFurnish
www.transformingthefuture.wordpress.com

4. Art Quarterly magazine for the National Art Collections Fund

5. Focus on fact is stifling schools, warns top head by Caroline Davies. Observer 08.03.09.

6. Devon County Council website pages: http://www.devon.gov.uk/index/cultureheritage/libraries.htm

7. UK Commission for Sustainable Development.

8. Devon CC target in Children and Young Person's Plan 2008 -2011 (p27)

EMPOWERING PEOPLE

1. Bruntland Commission 1988 definition of Sustainable Development. http://en.wikipedia.org/wiki/Brundt-land_Commission

2. Devon Community Strategy is available on Devon County Council's website: http://www.devon.gov.uk/index/councildemocracy/neighbourhoods-villages/community_development/community_strategy_-_have_your_say.htm

3. Collapse: How Societies Choose to Fail or Succeed (2005) Jared M. Diamond

4. The International Council for Local Environmental Initiatives: www.iclei.org

5. Plan B 3.0 – Mobilizing to Save Civilization (2008), Lester R. Brown. Earth Policy Institute Free download version at www.earth-policy.org/index.php?/books/pb/pb_table_of_contents

6. NCVO (National Council for Voluntary Organisations). www.ncvo-vol.org.uk/about/index.asp?id=12788

7. Britain on the Couch: Why We're Unhappier Compared with 1950, Despite Being Richer - A Treatment for the Low-serotonin Society. (1998) Oliver James

8. If. Rudyard Kipling. http://www.kipling.org.uk/po-ems_if.htm

9. Plan B 3.0 – Mobilizing to Save Civilization. (2008)
Lester R. Brown 2008 p266

GLOSSARY OF KEY TERMS

AD

Anaerobic Digestion. A method of treating animal and human sewerage wastes to produce methane gas (a valuable energy source).

Atmos Project

A TTT project-based plan for the regeneration of the former Dairy Crest Site in Totnes. It takes its name from Isambard Brunel's atmospheric air and stream driven power system associated with the 19th c. South Devon Railway.

Assumption

A calculated guess at something that is believed to be true. A possible driver of change into the future.

Biodiversity

The range of natural living organisms or wildlife present in a given ecological system.

Contingency

Planning for an unknown event, in particular a problem, emergency or expense that needs to be dealt with.

Climate Change

A change in the weather over periods of time that range from decades to millions of years. It can be a change in the average weather or a change in the distribution of weather events. In recent usage, climate change usually refers to 'global warming'.

CO2

The Chemical term for Carbon Dioxide, a greenhouse gas.

DCC

Devon County Council.

Energy Descent

Planned reduction in the use and dependence on non-renewable energy supplies (eg coal, nuclear, oil and gas).

Energy Security

Preparations and arrangements to ensure adequate energy supplies will be available to meet essential needs over time.

Food Security

Confirmed availability of food and one's access to it. A household is considered food secure when its occupants do not live in hunger or fear of starvation.

Fossil Fuels

Coal, oil and natural gas and peat, are non-renewable sources of energy, formed from plants and animals that lived up to 300 million years ago.

Global warming

Is caused by high levels of 'Greenhouse gases' in the atmosphere. This is considered to be due to human activities when we burn excessive amounts of fossil fuels to provide energy for transport, heating, to power industry and produce food.

Greenhouse Gases

Gases in an atmosphere that absorb and emit heat radiation. This process is the fundamental cause of the greenhouse effect. The main greenhouse gases in the Earth's Atmosphere are water vapour, carbon dioxide, methane, nitrous oxide and ozone.

LDF

Local Development Framework. A folder of local development documents prepared by local authorities that outline the spatial planning strategy for the local area.

LETS

Local Economic Trading System

Localisation

A process of refocusing policies and practices for the economy and society from a local market economy, rather than a wider (regional, national etc) perspective.. Where local needs are met locally

Inner Transition

Personal awareness and understanding that our outer actions, and therefore the external systems for living that we create, are shaped by our inner worldview and belief system. Likewise our inner world is affected by the outer world.

Oil Age

The period of time when we have access to and use petroleum oil to produce energy.

PC

Parish Council.

Peak Oil

The point of maximum production of petroleum oil from the earth, after which availability and production declines. Estimated to have been July 11th 2008

PSV

Public Service Vehicle (e.g. public bus)

Relocalisation

The process of rebuilding a localized economy and society. See localisation.

Resilience

The ability of a system (individual, economy, town or city), to withstand shock from the outside.

Runaway Climate Change

A theory of how things might go badly wrong for the planet if a relatively small warming of the earth upsets the normal checks and balances that keep the climate in equilibrium. As the atmosphere heats up, more greenhouse gases are released from the soil and seas. Plants and trees that take carbon dioxide out of the atmosphere die back, creating a vicious circle as the climate gets hotter and hotter.

SHDC

South Hams District Council.

TC

Town Council.

Tipping point

This is where a small amount of warming sets off unstoppable changes, for example the melting of the ice caps. Once the temperature rises a certain amount then all the ice caps will melt. The tipping point in many scientists' view is the 2°C rise that the EU has adopted as the maximum limit that mankind can risk.

Totnes and District

Totnes Town and its surrounding 15 parishes which comprise the traditional market economic system as identified in the government's Market and Coastal Town Initiative of 2001. Ashprington, Berry Pomeroy, Cornworthy, Dartington, Dean Prior, Diptford, Halwell & Moreleigh, Harberton & Harbertonford, Littlehempston, Marldon, North Huish, Rattery, South Brent, Staverton, Stoke Gabriel and Totnes.

Toxic Debt

Large debt that is un-repayable (and generally written off).

Transition

The process of change.

Transition Initiative

A community in a process of imagining and creating a future that addresses the twin challenges of diminishing oil and gas supplies and climate change, and creates the kind of community that we would all want to be part of.

Transition Culture

An evolving exploration into the head, heart and hands of energy descent. The emerging transition model in its many manifestations.

Transition Network

A group of Transition Initiatives set up to inspire, encourage, connect, support and train communities as they consider, adopt, adapt and implement the transition model in order to establish a Transition Initiative in their locality.

Transition Town

A Town based Community Initiative.

TTT

Transition Town Totnes.

TRESOC

Totnes Renewable Energy Society. A TTT project associated with the Energy group.

Energy & Power Units in SI (Systeme Internationale)

one-kilowatt-hour
1kWh 3,600,000 Joules

one-kilowatt-hour per day
1kWh/d (1,000/24) Watts

one-kilowatt-hour per year 1kWh/y
(1,000/8,784) Watts

one-megawatt-hour per day
1MWh/d (1,000,000/24) Watts

one-megawatt-hour per year
1MWh/y (1,000,000/8,784) Watts

one-gigawatt-hour per day 1GWh/d
(1,000,000,000/24) Watts

one-gigawatt-hour per year
1GWh/d (1,000,000,000/8,784) Watts

one-terawatt-hour per day
1TWh/d (1,000,000,000,000/24) Watts

one-terawatt-hour per day
1TWh/d (1,000,000,000,000/8,784) Watts

CREDITS:
PHOTOGRAPHS, ILLUSTRATIONS AND GRAPHICS

Thank you to everyone who has lifted the text with pictures:

Lou Brown provided a bank of stunning photographs of Totnes and Dartington.

Jenny Band created a series of amusing yet poignant cartoons.

Richard Hodgson contributed many drawings and pieces of colourful artwork.

Ernest Goh enhanced photographs to create visions of Totnes in 2030.

Students from the Grove School made some wonderful pictures.

Totnes Image Bank allowed us to use some of their collection of old photographs.

The Totnes Times, Sally Hewitt, Caspar Hodgson, Neil Chadbourne, Jim Carefrae and **Jynja Claderon** allowed us to use their photographs.

Totnes Town Council and **LED Architects** allowed use of their illustrations for plans.

Mark Thurston of Geofutures turned data and concepts into maps.

Sustainable Energy Without the Hot Air allowed open use of their illustrations.

The Government Office for the South West allowed us to use their maps.

The Tellus Institute allowed us to use their Happiness Graph.

Julie Brown allowed us to use her Food Zones Diagram and ideas.

Ishka Michocka provided clever and attractive graphics throughout these pages.

NOTES & IDEAS

NOTES & IDEAS

NOTES & IDEAS